™

References for the Rest of Us!®

BESTSELLING BOOK SERIES

Do you find that traditional reference books are overloaded with technical details and advice you'll never use? Do you postpone important life decisions because you just don't want to deal with them? Then our *For Dummies®* business and general reference book series is for you.

For Dummies business and general reference books are written for those frustrated and hard-working souls who know they aren't dumb, but find that the myriad of personal and business issues and the accompanying horror stories make them feel helpless. *For Dummies* books use a lighthearted approach, a down-to-earth style, and even cartoons and humorous icons to dispel fears and build confidence. Lighthearted but not lightweight, these books are perfect survival guides to solve your everyday personal and business problems.

> *"More than a publishing phenomenon, 'Dummies' is a sign of the times."*
>
> — The New York Times

> *"A world of detailed and authoritative information is packed into them…"*
>
> — U.S. News and World Report

> *"…you won't go wrong buying them."*
>
> — Walter Mossberg, Wall Street Journal, on For Dummies books

Already, millions of satisfied readers agree. They have made For Dummies the #1 introductory level computer book series and a best-selling business book series. They have written asking for more. So, if you're looking for the best and easiest way to learn about business and other general reference topics, look to For Dummies to give you a helping hand.

Wiley Publishing, Inc.

Spanish

FOR

DUMMIES®

Spanish
FOR
DUMMIES®

by Susana Wald
and
the Language Experts at Berlitz
Berlitz Series Editor: Juergen Lorenz

Wiley Publishing, Inc.

Spanish For Dummies®

Published by
Wiley Publishing, Inc.
909 Third Avenue
New York, NY 10022
www.wiley.com

Copyright © 2000 by Wiley Publishing, Inc., Indianapolis, Indiana

Published simultaneously in Canada

For general information on our other products and services or to obtain technical support, please contact our Customer Care Department within the U.S. at 800-762-2974, outside the U.S. at 317-572-3993, or fax 317-572-4002.

Wiley also publishes its books in a variety of electronic formats. Some content that appears in print may not be available in electronic books.

Library of Congress Cataloging-in-Publication Data:

Library of Congress Control Number: 99-67159

ISBN: 0-7645-5194-9

Manufactured in the United States of America

10 9

1B/RV/QY/QS/IN

About the Authors

Susana Wald is a writer and a simultaneous and literary translator in Hungarian, Spanish, English, and French. As a publisher, she has been working with books and authors for many years. She has been a teacher in Chile and Canada and has known the joy of learning from her students and their untiring enthusiasm and tolerance. She is also an artist and has had her work shown in many countries in North, Central, and South America and in Europe.

Berlitz has meant excellence in language services for more than 120 years. At more than 400 locations and in 50 countries worldwide, Berlitz offers a full range of language and language-related services, including instruction, cross-cultural training, document translation, software localization, and interpretation services. Berlitz also offers a wide array of publishing products, such as self-study language courses, phrase books, travel guides, and dictionaries.

The world-famous Berlitz Method® is the core of all Berlitz language instruction. From the time of its introduction in 1878, millions have used this method to learn new languages. For more information about Berlitz classes and products, please consult your local telephone directory for the Language Center nearest you or visit the Berlitz Web site at www.berlitz.com, where you can enroll in classes or shop directly for products online.

Author's Acknowledgments

I would like to thank Berlitz and Wiley for the splendid idea of publishing these truly novel books. My thanks go as well to Jean Antonin Billard greatest among the greatest translators, who had the kindness of recommending my skills to Berlitz. I must mention as well that I owe Juergen Lorenz, at Berlitz, the structure of the text, as well as his friendly help with its first birthpangs.

And I thank from the heart the unflagging editorial help of Kathy Cox, at Wiley, who kept my spirit from sinking at all times, as well as Tammy Castleman, Patricia Pan, Billie Williams, and Kathleen Dobie who contributed their excellent copy editing skills. Thanks and excuses are also due to my lifetime partner, Ludwig Zeller, who for months saw mostly the back of my head while my face was glued to the monitor of my computer. May we all have a happy life.

Susana Wald

Berlitz would like to thank: Susana Wald, our author, for her tireless dedication to creating Spanish For Dummies. Jordi Quesada, for being bilingual in one language, Spanish — both Castillian and Latin American — and applying those skills to a fine editing job. Our NY audio producer, Paul Ruben, who developed the audio CD, bringing the written Spanish language to life! Our editors, Juergen Lorenz and Sheryl Olinsky Borg, for their professionalism and commitment to putting this challenging and exciting project together. And our deep appreciation goes to the staff at Wiley, especially Holly McGuire, Pam Mourouzis, and Kathy Cox, who guided Spanish For Dummies from start to finish!

Publisher's Acknowledgments

We're proud of this book; please send us your comments through our online registration form located at www.dummies.com/register.

Some of the people who helped bring this book to market include the following:

Acquisitions, Editorial, and Media Development

Project Editor: Kathleen M. Cox

Acquisitions Editor: Holly McGuire

Senior Copy Editor: Tamara S. Castleman

Copy Editors: Kathleen Dobie, Patricia Pan, Billie Williams

Technical Editor: Juergen Lorenz, series editor at Berlitz

Acquisitions Coordinator: Karen Young

Cover Coordinator: Jonathan Malysiak

Media Development Editor: Marita Ellixson

Editorial Manager: Pamela Mourouzis

Editorial Assistant: Carol Strickland

Reprint Editor: Bethany Andre

Production

Project Coordinator: Shawn Aylsworth

Layout and Graphics: Amy M. Adrian, Angela F. Hunckler, Clint Lahnen, Barry Offringa, Jill Piscitelli, Brent Savage, Jacque Schneider, Michael A. Sullivan, Maggie Ubertini, Erin Zeltner

Proofreaders: Laura Albert, Beth Baugh, John Greenough, Marianne Santy

Indexer: Janet Perlman

Special Help
Sherry Gomoll, Amanda Foxworth, Seta Frantz, Linda Stark

Publishing and Editorial for Consumer Dummies
Diane Graves Steele, Vice President and Publisher, Consumer Dummies
Joyce Pepple, Acquisitions Director, Consumer Dummies
Kristin A. Cocks, Product Development Director, Consumer Dummies
Michael Spring, Vice President and Publisher, Travel
Brice Gosnell, Publishing Director, Travel
Suzanne Jannetta, Editorial Director, Travel

Publishing for Technology Dummies
Andy Cummings, Acquisitions Director

Composition Services
Gerry Fahey, Vice President, Production Services
Debbie Stailey, Director of Composition Services

Contents at a Glance

Cartoons at a Glance

By Rich Tennant

The 5th Wave By Rich Tennant
@RICHTENNANT

"I just think if we're going to be in a foreign country, we should know their units of measurement better. By the way, how's your Grande Espresso?"

page 205

The 5th Wave By Rich Tennant
@RICHTENNANT

"I'm so proud of Ted. He ordered our entire meal in Spanish, and everything came out perfect— from the sushi appetizers to the noodle and wonton soup with shrimp tempura."

page 41

The 5th Wave By Rich Tennant
@RICHTENNANT

"I know it's a popular American expression, but you just don't say 'Hasta la vista, baby'—to a nun."

page 7

The 5th Wave By Rich Tennant
@RICHTENNANT

"I called ahead and told Morris I'd love to have flautas for dinner tonight, so we'll see how he did."

page 319

The 5th Wave By Rich Tennant
@RICHTENNANT

"Do you mind NOT practicing your 'Olé's' while I'm vacuuming?"

page 339

Cartoon Information:
Fax: 978-546-7747
E-Mail: richtennant@the5thwave.com
World Wide Web: www.the5thwave.com

Table of Contents

Introduction

As society becomes more international in nature, knowing how to say at least a few words in other languages becomes increasingly useful. Inexpensive airfares make travel abroad a more realistic option. Global business environments necessitate overseas travel. You just may have friends and neighbors who speak other languages, or you may want to get in touch with your heritage by learning a little bit of the language that your ancestors spoke.

Whatever your reason for wanting to acquire some Spanish, *Spanish For Dummies* can help. Two experts at helping readers develop knowledge — Berlitz, experts in teaching foreign languages; and IDG Books Worldwide, Inc., publishers of the best-selling *For Dummies* series — have teamed up to produce a book that gives you the skills you need for basic communication in Spanish. We're not promising fluency here, but if you want to greet someone, purchase a ticket, or order off a menu in Spanish, you need look no further than *Spanish For Dummies*.

What's Special about Spanish

Spanish is one of the great European languages, rich in heritage from its more than nine centuries of existence. This is the language that comes from the region of Spain we call Castile. It is also the language of great literature.

The first European novel — as a matter of fact, the first novel in the modern sense — was written in Spanish by Miguel de Cervantes. You've probably heard about Don Quixote, the "enthusiastic visionary." His adventures have even become part of the English language. The word *quixotic* describes someone with an odd, eccentric, or utterly-regardless-of-material-interests attitude.

Spanish is also the language of great poets. Many Nobel Prize winners in both the sciences and in literature are Spanish-speaking. Two Nobel Prize winners for literature are poets from Chile: Gabriela Mistral and Pablo Neruda.

As Christopher Columbus and other Spanish explorers came to the New World, Spanish became the language of all the peoples from Florida to Tierra del Fuego (with the exception of Brazil, where Portuguese is spoken).

When you go to places like Argentina, Bolivia, Chile, Uruguay, Paraguay, Peru, Ecuador, Colombia, Venezuela, Mexico, Guatemala, Puerto Rico, Cuba, Costa Rica, Panama, Honduras, or Nicaragua, you'll be speaking in or spoken to in Spanish. If you visit cities like Santiago de Chile, Montevideo, Asuncion, Buenos Aires, Lima, Caracas, Bogota, Mexico City, Quito, San Juan, and many, many others, all the people you find speak Spanish.

So you have several reasons to embrace this beautiful language. You may want to understand the culture and the people. You may also want your Spanish-speaking friends to understand you, in their own language.

About This Book

This book will help you reach moments of true understanding in a different language. Use the text as a language and cultural guide for those moments when you really need to know how and why things are done. This book concentrates on Latin American Spanish, meaning the Spanish spoken in Central and South American countries.

This book is not a class that you have to drag yourself to twice a week for a specified period of time. You can use *Spanish For Dummies* however you want to, whether your goal is to know some words and phrases to help you get around when you visit the countries of Central or South America, travel to Spain, or simply want to be able to say, "Hello, how are you?" to your Spanish-speaking neighbor. Go through this book at your own pace, reading as much or as little at a time as you like. You don't have to trudge through the chapters in order, either; just read the sections that interest you.

And don't forget to practice by using the CD at the back of this book for help in pronunciation and inflection. The only way to really know and love a language is to speak it. Throughout the book, we give you lots of words, phrases, and dialogs, complete with pronunciations. Only a sampling of them are on the CD, but we've provided a broad selection that should serve most of your basic needs.

Note: If you've never taken Spanish lessons before, you may want to read the chapters in Part I before tackling the later chapters. Part I gives you some of the basics that you need to know about the language, such as how to pronounce the various sounds.

Why We Wrote This Book

Language exposes you to every aspect of the human condition, allowing you to study the past, understand the present, and ponder the future. You will find that language sometimes changes how people express various emotions and conditions. All people are connected through their ability to speak, but you can go one step further — to understanding — by being able to communicate in another language. Very few things are as exciting as that!

The best way to learn a language is to immerse yourself in it. Listen to the way Spanish sounds, concentrate on the pronunciation, look at how it's written. By listening and repeating, you'll enter a new world of ideas and peoples. Acquiring Spanish through immersion really does feel like a sort of magic.

Conventions Used in This Book

To make this book easy for you to navigate, we've set up a couple of conventions:

- Spanish terms are set in **boldface** to make them stand out.
- Pronunciations, set in *italics,* follow the Spanish terms.
- Verb conjugations (lists that show you the forms of a verb) are given in tables in this order: the "I" form, the "you" (singular) form, the "he/she/it" form, the "we" form, the "you" (plural/formal) form, and the "they" form. Pronunciations follow in the second column. Here's an example:

Conjugation	Pronunciation
yo llevo	yoh <u>yeh</u>-bvoh
tú llevas	too <u>yeh</u>-bvahs
él, ella, uno, usted lleva	ehl, <u>eh</u>-yah, <u>oo</u>-noh, oos-<u>tehd</u> <u>yeh</u>-bvah
nosotros llevamos	noh-<u>soh</u>-trohs yeh-<u>bvah</u>-mohs
vosotros lleváis	bvoh-<u>soh</u>-trohs yeh-<u>bva</u>ees
ellos, ellas llevan	<u>eh</u>-yohs, <u>eh</u>-yahs <u>yeh</u>-bvahn

Language learning is a peculiar beast, so this book includes a few elements that other *For Dummies* books do not. Following are the new elements that you'll find:

- **Talkin' the Talk dialogs:** The best way to learn a language is to see and hear how it's used in conversation, so we include dialogs throughout the book. The dialogs come under the heading "Talkin' the Talk" and show you the Spanish words, the pronunciation, and the English translation.

- ✔ **Words to Know blackboards:** Memorizing key words and phrases is also important in language learning, so we collect the important words that appear in a chapter (or section within a chapter) and write them on a "chalkboard," with the heading "Words to Know."

- ✔ **Fun & Games activities:** If you don't have actual Spanish speakers to practice your new language skills on, you can use the Fun & Games activities to reinforce what you learn. These word games are fun ways to gauge your progress.

Also note that because each language has its own ways of expressing ideas, the English translations that we provide for the Spanish terms may not be exactly literal. We want you to know the gist of what's being said, not just the words that are being said. For example, you can translate the Spanish phrase **de nada** *(deh nah-dah)* literally as "of nothing," but the phrase really means "you're welcome." This book gives the "you're welcome" translation.

Foolish Assumptions

To write this book, we had to make some assumptions about who you are and what you want from a book called *Spanish For Dummies.* Here are the assumptions that we've made about you:

- ✔ You know no Spanish — or if you took Spanish back in school, you don't remember a word of it.

- ✔ You're not looking for a book that will make you fluent in Spanish; you just want to know some words, phrases, and sentence constructions so that you can communicate basic information in Spanish.

- ✔ You don't want to have to memorize long lists of vocabulary words or a bunch of boring grammar rules.

- ✔ You want to have fun and learn a little bit of Spanish at the same time.

If these statements apply to you, you've found the right book!

How This Book Is Organized

This book is divided by topic into parts, and then into chapters. The following sections tell you what types of information you can find in each part.

Part I: Getting Started

This part lets you get your feet wet by giving you some Spanish basics: how to pronounce words, what the accents mean, and so on. We even boost your confidence by reintroducing you to some Spanish words that you probably already know. Finally, we outline the basics of Spanish grammar that you may need to know when you work through later chapters in the book.

Part II: Spanish in Action

In this part, you begin learning and using Spanish. Instead of focusing on grammar points, as many language textbooks do, this part focuses on every-day situations that you might find yourself in if you were living in a Spanish-speaking country or dealing with your Spanish-speaking neighbors. This part hones your small-talk skills and takes you on shopping and dining excursions. At the end of this part, you should be able to do some basic navigation in the Spanish language.

Part III: Spanish on the Go

This part gives you the tools you need to take your Spanish on the road, whether it's to a local Spanish restaurant or to a museum in Mexico. This part is devoted to the traveler in you, helping you to survive the Customs process, check into hotels, nab a taxi, exchange dollars for pesos, and have a great time doing it. Sprinkled throughout are cultural tidbits that introduce you to people, places, and things that are important in Spanish-speaking cultures.

Part IV: The Part of Tens

If you're looking for small, easily digestible pieces of information about Spanish, this part is for you. Here, you can find ten ways to speak Spanish quickly, ten useful Spanish expressions to know, and ten celebrations worth joining.

Part V: Appendixes

This part of the book includes important information that you can use for reference. We include verb tables, which show you how to conjugate a regular verb, and then how to conjugate those verbs that stubbornly don't fit the pattern. We also provide a listing of the tracks that appear on the audio CD that comes with this book so that you can find out where in the book those dialogs are and follow along. We give you a mini-dictionary in both Spanish-to-English and English-to-Spanish formats. And finally, we give you a brief overview of the 20 countries where Spanish is spoken.

Icons Used in This Book

You may be looking for particular information while reading this book. To make certain types of information easier for you to find, we've placed the following icons in the left-hand margins throughout the book:

This icon highlights tips that can make learning Spanish easier.

Languages are full of quirks that may trip you up if you're not prepared for them. This icon points to discussions of these weird grammar rules.

If you're looking for information and advice about culture and travel, look for these icons. They draw your attention to interesting tidbits about the countries in which Spanish is spoken.

The audio CD that comes with this book gives you the opportunity to listen to real Spanish speakers so that you can get a better understanding of what Spanish sounds like. This icon marks the Talkin' the Talk dialogs that you can find on the CD.

Where to Go from Here

Learning a language is all about jumping in and giving it a try (no matter how bad your pronunciation is at first). So make the leap! Start at the beginning, pick a chapter that interests you, or pop the CD into your stereo or computer and listen to a few dialogs. Just make sure that you have fun!

Part I
Getting Started

The 5th Wave   By Rich Tennant

"I know it's a popular American expression, but you just don't say 'Hasta la vista, baby'—to a nun."

In this part . . .

This part lets you get your feet wet by giving you some Spanish basics: how to pronounce words, what the accents mean, and so on. We even boost your confidence by reintroducing you to some Spanish words that you probably already know. Finally, we outline the basics of Spanish grammar that you may need to know when you work through later chapters in the book.

Chapter 1

You Already Know a Little Spanish

*1*f you're familiar with the term "Latin Lover," you may not be surprised to know that Spanish is called a Romance language. But the romance we're talking about here isn't exactly the Latin Lover type — unless you love to learn Latin.

Spanish (as well as several other languages such as Italian, French, Romanian, and Portuguese) is a Romance language because it has its origins in the Latin of ancient Rome. Because of that common origin, Romance languages have many similarities in grammar and the way they sound. (The fact that they all sound so romantic when spoken is purely a bonus!) For example, **casa** (*kah-sah),* the word for "house," is identical in looks, meaning, and sound whether you speak Portuguese, Italian, or Spanish.

The differences in the Romance languages are not terribly difficult to overcome, especially in South America. Any Spanish-speaking American can talk with a Portuguese-speaking Brazilian, and they will understand each other even if the other person sounds a bit funny. Still, each Romance language is different from its sister languages. Spanish is a language that comes from a region of Spain called Castile. So in Spain and some Latin American countries, such as Argentina, they call the language **castellano** (*kahs-teh-yah-noh),* which means Castilian.

This book concentrates on the Spanish spoken in Latin America. Throughout the book, we also explore the differences in the words used in these 19 countries and mention some variations in pronunciation. Latin America consists of all of the Western Hemisphere with the exception of Canada; the United States; the British and French-speaking Guyanas; and a few islands in the Caribbean, such as Jamaica, Haiti, and Curaçao, where English, French, or Dutch are spoken.

This chapter is the foundation for the other chapters in the book. Subsequent chapters in this book discuss pronunciation, gestures, and body language. We also give you a few quickie phrases that show Spanish speakers you're one of their bunch.

You Already Know Some Spanish!

The English language is like an ever-growing entity that, with great wisdom, absorbs what it needs from other cultures and languages. English is also a language that is like a bouquet of flowers plucked from many different roots. One of these roots is Latin, which 2,000 years ago was spread all over Europe by the Romans and later by scholars of the Middle Ages.

Because all of these live elements exist in the root of the language, you can find many correspondences between English and Spanish in the words that come from both Latin and French roots. These words can cause both delight and embarrassment. The delight comes in the words where the coincident sounds also give similar meanings. The embarrassment comes from words where the sounds and even the roots are the same, but the meanings are completely different.

Among the delightful discoveries of similarities between the languages are words like **soprano** *(soh-prah-noh)* (soprano), **pronto** *(prohn-toh)* (right away; soon), and thousands of others that differ by just one or two letters such as **conclusión** *(kohn-kloo-seeohn)* (conclusion), **composición** *(kohm-poh-see-see-ohn)* (composition), **libertad** *(lee-bvehr-tahd)* (liberty), **economía** *(eh-koh-noh-meeah)* (economy), **invención** *(een-bvehn-seeohn)* (invention), and **presidente** *(preh-see-dehn-teh)* (president).

Beware of false friends

The trouble begins in the world of words that French linguists have designated as *false friends*. You can't trust fool's gold, false friends, or all word similarities. Within the groups of false friends, you may find words that look very similar and even have the same root, yet mean completely different things. One that comes to mind is the word **actual,** which has very different meanings in English and Spanish. In English, you know that it means "real; in reality; or the very one." Not so in Spanish. **Actual** *(ahk-tooahl)* in Spanish means present; current; belonging to this moment, this day, or this year.

So, for example, when you say *the actual painting* in English, you're referring to the real one, the very one people are looking at or want to see. But, when you say **la pintura actual** *(lah peen-too-rah ahk-tooahl)* in Spanish, you're referring to the painting that belongs to the current time, the one that follows present day trends — a modern painting.

Another example is the adjective "embarrassed," that in English means ashamed or encumbered. In Spanish, **embarazada** *(ehm-bvah-rah-sah-dah)* is the adjective that comes from the same root as the English word, yet its use nowadays almost exclusively means "pregnant." So you can say in English that you are a little embarrassed, but in Spanish you can't be just a little **embarazada.** Either you're pregnant or you're not.

Recognize some crossover influence

Word trouble ends at the point where a word originating in English is absorbed into Spanish or vice versa. The proximity of the United States to Mexico produces a change in the Spanish spoken there. An example is the word *car.* In Mexico, people say **carro** *(kah-rroh).* In South America, on the other hand, people say **auto** *(ahoo-toh).* In Spain, people say **coche** *(koh-cheh).*

Here are just a few examples of Spanish words that you already know because English uses them, too:

- ✔ You've been to a **rodeo** *(roh-deh-oh)* or a **fiesta** *(feeehs-tah).*
- ✔ You've probably taken a **siesta** *(seeehs-tah)* or two.
- ✔ You probably know at least one **señorita** *(seh-nyoh-ree-tah),* and you surely have an **amigo** *(ah-mee-goh).* Maybe you'll even see him **mañana** *(mah-nyah-nah).*
- ✔ You already know the names of places like **Los Angeles** *(lohs ahn-Heh-lehs)* (the angels), **San Francisco** *(sahn frahn-sees-koh)* (St. Francis), **La Jolla** *(la Hoh-yah)* (the jewel), **Florida** *(floh-ree-dah)* (the blooming one), and **Puerto Rico** *(pooehr-toh ree-koh)* (rich harbor).
- ✔ You've eaten a **tortilla** *(tohr-tee-lyah),* a **taco** *(tah-koh),* or a **burrito** *(bvoo-rree-toh).*
- ✔ You fancy the **tango** *(tahn-goh),* the **bolero** *(bvo-leh-roh),* or the **rumba** *(room-bvah),* or you may dance the **cumbia** *(koom-bveeah).*
- ✔ You have a friend named **Juanita** *(Hooah-nee-tah),* **Anita** *(ah-nee-tah),* or **Clara** *(klah-rah).*

Reciting Your ABCs

Correct pronunciation is key to avoiding misunderstandings. The following sections present some basic guidelines for proper pronunciation.

Next to the Spanish words throughout this book, the pronunciation is in parentheses, which we call *pronunciation brackets*. Within the pronunciation brackets, we separate all the words that have more than one syllable with a hyphen, like this: *(kah-sah)*. An underlined syllable within the pronunciation brackets tells you to accent, or stress, that syllable. We say much more about stress later in this chapter. In the meantime, don't let yourself get stressed out (pardon the pun). We explain each part of the language separately, and the pieces will quickly fall into place. Promise!

In the following section we comment on some letters of the alphabet from the Spanish point of view. The aim is to help you to understand Spanish pronunciations. Here is the basic Spanish alphabet and its pronunciation:

a *(ah)*	**b** *(bveh)*	**c** *(seh)*	**d** *(deh)*
e (eh)	**f** *(eh-feh)*	**g** *(Heh)*	**h** *(ah-cheh)*
i (ee)	**j** *(Hoh-tah)*	**k** *(kah)*	**l** *(eh-leh)*
m *(eh-meh)*	**n** *(eh-neh)*	**ñ** *(eh-nyeh)*	**o** *(oh)*
p *(peh)*	**q** (koo)	**r** *(eh-reh)*	**s** *(eh-seh)*
t *(teh)*	**u** *(oo)*	**v** *(bveh)*	**w** *(doh-bleh bveh) (oo – bveh doh-bvleh) (Spain)*

x *(eh-kees)*   **y** *(ee gree eh-gah)* **z** *(seh-tah)*

Spanish also includes some double letters in its alphabet: **ch** *(cheh)*, **ll** *(ye)*, and **rr** *(a trilled r)*.

We don't go through *every* letter of the alphabet in the sections that follow, only those that you use differently in Spanish than in English. The differences can lie in pronunciation, the way they look, in the fact that you seldom see the letters, or that you don't pronounce them at all.

Consonants

Consonants tend to sound the same in English and Spanish. We explain the few differences that you can find.

Inside the Spanish-speaking world itself, you'll find that consonants may be pronounced differently than in English. For example, in Spain the consonant **z** is pronounced like the **th** in the English word *thesis*. (Latin Americans don't use this sound; in all 19 Spanish-speaking countries on this hemisphere, **z** and **s** sound the same.)

In the Spanish speaker's mind, a consonant is any sound that needs to have a vowel next to it when you pronounce it. For example, saying the letter **t** by itself may be difficult for a Spanish speaker. To the Spanish ear, pronouncing **t** sounds like **te** *(teh)*. Likewise, the Spanish speaker says **ese** *(eh-seh)* when pronouncing the letter **s**.

Only a few consonants in Spanish differ from their English counterparts. The following sections look more closely at the behavior and pronunciation of these consonants.

The letter K

In Spanish, the letter **k** is used only in words that have their origin in foreign languages. More often than not, this letter is seen in **kilo** *(kee-loh)*, meaning *thousand* in Greek. An example is **kilómetro** *(kee-loh-meh-troh)* (kilometer) — a thousand-meter measure for distance.

The letter H

In Spanish, the letter **h** is *always* mute. That's it!

The pronunciation brackets throughout this book often include the letter **h**. These h's generally signal certain vowel sounds, which we cover later in this chapter. In the pronunciation brackets, the Spanish **h** simply doesn't appear, because it's mute.

Following are some examples of the Spanish "h":

- **Huayapan** *(ooah-yah-pahn)* (name of a village in Mexico)
- **hueso** *(ooeh-soh)* (bone)
- **huevo** *(ooeh-bvoh)* (egg)

The letter J

The consonant **j** sounds like a guttural **h**. Normally you say **h** quite softly, as though you were just breathing out. Now, say your **h**, but gently raise the back of your tongue, as if you were saying **k**. Push the air out real hard, and you'll get the sound. Try it! There — it sounds like you're gargling, doesn't it?

To signal that you need to make this sound, we use a capital letter *H* within the pronunciation brackets.

Now try the sound out on these words:

- **Cajamarca** *(kah-Hah-mahr-kah)* (the name of a city in Peru)

- **cajeta** *(kah-Heh-tah)* (a delicious, thick sauce made of milk and sugar)

- **cajón** *(kah-Hohn)* (big box)

- **jadeo** *(Hah-deh-oh)* (panting)

- **Jijón** *(Hee-Hohn)* (the name of a city in Spain)

- **jota** *(Hoh-tah)* (the Spanish name for the letter **j**; also the name of a folk dance in Spain.)

- **tijera** *(tee-Heh-rah)* (scissors)

The letter C

The letter **c,** in front of the vowels **a, o,** and **u,** sounds like the English **k.** We use the letter *k* in the pronunciation brackets to signal this sound. Following are some examples:

- **acabar** *(ah-kah-bvahr)* (to finish)

- **café** *(kah-feh)* (coffee)

- **casa** *(kah-sah)* (house)

- **ocaso** *(oh-kah-soh)* (sunset)

When the letter **c** is in front of the vowels **e** and **i,** it sounds like the English **s.** In the pronunciation brackets, we signal this sound as *s.* Following are some examples:

- **acero** *(ah-seh-roh)* (steel)

- **cero** *(seh-roh)* (zero)

- **cine** *(see-neh)* (cinema)

In much of Spain — primarily the north and central parts — the letter **c** is pronounced like the *th* in *thanks* when placed before the vowels **e** and **i.**

The letters S and Z

In Latin American Spanish, the letters **s** and **z** always sound like the English letter **s.** We use the letter *s* in the pronunciation brackets to signal this sound. Following are some examples:

- **asiento** *(ah-seeehn-toh)* (seat)

- **sol** *(sohl)* (sun)

- **zarzuela** *(sahr-sooeh-lah)* (Spanish-style operetta)

In Spain, **z** also has the sound of the *th* in *thanks,* rather than the **s** sound prevalent in Latin America.

The letters B and V

The letters **b** and **v** are pronounced the same, the sound being somewhere in-between the two letters. This in-between is a fuzzy, bland sound — closer to **v** than to **b**. If you position your lips and teeth to make a **v** sound, and then try to make a **b** sound, you'll have it. To remind you to make this sound, we use *bv* in our pronunciation brackets, for both **b** and **v**. Here are some examples:

- **cabeza** *(kah-bveh-sah)* (head)
- **vida** *(bvee-dah)* (life)
- **violín** *(bveeoh-leen)* (violin)

The letter Q

Spanish doesn't use the letter **k** very much; when the language wants a **k** sound in front of the vowels **e** and **i**, it unfolds the letter combination **qu**. So when you see the word **queso** *(keh-soh)* (cheese), you immediately know that you say the **k** sound. Here are some examples of the Spanish letter **q,** which we indicate by the letter *k* in pronunciation brackets.:

- **Coquimbo** *(koh-keem-bvoh)* (the name of a city in Chile)
- **paquete** *(pah-keh-teh)* (package)
- **pequeño** *(peh-keh-nyoh)* (small)
- **tequila** *(teh-kee-lah)* (Mexican liquor, spirits)

The letter G

In Spanish the letter **g** has a double personality, like the letter **c.** When you combine the letter **g** with a consonant or when you see it in front of the vowels **a, o,** and **u,** it sounds like the **g** in *goose.* Here are some examples:

- **begonia** *(bveh-goh-neeah)* (begonia)
- **gato** *(gah-toh)* (cat)
- **gracias** *(grah-seeahs)* (thank you)
- **pagado** *(pah-gah-doh)* (paid for)

The **g** changes personality in front of the vowels **e** and **i**. It sounds like the Spanish **j**, which we signal with the capital *H* in our pronunciation brackets.

 ✔ **agenda** *(ah-Hehn-dah)* (agenda; date book)

 ✔ **gerente** *(Heh-rehn-teh)* (manager)

To hear the sound **g** (as in *goat*) in front of the vowels **e** and **i,** you must insert a **u,** making **gue** and **gui.** To remind you to make the goat sound (no, no, not *mmehehe,* but **g**) we use *gh* in our pronunciation brackets. Some examples:

 ✔ **guía** *(gheeah)* (guide)

 ✔ **guiño** *(ghee-nyoh)* (wink)

 ✔ **guerra** *(gheh-rrah)* (war)

Double consonants

Spanish has two double consonants: **ll** and **rr.** They are considered a singular letter, and each has a singular sound. Because these consonants are considered singular, they stick together when you separate syllables. For example, the word **calle** *(kah-yeh)* (street) appears as **ca-lle.** And **torre** *(toh-rreh),* (tower) separates into **to-rre.**

The letter LL

The **ll** consonant sounds like the **y** in the English word *yes,* except in Argentina and Uruguay.

Argentineans and Uruguayans pronounce this consonant as the sound that happens when you have your lips pursed to say **s** and then make the **z** sound through them. Try it. Fun, isn't it? But really, the sound isn't that difficult to make, because you can find the English equivalent in words like *measure* and *pleasure.* The way you say those **s** sounds is exactly how **ll** is pronounced in Argentina and Uruguay.

Throughout this book, we use the sound like the English **y** in the word *yes,* which is how **ll** is pronounced in 18 of the 20 Spanish-speaking countries. In the pronunciation brackets, we use *y* to signal this sound.

Now try the **ll** sound, using the *y* sound, in the following examples:

 ✔ **brillo** *(bree-yoh)* (shine)

 ✔ **llama** *(yah-mah)* (flame; also the name of an animal in Peru)

 ✔ **lluvia** *(yoo-bveeah)* (rain)

The letter RR

The **rr** sounds like a strongly rolled **r**. In fact, every **r** is strongly rolled in Spanish, but the double one is the real winner. To roll an **r**, curl your tongue against the roof of your mouth as you finish the **r** sound. It should trill.

An easy way to make this sound is to say the letter **r** as though you were pretending to sound like an outboard motor. There. You have it! Spanish speakers take special pleasure in rolling their **rr**'s. One fun thing about **rr** is that no words begin with it. Isn't that a relief! In pronunciation brackets we simply signal this sound as *rr*.

Play with these words:

- **carrera** *(kah-rreh-rah)* (race; profession)
- **correo** *(koh-rreh-oh)* (mail, post)
- **tierra** *(teeeh-rrah)* (land)

The letter Y

This letter represents sounds that are very similar to those of **ll**. The people of both Argentina and Uruguay pronounce this sound differently from the rest of Latin America. We advise that you pronounce it as the English **y** in *yes* and *you*. In the pronunciation brackets, we signal this sound as *y*. Following are some examples:

- **playa** *(plah-yah)* (beach)
- **yema** *(yeh-mah)* (yolk; also finger tip)
- **yodo** *(yoh-doh)* (Iodine)

In Spanish, the letter **y** is never a vowel, always a consonant.

The letter Ñ

When you see a wiggly line on top of the letter **n** that looks like **ñ**, use the **ny** sound that you use for the English word *canyon*. The wiggly line is called a **tilde** *(teel-deh)*. In pronunciation brackets, we show this sound as *ny*. Following are some examples:

- **cuñado** *(koo-nyah-doh)* (brother-in-law)
- **mañana** *(mah-nyah-nah)* (tomorrow)
- **niña** *(nee-nyah)* (girl)

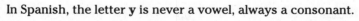

Vowels

If you want your Spanish to sound like a native's, you have to concentrate on your *vowels.*

The biggest difference between English and Spanish is almost certainly in the way the vowels are written and pronounced. By now, you may be well aware that one vowel in English can have more than one sound. Look, for instance, at *fat* and *fate.* Both words have the vowel **a,** but they're pronounced much differently from each other. The good news is that in Spanish, you always say the vowels one way, and one way only.

The upcoming sections discuss the five vowels — which are the only vowel sounds in Spanish. They are **a** *(ah),* **e** *(eh),* **i** *(ee),* **o** *(oh),* **u** *(oo).* Spanish sees each of these vowels by itself and makes other sounds by combining the vowels in twos.

The vowel A

As children, almost everybody sings their ABCs. In Spanish, the English **a** that starts off the song, is pronounced *ah.* The easiest way to remember how to pronounce the letter **a** in Spanish is to sing the chorus of the Christmas carol "Deck the Halls" to yourself. You remember the chorus, don't you? *Fa la la la la, la la, la la.* We write this sound as *ah* in the pronunciation brackets.

Following are some sample words to practice. Remember that you pronounce each and every **a** exactly the same way.

- **Caracas** *(kah-rah-kas)* (a city in Venezuela)
- **mapa** *(mah-pah)* (map)
- **Guadalajara** *(gooah-dah-lah-Hah-rah)* (a city in Mexico)

The vowel E

To get an idea of how the Spanish **e** sounds, smile gently, open your mouth a bit and say "eh." The sound should be like the **e** in the English word *pen.* In our pronunciation brackets, this vowel appears as *eh.*

Try these:

- **pelele** *(peh-leh-leh)* (rag doll; puppet)
- **pelo** *(peh-loh)* (hair)
- **seco** *(seh-koh)* (dry)

The vowel I

In Spanish the vowel i sounds like the **ee** in *seen,* but just a touch shorter. To give you an example, when English speakers say *feet* or *street,* the Spanish speaker hears what sounds like almost two i's.

We signal this sound as *ee* in our pronunciation brackets. Following are some examples:

- **irritar** *(ee-rree-tahr)* (to irritate)
- **piña** *(pee-nyah)* (pineapple)
- **pintar** *(peen-tahr)* (to paint)

The vowel O

The Spanish put their mouths in a rounded position, as if to breathe a kiss over a flower, and keeping it in that position, say **o.** It sounds like the **o** in *floor,* but a bit shorter. We signal this sound as *oh* in the pronunciation brackets.

Try practicing the sound on these words:

- **coco** *(koh-koh)* (coconut)
- **Orinoco** *(oh-ree-noh-koh)* (a river in Venezuela)
- **Oruro** *(oh-roo-roh)* (a city in Bolivia)
- **toronja** *(toh-rohn-Hah)* (grapefruit)

The vowel U

The fifth and last vowel in Spanish is the **u,** and it sounds like the **oo** in *moon* or *raccoon,* but just a touch shorter. *Oo,* we think you've got it! We write this sound as *oo* in the pronunciation brackets. Here are some examples of the **u** sound:

- **cuna** *(koo-nah)* (cradle)
- **cuñado** *(koo-nyah-doh)* (brother-in-law)
- **cúrcuma** *(koor-koo-mah)* (turmeric)
- **curioso** *(koo-reeoh-soh)* (curious)
- **fruta** *(froo-tah)* (fruit)
- **luna** *(loo-nah)* (moon)
- **tuna** *(too-nah)* (prickle pear)

Isn't it **curioso** that, in Spanish, **fruta** is fruit and so is **tuna**?

The diphthongs

Good grief, you say, what's *that?*

Diphthong comes from Greek, where *di* means two, and *thong* comes from a very similar word meaning sound or voice. (Don't worry, we had to look it up in the dictionary ourselves.) Very simply, it means *double sound.* There. That's easier.

The Spanish word is **diptongo** *(deep-tohn-goh)*. **Diptongos** are the combination of two vowels, from the Spanish-speaking point of view. For instance, **i** and **o** combine to make **io** as in **patio** *(pah-teeoh)* (courtyard or patio.)

Joining the weak to the strong

Diptongos are always made up of a weak and a strong vowel. Calling vowels "weak" or "strong" is a convention of the Spanish language. The convention comes from the fact that the so-called strong vowel is always dominant in the diphthong. To the Spanish speaker, **i** and **u** are weak vowels, leaving **a, e,** and **o** as strong ones.

To visualize this weak or strong concept, consider a piccolo flute and a bass horn. The sound of the piccolo is definitely more like the Spanish **i** and **u**, while the base horn sounds more like the Spanish **a, e,** and especially **o**.

Any combination of one strong and one weak vowel is a **diptongo** *(deep-tohn-goh),* which means that they will belong together in the same syllable. In fact, they're not only together, they're stuck like superglue; they can't be separated.

In the **diptongo,** the stress falls on the strong vowel (more about stress later in this chapter). An accent mark alerts you when the stress falls on the weak vowel. (More about accents later, too.) In the combination of two weak vowels, the stress is on the second one.

Try these examples of diphthongs:

- **bueno** *(bvooeh-noh)* (good)
- **cuando** *(kooahn-doh)* (when)
- **fiar** *(feeahr)* (sell on credit)
- **fuera** *(fooeh-rah)* (outside)
- **suizo** *(sooee-soh)* (Swiss)
- **viudo** *(bveeoo-doh)* (widower)

Separating the strong from the strong

When two strong vowels are combined, they don't form a diphthong. Instead, the vowels retain their separate values, so you must put them into separate syllables. Here are some examples:

- ✔ **aorta** *(ah-ohr-tah)* (aorta) (See! Just as in English!)
- ✔ **feo** *(feh-oh)* (ugly)
- ✔ **marea** *(mah-reh-ah)* (tide)
- ✔ **mareo** *(mah-reh-oh)* (dizziness)

Did you notice in the previous list how changing one letter, in **marea** and **mareo,** for example, can change the meaning of a word? This letter phenomenon occurs in Spanish, just as in English. Finding such words is fun. In the case of the previous list, at least the two words come from the same root **mar** *(mahr)* (sea). And, associating the tide to one's dizziness isn't all that difficult. But in other places you can have oceans of difference. Here are some more examples: **casa** *(kah-sah)* (house) and **cosa** *(koh-sah)* (thing); and **pito** *(pee-toh)* (whistle), **pato** *(pah-toh)* (duck), and **peto** *(peh-toh)* (bib or breastplate.)

Pronunciation and Stress

In Spanish, one syllable is stressed in every word. *Stress* is the accent that you put on a syllable as you speak it. One syllable always gets more stress than the others. In single-syllable words, finding the stress is easy. But many words have more than one syllable, and that's when the situation becomes stressful.

Looking for stress, normally

Can you believe that you're *looking* for stress? In Spanish, the right stress at the right time is a good thing, and fortunately, stress in Spanish is easy to control. If you have *no* written accent, you have two possibilities:

- ✔ The word is stressed next to the last syllable if it ends in a vowel, an **n**, or an **s.** Here are some examples:
  - • **camas** *(kah-mahs)* (beds)
  - • **mariposas** *(mah-ree-poh-sahs)* (butterflies)
  - • **pollo** *(poh-yoh)* (chicken)

✔ The word is stressed on the last syllable when it ends in a consonant that is *not* an **n** or **s.** Look at these examples:

- **cantar** *(kahn-<u>tahr</u>)* (to sing)
- **feliz** *(feh-<u>lees</u>)* (happy)

If a word is *not* stressed in either of these two ways, the word will have an accent mark on it to indicate where you should place the stress.

Looking for accented vowels

One good thing about having the accent mark on a vowel is that you can tell immediately where the stress is, just by looking at the word.

The accent mark does not affect how the vowel is pronounced, just which syllable is stressed.

Here are some examples of words with accent marks on a vowel:

✔ **balcón** *(bahl-<u>kohn</u>)* (balcony)

✔ **carácter** *(kah-<u>rahk</u>-tehr)* (character, personality)

✔ **fotógrafo** *(foh-<u>toh</u>-grah-foh)* (photographer)

✔ **pájaro** *(<u>pah</u>-Hah-roh)* (bird)

Understanding accents on diphthongs

An accent in a diphthong shows you which vowel to stress. Take a look at these examples:

✔ **¡Adiós!** *(ah-dee<u>ohs</u>)* (Good bye!)

✔ **¡Buenos días!** *(bvoo<u>eh</u>-nohs <u>dee</u>ahs)* (Good morning!)

✔ **¿Decía?** *(deh-<u>see</u>ah)* (You were saying?)

✔ **tía** *(<u>tee</u>ah)* (aunt)

¡Punctuation Plus!

Did you notice the unfamiliar punctuation in **¡Buenos días!, ¿Decía?,** and **¡Adiós!?** Spanish indicates the mood (or tone) of what you're saying both at the beginning and at the end of the phrase that is a question or an exclamation, as in **¿Decía?** *(deh-_seeah_)* (You were saying?) or **¡Decía!** *(deh_see_-ah)* (You were saying!).

As far as we know, Spanish is the only language that provides this sort of punctuation. However, this punctuation is very useful when you have to read something aloud because you know beforehand how to modulate your voice when the phrase is coming up.

This punctuation is the verbal equivalent of making gestures, which you can see in the following examples:

- **¿Dónde está?** *(_dohn_-deh ehs-_tah_)* (Where is it?)
- **¡Qué maravilla!** *(keh mah-rah-_bvee_-yah)* (How wonderful!)

Some Basic Phrases to Know

The following phrases can get you through a number of awkward pauses as you think of the right word:

- **¡Olé!** *(oh- _leh_)* (Great!; Superb!; Keep going!) This very Spanish expression is used during bullfights in Mexico and Peru.
- **¿Quiubo?** *(kee _oo_-boh)* (Hello, what's happening?)
- **¿De veras?** *(deh _bveh_-rahs)* (Really?) This phrase signals slight disbelief.
- **¡No me digas!** *(noh meh _dee_-gahs)* (You don't say!) This phrase also means disbelief.

Fun & Games

Try to match these Spanish letters with the English letters they sound like. Draw a line from the Spanish letter to its English sound equivalent. Then give a Spanish word that uses that sound.

Spanish Letters	English Letter	Spanish Word
ll	e	→ piña (pineapple)
j	H →	tijera (Scissors)
i	s	zarzuela (operta)
z	k →	qué tal (How are things)
q	y →	brillo (Shine)

Chapter 2

The Nitty Gritty: Basic Spanish Grammar

Studying a language is similar to driving a car. After you get used to all the gadgets and gauges, driving becomes second nature, and fun, to boot. You don't even think about how you make your car go from Point A to Point B. Spanish is the same. You read the chatty parts and — without much thought — the language becomes second nature.

However, driving involves more than making a car move. You also have to incorporate the nitty-gritty elements of driving — like obeying traffic rules. The nit-picky part of any language — the traffic rules, so to speak — is grammar.

To be honest, studying grammar isn't the most enjoyable part of discovering a language. Just keep in mind that what you get from the nitty-gritty of this grammar chapter is useful in other places, too. And, remember that you don't need to chew your way through this chapter in one single meal. You can go to another part of the book, and when we want to draw your attention to something in this chapter, we tell you. (We provide cross-references throughout the book.)

Then again, you may be the kind of person who truly enjoys grammar and structure. If so, you're in for a treat!

Simple Sentence Construction

When you meet people, naturally, you want to talk to them. And how do you go about that? In sentences, of course. You make a statement, you ask a question (When someone questions you, you answer, right? Most people do, and that's how conversations get started.) In Spanish, as in English, you form a sentence by combining a subject, a verb, and perhaps further descriptive information. For example:

> **La casa es grande.** *(lah kah-sah ehs grahn-deh)* (The house is big.)

Here, the subject of the sentence is **la casa** *(lah kah-sah)* (the house); then comes the verb, **es** *(ehs)* (is); after that comes the adjective, **grande** *(grahn-deh)* (big), which describes the house. In Spanish, the three basic parts of a sentence go in this order.

Here are some more examples:

- ✔ **La mujer es bella.** *(lah moo-Hehr ehs bveh-yah)* (The woman is beautiful.)
- ✔ **El hombre es buen mozo.** *(ehl ohm-bvreh ehs bvooehn moh-soh)* (The man is handsome.)
- ✔ **Las calles son largas.** *(lahs kah-yehs sohn lahr-gahs)* (The streets are long.)

Forming Questions

We have some good news for you: Forming a question in Spanish is easy. All you have to do is reverse the order of the verb and the subject. Where you say **Ésta es . . .** *(ehs-tah ehs)* in a regular sentence, for a question you say **¿Es ésta . . .?** *(ehs ehs-tah)*. This works the same as it does in English, when you say "This is . . ." and "Is this . . .?"

Check out this example

> **Esta es la puerta.** *(ehs-tah ehs lah poo-ehr-tah)* (This is the door.)

> **¿Es ésta la puerta?** *(ehs ehs-tah lah poo-ehr-tah)* (Is this the door?)

Now, suppose you want to answer in the negative. All you have to do is insert the word **no** *before* the verb (almost the way you do in English, but easier). An example:

> **¿Es ese el carro?** *(ehs eh-seh ehl kah-rroh)* (Is that the car?)

> **No, ese no es el carro.** *(noh eh-seh noh ehs ehl kah-rro)* (No, that is not the car.)

English often includes the verb "do" in questions, but Spanish makes things easier on you. In Spanish, the word "do" is understood as part of the verb:

¿Vas al cine? *(bvahs ahl see-neh)* (Do you go to the movies?)

Sí, voy. *(see bvohy ahl see-neh)* (Yes, I [do] go.)

In English, "Yes, I do" can mean many things (going to the movies, using your computer, making a phone call, and so on).

In Spanish you are a bit more specific:

¿Va tu padre al cine? *(bvah too pah-dreh ahl see-neh)*
(Does your father go to the movies?)

No, no va. *(noh noh bvah)* (No, he doesn't go.)

The following sentences were affirmative statements, previously in this chapter, and now we're using them to demonstrate the questioning (interrogative) and denying (negative) moods:

- **¿Es bella la mujer?** *(ehs bveh-yah lah moo-Hehr)*
  (Is the woman beautiful?)

  La mujer no es bella. *(lah moo-Hehr noh ehs bveh-yah)* (The woman is not beautiful.)

- **¿Es buen mozo el hombre?** *(ehs bvooehn moh-soh ehl ohm-bvreh)*
  (Is the man handsome?)

  El hombre no es buen mozo. *(ehl ohm-bvreh noh ehs bvooehn moh-soh)*
  (The man is not handsome.)

- **¿Son largas las calles?** *(sohn lahr-gahs lahs kah-yehs)*
  (Are the streets long?)

- **Las calles no son largas.** *(lahs kah-yehs noh sohn lahr-gahs)*
  (The streets are not long.)

Introducing Regular and Irregular Verbs

Spanish verbs all end with one of three letter combinations: **-ar, -er,** or **-ir.** You find both regular and irregular verbs with all three endings. As you may guess, regular verbs all form different tenses (past, present, future) and persons (I/we, you, he/she/they) in the same way — a process called *conjugation.* So, if you know how to conjugate one regular verb, you can determine the conjugation of all regular verbs like it.

The form of *irregular verbs,* however, can change when you least expect it. Ultimately, you need to memorize the conjugation of each irregular verb to ensure that you use it correctly. (Don't worry if you make a mistake; most Spanish speakers can figure out what you want to say even if your verb ending is not quite right.)

Regular verbs

In all regular verbs in Spanish, the first section of the word — its *root* — stays constant. For example, the verb **trabajar** *(trah-bvah-Hahr)* (to work) is a regular verb ending in **-ar.** The root *trabaj-* stays the same throughout conjugation. The following table shows you how you conjugate this verb — and all other regular verbs ending with **-ar.**

Conjugation	*Pronunciation*
Present tense:	
yo trabaj**o** *(to work)*	yoh trah-<u>bvah</u>-Hoh
tú trabaj**as**	too trah-<u>bvah</u>-Hahs
él, ella, ello, uno, trabaj**a**	ehl, <u>eh</u>-yah, <u>eh</u>-yoh, <u>oo</u>-noh, oos-<u>tehd</u> trah-usted <u>bvah</u>-Hah
nosotros trabaj**amos**	noh-<u>soh</u>-trohs trah-bvah-<u>Hah</u>-mohs
vosotros trabaj**áis**	bvoh-<u>soh</u>-trohs trah-bvah-<u>Hah</u>ees
ellos, ellas, ustedes trabaj**an**	<u>eh</u>-yohs, <u>eh</u>-yahs, oos-<u>teh</u>-dehs trah-<u>bvah</u>-Hahn
Past tense:	
yo trabaj**é**	yoh trah-bvah-<u>Heh</u>
tú trabaj**aste**	too trah-bvah-<u>Hahs</u>-teh
él, ella, ello, uno, usted trabaj**ó**	ehl, <u>eh</u>-yah, <u>eh</u>-yoh, <u>oo</u>-noh, oos-<u>tehd</u> trah-bvah-<u>Hoh</u>
nosotros trabaj**amos**	noh-<u>soh</u>-trohs trah-bvah-<u>Hah</u>-mohs
vosotros trabaj**ásteis**	bvoh-<u>soh</u>-trohs trah-bvah-<u>Hahs</u>-tehees
ellos, ellas, ustedes trabaj**aron**	<u>eh</u>-yohs, <u>eh</u>-yahs, oos-<u>teh</u>-dehs trah-bvah-<u>Hah</u>-ron

Conjugation	*Pronunciation*
Future tense:	
yo trabaj**aré**	yoh trah-bvah-<u>Hah</u>-reh
tú trabaj**arás**	too trah-bvah-<u>Hah</u>-rahs
él, ella, ello, uno, usted trabaj**ará**	ehl, <u>eh</u>-yah, <u>eh</u>-yoh, <u>oo</u>-noh, oos-<u>tehd</u> trah-bvah-<u>Hah</u>-rah
nosotros trabaj**aremos**	noh-<u>soh</u>-trohs trah-bvah-<u>Hah</u>-<u>reh</u>-mohs
vosotros trabaj**aréis**	bvoh-<u>soh</u>-trohs trah-bvah-Hah-rehees
ellos, ellas, ustedes trabaj**arán**	<u>eh</u>-yohs, <u>eh</u>-yahs, oos- <u>teh</u>-dehs trah-bvah-<u>Hah</u>-ran

Talkin' the Talk

Rosario is interested in Alejandro's job. It pays well, and Alejandro has a great deal of free time.

Rosario:	**¿Dónde trabajas?**
	<u>dohn</u>-deh trah-<u>bvah</u>-Hahs
	Where do you work?
Alejandro:	**Trabajo en mi casa.**
	trah-<u>bvah</u>-Hoh ehn mee <u>kah</u>-sa
	I work at home.
Rosario:	**¿Siempre trabajaste en tu casa?**
	see-<u>ehm</u>-preh trah-bvah-<u>Hahs</u>-teh ehn too <u>kah</u>-sah
	Did you always work at home?
Alejandro:	**No, pero desde hoy trabajaré en mi casa.**
	noh <u>peh</u>-roh <u>dehs</u>-deh oy trah-bvah-Hah-<u>reh</u> ehn mee <u>kah</u>-sah
	No, but from [today] now on, I'll work at home.
Rosario:	**¿Juan y tú trabajarán juntos?**
	Hooahn ee too trah-bvah-Hah-<u>rahn</u> <u>Hoon</u>-tohs
	Will Juan and you work together?
Alejandro:	**Juan trabajará en su oficina y yo en la casa.**
	Hooahn trah-bvah-Hah-<u>rah</u> ehn soo oh-fee-<u>see</u>-nah ee yoh ehn <u>kah</u>-sah
	Juan will work in his office, and I will work at home.

Irregular verbs

In irregular verbs, the root, and at times the endings of the verb keep changing, which complicates matters.

An example is the verb **tener** _(teh-nehr)_ (to have). As the following table shows, the root of the verb, **ten-,** changes into **teng-** and **tien-.** Look carefully at the endings though, and you can see that some things remain the same.

Conjugation	_Pronunciation_
Present tense:	
yo ten**go**	yoh tehn-goh
tú tien**es**	too teeeh-nehs
él, ella, ello, uno, usted tien**e**	ehl, eh-yah, eh-yoh, oo-noh, oos-tehd tee eh-neh
nosotros ten**emos**	noh-soh-trohs teh-neh-mohs
vosotros ten**éis**	bvoh-soh-trohs teh-nehees
ellos, ellas, ustedes tien**en**	eh-yohs, eh-yahs, oos-teh-dehs teeeh-nehn
Past tense:	
yo tu**ve**	yoh too-bveh
tú tu**viste**	too too-bvees-teh
él, ella, ello, uno, usted tu**vo**	ehl, eh-yah, eh-yoh, oo-noh, oos-tehd too-bvoh
nosotros tu**vimos**	noh-soh-trohs too-bvee-mohs
vosotros tu**visteis**	bvoh-soh-trohs too-bvees-tehees
ellos, ellas, ustedes tu**vieron**	eh-yohs, eh-yahs, oos-teh-dehs too-bvee eh-rohn
Future tense:	
yo ten**dré**	yoh tehn-dreh
tú ten**drás**	too tehn-drahs
él, ella, ello, uno, usted ten**drá**	ehl, eh-yah, eh-yoh, oo-noh, oos-tehd tehn-drah
nosotros ten**dremos**	noh-soh-trohs tehn-dreh-mohs
vosotros ten**dréis**	bvoh-soh-trohs tehn-drehees
ellos, ellas, ustedes ten**drán**	eh-yohs, eh-yahs, oos-teh-dehs tehn-drahn

Another Spanish verb that means "to have" is **haber** *(ah-bvehr)*. Though its meaning is the same as **tener,** conjugated in the preceding table, **haber** is often used in the conjugation of other verbs — as is the case with the English verb "to have," which can be used in such English conjugations as, "He has written" or "I have stopped."

Talkin' the Talk

In the following conversation, Verónica tells Javier about her new job, using several tenses of the verb **trabajar.**

Verónica: **¡Ya tengo trabajo!**
yah <u>tehn</u>-goh trah-<u>bvah</u>-Hoh
I already have a job!

Javier: **¿Dónde tienes trabajo?**
<u>dohn</u>-deh tee<u>eh</u>-nehs trah-<u>bvah</u>-Hoh
Where do you have a job?

Verónica: **En una tienda.**
ehn <u>oo</u>-nah tee<u>eh</u>n-dah
In a store.

Javier: **¿En qué trabajas en la tienda?**
ehn keh trah-<u>bvah</u>-Hahs ehn lah tee<u>eh</u>n-dah
What do you do at the store?

Verónica: **Trabajo en ventas.**
trah-<u>bvah</u>-Hoh ehn <u>bvehn</u>-tahs
I work in sales.

Javier: **¿Trabajaste en ventas antes?**
trah-bvah-<u>Hahs</u>-teh ehn <u>bvehn</u>-tahs <u>ahn</u>-tehs
Did you work in sales before?

Verónica: **Sí, tengo alguna experiencia en ventas.**
see <u>tehn</u>-goh ahl-<u>goo</u>-nah ehks-peh-ree<u>eh</u>n-seeah
ehn <u>bvehn</u>-tahs
Yes, I have some experience in sales.

Javier: **Ahora tendrás experiencias nuevas.**
ah-<u>oh</u>-rah tehn-<u>drahs</u> ehks-peh-ree<u>eh</u>n-seeahs
noo<u>eh</u>-bvahs
Now you will have new experiences.

Verónica:	**Sí, espero que tendré mucha experiencia.**
	see ehs-<u>peh</u>-roh keh tehn-dreh moo-chah ehks-peh-ree<u>ehn</u>-seeah
	Yes, I hope I'll have much experience.

Él or Ella? Pronouns in Hiding

For the most part, the Spanish language stays quite regular and to the point, which makes it easy to learn and speak. However, Spanish often hides the pronouns he, she, and it. The easy part with Spanish is that you don't have to say the pronoun — you can make a good guess about the intended pronoun simply from the verb form.

In English, you always use the pronoun before the verb. Not so in Spanish. Because each pronoun has its own verb form, Spanish generally omits the pronoun. Therefore, you say **Voy al cine**, for "I go to the movies." Here are some other examples:

- **Están de vacaciones.** *(ehs-<u>tahn</u> deh bvah-kah-see<u>oh</u>-nehs.)* (They are on vacation.)

- **No es el carro.** *(noh ehs ehl <u>kah</u>-rroh)* (It is not the car.)

- **¿Tienen vino?** *(tee<u>eh</u>-nehn <u>bvee</u>-noh)* (Do they or you [formal] have wine?)

Figuring out Spanish pronouns is much like playing hide-and-seek. For a language that gives every word a specific gender, Spanish still manages to hide the gender of the doer of its verbs. In the sentence **Trabaja en ventas,** you know that someone or something is working in sales, but you don't know if it is a woman, a man, a cat, or a computer. In English you use he, she, and it to know who (or what) performs the action, but Spanish generally omits the pronoun. But because each pronoun has its own verb form, when you say, **Voy al cine**, I understand that you're saying "*I* go to the movies," based on the form of the verb.

That Whole Gender Thing

What Spanish lacks in pronouns, it makes up for by being very specific in other parts of a sentence.

You see, in Spanish, not just people, but everything in creation has gender!

When you refer to people and animals, understanding gender use in Spanish is easy because gender is a part of their essence — just as with flowers;

everyone knows that flowers are pollinated, needing both genders to produce fruit and seeds.

So why not refer to all things that grow with names that are marked by gender? And if things that grow have gender, why not give everything (and every word) that privilege? Many languages spread this gender thing into their universe. English isn't the only exception — it simply belongs to those languages that don't.

A noun's gender conditions everything around it, just as your own gender conditions your lifestyle. For example, in English, the word "piano" has no gender. But in Spanish, the word *piano* (peeah-noh) ends in an *o,* and can therefore only be male. Consequently, *piano* has a male definite article before it **el piano,** (*ehl peeah-noh*) (the piano) or the male indefinite article **un piano** (*oon peeah-noh*) (a piano).

Lots about articles

In English, you use the articles *the* and *a* or *an* without knowing the subject's gender, or even caring whether a plural or singular word comes after it — very comfortable, but also very vague. However, with Spanish articles, you can point out when you're referring to one or several specific beings or things, and in the same breath, you can specify their gender.

In Spanish, your reward for this precision is variety. It's a "more is better" kind of policy — you have four different ways to say *the:* "The" can precede "the girl," "the girls," "the boy," "the boys," or any other subject you want to stick in!

- ✔ **el** *(ehl)* (the male *the,* singular)
- ✔ **la** *(lah)* (the female *the,* singular)
- ✔ **los** *(lohs)* (the male *the,* plural)
- ✔ **las** *(lahs)* (the female *the,* plural)

And, four ways to say *a* or *an:*

- ✔ **un** *(oon)* (the male *a* or *an*)
- ✔ **una** *(oo-nah)* (the female *a* or *an*)
- ✔ **unos** *(oo-nohs)* (the plural of *un*)
- ✔ **unas** *(oo-nahs)* (the plural of *una*)

So how do you know when to use which article? It's easy. When the noun ends in **o** — it's male. If a word ends in **a,** it's female. (Some exceptions to this rule exist, but they're pretty easy to figure out because they follow another rule — the **ma, pa, ta** rule — which holds that words ending in **ma, pa,** and **ta** are likely to be masculine even though **a** is the last letter.) The easy part to remember is that when you see an "s" at the end of the word, you know the word is plural. Here are some examples:

✔ **el niño** *(ehl nee-nyoh)* (the boy)

los niños *(lohs nee-nyohs)* (the boys [or the children])

un niño *(oon nee-nyoh)* (a boy)

unos niños *(oo-nohs nee-nyohs)* (some boys [or children])

✔ **la niña** *(lah nee-nyah)* (the girl)

las niñas *(lahs nee-nyahs)* (the girls)

una niña *(oo-nah nee-nyah)* (a girl)

unas niñas *(oo-nahs nee-nyahs)* (some girls)

Look at the **los niños** entry in the preceding list and notice that the translation is plural for both "the boys" and "the children." When you have mixed company (both the male and females genders are present), you use the male plural article. So **los niños** can mean "boys" or "boys and girls." You follow the same pattern with unos.

Okay, okay, so Spanish and English are both vague in places, you say. And Spanish speakers say, sorry, that's the way it is. Languages, like people, all reserve the right to be vague at times.

Spanish is a melodious language. It doesn't like to have two consonants at the end of a word, so it inserts a vowel between them — as in **mujer, mujeres.** So when a noun ends in a consonant, before adding the **s** to turn it into a plural, Spanish inserts an **e.** Following are some examples:

✔ **la mujer** *(lah moo-Hehr)* (the woman)

una mujer *(oo-nah moo-Hehr)* (a woman)

unas mujeres *(oo-nahs moo-Heh-rehs)* (some women)

✔ **el pan** *(ehl pahn)* (the bread)

los panes *(lohs pah-nehs)* (the breads)

un pan *(oon pahn)* (a bread)

unos panes *(oo-nohs pah-nehs)* (some breads)

✔ **el canal** *(ehl kah-nahl)* (the channel)

> **los canales** *(lohs kah-nah-lehs)* (the channels)
>
> **un canal** *(oon kah-nahl)* (a channel)
>
> **unos canales** *(oo-nohs kah-nah-lehs)* (some channels)
>
> ✔ **el doctor** *(ehl dohk-tohr)* (the doctor)
>
> **los doctores** *(lohs dohk-toh-rehs)* (the doctors)
>
> **un doctor** *(oon dohk-tohr)* (a doctor)
>
> **unos doctores** *(oo-nohs dohk-toh-rehs)* (some doctors)

You may not be aware of this, but you already know how to make plurals of these nouns: Simply add **s** to both the article and to the noun.

Words to Know

el niño	ehl nee-nyo	the boy
la niña	lah nee-nyah	the girl
la mujer	lah moo-Hehr	the woman
el hombre	ehl ohm-breh	the man
los vinos	lohs bvee-nohs	the wines
el camino	ehl kah-mee-noh	the road
las casas	lahs kah-sahs	the houses
los autos	lohs ahoo-tohs	the cars

A professional job

When a male word for a profession comes up, you form the female term by adding an "a" to the end of the word. Thus, "doctor" becomes **doctora**. From there, you know already how to find your articles:

✔ **la doctora** *(lah dohk-toh-rah)* (the female doctor)

✔ **una doctora** *(oo-nah dohk-toh-rah)* (a female doctor)

✔ **las doctoras** *(lahs dohk-toh-rahs)* (the female doctors)

✔ **unas doctoras** *(oo-nahs dohk-toh-rahs)* (some female doctors)

Not as tough as it looks, is it?

Adjectives

A *noun* tells you what you're talking about, and a *pronoun* tells whom you're talking about. But, adjectives are more fun. They tell you what these things and people *are like*. Adjectives are the essence of gossip!

When you talk or gossip in Spanish, you're very specific about gender and number. In fact, even adjectives get to show their gender and number.

Suppose that you want to say, "I have a white car." In Spanish you say, **Tengo un carro blanco** (*tehn*-goh oon *kah*-rroh *bvlahn*-koh). (Remember, because it ends in *o*, carro is masculine. A masculine noun gets a masculine adjective: **blanco** (*bvlahn*-koh).

Before we discuss how to talk about more than one house, more than one woman, or more than one car, we need to show you some numbers.

No, no! Not math — just numbers!

Numbers: When Everything Counts

You can get by with asking for one thing, or more than one thing, or even some things . . . for a while. But eventually you'll want to ask for two things, or ten things, or even more. When numbers are important, you need to know how to say them, so we show you how to count from one to ten in Spanish:

Is Casablanca a big, white house?

You know about *Casablanca,* don't you? You know it's a film where Ingrid Bergman and Humphrey Bogart say goodbye to each other endlessly? Well you're right, but there's more.

Casablanca is also the place where all the movie's tearful events take place — a Moroccan harbor on the Atlantic coast of Africa. The city's name in Arabic is Dar El-Beida (*dahr ehl-bvehee-dah*). Sorry, we're not translating the city's Arabic name, but imagine Casablanca as a place with white-washed houses all around the harbor.

And do you know how to say "the white house" in Spanish? Of course you do! **¡la casa blanca!**

1. **uno** *(oo-noh)* (one)

2. **dos** *(dohs)* (two)

3. **tres** *(trehs)* (three)

4. **cuatro** *(kooah-troh)* (four)

5. **cinco** *(seen-koh)* (five)

6. **seis** *(sehees)* (six)

7. **siete** *(seeeh-teh)* (seven)

8. **ocho** *(oh-choh)* (eight)

9. **nueve** *(nooeh-bveh)* (nine)

10. **diez** *(deeehs)* (ten)

Earlier in this chapter, we say that, with adjectives (as with other Spanish words), you need to be very specific about gender and number. You already know about gender; here's how to handle number.

When you talk about things in the plural, you add the letter *s* to the adjective to show that you're talking about more than one. So, **blanco** *(bvlahn-koh)* becomes **blancos** *(bvlahn-kohs)*, **alta** *(ahl-tah)* becomes **altas** *(ahl-tahs),* and so on. More examples follow:

- ✔ **Las dos mujeres son altas.** *(lahs dohs moo-Heh-rehs sohn ahl-tahs)* (The two women are tall.)

- ✔ **Ocho hombres altos van en un auto rojo.**
  (oh-choh ohm-bvrehs ahl-tohs bvahn ehn oon ahoo-toh roh-Hoh)
  (Eight tall men go in a red car.)

- ✔ **Las dos casas son grandes.** *(lahs dohs kah-sahs sohn grahn-dehs)* (The two houses are large.)

- ✔ **Los tres caminos son largos.** *(lohs trehs kah-mee-nohs sohn lahr-gohs)* (The three roads are long.)

It's You, You Know: The Tú/Usted Issue

People use both body language and spoken language to convey how they want a relationship to develop.

Relationships tend to be more formal in Spanish than in English. If you need to be formal in English you have to show it by your body movements, or by the tone of your voice. In Spanish, the distinction between **tú** *(too)* and **usted** *(oos-tehd)* allows you to introduce this formality right into the language.

In the olden days, English speakers said *thou* and *you*. People said *thou* to their beloved and *you* to their beloved's parents. Anyone listening to a conversation knew whether the speakers were intimate or had a more formal relationship.

Spanish speakers kept this habit. Spanish speakers say **tú** *(too)* as English speakers used to say "thou" and **usted** *(oos-tehd)* to signify a more respectful way of talking to someone, such as a new acquaintance, an older person, or someone they consider to be of higher rank.

Human relations are rigged with feelings. Only you know when you want to be more personal with someone. The beauty of Spanish is that you have a verbal means to manifest these feelings.

At some point in a relationship between people who speak Spanish, a shift occurs from the formal **usted** to the more informal and intimate **tú**. Two people of the same age, the same rank, or the same educational level, or people who wish to express a certain intimacy, very soon arrive at a point where they want to talk to each other in a more informal or intimate manner. It is at this point that they use the word **tú** when addressing each other. In Spanish we call this **tutearse** *(too-tehahr-seh),* that is, "to talk *tú*." Most adults address children using **tú**. These formalities make relationships more graceful and more varied. Being graceful in your speech and your relationships is much appreciated in Spanish-speaking places.

On the other hand, if you don't want to have a closer, more intimate relationship with someone, or if you want to keep the relationship more professional and less chummy, you should stick to calling that person **usted**.

Following are some examples of sentences that use **tú** and **usted**:

- ✔ **¿Cómo se llama usted?** *(koh-moh seh yah-mah oos-tehd)* (What's your name? [Respectful])

- ✔ **¿Vas tú con Juan en el auto rojo?** *(bvahs too kohn Hooahn ehn ehl ahoo-toh roh-Hoh)* (Do you go with Juan in the red car? [Friendly, intimate])

- ✔ **Usted tiene una casa muy bella.** *(oos-tehd teeeh-neh oo-nah kah-sah mooy bveh-yah)* (You [singular] have a very beautiful house [Respectful, formal].)

When people in Spain want to address several persons, they use the word **vosotros** *(bvoh-soh-trohs),* which is the informal "you," in the plural. Spanish-speaking Americans almost never use **vosotros.**

When in Spain, vosotros rules

The pronoun **vosotros** is used in spoken Spanish in Spain only. In all other Spanish-speaking countries, **vosotros** is taught in the schools, but never used in normal conversation. In Latin America, you hear **ustedes**; there is no distinction between formal and informal in the plural you.

Here are all the various *you* forms using **trabajar** (to work) as an example:

> **tú trabajas** (you work), which is singular, informal

usted trabaja (you work), which is singular, formal

vosotros trabajáis (you work), which is plural, informal in Spain only

ustedes trabajan (you work), which is plural, formal in Spain, formal AND informal in Latin America)

You may hear a variation of the **vosotros** in Argentina or Colombia, **Vos trabajás** (you work). From a grammatical standpoint, this form is totally incorrect, so don't try to copy it.

One of the main differences between the Spain Spanish way of addressing several people and the Spanish-speaking American one is that in Spanish America, people say **ustedes** (meaning "you," in the plural — but "they" in conjugation). This **ustedes** can be a formal way of addressing two or more people, or it can be very informal. The situation dictates the difference. Here are some examples:

> ✔ **¿Adónde van ustedes dos?** (*ah <u>dohn</u>-deh bvahn oos-<u>teh</u>-dehs dohs*) (Where are the two of you going?) (Can be very informal, or formal)

> ✔ **¿Tú viajas en el auto?** (*too bvee<u>ah</u>-Hahs ehn ehl <u>ah</u>oo-toh*) (Do you travel in the car?) (Informal, close)

> ✔ **¿A usted le gusta el tango?** (*ah oos-<u>tehd</u> leh <u>goos</u>-tah ehl <u>tahn</u>-goh*) (Do you like the tango?) (Formal)

In written texts you may find the words **usted** and **ustedes** in their abbreviated forms (**Ud.** for **usted,** and **Uds.** for **ustedes**). When you read these abbreviations aloud, you say the whole word.

Congratulations, you're becoming a Spanish grammarian! (Grammar may not be glamorous, but you can't beat it as a means of making sure you understand and are understood when visiting your Spanish-speaking neighbors and friends.)

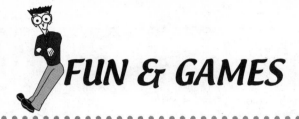

FUN & GAMES

Suppose you want to say "I have a white house."

You already know how to say it! In Spanish you say, **"Tengo una casa blanca"** *(tehn-goh oo-nah kah-sah bvlahn-kah)*. You know *la casa (lah kah-sah)* is female, because it ends in **a**. Therefore, the adjective, **blanca** *(bvlahn-kah)*, is also female.

The following examples further illustrate my point about the gender of adjectives. Just select the appropriate adjective to fill in the blank in the sentence:

✔ **Tengo una caja (blanca, blanco).** I have a white box.

✔ **Mi auto no es (blanca, blanco).** My car is not white.

✔ **La mujer es (alta, alto).** The woman is tall.

✔ **El hombre es (alta, alto).** The man is tall.

Part II
Spanish in Action

The 5th Wave   By Rich Tennant

"I'm so proud of Ted. He ordered our entire meal in Spanish, and everything came out perfect – from the sushi appetizers to the noodle and wonton soup with shrimp tempura."

In this part . . .

In this part, you begin learning and using Spanish. Instead of focusing on grammar points as many language textbooks do, this part focuses on everyday situations that you might find yourself in if you were living in a Spanish-speaking country or dealing with your Spanish-speaking neighbors. This part hones your small-talk skills and takes you on shopping and dining excursions. At the end of this part, you should be able to do some basic navigation in the Spanish language.

Chapter 3

¡Buenos Días! Hello! Greetings and Introductions

- -

In This Chapter

▶ Naming names

▶ Making introductions

▶ Speaking formally or informally

▶ Being you: **ser** *(sehr)* (to be); being there: **estar** *(ehs-tahr)* (to be)

▶ Mentioning cities, countries, and nationalities

- -

Meeting and greeting go hand in hand!

In Latin America especially, *how* you greet people matters a great deal. Latin Americans tend to be very respectful of each other and of strangers. So as a rule, when you greet someone for the first time in Latin America, it's best not to say "Hello!" — a greeting that is quite informal.

Greetings: Formal or Friendly

As you begin a relationship, Latin Americans believe that keeping a certain distance is best. Only when you already know the person should you use the friendlier, informal phrases. Because Latins look at building relationships this way, try to respect that view when you're in Spanish-speaking countries or with Latins in the United States. It's just being polite, Latin-style. A relationship with a customer in a business situation, however, is always formal.

Latins don't use *tú (too),* the informal "you" (refer to Chapter 2) when addressing someone they respect and have never met. And they don't greet each other informally on the first occasion they meet.

Latin Americans know that people in the States tend to treat each other very informally, so some may treat you as someone they already know. You may feel a bit leery of this behavior, though: The uncharacteristic informality may make you wonder whether there's some special reason for treating you with such familiarity. On the other hand, an overly friendly Spanish-speaker may simply be trying to put you at ease.

Talkin' the Talk

In this conversation, Pepe is formally introducing Lucía and Fernando to Mr. Kendall.

Pepe:	**Buenas tardes. ¿El señor Kendall?**
	bvooeh-nahs tahr-dehs ehl seh-nyohr Kendall
	Good afternoon. Mr. Kendall?
Mr. Kendall:	**Sí, me llamo Kendall.**
	see meh yah-moh Kendall
	Yes, my name is Kendall.
Pepe:	**Permítame que le presente al señor Fernando Quintana Martínez.**
	pehr-mee-tah-me keh leh preh-sehn-teh ahl seh-nyohr fehr-nahn-doh keen-tah-nah mahr-tee-nehs
	Allow me to introduce Mr. Fernando Quintana Martínez.
Mr. Kendall:	**Mucho gusto.**
	moo-choh goos-toh
	A pleasure.
Pepe:	**Esta es la señora de Kendall.**
	ehs-tah ehs lah seh-nyoh-rah deh Kendall
	This is Mrs. Kendall.
	Esta es la señora Lucía Sánchez de Quintana.
	ehs-tah ehs lah seh-nyoh-rah loo-seeah sahn-ches deh keen-tah-nah
	This is Mrs. Lucía Sánchez de Quintana.
Mrs. Kendall:	**Mucho gusto, señora.**
	moo-choh goos-toh seh-nyoh-rah
	A pleasure, ma'am.

Talkin' the Talk

Listen to how John and Julia, two teenagers, greet each other informally:

John: **¡Hola! ¿Cómo te llamas?**
_oh_-lah! _koh_-moh teh _yah_-mahs
Hi! What's your name?

Julia: **Me llamo Julia. ¿Y tú?**
meh _yah_-moh _Hoo_-leeah ee too
My name is Julia. And yours?

John: **Yo me llamo John.**
yoh meh _yah_-moh John
My name is John.

Using Names and Surnames

Latin Americans are generally easygoing people who love to converse. Feel free to initiate contact with them, using the greetings we present in this chapter. If you feel interest on both your part and theirs to keep the contact going, then you can introduce yourself, but wait for your acquaintance to give you his or her name. Only if the other person doesn't give you his or her name should you ask what it is. In some specific situations, a third person introduces you, but usually you are expected to introduce yourself. In this chapter, we show you several ways that introductions can happen.

As we get into the names issue, we need to clear up one little thing. When you meet someone, he or she probably will tell you just his or her first name, or maybe only part of it — **Carmen** (_kahr_-mehn), instead of **María del Carmen** (mah-_reeah_ dehl _kahr_-mehn). But, as you get to know people better, you will learn their surnames, as well.

A new acquaintance usually expresses some caution in the beginning by giving you only a partial name. When you receive the full name and the two surnames, you know you have a complete introduction.

These little maneuvers take place because, in the Spanish-speaking world, it isn't customary to wait to be introduced to someone before you talk to him or her. An introduction as such isn't necessary. When a third party does introduce you, it's just meant to make your contact with the new acquaintance much faster.

What's in a name?

Suppose that you meet a woman named **María del Carmen Fernández Bustamante** *(mah-<u>reeah</u> dehl <u>kahr</u>-mehn fehr-<u>nahn</u>-dehs bvoos-tah-<u>mahn</u>-teh)*. You can tell that you may call her **señorita** *(seh-nyoh-<u>ree</u>-tah)*, or Miss Fernández *(fehr-<u>nahn</u>-dehs)* because of the three-part structure of her name. (In an English-speaking country, she would rearrange her name to María del Carmen Bustamante Fernández because English speakers put the father's name at the end, and use the person's *last name* as a reference.

So far, so good. But if Miss Fernández marries, she adds on more names. In our example, she marries **señor** *(seh-<u>nyohr</u>)* (Mr.) **Juan José García Díaz** *(Hooahn Hoh-<u>seh</u> gahr-<u>seeah</u> deeahs)*. She is still called Fernández, but after her father's name she adds **de** *(deh)* (of) and her husband's surname, which is García. Now, she is **señora María del Carmen Fernández de García** *(mah-<u>reeah</u> dehl <u>kahr</u>-mehn fehr-<u>nahn</u>-dehs deh gahr-<u>seeah</u>)*.

Note that Spanish speakers capitalize **señor** or **señora** when abbreviated the way people in the States capitalize Mr. and Mrs.

Within the social circles of some countries, the surname of a married woman's husband gets more emphasis; in other places, her father's surname is stressed. For example, you hear the husband's surname used more often in Argentina than in Mexico.

The effect of these conventions is that women keep their family names, which are considered very important and meaningful. A child's surnames indicate both his or her father and mother. Señor García, in our example, has a child, Mario, by a previous marriage to a woman whose surname was Ocampo. Because children carry the surnames of both parents, Mario is called Mario García Ocampo. And when señor García and María del Carmen Fernández de García's daughter, Ana, is born, her name is Ana García Fernández. Ana and Mario are siblings, having the same father and different mothers. The Spanish use of both the father' and mother's surnames immediately indicates the relationship between the siblings.

Among Spanish speaking peoples, using both parents' first names for their same-sex children is customary. So, in a family where the mother, Marta Inés, has three daughters, she may call one Marta Julieta, another Marta Felicia, and the third Marta Juana. When the father's name is used for the son, the two are called identical names, because "Jr." is not used in Spanish. But you can tell the men apart because their *mother's surnames* are different.

Introducing the verb llamarse

Now is a good time to include the conjugation of the **llamarse** (yah-_mahr_-seh), the equivalent of "name is," which you use when you introduce yourself.

The verb **llamar** is a regular **-ar** verb; however, the **se** at the end of it tells you that the verb is reflexive, which makes it irregular, too (nobody said grammar was easy). In case your memory needs to jog a little, a reflexive verb is one that acts on the noun (or object) of the sentence. For instance, the sentence **yo me llamo** (yo meh _yah_-moh) literally means "I call myself." In this case, "I" is the subject of the sentence and "call myself" reflects back to "I." Anytime you see the **se** at the end of a verb, you simply put the reflexive pronoun (**me** in the example sentence) in front of the verb. For more on reflexive verbs, see Chapter 16.

Take a look at the following table for the conjugation of **llamarse** in the present tense. Pay attention to the reflexive pronouns — they stay the same for all regular **-ar** verbs.

Conjugation	Pronunciation
yo me llamo	yoh meh _yah_-moh
tú te llamas	too teh _yah_-mahs
él, ella, ello, uno, usted se llama	ehl, _eh_-yah, _eh_-yo, _oo_-noh, _oos_-tehd seh _yah_-mah
nosotros nos llamamos	noh-_soh_-trohs nohs yah-_mah_-mohs
vosotros os llamáis	bvoh-_soh_-trohs ohs yah-_mahees_
ellos, ellas, ustedes se llaman	_eh-yohs_, _eh_-yahs, oos-_teh_-dehs seh _yah_-mahn

Introductions: Solemn and Social

Some situations call for a certain level of solemnity. An example is when one is being introduced to a very important or famous person.

Like English, a few, specific phrases signal this formality, as the following examples demonstrate:

✔ **¿Me permite presentarle a . . . .?** (meh pehr-_mee_-teh preh-sehn-_tahr_-leh ah) (May I introduce. . . .?)

✔ **Es un gusto conocerle.** (ehs oon _goos_-toh koh-noh-_sehr_-leh) (It's a pleasure to meet you.)

✔ **El gusto es mío.** (ehl _goos_-toh ehs _mee_oh) (The pleasure is mine.)

My name is Is, isn't it?

When, in English, you say, "I introduce myself," you're using a reflexive form of the verb "introduce," and so you say "myself." Likewise, when Pedro says **"me llamo Pedro"** *(meh yah-moh peh-droh),* the word **me** *(meh)* means "myself." (See Chapter 16 for details about reflexive verbs.)

Often, beginning Spanish speakers say, **"Me llamo es,"** using a mistakenly literal translation of "my name is." But, note that **me** in Spanish means "to me" or "myself" — it never means "I." **Llamo** is the first person of the singular of a verb, so **me llamo** can be translated as "I call myself." Even in English, you don't add "is" to that. Right?

Introducing yourself formally

Introducing yourself formally means that you don't talk in a chummy, informal way to a person with whom you have no relationship as yet. Unlike a child, you use the formal way of introducing yourself because you want to keep a certain distance, just in case you decide later on that you don't want a closer relationship with this person.

People who don't know each other use *usted* (oos-<u>tehd</u>) — the formal form of "you" — and its verbal form when addressing one another.

Talkin' the Talk

In a more formal situation, people introduce each other differently. Listen to Pedro García Fernández as he approaches a table at a sidewalk cafe with a person already sitting there.

Pedro: **¿Me permite?**
              meh pehr-<u>mee</u>-teh
              May I?

Jane: **Sí, ¡adelante!**
              see, ah-deh-<u>lahn</u>-teh
              Yes, [go] ahead!

Pedro:	**Buenas tardes. Me llamo Pedro García Fernández.**
	bvoo<u>eh</u>-nahs <u>tahr</u>-dehs meh <u>yah</u>-moh <u>peh</u>-droh gahr-<u>seeah</u> fehr-<u>nahn</u>-dehs
	Good afternoon. My name is Pedro García Fernández.
Jane:	**Mucho gusto, señor García.**
	<u>moo</u>-choh <u>goos</u>-toh seh-<u>nyohr</u> gahr-<u>seea</u>h
	Nice to meet you, Mr. García.
Pedro:	**Y usted ¿cómo se llama?**
	ee oos-<u>tehd</u> <u>koh</u>-moh seh <u>yah</u>-mah
	And what's your name?
Jane:	**Me llamo Jane Wells.**
	meh <u>yah</u>-moh Jane Wells
	My name is Jane Wells.
Pedro:	**Mucho gusto.**
	<u>moo</u>-choh <u>goos</u>-toh
	A pleasure.

Note: People commonly describe children with diminutives, as we explain in Chapter 2.

When you're talking to a child, you speak less formally. The adult speaker may be identified by the insertion of **don** in front of his name. Calling someone **don** (or the feminine form, **doña**) can be a way of showing that you're addressing an older and respected person. (To the child, the adult looks old.)

Capitalize abbreviations.

Only in abbreviations (as well as proper names) do Spanish speakers use use capitals. Here's how it goes:

		señorita	Srta.
		usted	Ud.
		ustedes	Uds.
señor	Sr.		
señora	Sra.		

Talkin' the Talk

Narr.:	Sr. Rivera and Sra. Salinas work in the same building. Here's how they might greet each other in hallway.
Sra. Salinas:	**Buenos días, Sr. Rivera. ¿Cómo está?** *bvooeh-nohs deeahs seh-nyohr ree-veh-rah koh-moh ehs-tah* Good morning, Mr. Rivera. How are you?
Sr. Rivera:	**Muy bien. ¿Y Ud.?** *mooy bveeehn ee oos-tehd* Very well. And you?
Sra. Salinas:	**Bien, gracias.** *bveeehn, grah-seeahs* Well, thank you.
Narr.:	John and Julia meet again by accident a few days later while on their way to school.
John:	**Buenos días. ¿Qué tal?** *bvooeh-nohs deeahs keh tahl* Good morning. How are things?
Julia:	**¡Ah, hola, John! ¿Cómo estás?** *ah oh-lah john koh-moh ehs-tahs* Ah, hello, John! How are you?
John:	**Bien. ¿Y tú?** *bveeehn ee tooh* Well. And you?
Julia:	**Bien.** *bveeehn* Well.

Free to Be the Way You Are

In Spanish, you have two ways to ask, "To be or not to be." You can say **Ser o no ser** *(sehr oh noh sehr),* when the state of being is unlikely to change (you will always be a person, for example), and you use **Estar o no estar** *(ehs-tahr o no ehs-tahr)* if the state of being is changeable (you won't always be tired).

To be permanent: ser

Ser refers to a kind of being that is *permanent,* like the fact that you are you. The word also refers to all things that are expected to be permanent, such as places, countries, and certain conditions or states of being, such as shape, profession, nationality, and place of origin. This permanent "to be" in Spanish is **ser** *(sehr):*

- ✔ **Soy mujer.** *(sohy moo-Hehr)* (I'm a woman.)
- ✔ **Soy Canadiense.** *(sohy kah-nah-dee-ehn-seh)* (I'm Canadian.)
- ✔ **Soy de Winnipeg.** *(sohy de Winnipeg)* (I'm from Winnipeg.)
- ✔ **Ellos son muy altos.** *(eh-yohs sohn mooy ahl-tohs)* (They are very tall.)
- ✔ **¿Ustedes son Uruguayos?** *(oos-teh-dehs sohn oo-roo-gooah-yohs)* (Are you [formal] Uruguayan?)
- ✔ **Ella es maestra.** *(eh-yah ehs mah-ehs-trah)* (She's a teacher.)
- ✔ **Eres muy bella.** *(eh-rehs mooy bveh-yah)* (You are very beautiful.)
- ✔ **Eres muy gentil.** *(eh-rehs mooy Hehn-teel)* (You are very kind.)

Conjugating ser (to Be)

The verb **ser** *(sehr)* (to be) is the one most frequently used in Spanish. And, of course, just like the English "to be," it's an irregular verb. (We discuss irregular verbs in Chapter 2.) The following table shows how **ser** is conjugated.

Americans all

You probably like to tell people where you're from, and you like to know where the people you meet are from, too.

Almost everyone likes to talk about nationalities. And when you talk about nationalities with Latin Americans, you're wise to remember one, crucial point: Latin Americans are Americans, too.

So, to say **americano** *(ah-meh-ree-kah-noh)* when you mean someone from the United States, doesn't quite cover the ground. You make yourself better understood if you say **norteamericano** *(nohr-teh-ah-meh-ree-kah-noh),* meaning "North American."

Conjugation	*Pronunciation*
yo soy	yoh sohy
tú eres	too eh-rehs
él, ella, ello, uno, usted es	ehl, eh-yah, eh-yoh, oo-noh, oos-tehd, ehs
nosotros somos	noh-soh-trohs soh-mohs
vosotros sois	bvoh-soh-trohs sohees
ellos, ellas, ustedes son	eh-yohs, eh-yahs, oos-teh-dehs sohn

Adios, pronouns

In an English sentence, you always use a noun or pronoun with a verb. You may already have noticed that Spanish does not. Because the verb form is different for each pronoun, Spanish frequently omits the pronoun.

Spanish verbs indicate the pronoun through their conjugation. English verbs don't. For example, in English, you say "*I sing,*" "*you sing,*" and "*we sing.*" In Spanish, you say, **canto** (I sing), **cantas** (you sing), and **cantamos** (we sing). Therefore, Spanish-speakers can understand you clearly even if you use only the verb. Using the pronoun in Spanish isn't wrong, although leaving it off is more informal and conversational. However, especially as you start practicing the language, using the pronoun may help you conjugate the verb correctly.

Talkin' the Talk

Now is a good time to practice the "permanent" way to be, so that it becomes second nature. (You wouldn't want your being to flitter away, would you?) Imagine that you're in a café, the meeting place for socializing in most Latin-American countries, and you can over-hear several conversations. Listening to the people at the first table, you hear the following:

Roberto: **¿Y usted Jane, de qué ciudad es?**
ee oos-<u>tehd</u> Jane deh keh seeoo-<u>dahd</u> ehs
And you, Jane, what city are you from?

Jane: **Soy de New Berlin, en el estado de Nueva York.**
sohy deh New Berlin ehn ehl ehs-<u>tah</u>-doh deh noo<u>eh</u>-bvah yohrk
I'm from New Berlin in New York state.

Roberto: **¿Es esa una ciudad grande?**
ehs <u>eh</u>-sah <u>oo</u>-nah seeoo-<u>dahd</u> <u>grahn</u>-deh
Is that a very large city?

Jane: **Es un pueblo chico, pero muy bonito.**
ehs oon poo<u>eh</u>-bvloh <u>chee</u>-koh <u>peh</u>-roh mooy bvoh-<u>nee</u>-toh
It's a small town, but it's very nice.

Roberto: **Bueno, esta es también una ciudad chica.**
bvoo<u>eh</u>-noh <u>ehs</u>-tah ehs tahm-bvee<u>ehn</u> <u>oo</u>-nah seeoo-<u>dahd</u> <u>chee</u>-kah
Well, this is also a small city.

Jane: **¡Para nada!, es bastante grande.**
<u>pah</u>-rah <u>nah</u>-dah ehs bvahs-<u>tahn</u>-teh <u>grahn</u>-deh
Not at all, it's quite big.

Words to Know

chico	<u>chee</u>-koh	little; small
grande	<u>grahn</u>-deh	big; large
bastante	bvahs-<u>tahn</u>-teh	quite; enough

Talkin' the Talk

Still at the café, you hear this conversation from another table:

Esperanza: **¿Es bueno el hotel Paraíso?**
ehs bvoo<u>eh</u>-noh ehl oh-<u>tehl</u> pah-ra<u>hee</u>-soh
Is the hotel Paraíso any good?

Esteban: **Sí, es un buen hotel.**
see ehs oon bvooehn <u>oh</u>-tehl
Yes, it's a good hotel.

Esperanza: **¿Es caro?**
ehs <u>kah</u>-roh
Is it expensive?

Esteban: **Es un poco caro.**
ehs oon <u>poh</u>-koh <u>kah</u>-roh
It's a little expensive.

Esperanza: **¿Es grande?**
ehs <u>grahn</u>-deh
Is it big?

Esteban: **No, no es muy grande.**
noh noh ehs mooy <u>grahn</u>-deh
No, it's not very big.

Esperanza: **¿Es un problema llamar allí?**
ehs oon proh-<u>bvleh</u>-mah yah-<u>mahr</u> ah-<u>yee</u>
Is it a problem to call there?

Esteban: **No, no es ningún problema.**
noh noh ehs neen-<u>goon</u> proh-<u>bvleh</u>-mah
No, it's no problem.

Words to Know

buen	bvooehn	good (male)
bueno	bvooeh-noh	good (male)
buena	bvooeh-nah	good (female)
caro	kah-roh	expensive
poco	poh-koh	a bit; small amount
ningún	neen-goon	none

A Second "Be" for Your Bonnet

Remember that Spanish is a very precise language. In Spanish, you have two forms of "to be," each with a different meaning, to supply more precision to your statements. Unlike in English, when you talk about *being* in Spanish, the verb you use removes any guesswork about what your meaning is.

As we discuss in the preceding section, when you speak of being someone or something *permanently* in Spanish, you use the verb **ser** *(sehr)*. But when you're talking about a state of being that is *not permanent* — such as being someplace (you won't be there forever), or being some temporary way (being ill, for instance) — you use the verb **estar** *(ehs-tahr)*. So in Spanish, it isn't "To be or not to be," but "To be forever **(ser)** or not forever **(estar)**."

So you know you can use one of two verbs to say "to be." We delve into the verb **ser** *(sehr)* in the previous section. The following table conjugates the present tense of the verb **estar**:

Conjugation	*Pronunciation*
yo estoy	yoh ehs-tohy
tú estás	too ehs-tahs
él, ella, ello, uno, usted está	ehl, eh-yah, eh-yoh, oo-noh, oos-tehd ehs-tah
nosotros estamos	noh-soh-trohs ehs-tah-mohs
vosotros estáis	bvoh-soh-trohs ehs-tahees
ellos, ellas, unos, ustedes están	eh-yohs, eh-yahs, oo-nohs, oos-teh-dehs ehs-tahn

We use this verb a great deal in this book, so we give you the simple past and future tenses, also. The following table provides conjugation of the past tense:

Conjugation	Pronunciation
yo estuve	yoh ehs-<u>too</u>-bveh
tú estuviste	too ehs-too-<u>bvees</u>-teh
él, ella, ello, uno, usted estuvo	ehl, <u>eh</u>-yah, <u>eh</u>-yoh, <u>oo</u>-noh, oos-<u>tehd</u> ehs-<u>too</u>-bvoh
nosotros estuvimos	noh-<u>soh</u>-trohs ehs-too-<u>bvee</u>-mohs
vosotros estuvisteis	bvoh-<u>soh</u>-trohs ehs-too-<u>bvees</u>-tehees
ellos, ellas, unos, ustedes estuvieron	<u>eh</u>-yohs, <u>eh</u>-yahs, <u>oo</u>-nohs, oos-<u>teh</u>-dehs ehs-too-bvee<u>eh</u>-rohn

Here's how you conjugate the future tense of **estar**:

Conjugation	Pronunciation
yo estaré	yoh ehs-tah-<u>reh</u>
tú estarás	too ehs-tah-<u>rahs</u>
él, ella, ello, uno, usted estará	ehl, <u>eh</u>-yah, <u>eh</u>-yoh, <u>oo</u>-noh, oos-<u>tehd</u> ehs-tah-<u>rah</u>
nosotros estaremos	noh-<u>soh</u>-trohs ehs-tah-<u>reh</u>-mohs
vosotros estaréis	bvoh-<u>soh</u>-trohs ehs-tah-<u>rehees</u>
ellos, ellas, unos, ustedes estarán	<u>eh</u>-yohs, <u>eh</u>-yahs, oos-<u>teh</u>-dehs ehs-tah-<u>rahn</u>

Talkin' the Talk

Here's a dialog to help you practice this new way of being, the one that isn't forever.

You're in the same café you imagined yourself in for the previous **ser** conversations — it's a popular place! — overhearing a different conversation.

Guillermo: **¿Cómo están ustedes?**
<u>koh</u>-moh ehs-<u>tahn</u> oos-<u>teh</u>-dehs
How are you?

Sra. Valdés: **Estamos muy bien, gracias.**
ehs-<u>tah</u>-mohs mooy bvee<u>ehn</u> <u>grah</u>-seeahs
We're very well, thank you.

Guillermo: **¿Están de paseo?**
ehs-<u>tahn</u> deh pah-<u>seh</u>-oh
Are you talking a walk?

Sra. Valdés: **Estamos de vacaciones.**
ehs-<u>tah</u>-mohs deh bvah-kah-see<u>oh</u>-nehs
We're on vacation.

Guillermo: **¿Están contentos?**
ehs-<u>tahn</u> kohn-<u>tehn</u>-tohs
Are you content?

Sra. Valdés: **Estamos muy felices.**
ehs-<u>tah</u>-mohs mooy feh-<u>lee</u>-sehs
We're very happy.

Guillermo: **¿Cómo está su hija?**
<u>koh</u>-moh ehs-<u>tah</u> soo <u>ee</u>-Hah
How is your daughter?

Sra. Valdés: **Más o menos, no está muy feliz.**
mahs oh <u>meh</u>-nohs noh ehs-<u>tah</u> mooy feh-<u>lees</u>
So-so, she's not very happy.

Talkin' the Talk

Everyone, at one time or another, needs to find a bathroom. Here's a sample of how such a conversation might sound. You are again at the cafe, this time in the back, near the bathroom.

Renata: **¿Está libre este baño?**
ehs-<u>tah</u> <u>lee</u>-bvreh <u>ehs</u>-teh <u>bvah</u>-nyoh
Is the bathroom free?

Elena: **No, está ocupado.**
noh ehs-<u>tah</u> oh-koo-<u>pah</u>-doh
No it's taken.

Renata: **¿Está libre el otro baño?**
ehs-<u>tah</u> <u>lee</u>-bvreh ehl <u>oh</u>-troh <u>bvah</u>-nyoh
Is the other bathroom free?

Elena: **Sí, está libre.**
see ehs-<u>tah</u> <u>lee</u>-bvreh
Yes, it's free.

Words to Know

el paseo	ehl pah-<u>seh</u>-oh	the walk
contento	kohn-<u>tehn</u>-toh	content; satisfied
feliz	feh-lees	happy
libre	lee-bvreh	free
ocupado	oh-koo-pah-doh	occupied; busy
este	<u>ehs</u>-teh	this one
otro	<u>oh</u>-troh	the other one

Speaking about Speaking: Hablar

To complete your conversations at the café, you need to know about the verb **hablar** (*ah-<u>bvlahr</u>*) (to speak; to talk). You'll be happy to know that **hablar** is a regular verb, so you don't need to memorize how it works. (We cover regular verbs in Chapter 2.) This verb is from the group that ends in **-ar**. The root of this verb is **habl-,** and the table that follows shows how it's conjugated in the present tense.

Conjugation	*Pronunciation*
yo hablo	yoh <u>ah</u>-bvloh
tú hablas	too <u>ah</u>-bvlahs
él, ella, ello, uno, usted habla	ehl, <u>eh</u>-yah, <u>eh</u>-yoh, <u>oo</u>-noh, oos-<u>tehd</u> <u>ah</u>-bvlah
nosotros hablamos	noh-<u>soh</u>-trohs ah-<u>bvlah</u>-mohs
vosotros habláis	bvoh-<u>soh</u>-trohs ah-<u>bvla</u>ees
ellos, ellas, unos, ustedes hablan	<u>eh</u>-yohs, <u>eh</u>-yahs, <u>oo</u>-nohs, oos-<u>teh</u>-dehs <u>ah</u>-bvlahn

Talkin' the Talk

In this conversation Kathleen and Lorenzo talk about talking.

Kathleen: **¿María habla mucho?**
mah-reeah ah-bvlah moo-choh
Does María talk a lot?

Lorenzo: **Sí, le encanta hablar.**
see leh ehn-kahn-tah ah-bvlahr
Yes, she loves to talk.

Kathleen: **Yo hablo mal el español.**
yoh ah-bvloh mahl ehl ehs-pah-nyohl
I speak Spanish badly.

Lorenzo: **¡Por el contrario, lo habla muy bien!**
pohr ehl kohn-trah-reeoh loh ah-bvlah mooy bveeehn
On the contrary, you speak it very well!

Words to Know

mucho	moo-choh	a lot; much
difícil	dee-fee-seel	difficult; hard
fácil	fah-seel	easy
la lengua	lah lehn-gooah	the language (Literally: the tongue)
el idioma	ehl ee-dee-oh-mah	the language
gustar	goos-tahr	to like

Talkin' the Talk

Back at that café, you hear more talk about speaking.

Antonia: **¿Habla usted español?**
<u>ah</u>-blah <u>oos</u>-tehd ehs-pah-<u>nyol</u>
Do you speak Spanish?

Reynaldo: **Sí. ¿Qué idiomas habla usted?**
see keh ee-dee-<u>oh</u>-mahs <u>ah</u>-blah oos-<u>tehd</u>
Yes. What languages do you speak?

Antonia: **Yo hablo inglés y francés.**
yoh <u>ah</u>-bvloh een-<u>glehs</u> ee frahn-<u>sehs</u>
I speak English and French.

Reynaldo: **Es muy difícil hablar inglés?**
ehs mooy dee-<u>fee</u>-seel <u>ah</u>-blahr een-<u>glehs</u>
Is it very difficult to speak English?

Antonia: **No, ¡es muy fácil!**
noh, ehs mooy <u>fah</u>-seel
No, it's very easy!

Reynaldo: **¿Y es difícil hablar francés?**
ee ehs dee-<u>fee</u>-seel <u>ah</u>-bvlahr frahn-<u>sehs</u>
And is it difficult to speak French?

Antonia: **No, no es en absoluto difícil.**
noh noh ehs ehn ahb-soh-<u>loo</u>-toh dee-<u>fee</u>-seel
No, it's not difficult all.

Reynaldo: **A mí me gusta mucho hablar español.**
ah mee meh <u>goos</u>-tah <u>moo</u>-choh <u>ah</u>-bvlahr ehs-pah-<u>nyohl</u>.
I like to speak Spanish.

Antonia: **A mí también.**
ah mee tahm-bvee<u>ehn</u>
So do I.

Words to Know

Ser de aquí	sehr deh ah-kee	To belong to this place; to live here
¿Cómo le va?	koh-moh leh brah	How are you doing?
¿Cómo van las cosas?	koh-moh brahn lahs koh-sahs	How are things [going]?
¿Cómo está usted?	koh-moh ehs-tah oos-tehd	How are you? (formal)
¿Cómo estás?	koh-moh ehs-tahs	How are you? (informal)
¿Qué tal?	keh tahl	How are things [Literally: How such]?
Más o menos	mahs oh meh-nohs	So-so [Literally: More or less]
¿Quiubo?	keeoo-bvoh	How are things [Literally: What was there]? (Chile)
¿Qué pasó?	keh pah-soh	How are things [Literally: What happened]? (Mexico)

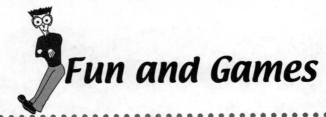

Fun and Games

Translate the English sentences below into Spanish. All the statements are based on information in this chapter. Sit back, relax, and marvel at how much Spanish you know.

Do these at your leisure. The idea is to fill in the Spanish version of the sentence you see in English.

Good afternoon! _____

My name is Kendall. _____

A pleasure, Mr. Kendall. _____

My name is María Luisa. _____

Where are you from? _____

I'm from Canada. _____

What city are you from? _____

I'm from New York. _____

Is that a very large city? _____

Yes, it is a very large city. _____

We are on vacation. _____

Are you satisfied? _____

We are very happy. _____

Chapter 4

Getting to Know You: Making Small Talk

· ·

In This Chapter

▶ Making small talk with a stranger

▶ Talking about yourself and your family

▶ Discussing weather, temperature, and seasons

▶ Starting with simple questions

· ·

Meeting new people and getting to know them can be stressful, especially when you have to converse in a language that isn't your own. Small talk is the universally recognized means of joining a new situation by discussing common, easily understood interests and concerns. Through small talk, you can better understand how the people you come to know live and go about their lives. This chapter helps you make small talk with your Spanish-speaking neighbors so that you can begin to achieve a better understanding all around.

Using the Key Questions: Seven Ws and an H

You may have heard about "The Five Ws," which represent the questions that you need to ask to cover the basic information about a situation (who, what, where, when, and why). We've added three more questions to this group that you may find useful when you meet someone. Here are the key questions:

✔ **¿Quién?** *(keee__hn__)* (Who?)

✔ **¿Qué?** *(keh)* (What?)

✔ **¿Dónde?** *(__dohn__-deh)* (Where?)

✔ **¿Cuándo?** *(koo__ahn__-doh)* (When?)

✔ **¿Por qué?** *(pohr keh)* (Why?)

✔ **¿Cómo?** *(koh-moh)* (How?)

✔ **¿Cuánto?** *(kooahn-toh)* (How much?)

✔ **¿Cuál?** *(kooahl)* (Which?)

The following are examples of how to use these words:

✔ **¿Quién es él?** *(keeehn ehs ehl)* (Who is he?)

✔ **¿Qué hace usted?** *(keh ah-seh oos-tehd)* (What do you do?)

✔ **¿Dónde viven?** *(dohn-deh bvee-bvehn)* (Where do you live?)

✔ **¿Cuándo llegaron?** *(kooahn-doh yeh-gah-rohn)* (When did you arrive?)

✔ **¿Por qué está aquí?** *(pohr keh ehs-tah ah-kee)* (Why are you [formal] here? Why is he [she, it] here?)

✔ **¿Cómo es el camino?** *(koh-moh ehs ehl kah-mee-noh)* (What's the road like?)

✔ **¿Cuánto cuesta el cuarto?** *(kooahn-toh kooehs-tah ehl kooahr-toh)* (How much is the room?)

✔ **¿Cuál hotel es mejor?** *(kooahl oh-tehl ehs meh-Hohr)* (Which hotel is better?)

All about accent marks

You may notice that some of the words we introduce in the previous section have accent marks over some vowels. Why did those words, which were used in questions, have an accent? The reason is to help you, and readers of Spanish in general, distinguish how the word is being used. For example,

You can use a word such as **quien** *(keeehn)*, which means "who," in two ways:

✔ In a sentence to refer to someone *who* did this or that. **Quien** has no accent when you use it this way.

✔ As a question — *Who* did it? — or as an exclamation — *Who* could have said that? To call your attention to the fact that *who* is being used as a question or an exclamation, it carries an accent, as in ¡**quién**! or ¿**quién**?

The treatment is the same for other words you use to make a question or an exclamation, such as "when?" **¿cuándo?** *(kooahn-doh)*; "what!" ¡**qué**! *(keh)*; "where?" **¿dónde?** *(dohn-deh)*; "why!" ¡**por qué**! (pohr keh); "how?" **¿cómo?** *(koh-moh)*; and "which?" **¿cuál?** *(kooahl)*.

Three useful sentences amid all the other talk

Sometimes, you may not understand what someone is saying. Or you bump into someone and wish to excuse yourself. The following courtesy phrases can come in handy:

- **No entiendo.** *(noh ehn-tee__ehn__-doh)* (I don't understand.)

- **Lo lamento.** *(loh lah-__mehn__-toh)* (I regret it; I'm sorry.)

- **¡Perdone!** (pehr-__doh__-neh) (Excuse me!) Say this when you bump into someone.

The accents don't change the way the words sound; you use them only in the written form of the language. When speaking, your *inflection*, or tone of voice, tells listeners how you're using the term in question.

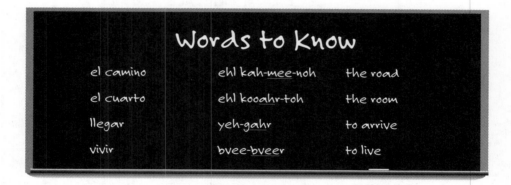

Words to Know

el camino	ehl kah-__mee__-noh	the road
el cuarto	ehl koo__ahr__-toh	the room
llegar	yeh-__gahr__	to arrive
vivir	bvee-__bveer__	to live

Talkin' the Talk

Carlos is on Flight Number 223, from Mendoza to Buenos Aires. He has introduced himself to his seatmates, so he knows their names, but he wants to make small talk about himself. Here's how such a conversation might go.

Carlos: **Qué vuelo tan agradable!**
            keh bvoo__eh__-loh tahn ah-grah-__dah__-bvleh
            . . . Such a pleasant flight!

Juan:	**Sí, es un viaje tranquilo.**
	see ehs oon bveeah-Heh trahn-kee-loh
	Yes, it's a peaceful trip.

Carlos:	**¿Viaja a menudo en avión?**
	bveeah-Hah ah meh-noo-doh ehn ah-bveeohn
	Do you fly often?

Juan:	**No, éste es mi primer vuelo.**
	noh, ehs-teh ehs mee pree-mehr bvooeh-loh
	No, this is my first time flying.

Carlos:	**¿De dónde es usted?**
	deh dohn-deh ehs oos-tehd
	Where are you from?

Juan:	**Soy de Buenos Aires. ¿Y usted?**
	sohy deh bvooeh-nohs ahee-rehs. ee oos-tehd
	I'm from Buenos Aires. And you?

Carlos:	**Yo soy de Nueva York . . .**
	yoh sohy deh nooeh-bvah yohrk.
	I'm from New York . . .
	. . . ¿cómo es Buenos Aires?
	koh-moh ehs bvooeh-nohs ahee-rehs
	. . . what's Buenos Aires like?

Juan:	**Es una ciudad grande y maravillosa.**
	ehs ooh-nah seeoo-dahd grahn-deh ee
	mah-rahbvee-yoh-sah
	It's a large and wonderful city.

Weather or Not, Here You Come

Weather is an obsession in temperate countries where conditions vary a great deal, and where it often gets to be, as Canadians like to say, "inclement." In warmer climates, weather is much less of an issue. Some cities in southern Mexico, for example, don't even do weather reports.

The tropics really have only two seasons: the rainy season and the dry season. When you travel, you may want to avoid the rainy season, which is also the time for hurricanes. Hurricanes are bothersome (if not downright dangerous!) on the coasts, and they bring a lot of rain into the highlands, where most of the cities are situated. In Mexico, the rainy season is from the end of May to November, really seting in by July and August.

South America has a region called The "South Cone" that includes Uruguay, Argentina, and Chile; the region is (you guessed it!) cone-shaped on the map. There, the weather is temperate — that is to say, warm in summer and cold in winter. Truly cold weather happens only very far south in areas where few people live. Summer in the South Cone coincides with North America's winter, and vice versa.

In Spain, as you all know, the "rain falls mainly on the plain." At least, that's how it was for Eliza Doolittle in *My Fair Lady*. Spain lies in the temperate zone, but just as the tropics have a rainy season an a dry season, Spain has rainy country and a dry country. The rain that falls on the plains occurs north of the Cantabrian mountains in an area of mild winters and cool summers. The rest of the country is hot and dry, while the coastal areas are just about perfect any time of year.

Talkin' the Talk

 Mario has just returned from a six-month assignment in Argentina. Now, back at his home office, Mario and his co-worker Rosa talk about the weather in Buenos Aires.

Rosa:	**¿Cómo es el clima de Buenos Aires?** *koh-moh ehs ehl klee-mah deh bvooeh-nohs ahee-rehs* What's Buenos Aires' climate like?
Mario:	**Es muy agradable y templado.** *ehs mooy ah-grah-dah-bvleh ee tehm-plah-doh* It's very pleasant and temperate.
Rosa:	**¿Llueve mucho?** *yooeh-bveh moo-choh* Does it rain a lot?
Mario:	**Sí, llueve todo el año, pero no mucho.** *see, yooeh-bveh toh-doh ehl an-nyoh, peh-roh noh moo-choh* Yes, there's rain all year round, but not too much.
Rosa:	**¿Y también hay sol?** *ee tahm-bveeehn ahy sohl* And is it also sunny?
Maria:	**Sí, hay sol casi todos los días.** *see ahy sohl kah-see toh-dohs lohs deeahs* Yes, it's sunny almost every day.

Rosa: **¿No nieva nunca?**
noh neeeh-bvah noon-kah
Does it ever snow?

Maria: **No, en Buenos Aires nunca nieva.**
noh ehn bvooeh-nohs ahee-rehs noon-kah neeeh-bvah
No, in Buenos Aires it never snows.

Talkin' the Talk

 Listen to Jane and Pedro in a cafe talking about their jobs.

Jane: **¿Dónde trabaja usted?**
dohn-deh trah-bvah-Hah oos-tehd
Where do you work?

Pedro: **Trabajo en México, soy ingeniero.**
trah-bvah-Hoh ehn meh-Hee-koh, sohy een-Heh-neeeh-roh
I work in Mexico [City], I'm an engineer.

Jane: **¿Para qué compañía trabaja?**
pah-rah keh kohm-pah-nyeeah trah-bvah-Hah
What company do you work for?

Pedro: **Soy empresario independiente.**
sohy ehm-preh-sah-reeoh een-deh-pehn-deeehn-teh
I'm an independent entrepreneur.

Jane: **¿Cuántos empleados tiene?**
kooahn-tohs ehm-pleh-ah-dohs teeeh-neh
How may many employees do you have?

Pedro: **Tengo nueve empleados. ¿Y usted qué hace?**
tehn-goh nooeh-bveh ehm-pleh-ah-dohs ee oos-tehd keh ah-seh
I have nine employees. What do you do?

Jane: **Soy dentista.**
sohy dehn-tees-tah
I'm a dentist.

Pedro:	**¿Y dónde tiene su consultorio?**
	ee dohn-deh teeeh-neh soo kohn-sool-toh-reeoh
	And where do you work?
Jane:	**En Puebla.**
	ehn Poo-eh-bvlah
	In Puebla.

The Verb Entender: To Understand/to Know About

Work and professions are always useful subjects for small talk. And when discussing these topics, you want to be sure that you understand each other, so you use the irregular verb **entender**. (You find the verb "to work" in Chapter 2.) **Entender** *(ehn-tehn-dehr)* (to understand) is an irregular verb, which you conjugate in the present tense as shown in the following table:

Conjugation	*Pronunciation*
yo entiendo	yoh ehn-teeehn-doh
tú entiendes	too ehn-teeehn-dehs
él, ella, ello, uno, usted entiende	ehl, eh-yah, eh-yoh, oo-noh,oos-tehd ehn-teeehn-deh
nosotros entendemos	noh-soh-trohs ehn-tehn-deh-mohs
vosotros entendéis	bvoh-soh-trohs ehn-tehn-dehees
ellos, ellas, ustedes entienden	eh-yohs, eh-yahs, oos-teh-dehs ehn-teeehn-dehn

Here are some examples to help you use the irregular verb **entender:**

- **Yo entiendo de enfermería.** *(yoh ehn-teeehn-doh deh ehn-fehr-meh-reeah)* (I know about nursing.)

- **Francisca entiende de cocina.** *(frahn-sees-kah ehn-teeehn-deh deh koh-see-nah)* (Francisca knows about cooking.)

- **Nosotros entendemos el problema.** *(noh-soh-trohs ehn-tehn-deh-mohs ehl proh-bvleh-mah)* (We understand the problem.)

- **Pedro no entiende.** *(peh-droh noh ehn-teeehn-deh)* (Pedro doesn't understand.)

- **Ellos entienden lo que decimos.** *(eh-yohs ehn-teeehn-dehn loh keh deh-see-mohs)* (They understand what we are saying.)

An understanding proverb

A buen entendedor, pocas palabras. *(ah bvooehn ehn-tehn-deh-dohr poh-kahs pah-lah-bvrahs.)* (Who knows, knows [Literally: To the one who understands, few words.])

This proverb comes in handy when you assume that the other person already knows about the issue you're discussing.

If we had to explain it with body language, we would say it's the equivalent of a knowing wink.

People and Families

The individual is the basic element of U.S. and Canadian societies. In Latin America, on the other hand, the family is the basic unit. People work, live, and function in consonance with their families. When visiting your Spanish-speaking neighbors, therefore, you'll be more comfortable if you pay attention to the way that Latinos stress the importance of the family and of family relationships.

Celebrations such as marriage, birth, and entering into society are carefully observed, and much energy and enthusiasm goes into them. May 10, Mothers' Day, for example, is one of the four most important holidays in Mexico. The other three are the Day of the Dead (November 2), Christmas, and Easter. Actually, holidays of all kinds sprinkle the calendar in warm countries, where people take advantage of any occasion to celebrate (see more about holidays in Chapter 20).

The following list gives basic names for family members:

- **padre** *(pah-dreh)* (father)
- **madre** *(mah-dreh)* (mother)
- **hijo** *(ee-Hoh)* (son)
- **hija** *(ee-Hah)* (daughter)
- **hermano** *(ehr-mah-noh)* (brother)
- **hermana** *(ehr-mah-nah)* (sister)
- **yerno** *(yehr-noh)* (son-in-law)
- **nuera** *(nooeh-rah)* (daughter-in-law)
- **nieto** *(neeeh-toh)* (grandson)

- **nieta** *(nee<u>eh</u>-tah)* (granddaughter)
- **cuñado** *(koo-<u>nyah</u>-doh)* (brother-in-law)
- **cuñada** *(koo-<u>nyah</u>-dah)* (sister-in-law)
- **primo** *(<u>pree</u>-moh)* (cousin [male])
- **prima** *(<u>pree</u>-mah)* (cousin [female])
- **padrino** *(pah-<u>dree</u>-noh)* (godfather)
- **madrina** *(mah-<u>dree</u>-nah)* (godmother)
- **tío** *(<u>tee</u>oh)* *(uncle)*
- **tía** *(<u>tee</u>ah)* *(aunt)*
- **abuelo** *(ah-bvoo<u>eh</u>-loh)* (grandfather)
- **abuela** *(ah-bvoo<u>eh</u>-lah)* (grandmother)

Talkin' the Talk

Shirley is visiting a family at their home for the first time. You may notice a certain amount of ceremony in the way people invite others into their homes.

Juan Carlos: **Mire, le invito a que conozca mi casa.**
<u>mee</u>-reh leh een-<u>bvee</u>-toh ah keh koh-<u>nohs</u>-kah mee <u>kah</u>-sah
Look, I'm inviting you to see my house.

Shirley: **Por favor, no quiero molestarle.**
pohr fah-<u>bvohr</u> noh kee<u>eh</u>-roh moh-<u>lehs</u>-tahr-leh
Please, I don't want to bother you.

Juan Carlos: **No es ninguna molestia, y así le presento mi familia.**
noh ehs neen-<u>goo</u>-nah moh-lehs-teeah ee ah-<u>see</u> leh preh-<u>sehn</u>-toh mee fah-<u>mee</u>-leeah
It's no bother, and this way I can introduce you to my family.

Shirley: **Pues si no le parece un abuso . . .**
pooehs see noh leh pah-<u>reh</u>-seh oon ah-<u>bvoo</u>-soh
Well, if you don't think I'm abusing [your hospitality]

Juan Carlos: **No, para nada, le insisto . . .**
noh <u>pah</u>-rah <u>nah</u>-dah leh een-<u>sees</u>-toh
Not at all, I insist . . .

Talkin' the Talk

Shirley has been invited into a beautiful, middle class, family house.

Juan Carlos: **Bueno, ya llegamos a la casa de mis padres.**
bvoo<u>eh</u>*-noh yah yeh-*<u>gah</u>*-mohs ah lah* <u>kah</u>*-sah deh mees* <u>pah</u>*-drehs*
Well, we're at my parents' house.

Shirley: **¡Qué bella casa! Parece muy antigua.**
keh <u>bveh</u>*-yah* <u>kah</u>*-sah pah-*<u>reh</u>*-seh mooy ahn-*<u>tee</u>*-gooah*
What a beautiful house! It seems very old.

Juan Carlos: **Sí, es una casa del siglo diecisiete.**
see ehs <u>oo</u>*-nah* <u>kah</u>*-sah dehl* <u>see</u>*-gloh deeeh-see-see*<u>eh</u>*-teh*
Yes, it's a seventeenth century house.

Shirley: **¡Qué patio tan bello!**
keh <u>pah</u>*-teeoh tahn* <u>bveh</u>*-yoh*
What a beautiful patio!

Juan Carlos: **Sí, el patio es muy tradicional.**
see ehl <u>pah</u>*-teeoh ehs mooy trah-dee-seeoh-*<u>nahl</u>
Yes, it's very traditional.

Vivir: The Verb to Live

It's natural once you've been invited to someone's house to invite them back to yours. And "where do you live?" is as frequent a question as "where do you work" when making small talk. The verb **vivir** *(bvee-*<u>bveer</u>*)* is a regular verb, and it means "to live." You can see how to conjugate its present tense in the following table.

Conjugation	*Pronunciation*
yo vivo	yoh <u>bvee</u>-bvoh
tú vives	too <u>bvee</u>-bvehs
él, ella, ello, uno, usted vive	ehl, <u>eh</u>-yah, <u>eh</u>-yoh, <u>oo</u>-noh, oos-<u>tehd</u> <u>bvee</u>-bveh
nosotros vivimos	noh-<u>soh</u>-trohs bvee-<u>bvee</u>-mohs
vosotros vivís	bvoh-<u>soh</u>-trohs bvee-<u>bvee</u>s
ellos, ellas, ustedes viven	<u>eh</u>-yohs, <u>eh</u>-yahs, oos-<u>teh</u>-dehs <u>bvee</u>-bvehn

Talkin' the Talk

After Shirley is introduced to the family, they will want to know where she lives, and they will invite her to come again:

Family member: **¿Dónde vives?**
dohn-deh bvee-bvehs
Where do you live?

Shirley: **Busco un departamento pequeño.**
*bvoos-koh oon deh-pahr-tah-mehn-toh
peh-keh-nyoh*
I'm looking for a small apartment.

Family member: **A la vuelta, arriendan un departamentito.**
*ah lah bvooehl-tah ah-rreeehn-dahn oon deh-
pahr-tah-mehn-tee-toh*
Around the corner, they rent a little apartment.

Shirley: **Bueno, voy a verlo.**
bvooeh-noh bvoy ah bvehr-loh
Good, I'm going to see it.

Family member: **Te va a gustar.**
teh bvah ah goos-tahr
You'll like it.

Shirley: **Bueno, no quiero molestar más, tengo que irme.**
*bvooeh-noh noh keeeh-roh moh-lehs-tahr mahs
tehn-goh keh eer-meh*
Well, I don't want to bother you any more, I
have to go.

Family member: **Aquí tienes tu casa.**
ah-kee teeeh-nehs too kah-sah
This is your home.

Shirley: **Muchas gracias.**
moo-chahs grah-seeahs
Thanks a lot.

Family member: **Te invito a que vengas mañana a tomar el tecito
con nosotros.**
*teh een-bvee-toh ah keh bvehn-gahs
mah-nyah-nah ah toh-mahr el teh-see-toh kohn
noh-soh-trohs*
I invite you to come tomorrow for [a small] tea
[with us].

Shirley:	**Lo haré con mucho gusto.**
	loh ah-<u>reh</u> kohn <u>moo</u>-choh <u>goos</u>-toh
	I'd love to.

A Little about Diminutives

In English when you want to say that something is small, you have to add the adjective "small" or "little" in front of the noun. Not so in Spanish. In that language, you add a few letters to the noun, called a *suffix*, meaning that you paste it to the end of the word. With that suffix, you create a *diminutive,* and people know that you're talking about something or someone small. The suffixes you add to the words are **ito** *(<u>ee</u>-toh)* or **ita** *(<u>ee</u>-tah)*. A boy **niño** *(<u>nee</u>-nyoh)* (boy/child) turns little when you add the suffix **niñito** *(neenyee-toh)* (little boy/child).

Diminutives are used in Spain and other Spanish-speaking countries, but not as profusely as in some Latin American countries — especially the ones near the Andes Mountain range, such as Chile, Peru, and Ecuador.

Talkin' the Talk

In all Latin American countries, children are an important part of the family. See how Shirley takes this fact into consideration.

Florencia:	**Dime Shirley, tienes hijos?**
	<u>dee</u>-meh Shirley tee<u>eh</u>-nehs <u>ee</u>-Hohs
	Tell me Shirley, do you have children?

Shirley:	**Tengo un hijo. Aquí está su foto.**
	<u>tehn</u>-goh oon <u>ee</u>-Hoh ah-<u>kee</u> ehs-<u>tah</u> soo <u>foh</u>-toh
	I have a son. Here's his photo.

Florencia:	**A ver . . . Un muchacho muy buen mozo.**
	ah bvehr oon moo-<u>chah</u>-choh mooy booehn <u>moh</u>-so
	Let's see . . . A good looking boy.

Shirley:	**Sí. ¿Y tú?**
	see ee too
	Yes. And you?

Florencia:	**Yo tengo una hija y un hijo.**
	yoh <u>tehn</u>-goh <u>oo</u>-nah <u>ee</u>-Hah ee oon <u>ee</u>-Hoh
	I have a daughter and a son.

Shirley: **¿Cuántos años tienen?**
koo*ahn*-tohs *ah*-nyohs tee*eh*-nehn
How old are they?

Florencia: **Mi hija tiene seis años y mi hijo tres. Allí viene mi hija.**
mee *ee*-Hah tee*eh*-neh *seh*ees *ah*-nyohs ee mee
ee-Hoh trehs a*hee* bvee*eh*-neh mee *ee*-Hah
My daughter is six and my son three. There comes my daughter.

Shirley: **Hola, ¿cómo te llamas?**
oh-lah *koh*-moh teh *yah*-mahs
Hello, what's your name?

Rosita: **Me llamo Rosita.**
meh *yah*-moh roh-*see*-tah
My name is Rosita.

Shirley: **¡Qué bello nombre, me gusta mucho!**
keh *bveh*-yoh *nohm*-breh meh *goos*-tah *moo*-choh
What a beautiful name, I like it very much!

A little here and a little there

These sets of words have identical meaning. It's a question of taste and sound which to choose.

allí *(ah-yee)*   **allá** *(ah-yah)*

(there)   (there)

aquí *(ah-kee)*   **acá** *(ah-kah)*

(here)   (here)

Fun & Games

You've been invited to attend a Spanish-speaking wedding. Both the bride and groom have very large families, so you have several relationships to figure out. The night before the wedding, your host quizzes you on question words and family members. Unscramble the English word below and then provide the Spanish translation.

- ✔ coinsu (female) _____
- ✔ chwih _____
- ✔ cleun _____
- ✔ draggundreath _____
- ✔ dreamthrong _____
- ✔ fatgodher _____
- ✔ franterdagh _____
- ✔ herfat _____
- ✔ hewn _____
- ✔ how _____
- ✔ hwy _____
- ✔ moodgreth _____
- ✔ nos _____
- ✔ ons-ni-awl _____
- ✔ owh _____
- ✔ redaught-ni-wal _____
- ✔ remoth _____
- ✔ resist _____
- ✔ robreth-ni-lwa _____
- ✔ sandgron _____
- ✔ sincou (male) _____
- ✔ strise-ni-wla _____
- ✔ thaw _____
- ✔ thredaug _____

Chapter 5
Dining Out and Going to Market

• •

• •

Food is an important element of any culture. Each country and region in Latin America has different-tasting food, making restaurant hopping and trying new dishes there among the most diverse experiences possible. The same is true in sunny Spain, where deep-fried fish, mountain-cured ham, and a variety of other tasty treats await you.

¡Buen Provecho! Enjoy Your Meal!

As with any cultural group, some peoples of Latin America are more interested in food than others. Mexicans are as devoted to their food as the French or the Chinese, even in very small places. They have very fine palates and can distinguish among many different fiery flavors. They also have an immense variety of ways to prepare the same foods, such as tortillas and beans, which are basic elements in their meals.

In Mexico you can eat **tortillas** *(tohr-tee-yahs)* — round, flat, soft, wafer-like bread made of corn — that are small and thick, and others that are immense and paper-thin, as well as all the sizes and thicknesses in between. Added to these variations are **tortillas** made of black or yellow corn. Mexicans, and Meso-Americans in general, employ their **tortillas** as eating utensils. They fold them ingeniously to use them as spoons, they pick up their food with them as we do with our forks, and after all is done, they proceed to *eat* their spoons! You try that with your spoon!

In Spain, at the **tapas** (*tah-pahs*) bars, where enticing treats are served with your drinks, everyone eats from the same dishes, though you can get your own **platos** (*plah-tohs*) (plate) if you ask for one.

Here are some other tastes that are popular in various Spanish-speaking countries:

- Argentineans and Chileans eat milder flavored and more European foods than do Mexicans.
- Peruvians and Bolivians like spice in their dishes.
- From the Rio Grande to Central America, the main fare is corn, which can be prepared a thousand ways, just as wheat is in the United States.
- From Colombia on south, potatoes, wheat, and barley join corn as the basis of foods.
- In Peru, you find a native grain called **quínoa** (*kee-noh-ah*), which is a bit like barley, and a flour called **chuño** (*choo-nyo*), made from freeze-dried potatoes.
- The best beef you can eat is in Argentina. Argentineans are enthusiastic beef eaters and really know how to prepare it so that it tastes superb.
- Spaniards commonly eat a mini-meal of appetizers called **tapas** (*tah-pahs*).

Table terms

You may find these phrases useful when you plan a meal:

- **¡A poner la mesa!** (*ah poh-nehr lah meh-sah*) (Set the table!)
- **Aquí están los platos y los vasos.** (*ah-kee ehs-tahn lohs plah-tohs ee lohs bvah-sohs*) (Here are the dishes and glasses.)
- **¿Qué cubiertos?** (*keh koo-bvee-ehr-tohs*) (What cutlery?)
- **Cuchara, cuchillo, tenedor, y cucharita.** (*koo-chah-rah koo-chee-yo teh-neh-dohr ee koo-chah-ree-tah*) (Spoon, knife, fork, and coffee or demitasse spoon.)
- **Aquí están las servilletas.** (*ah-kee ehs-tahn lahs sehr-bvee-yeh-tahs*) (Here are the napkins.)
- **Más sal en el salero.** (*mahs sahl ehn ehl sah-leh-roh*) (More salt in the salt shaker.)

CULTURAL WISDOM

When shall we eat what?

Sometimes the same word has a different meaning from country to country. **Desayuno** in Argentina is a light breakfast — what hotels call a Continental breakfast. In Mexico, a **desayuno** is even lighter, often just a cup of coffee or juice. So, in Mexico, around ten o'clock or so, people sit down to a meal that is a lot like breakfast in the United States: juice or fruit, eggs with sauces, steak, plus lots of tortillas. Mexicans call this meal **almuerzo**.

In South America, **almuerzo** is simply lunch, and it's eaten around noon or one o'clock. In Spain, **almuerzo** is a late breakfast. In Uruguay an **almuerzo** is soup, a main dish with meats or fish, and a dessert.

Comida in Chile is a meal that you eat in the evening, and may again be soup, a main dish, and dessert. The same word in Mexico signifies a meal taken between two and four o'clock in the afternoon. It's a hearty affair, with appetizers, soup, main dish, dessert, and leads to an immediate *siesta*. In Spain, **comida** is lunch.

Cena is supper, eaten late, between eight and ten in the evening. In some countries, you have just fruit at this time, but some families do eat a main dish and dessert.

Phrases for food and drink

Here are some common terms connected with meals:

- ✔ **almuerzo** *(ahl-moo<u>ehr</u>-soh)* (lunch)
- ✔ **cena** *(<u>seh</u>-nah)* (supper)
- ✔ **comida** *(koh-<u>mee</u>-dah)* (dinner)
- ✔ **desayuno** *(deh-sah-<u>yoo</u>-noh)* (breakfast)
- ✔ **tengo sed** *(<u>tehn</u>-goh sehd)* (I'm thirsty)
- ✔ **tiene hambre** *(tee <u>eh</u>-neh <u>ahm</u>-bvreh)* (he/she's hungry)

You may hear these phrases, or speak them yourself, when giving or receiving foods and beverages:

- ✔ **¡Buen provecho!** *(bvooehn proh-<u>bveh</u>-choh)* (Enjoy your meal! — the equivalent of the French *Bon appetit!*)
- ✔ **¿Con qué está servido?** *(kohn keh ehs-<u>tah</u> sehr-<u>bvee</u>-doh)* (What does it come with?)
- ✔ **Está caliente.** *(ehs-<u>tah</u> kah-lee <u>ehn</u>-teh)* (It's hot [temperature].)
- ✔ **Está frío.** *(ehs-<u>tah</u> freeoh)* (It's cold.)

 ✔ **Está picante.** *(ehs-tah pee-kahn-teh)* (It's hot (flavor/spicy.)

 ✔ **Es sabroso.** *(ehs sah-bvroh-soh)* (It's tasty.)

 ✔ **Lamento, no tenemos . . .** *(lah-mehn-toh noh teh-neh-mohs)*
 (Sorry, we don't have any . . .)

 ✔ **¿Qué ingredientes tiene?** *(keh een-greh-dee ehn-tehs tee eh-neh)*
 (What are the ingredients?)

 ✔ **¿Qué más trae el plato?** *(keh mahs trah-eh ehl plah-toh)*
 (What else is in the dish?)

These words can help you when you're ordering something to drink:

 ✔ **Escoger un vino.** *(ehs-koh-Hehr oon bvee-noh)* (Choose a wine)

 ✔ **¡Salud!** *(sah-lood)* (Cheers!)

 ✔ **Tomar un refresco.** *(toh-mahr oon reh-frehs-koh)* (Drink a soda pop)

 ✔ **Tomar un trago.** *(toh-mahr oon trah-goh)* (Have a drink [alcoholic])

 ✔ **Un vaso de agua.** *(oon bvah-soh deh ah-gooah)* (A glass of water)

 ✔ **Un vaso de leche.** *(oon bvah-soh deh leh-cheh)* (A glass of milk)

Three Verbs Used at the Table

Insofar as talking about drinking goes, in Spanish, you do it with two verbs.
One is **tomar** *(toh-mahr)*; the other is **beber** *(bveh-bvehr)*.

To take and to drink: The verb tomar

Tomar *(toh-mahr)* means literally "to take" and often means exactly that. But
when you say **tomar un refresco** *(toh-mahr oon reh-frehs-koh)*, you're talking
about drinking a soda, not literally taking one, and you know that's what you
mean because **tomar** is followed by something you drink. So **tomar** is a verb
with a certain imprecision.

Tomar is a regular verb of the **-ar** *(ahr)* group. The root of the verb is **tom-**
(tohm), as you can see from the table that follows:

Conjugation	Pronunciation
yo tomo	yoh toh-moh
tú tomas	too toh-mahs

él, ella, ello, uno, usted toma	ehl, <u>eh</u>-yah, <u>eh</u>-yoh, <u>oo</u>-noh, oos-<u>tehd</u> <u>toh</u>-mah
nosotros tomamos	noh-<u>soh</u>-trohs toh-<u>mah</u>-mohs
vosotros tomáis	bvoh-<u>soh</u>-trohs toh-<u>mah</u>-ees
ellos, ellas, ustedes toman	<u>eh</u>-yohs, <u>eh</u>-yahs, oos-<u>teh</u>-dehs <u>toh</u>-mahn

For drinking only: The verb beber

In the case of the verb *beber,* you can have no doubts: This verb applies to drinking only.

Beber *(bveh-<u>bvehr</u>)* is also a regular verb; it's from the **-er** *(ehr)* group. The root of the verb is: **beb-** *(bvehbv),* as you can see in the following table:

Conjugation	*Pronunciation*
yo bebo	yoh <u>bveh</u>-bvoh
tú bebes	too <u>bveh</u>-bvehs
él, ella, ello, uno, usted bebe	ehl, <u>eh</u>-yah, <u>eh</u>-yoh, <u>oo</u>-noh oos-<u>tehd</u> <u>bveh</u>-bveh
nosotros bebemos	noh-<u>soh</u>-trohs bveh-<u>bveh</u>-mohs
vosotros bebéis	bvoh-<u>soh</u>-trohs bveh-<u>bveh</u>ees
ellos, ellas, ustedes beben	<u>eh</u>-yohs, <u>eh</u>-yahs, oos-<u>teh</u>-dehs <u>bveh</u>-bvehn

For eating: The verb comer

Comer *(<u>kohm</u>-ehr)* means "to eat." A regular verb from the **-er** *(ehr)* group, the root of this verb is **com** *(kohm),* as the following table shows:

Conjugation	*Pronunciation*
yo como	yoh <u>koh</u>-moh
tú comes	too <u>koh</u>-mehs
él, ella, ello, uno, usted come	ehl, <u>eh</u>-yah, <u>eh</u>-yoh, <u>oo</u>-noh, oos-<u>tehd</u> <u>koh</u>-meh
nosotros comemos	noh-<u>soh</u>-trohs koh-<u>meh</u>-mohs
vosotros coméis	bvoh-<u>soh</u>-trohs koh-<u>meh</u>ees
ellos, ellas, ustedes comen	<u>eh</u>-yohs, <u>eh</u>-yahs, oos-<u>teh</u>-dehs <u>koh</u>-mehn

At the Restaurant: Trying Exotic Foods

A menu in a foreign language can be intimidating. But Latin America has many tasty and exotic foods that you won't want to miss. This list identifies the most popular ones:

- **Agua** (*ah-gooah*) in Mexico can mean "water," which is its exact translation, but it can also be a beverage made with water, fruit, and sugar. All fruits, and some vegetables even, make refreshing **aguas** (*ah-gooahs*).

- **Aguita** (*ah-goo-ee-tah*) little water, in Chile can be an herb tea, served after a meal.

- **Empanada** (*ehm-pah-nah-dah*) actually means "in bread." In Mexico, an **empanada** is a folded and stuffed corn tortilla. You can get **empanadas** made out of wheat dough, which is then folded and stuffed, in Argentina and Chile. Argentinians like theirs small. Chileans make theirs big. Either way, they're delicious!

- In Spain, a **tortilla** (*tohr-tee-yah*) is a potato, onion, and egg omelette that's often served at room temperature.

- In Mexico, **elote** (*eh-loh-teh*) is the name of tender corn, the kind you eat from the cob. The same thing in Argentina, Chile, Peru, and Bolivia is called **choclo** (*choh-kloh*).

- Green beans in Mexico are called **ejotes** (*eh-Hoh-tehs*). In South America, you find them under names like **porotos verdes** (*poh-roh-tohs bvehr-dehs*), or **porotitos** (*poh-roh-tee-tohs*). When the beans are dry, they're called **porotos** (*poh-roh-tohs*) in most of Spanish-speaking America, except in Mexico, where they are known as **frijoles** (*free-Hoh-lehs*). Nowhere else can you see as great a variety of beans as in a Peruvian market. They come in enough colors and shapes and sizes to make your mouth water. You may want to try them all.

- In Chile, **filete** (*fee-leh-teh*) is the cut of beef called "sirloin" in the United States. In Argentina, the same cut is called **lomo** (*loh-moh*).

- The basic Argentinean meal is **bife, con papas y ensalada** (*bvee-feh kohn pah-pahs ee ehn-sah-lah-dah*), which translates to "grilled steak, with potatoes and salad." On an Argentinean grill, you're likely to find a number of meats familiar to you, along with others that you probably never have eaten. Among the more exotic are **chinchulín** (*cheen-choo-leen*), which is braided and grilled beef bowels. ¡Delicioso! Another delicacy is **molleja** (*moh-lyeh-Hah*), which is the thyroid gland of a cow.

- In Mexico, **molleja** (*moh-yeh-Hah*) is chicken gizzard. And in Chile, the same chicken gizzard is **contre** (*kohn-treh*).

✔ The liver that you eat in Chile is called **pana** *(pah-nah);* in most other places in Latin America, liver is **hígado** *(ee-gah-doh).*

✔ In Spain, **jamón serrano** *(Ha-mohn seh-rran-oh),* salt cured ham typical of the mountain regions, is a great delicacy.

If you love fish and seafood, the places to go are Chile and Peru. The best fish in the world swim in the Humboldt Current, coming from Antarctica.

✔ You find delights such as **loco** *(loh-koh),* a truly gigantic scallop, and **congrio** *(kohn-greeoh),* or "conger eel," a type of fish.

✔ You can also find **albacora** *(ahl-bvah-koh-rah)* (swordfish), **cangrejo** *(kahn-greh-Hoh)* (giant crab), **jaiba** *(Hahee-bvah)* (small crab), **langosta** *(lahn-gohs-tah)* (lobster); **langostino** *(lahn-gohs-tee-noh)* (prawn), **camarón** *(kah-mah-rohn)* (shrimp), and other delights to crowd your **sopa marinera** *(soh-pah mah-ree-neh-rah)* (fish soup).

✔ In Peru, they make **ceviche** *(seh-bvee-cheh),* out of raw fish or raw seafood. **Ceviches** come in many varieties. One commonality is that Latinos like their **ceviche** very hot. In **ceviche,** raw fish or seafood is marinated in lemon juice, salt, and hot peppers. The fish or seafood is still raw after this treatment, but it looks less transparent, as though it were cooked. Sensational!

You also may wish to order some of these specialties:

✔ Called **aguacate** *(ah-gooah-kah-teh)* in Mexico and **palta** *(pahl-tah)* in Argentina, Uruguay, and Chile, it's still the same "avocado."

✔ In the south of Mexico, when you say **pan** *(pahn),* meaning "bread," people usually think of something that the baker made to taste sweet. In South America, **pan** is closer to what you eat in the States.

✔ **Torta** *(tohr-tah)* in Mexico is a sandwich in a bun (a "sandwich" is made with bread baked in a mold and sliced.) But most everywhere else in Latin America, **torta** *(tohr-tah)* means "cake," and **sandwich** means "sandwich" (no matter how it's served).

✔ **Memelas** *(meh-meh-lahs)* in Mexico are **tortillas** that are pinched on the side to form a hollow, which is filled with pastes and delicacies.

✔ **Gazpacho** *(gahs-pah-choh),* is a chilled vegetable soup from Spain flavored with olive oil, garlic, and vinegar.

✔ In Spain, **paella** *(pah-eh-yah)* is a favorite dish made of seafood and saffron rice.

About sauces: Hot, cold, and spicy!

Some people say that what's truly special about Latin American foods is the sauces. This statement is especially true of the sauces served in Mexico, which have an infinite variety of flavors and textures.

Moles: Served hot and HOT!

Mole (*moh-leh*), a word used in Mexico, means "sauce." These Mexican moles are served hot with meats and chicken:

✔ **Mole negro** (*moh-leh neh-groh*) (black mole) looks black — naturally! — and is made with all toasted ingredients: cocoa, chilies, almonds, onions, garlic, and bread. It can be very spicy or less so.

✔ **Mole colorado** (*moh-leh koh-loh-rah-doh*) (red mole) looks red and is made with chilies. It is spicy hot! The sauce is also called **coloradito**.

✔ **Mole amarillo** (*moh-leh ah-mah-ree-lyoh*) (yellow mole) is orangy yellow. You make it with almonds and raisins, among other ingredients. Generally, it is only mildly spicy.

✔ **Mole verde** (*moh-leh bvehr-deh*) (green mole) is made with green tomatoes, green chilies (hot peppers), and coriander (cilantro) and looks green. It can be very spicy or mildly hot.

Mexicans don't eat **moles** every day. These delicacies are served only on special occasions. Tourists are luckier. They can find them all the time.

Cold sauces for seasoning: Still Hot!

Mexicans bring some cold sauces to the table to add more spice to your food.

✔ **Pico de gallo** (*pee-koh deh gah-lyoh*), which translates as "rooster's beak," is made totally with vegetables. It looks red, green, and white, because it's made with tomatoes, jalapeño peppers, coriander, and onions. Hot!

✔ **Guacamole** (*gooah-kah-moh-leh*) needs no translation. It's the dip made with avocado, chili (*chee-leh*) "hot pepper," coriander (cilantro), lemon, and salt. It's sometimes spicy hot.

✔ **Salsa verde** (*sahl-sah bvehr-deh*) green sauce made with green tomatoes, chilies, and coriander. Hot!

✔ **Salsa roja** (*sahl-sah roh-Hah*) red sauce is made with red tomatoes and chilies. Hot!

Getting What You Want: The Verb Querer

The verb **querer** *(keh-rehr)* is often used to convey "to want" or "to wish."

Querer is an irregular verb. Notice that the root **quer-** *(kehr)* is transformed into **quier-** *(keeehr)* with some pronouns.

Conjugation	Pronunciation
querer	keh-rehr
yo quiero	yoh keeeh-roh
tú quieres	too keeeh-rehs
él, ella, ello, uno, usted quiere	ehl, eh-yah, eh-yoh, oo-noh, oos-tehd keeeh-reh
nosotros queremos	noh-soh-trohs keh-reh-mohs
vosotros queréis	bvoh-soh-trohs keh-rehees
ellos, ellas, ustedes quieren	eh-yohs, eh-yahs, oos-teh-dehs keeeh-rehn

Talkin' the Talk

Señor Porter wants to take his wife to a nice restaurant on her birthday. Listen in as he calls the restaurant to make reservations.

Señor Porter: **Quiero reservar una mesa para dos personas.**
keeeh-roh reh-sehr-bvahr oo-nah meh-sah pah-rah dohs pehr-soh-nahs
I want to reserve a table for two people.

Waiter: **¡Cómo no! ¿Para qué hora será?**
koh-moh noh pah-rah keh oh-rah seh-rah
Of course! At what time?

Señor Porter: **Para las ocho de la noche.**
pah-rah lahs oh-choh deh lah noh-cheh
At eight o'clock in the evening.

Waiter: **¿A nombre de quién?**
ah nohm-bvreh deh keeehn
Under what name?

Señor Porter: **El señor Porter.**
ehl <u>seh</u>-nyohr Porter
Mr. Porter.

Waiter: **Bien, les esperamos.**
bvee<u>ehn</u> lehs ehs-peh-<u>rah</u>-mohs
Good, we'll wait for you.

Señor Porter: **Muchas gracias.**
<u>moo</u>-chahs <u>grah</u>-seeahs
Many thanks.

The vast majority of restaurants in Latin America do not require reservations.

Ordering beverages

Many people like to order an aperitif, or cocktail, before dinner. Most aperitifs served in Spanish-American restaurants are similar to those you drink at home. Exceptions are the local liquors such as **aguardiente** (ah-gooahr-dee<u>ehn</u>-teh), which translates as "fire water," and is made out of grapes, **tequila** (teh-<u>kee</u>-lah) and **mezcal** (mehs-<u>kahl</u>), both made from cacti, or **pisco** (<u>pees</u>-koh), a liquor also made out of grapes, and the cocktails prepared with these liquors. In Chile and Peru, people like pisco sour, a cocktail made with pisco, sugar, and lemon juice.

Calling a waiter

A waiter in Argentina is a **mozo** (<u>moh</u>-soh) or "young man."

But, calling someone **mozo** in Chile is offensive. In Chile, you say, **garzón** (gahr-<u>sohn</u>), which is derived from the French word for "young man" — the similarly spelled and identically pronounced garçon.

If you call the waiter by either of these terms in Mexico, he may not react. You can better get his attention by saying **joven** (<u>Hoh</u>-bvehn), meaning "young," even if he isn't so young.

In Spain, a waiter is a **camarero** (kah-mah-<u>reh</u>-roh).

When a woman is serving you, call her simply **señorita** (seh-nyoh-<u>ree</u>-tah), Miss, no matter where you are.

Talkin' the Talk

If you want to order a beverage to drink with your food, you may participate in a conversation similar to this one.

Waiter:	**¿Quieren algo para beber?**
	keeeh-rehn ahl-goh pah-rah bveh-bvehr
	Do you want anything to drink?
	¿Se sirven un agua de frutas?
	seh seer-bvehn oon ah-gooah deh froo-tahs
	Would you like a diluted fruit juice?
Señora Porter:	**No, yo quiero un vaso de vino tinto.**
	noh yoh keeeh-roh oon bvah-soh de bvee-noh teen-toh
	No, I want a glass of red wine.
Waiter:	**Muy bien, ¿y usted?**
	mooy bveeehn ee oos-tehd
	Very well, and you?
Señor Porter:	**Yo quiero una cerveza.**
	yoh keeeh-roh oo-nah sehr-bveh-sah
	I want a beer.
Waiter:	**¿Lager o negra?**
	lah-gehr oh neh-grah
	Lager or dark?
Señor Porter:	**Prefiero negra.**
	preh-feeeh-roh neh-grah
	I prefer dark.

Talkin' the Talk

Now for great eating! You can use the following conversation as an example to order some soup or salad.

Waiter:	**¿Están listos para ordenar?**
	ehs-tahn lees-tohs pah-rah ohr-deh-nahr
	Are you ready to order?
Señora Porter:	**Yo quiero una ensalada mixta.**
	yoh keeeh-roh oo-nah ehn-sah-lah-dah meeks-tah
	I want a mixed [several vegetables] salad.

Señor Porter:	**Y para mí una sopa de mariscos.** *ee pah-rah mee oo-nah soh-pah deh mah-rees-kohs* And for me, seafood soup.
Waiter:	**¿Y de plato fuerte?** *ee deh plah-toh fooehr-teh* And as the main course?
Señor Porter:	**¿Qué nos recomienda?** *keh nohs reh-koh-meeehn-dah* What do you suggest?
Waiter:	**Tenemos dos platos especiales: mole amarillo con carne de res y huachinango a la ver-acruzana.** *teh-neh-mohs dohs plah-tohs ehs-peh-seeah-lehs moh-leh ah-mah-ree-lyoh kohn kahr-neh deh rehs ee ooah-chee-nahn-goh ah lah bveh-rah-kroo-sah-nah* We have two specials: yellow mole with beef and red snapper Veracruz style.
Señora Porter:	**¿Qué es el huachinango a la veracruzana?** *keh ehs ehl ooah-chee-nahn-goh ah lah bveh-rah-kroo-sah-nah* What is red snapper Veracruz style?
Waiter:	**Es pescado con tomates, chile, cilantro, y cebolla.** *ehs pehs-kah-doh kohn toh-mah-tehs chee-leh see-lahn-troh ee seh-bvoh-yah* It's fish with tomatoes, hot peppers, coriander (cilantro), and onions.
Señora Porter:	**Yo quiero pollo frito.** *yoh keeehh-roh poh-yoh free-toh* I want fried chicken.
Waiter:	**No tenemos pollo frito. Tenemos pollo asado en salsa de mango.** *noh teh-neh-mohs poh-yoh free-toh teh-neh-mohs poh-yoh ah-sah-doh ehn sahl-sah deh mahn-goh* We don't have fried chicken. We have broiled chicken with mango sauce.

Señora Porter:	**¿Con qué está acompañado?**
	kohn keh ehs-<u>tah</u> ah-kohm-pah-<u>nyah</u>-doh
	What does it come with?
Waiter:	**Con elotes frescos, y calabazas entomatadas.**
	kohn eh-loh-tehs <u>frehs</u>-kohs ee
	kah-lah-<u>bvah</u>-sahs ehn-toh-mah-<u>tah</u>-dahs
	With fresh corn, and zucchini in tomato sauce.
Señora Porter:	**Bueno, voy a probar el pollo con mango.**
	bvoo<u>eh</u>-noh, bvohy ah proh-<u>bvahr</u> ehl
	<u>poh</u>-yoh kohn <u>mahn</u>-goh
	Good, I'll try the chicken with mango.

Talkin' the Talk

You may have an exchange like the following as you pay your bill.

Señor Porter:	**Joven, ¿nos trae la cuenta por favor?**
	<u>Hoh</u>-bveh nohs <u>trah</u>-eh lah koo<u>ehn</u>-tah
	pohr fah-<u>bvohr</u>
	Waiter, will you bring us the check please?
Waiter:	**Ya vuelvo con la cuenta.**
	yah bvoo-<u>ehl</u>-bvoh kohn lah
	koo<u>ehn</u>-tah
	I'll be back with the check.
Señor Porter:	**¿Aceptan tarjetas de crédito?**
	ah-<u>sehp</u>-tahn tahr-<u>Heh</u>-tahs deh
	<u>kreh</u>-dee-toh
	Do you accept credit cards?
Waiter:	**No, lo lamento mucho, aquí no aceptamos tarjetas de crédito.**
	noh loh lah-<u>mehn</u>-toh <u>moo</u>-choh ah-<u>kee</u>
	noh ah-sehp-<u>tah</u>-mohs tahr-<u>Heh</u>-tahs
	deh <u>kreh</u>-dee-toh
	No, I'm very sorry; we don't take credit cards.
Señora Porter [a bit later]:	**¿Ya pagamos la cuenta?**
	yah pah-<u>gah</u>-mohs lah koo-<u>ehn</u>-tah
	We paid the check already?

Señor Porter:	**Ya la pagué.**
	yah lah pah-gheh
	I paid it already.
Señora Porter:	**¿Dejamos propina?**
	deh-Hah-mohs proh-pee-nah
	Did we leave a tip?
Señor Porter:	**Sí dejé propina.**
	see deh-Heh proh-pee-nah
	Yes, I left a tip.

CULTURAL WISDOM

Corny tortillas and other food facts

The Spanish-speaking countries we talk about in this book have different climates, cultures, and peoples, and, especially, different foods. To cover the variety of food and drink available would take a whole book — at least. We don't have even half a book to devote to food, so don't be surprised if we don't mention that Guatemalan dish you tried last month.

And, if you do find your favorite Spanish-American dish in this book, or in its country of origin, don't be surprised if it's somewhat different from the dish you tried in an ethnic restaurant in the States or Canada.

The humble **tortilla** (*tohr-tee-yahs*) is one example of how foods differ. In Canada, Mexican food is often served on tortillas made from wheat. And, although you may find wheat tortillas in the north of Mexico, more often than not, Mexicans themselves eat corn tortillas. In Spain, however, a **tortilla** is an omelette, having nothing to do with the popular corn or wheat wraps of Latin America.

You also may find out that food in Latin America doesn't taste like the stuff you get in the chain eateries that offer Latin food. In its own country, a dish is usually made fresh, and to the taste of the locals.

Hamburgers are called — not surprisingly — **hamburguesas** *(ahm-bvoor-gheh-sahs),* and may also be different from those you eat at home. They may be close, but they're not the same. And they may be quite expensive by local standards. Don't worry if your taste runs to the traditional meat and potatoes — at better restaurants you can always find food quite similar to what you're accustomed to.

Of course, at the inexpensive places the locals eat in, you are likely to find only the local fare. If you're like us, though, this is your idea of fun.

Taking a bathroom break

Inevitably, you want to wash your hands, freshen your makeup, or do something else that requires the use of a public bathroom. Bathrooms in Latin America are very similar to those in the States and Canada — the more expensive the restaurant, the more elegant the bathroom. The following phrases can help you find the room you need.

✔ **¿Dónde están los baños?** (*dohn-deh ehs-tahn lohs bvah-nyohs*) (Where are the bathrooms?)

✔ **Los baños están al fondo, a la derecha.** (*lohs bvah-nyohs ehs-tahn ahl fohn-doh ah lah deh-reh-chah*) (The bathrooms are at the back, to the right.)

✔ **¿Es este el baño?** (*ehs ehs-teh ehl bvah-nyoh*) (Is this the bathroom?)

✔ **No, este no es el baño. Es ese.** (*noh ehs-teh noh ehs ehl bvah-nyoh ehs eh-se*) (No, this is not the bathroom. It's that one.)

Using the Shopping Verb: Comprar

Comprar (*kohm-prahr*) means "to shop," and **Ir de compras** (*eer deh kohm-prahs*) means "to go shopping." **Comprar** is a regular verb of the **-ar** (*ahr*) group. The root of the verb is **compr-** (*kohmpr*). Here's how you conjugate **comprar** in the present tense:

Conjugation	*Pronunciation*
yo compro	yoh kohm-proh
tú compras	too kohm-prahs
él, ella, ello, uno, usted compra	ehl, eh-yah, eh-yoh, oo-noh, oos-tehd kohm-prah
nosotros compramos	noh-soh-trohs kohm-prah-mohs
vosotros compráis	bvoh-soh-trohs kohm-prahees
ellos, ellas, ustedes compran	eh-yohs, eh-yahs, oos-teh-dehs kohm-prahn

Using shopping terms

These phrases, based on **ir de compras** (*eer deh kohm-prahs*) (to go shopping), can help you at the market.

✔ **Fue de compras.** *(fooeh deh koh<u>m</u>-prahs)* (She or he is out shopping.)

✔ **¡Voy de compras!** *(bvoy deh koh<u>m</u>-prahs)* (I'm going shopping!)

✔ **¡Vamos de compras al mercado!** *(<u>bvah</u>-mohs deh koh<u>m</u>-prahs ahl-mehr-<u>kah</u>-do)* (Let's go shopping at the market!)

At the Market

In this section you visit markets that may be open or under a roof, but are more informal than supermarkets. Also, in these markets, vendors are salespeople, not just cashiers, and they may approach you to sell you goods you may or may not want. When you don't want something you can simply say one of the following:

✔ **Ahora no, gracias.** *(ah-<u>oh</u>-rah noh <u>grah</u>-seeahs)* (Not now, thank you.)

✔ **Ya tengo, gracias.** *(yah <u>tehn</u>-goh <u>grah</u>-seeahs)* (I already have some, thanks.)

✔ **No me interesa, gracias.** *(no meh een-teh-<u>reh</u>-sah <u>grah</u>-seeahs)* (It doesn't interest me, thank you.)

✔ **Más tarde, gracias.** *(mahs <u>tahr</u>-deh <u>grah</u>-seeahs)* (Later, thank you.)

✔ **No me gusta, gracias.** *(noh meh <u>goos</u>-tah <u>grah</u>-seeahs)* (I don't like it, thanks.)

✔ **No me moleste, ¡por favor!** *(noh meh moh-<u>lehs</u>-teh pohr fah-<u>bvohr</u>)* (Don't bother me, please!)

You may love markets where you're surrounded by vendors and other people, and enjoy an environment so different from what you're used to. Depending where you go, these markets may be full of folks wearing clothes you probably have not seen before, talking and behaving in ways that are new to you.

In most markets in Latin America, merchandise is piled in colorful mountains. You may choose from these items at your leisure.

In supermarkets, prices are clearly posted. In other markets, they probably are not, although this practice varies from country to country. In some places, where prices are not marked, you may be able to negotiate a price by simply protesting that it's too high. The vendors are interested in selling, so they allow some discount.

When you go to the market, it's a good idea to bring your own shopping bags or baskets to carry away the stuff you buy. Supermarkets provide bags, of course, but at the more informal markets, the vendor simply packs the stuff you buy but doesn't provide a larger container to carry it away. Wherever this is the rule, you can find stalls that sell bags or baskets of all sizes. More often than not, you want to take these bags home with you — many of them are handmade and quite beautiful.

Buying fruit

Here are the names of fruits you find at the market:

- **la cereza** *(lah seh-reh-sah)* (the cherry)
- **la ciruela** *(lah see-ro-eh-lah)* (the plum)
- **el durazno** *(ehl doo-rahs-noh)* (the peach); **el melocotón** *(ehl meh-loh-koh-tohn)* [in Spain]
- **la fresa** *(la freh-sah)* (the strawberry) [Mexico, Central America, and Spain]
- **la frutilla** *(lah froo-tee-yah)* (the strawberry) [from Colombia to the South Pole]
- **la guayaba** *(lah gooah-yah-bvah)* (the guava)
- **el higo** *(ehl ee-goh)* (the fig)
- **la lima** *(lah lee-mah)* (lime)
- **el limón** *(ehl lee-mohn)* (the lemon)
- **el mango** *(ehl mahn-goh)* (the mango)
- **la manzana** *(lah mahn-sah-nah)* (the apple)
- **el melón** *(ehl meh-lohn)* (the melon)
- **la mora** *(lah moh-rah)* (the blackberry)
- **la naranja** *(lah nah-rahn-Hah)* (the orange)
- **la papaya** *(lah pah-pah-yah)* (the papaya)
- **la pera** *(lah peh-rah)* (the pear)
- **el plátano** *(ehl plah-tah-noh)* (the banana)
- **el pomelo** *(ehl poh-meh-loh)* (the grapefruit [in Mexico])
- **la sandía** *(lah sahn-deeah)* (the watermelon)
- **la toronja** *(lah toh-rohn-Ha)* (the grapefruit) [in Mexico]
- **la tuna** *(lah too-nah)* (the prickly pear)
- **la uva** *(lah oo-bvah)* (the grape)

CULTURAL WISDOM

Yes, we have bananas!

The bananas that reach the Canadian and American markets are just one kind of the wide variety of shapes, sizes, and tastes available in countries near the tropics. Some bananas come with very fine skin and go by such nicknames as "nylon"; others have really heavy skins. **Plátano macho** *(plah-tah-noh mah-choh),* which translates as "male banana," is a huge, long banana often served fried in Cuba and other places.

In Lima, Peru, one of the authors of this book noticed some tiny things she didn't recognize. So she asked the vendor, **"¿Cuánto?"** *(kooahn-toh?)* (How much?), and the vendor said, **"A sol la manito."** *(ah sohl lah mah-nee-toh.)* ("One sol, each hand.") Susana willingly paid the **sol,** which is very little money, and in return got five little things that, sure enough, looked like a child's hand. They were bananas. Sweet as honey.

Buying vegetables

Fresh vegetables are always good. You can easily find the following:

- **las acelgas** *(lahs ah-sehl-gahs)* (the swiss chard)
- **el aguacate** *(ehl ah-gooah-kah-teh)* (the avocado)
- **el ají** *(el ah-Hee)* (the hot pepper [South America])
- **el ajo** *(ehl ah-Hoh)* (the garlic)
- **el brócoli** *(ehl bvroh-koh-lee)* (the broccoli)
- **la calabacita** *(lah kah-lah-bvah-see-tah)* (the zucchini [Mexico])
- **la calabaza** *(lah kah-lah-bvah-sah)* (the pumpkin [Central America and Mexico])
- **las cebollas** *(lahs seh-bvoh-yahs)* (the onions)
- **el chile** *(chee-leh)* (the hot pepper [Mexico and Guatemala])
- **el chile morrón** *(ehl chee-leh moh-rrohn)* (the sweet pepper [Mexico])
- **la col** *(lah kohl)* (the cabbage [Mexico])
- **la coliflor** *(lah koh-lee-flohr)* (the cauliflower)
- **la espinaca** *(lah ehs-pee-nah-kah)* (the spinach)
- **la lechuga** *(lah leh-choo-gah)* (the lettuce)
- **las papas** *(lahs pah-pahs)* (the potatoes); **patatas** *(pah-tah-tahs)* in Spain
- **la palta** *(lah pahl-tah)* (the avocado [South America])

- **el pimentón** *(ehl pee-mehn-tohn)* (the sweet pepper [Argentina, Chile, and Uruguay])
- **el repollo** *(ehl reh-poh-yoh)* (the cabbage [Argentina and Chile])
- **la zanahoria** *(lah sah-nah-oh-reeah)* (the carrot)
- **el zapallito** *(ehl sah-pah-yee-toh)* (zucchini [Uruguay and Argentina])
- **el zapallo** *(ehl sah-pah-yoh)* (the pumpkin [South America])

Shopping for fish

These terms can help you when you're selecting fish:

- **el camarón** *(kah-mah-rohn)* (shrimp); **gambas** *(gahm-bahs)* in Spain
- **el congrio** *(ehl kohn-greeoh)* (conger eel [coasts of Chile and Peru])
- **el huachinango** *(ehl ooah-chee-nahn-goh)* (red snapper)
- **el langostino** *(ehl lahn-gohs-tee-noh)* (prawn)
- **el marisco** *(ehl mah-rees-koh)* (seafood)
- **el pescado** *(ehl pehs-kah-doh)* (fish)
- **la trucha** *(lah troo-chah)* (trout)

Talkin' the Talk

Latin Americans prepare fish and seafood in a variety of ways, all of them delicious. Here's how Amalia shops for fish.

Amalia: **¿Cuánto cuesta el pescado?**
          koo ahn-toh kooehs-tah ehl pehs-kah-doh
          How much is the fish?

Vendor: **Treinta pesos el kilo.**
          treheen-tah peh-sohs ehl kee-loh
          Thirty pesos per kilo.

Amalia: **Lo quiero fileteado, sin espinas.**
          loh keeeh-roh fee-leh-teh-ah-doh seen ehs-pee-na
          I want it filleted, boneless.

Vendor:	**¿Se lleva la cabeza para la sopa?**
	seh yeh-bvah lah kah-bveh-sah pah-rah lah soh-pah
	Will you take the head for the soup?
Amalia:	**Sí, aparte, por favor.**
	see ah-pahr-teh pohr fah-bvohr
	Yes, separately, please.

Knowing the measures: Weight and volume

Since some year in the nineteenth century, the United States is supposedly on the metric system, like most of the world. But because this has not become a general custom, you may need some explanations about measures, which we're happy to provide.

A **kilo** (_kee_-loh) is a bit more than two pounds. **Kilo** actually comes from the word _kilogram_, which means one thousand grams. One gram is **un gramo** (_oon grah_-moh). One gram is a very small amount. It's roughly equivalent to the weight of the water filling a thimble. A **litro** (_lee_-troh) or "liter," like a quart, is four cups. Here's a list of other quantities:

- **una docena** (_oo-nah doh-seh-nah_) (a dozen)
- **media docena** (_meh-deeah doh-seh-nah_) (a half dozen)
- **una cincuentena** (_oo-nah seen-kooehn-teh-nah_) (fifty; 50)
- **una centena** (_oo-nah sehn-teh-nah_) (one hundred; 100)
- **un millar** (_oon mee-yahr_) (one thousand; 1,000)

Talkin' the Talk

 Listen as Amalia bargains with a vendor over oranges at a fruit and vegetable stand.

Amalia:	**¿A cuánto las naranjas?**
	ah kooahn-toh lahs nah-rahn-Hahs
	How much for the oranges?
Vendor:	**A diez pesos las veinticinco.**
	ah deeehs peh-sohs lahs bveheen-tee-seen-koh
	Ten pesos for twenty five.

Amalia:	**¿A cuánto los aguacates?** *ah koo<u>ahn</u>-toh lohs ah-gooah-<u>kah</u>-tehs* How much for the avocados?
Vendor:	**Quince pesos el kilo.** *<u>keen</u>-seh <u>peh</u>-sohs ehl <u>kee</u>-loh* Fifteen pesos for one kilo.
Amalia:	**¡Es muy caro!** *ehs mooy <u>kah</u>-roh* It's very expensive.
Vendor:	**Esá más barato que ayer.** *ehs mahs bvah-<u>rah</u>-toh keh ah-<u>yehr</u>* It's cheaper than yesterday.
Amalia:	**¿Tiene plátanos?** *tee<u>eh</u>-neh <u>plah</u>-tah-nohs* Do you have bananas?
Vendor:	**¿Sí, de cuáles?** *see deh koo<u>ah</u>-lehs* Yes, which kind?
Amalia:	**De esos. ¿Cuánto?** *deh <u>eh</u>-sohs koo<u>ahn</u>-toh koo<u>ehs</u>-tahn* Those. How much?
Vendor:	**Tres pesos el kilo.** *trehs <u>peh</u>-sohs ehl <u>kee</u>-loh* Three pesos the kilo.
Amalia:	**Medio kilo, por favor. Los ajos, ¿a cuánto?** *<u>meh</u>-deeoh <u>kee</u>-loh porh fah-<u>bvohr</u>. lohs <u>a</u>-Hos ah koo<u>ahn</u>-toh* A half kilo please. How much is the garlic?
Vendor:	**A cinco pesos el ramillete.** *ah <u>seen</u>-koh <u>peh</u>-sohs ehl rah-mee-<u>yeh</u>teh* 5 pesos per bunch [of heads.]

At the Supermercado

Of course, you can also buy groceries at the **supermercado** *(soo-pehr-mehr-<u>kah</u>-doh)*, where you proceed very much as you do in the United States. You may also find food there that you are more accustomed to. The supermarket is a good place to go for things like cereals and canned goods.

Following are some words and phrases that can help you at the supermarket:

- **el arroz** *(ehl ah-<u>rrohs</u>)* (the rice)
- **el atún** *(ehl ah-<u>toon</u>)* (the tuna)
- **el fideo** *(ehl fee-<u>deh</u>-oh)* (the pasta)
- **los cereales** *(lohs seh-reh-<u>ah</u>-lehs)* (the cereals)
- **las galletas** *(lahs gah-<u>yeh</u>-tahs)* (the cookies or crackers)
- **la leche** *(lah <u>leh</u>-cheh)* (the milk)
- **pagar** *(pah-<u>gahr</u>)* (to pay)
- **el pasillo** *(ehl pah-<u>see</u>-yoh)* (the aisle)
- **las sardinas** *(lahs sahr-<u>dee</u>-nahs)* (the sardines)
- **el vino** *(ehl <u>bvee</u>-noh)* (the wine)
- **el vuelto** *(ehl <u>bvooehl</u>-toh)* (change [as in money back]); *la vuelta (lah <u>bvoo</u>-ehl-tah)* in Spain
- **las ollas** *(lahs <u>oh</u>-yas)* (pots)
- **el tercer pasillo** *(ehl tehr-<u>sehr</u> pah-<u>see</u>-yoh)* (the third aisle)
- **Al fondo** *(ahl <u>fohn</u>-doh)* (At the back)
- **Gracias, aquí está su vuelto.** *(<u>grah</u>-seeahs ah-<u>kee</u> ehs-<u>tah</u> soo bvoo<u>ehl</u>-toh)* (Thanks, here's your change.)

Talkin' the Talk

A popular chicken dish in many Latin American countries is **arroz con pollo** *(ah-<u>rros</u> kohn <u>poh</u>-yoh)* (rice with chicken) Amalia has this conversation when she buys the chicken.

Amalia:	**¿Cuánto cuesta el pollo?**
	koo<u>ahn</u>-toh koo<u>ehs</u>-tah ehl <u>poh</u>-yoh
	How much is the chicken?

Vendor:	**A veinte el kilo.**
	ah <u>bveh</u>een-teh ehl <u>kee</u>-loh
	Twenty per kilo.

Amalia:	**Este, ¿cuánto es?**
	<u>ehs</u>-teh, koo<u>ahn</u>-toh ehs
	This one, how much?

Vendor:	**Cuarenta pesos. ¿Lo quiere cortado?**
	kooah-rehn-tah peh-sohs loh keeeh-reh
	kohr-tah-doh
	Forty pesos. You want it cut up?

Amalia:	**Sí, lo quiero en pedazos, la pechuga aparte.**
	see loh keeeh-roh ehn peh-dah-sohs lah
	peh-choo-gah ah-pahr-teh
	Yes, I want it in pieces, the breast separate.

Vendor:	**¿La pechuga la preparamos para hacer bistecs?**
	lah peh-choo-gah lah preh-pah-rah-mohs pah-rah
	ah-sehr bees-tehks
	Should we prepare the breast to make fillets?

Amalia:	**No, mejor entera.**
	noh meh-Hohr ehn-teh-rah
	No, better in one piece.

Numbers to Know

You can't shop or do much of anything without running into a number sooner or later. The table that follows gives you a numbered list for when it counts

From 1 to 10:

uno	oo-noh	1
dos	dohs	2
tres	trehs	3
cuatro	kooah-troh	4
cinco	seen-koh	5
seis	sehees	6
siete	see-eh-teh	7
ocho	oh-choh	8
nueve	nooeh-bveh	9
diez	dee-ehs	10

From 11 to 20:

once	ohn-seh	11

doce	<u>doh</u>-seh	12
trece	<u>treh</u>-seh	13
catorce	kah-<u>tohr</u>-seh	14
quince	<u>keen</u>-seh	15
dieciséis	deeeh-see-<u>se</u>hees	16

From 11 to 20:

diecisiete	deeeh-see-see<u>eh</u>-teh	17
dieciocho	deeeh-see<u>oh</u>-choh	18
diecinueve	deeeh-see-<u>nooeh</u>-bveh	19
veinte	<u>bveh</u>een-teh	20

From 21 to 25:

veintiuno	bveheen-tee<u>oo</u>-noh	21
veintidos	bveheen-tee-<u>dohs</u>	22
veintitres	bveheen-tee-<u>trehs</u>	23
veinticuatro	bveheen-tee-koo<u>ah</u>-troh	24
veinticinco	bveheen-tee-<u>seen</u>-koh	25

From 35 to 40:

treinta y cinco	<u>treh</u>een-tah ee <u>seen</u>-koh	35
treinta y seis	<u>treh</u>een-tah ee sehees	36
treinta y siete	<u>treh</u>een-tah ee see<u>eh</u>-teh	37
treinta y ocho	<u>treh</u>een-tah ee <u>oh</u>-choh	38
treinta y nueve	<u>treh</u>een-tah ee <u>nooeh</u>-bveh	39
cuarenta	kooah-<u>rehn</u>-tah	40

From 10 to 100, in tens:

diez	dee<u>ehs</u>	10
veinte	<u>bveh</u>een-teh	20
treinta	<u>treh</u>een-tah	30
cuarenta	kooah-<u>rehn</u>-tah	40
cincuenta	seen-koo<u>ehn</u>-tah	50

sesenta	seh-<u>sehn</u>-tah	60
setenta	seh-<u>tehn</u>-tah	70
ochenta	oh-<u>chehn</u>-tah	80
noventa	noh-<u>bvehn</u>-tah	90
cien	see<u>ehn</u>	100
Other numbers:		
trescientos	trehs-see<u>ehn</u>-tohs	300
quinientos	kee-nee<u>ehn</u>-tohs	500
setecientos	seh-teh-see<u>ehn</u>-tohs	600
ochocientos	oh-choh-see<u>ehn</u>-tohs	800
mil	meel	1,000
dos mil	dohs meel	2,000
siete mil	see<u>eh</u>-teh meel	7,000
treinta mil	<u>treh</u>een-tah meel	30,000
un millón	oon mee-<u>yohn</u>	1,000,000
diez millones	dee<u>eh</u>s mee-<u>yoh</u>-nehs	10,000,000

Fun and Games

A Spanish-speaking friend has come to visit you. To celebrate, you take him to a fancy restaurant. Of course, the menu is in English, and your friend asks you to translate several items. Write the Spanish words in the blank following each menu item:

Beef _____

Coffee _____

Fried chicken _____

Green sauce _____

Apples _____

Beer _____

Bananas _____

After translating the menu, your friend chooses his meal. Now translate his choices into English for the waiter:

Un vaso de agua _____

Un vaso de leche _____

Una ensalada mixta _____

Mole amarillo con pollo _____

Calabaza _____

Chapter 6

Shopping Made Easy

· ·

In This Chapter

▶ Shopping at the department store

▶ Asking for help

▶ Trying things on

▶ Checking sizes, colors, materials, items

▶ Using the verbs **probar** and **llevar**

▶ Expressing superlatives

· ·

*E*ven experienced shoppers can enjoy new ways to shop and new stores to shop at. Shopping beyond the borders of the Unites can be entertaining, and you can find some great bargains. But whether shopping is fun or hard work for you, in this chapter, we explain how to go about it Latin style!

In Latin American cities, you are likely to find that the shopping process resembles what you're used to. A worldwide trend seeks to make shopping faster, more abundant, and more varied. In larger cities like Buenos Aires *(bvooeh-nohs ahee-rehs)*, Caracas *(kah-rah-kahs)*, and Santiago de Chile *(sahn-teeah-goh deh chee-leh)* stores and market places have clothes and objects in styles that may be new and different from what you have already seen. And if you like to shop the way you are used to, you usually find department stores and supermarkets that carry merchandise that feels exotic but is still familiar.

In smaller places, or in villages and other areas where traditional ways of exchanging goods at an open-air market are still in use, you enter a new kind of shopping world — one full of surprises. At times, the merchandise may seem unfamiliar to the point of making it difficult to recognize what an item is and what it's used for. And the shopping style also differs from what you're used to. This is what we call fun time!

Shopping at the Department Store

I have a friend of the "shop till you drop" variety. When she travels, she always checks out the local department stores. In larger cities, local department stores are ideal places to see how and where the locals get their clothes and other necessities.

By contrast, if you want exotic items sold the old-fashioned way, a department store is not the best place to go. Exotic clothes and objects are sold in markets where the whole shopping operation is different. We cover traditional markets later in this chapter.

In department stores, you find the prices clearly posted and labeled. And you can surely find items that have local flavor.

Labels are not taken as seriously in all countries as they are in Canada or the States. Often, you may find merchandise that doesn't have all the information you need. Information the salesperson gives you may be just as fuzzy, simply because the United States and Canada put more emphasis on certain things than other countries do. Trust your senses and your experience.

These phrases can help you at a department store:

- **¿Dónde está la entrada?** *(dohn-deh ehs-tah lah ehn-trah-dah)* (Where's the entrance?)

- **¿Dónde está la salida?** *(dohn-deh ehs-tah lah sah-lee-dah)* (Where's the exit?)

- **empuje** *(ehm-poo-Heh)* (push)

- **tire** *(tee-reh)* (pull)

- **jale** *(Hah-leh)* (pull [Mexico])

- **el ascensor** *(ehl ah-sehn-sohr)* (the elevator)

- **la escalera mecánica** *(lah ehs-kah-leh-rah meh-kah-nee-kah)* (the escalator)

- **el vendedor** *(ehl bvehn-deh-dohr)* or **la vendedora** *(lah bvehn-deh-doh-rah)* (the salesperson [male and female])

- **la caja** *(lah kah-Hah)* (the check out stand)

Suppose that you are planning your day, and you want to know the store's hours. Here's how to ask for that information:

- **¿A qué hora abren?** *(ah keh oh-rah ah-bvrehn)* (At what time do you [formal] open?)

- **¿A qué hora cierran?** *(ah keh oh-rah seeeh-rrahn)* (At what time do you [formal] close?)

In the United States and Canada, you are probably used to browsing and shopping by yourself. In some places in Latin America, the salesperson wants to help you as soon as you enter the department. If you find the person insistent, my advice is to let yourself be helped. The salespeople are not trying to impose anything on you; quite to the contrary, they can be very involved and helpful. Let yourself feel like royalty, being pampered as you shop.

On the other hand, if you only want to browse, be firm about refusing help.

Talkin' the Talk

Here's how to tell a sales person that you want just to browse around the store.

Salesperson: **¿Busca algo en especial?**
bvoos-kah ahl-goh ehn ehs-peh-seeahl
Looking for something special?

Silvia: **Quiero mirar no más.**
keeeh-roh mee-rahr noh mahs
I just want to look.

Salesperson: **Me llama cuando me necesita.**
meh yah-mah kooahn-doh meh neh-seh-see-tah
Call me when you need me.

Silvia: **Sí, le voy a llamar, gracias.**
see leh bvohy ah yah-mahr grah-seeahs
Yes, I'll call you, thank you.

Using the Verb Probar (To Try)

The verb **probar** *(proh-bvahr)* (to try, to try on, or to taste) is one that you may use quite a lot when shopping.

Probar's root changes from *pro- (proh)* to *prue- (prooeh)* in some tenses, so it's an irregular verb. Here is the conjugation:

Conjugation	*Pronunciation*
yo pruebo	yoh prooeh-bvoh
tú pruebas	too prooeh-bvahs

él, ella, ello, uno, usted prueba	ehl _eh_-yah _eh_-yoh _oo_-noh oos-_tehd_ proo_eh_-bvah
nosotros probamos	noh-_soh_-trohs proh-_bvah_-mohs
vosotros probáis	bvoh-_soh_-trohs proh-_bvahees_
ellos, ellas, ustedes prueban	_eh_-yohs _eh_-yahs oos-_teh_-dehs proo_eh_-bvahn

Once you know how to use **probar**, you can ask to try on anything before you buy it, which is important to do when shopping in Latin America. Different people have different shapes, and some cuts may look different on Latins than on you.

Talkin' the Talk

You want the section of the store with the goods you are looking for. Here's how you might ask where it is:

Silvia: **¿Dónde están los vestidos de señora?**
dohn-deh ehs-_tahn_ lohs bvehs-_tee_-dohs deh seh-_nyoh_-rah
Where are the ladies' clothes?

Salesperson: **En el quinto piso.**
ehn ehl _keen_-toh _pee_-soh
On the fifth floor.

Silvia: **¿Dónde está la ropa de hombre?**
dohn-deh ehs-_tah_ lah _roh_-pah deh _ohm_-bvreh
Where are the men's clothes?

Salesperson: **En el cuarto piso.**
ehn ehl koo_ahr_-toh _pee_-soh
On the fourth floor.

Silvia: **¿Dónde encuentro artículos de tocador?**
dohn-deh ehn-koo_ehn_-troh ahr-_tee_-koo-lohs deh toh-kah-_dohr_
Where do I find toiletries?

Salesperson: **Al fondo, a la izquierda.**
ahl _fohn_-doh ah lah ees-kee_ehr_-dah
At the back, to the left.

Silvia:	**Busco la sección de ropa blanca.**
	bvoos-koh lah sehk-seeohn deh roh-pah bvlahn-kah
	I'm looking for sheets and towels.

Salesperson:	**Un piso más arriba.**
	oon pee-soh mahs ah-rree-bvah
	One floor up.

Silvia:	**¿Venden electrodomésticos?**
	bvehn-dehn eehl-ehk-troh-doh-mehs-tee-kohs
	Do you sell appliances?

Salesperson:	**Sí, en el último piso.**
	see ehn ehl ool-tee-moh pee-soh
	Yes, on the top floor.

Creating a colorful you

The colors in Spanish-speaking countries are sun-warmed and vibrant. Shopping for clothes and other goods requires some familiarity with describing these colors so you can select the best match for your needs and personality. Table 6-1 gives you a handle on the Spanish color palette:

Table 6-1	Selecting Your Colors	
Color	*Pronunciation*	*Translation*
blanco	*bvlahn-koh*	white
negro	*neh-groh*	black
gris	*grees*	grey
rojo	*roh-Hoh*	red
azul	*ah-sool*	blue
verde	*bvehr-deh*	green
morado	*moh-rah-doh*	purple
violeta	*bveeoh-leh-tah*	violet, purple
café	*kah-feh*	brown
marrón	*mah-rrohn*	brown (Argentina)
amarillo	*ah-mah-ree-yoh*	yellow
naranja	*nah-rahn-Hah*	orange

(continued)

Table 6-1 (continued)

Color	Pronunciation	Translation
rosado	roh-_sah_-doh	pink
celeste	seh-_lehs_-teh	sky blue
claro	_klah_-roh	light
oscuro	ohs-_koo_-roh	dark

Talkin' the Talk

Silvia accidentally split her skirt bending down to pick up some boxes at work. She needs a new one quick — one with pockets to hold the art supplies she needs as a graphic designer. She asks a salesperson for help:

Silvia: **¿Me ayuda por favor?**
meh ah-_yoo_-dah porh fah-_bvohr_
Will you help me, please?

Busco una falda, con bolsillos.
bvoos-koh _oo_-nah _fahl_-dah kohn bvohl-_see_-yohs
I'm looking for a skirt, with pockets.

Salesperson: **¿Qué talla tiene?**
keh _tah_-yah tee_eh_-neh
What's your size?

Silvia: **Talla doce americana.**
tah-yah _doh_-seh ah-meh-ree-_kah_-nah
Size twelve, American.

Salesperson: **¿Me permite medirla, para estar seguras?**
meh pehr-_mee_-teh meh-_deer_-lah _pah_-rah ehs-_tahr_ seh-_goo_-rahs
May I take your size so we can know for sure?

Ah, su talla es treinta y ocho.
ah soo _tah_-yah ehs _treheen_-tah ee _oh_-choh
Ah, your size is thirty eight.

¿Qué color busca?
keh koh-_lohr_ _bvoos_-kah
What color are you looking for?

Silvia: **Rojo.**
<u>roh</u>-Hoh
Red.

Salesperson: **La quiere con flores?**
lah kee<u>eh</u>-reh kohn <u>floh</u>-rehs
Do you want it with flowers?

Silvia: **No, lisa, por favor.**
noh <u>lee</u>-sah pohr fah-<u>bvohr</u>
No, plain, please.

Words to Know

ayudar	ah-yoo-<u>dahr</u>	to help
más	mahs	more
menos	<u>meh</u>-nohs	less
la falda	lah <u>fahl</u>-dah	the skirt
el bolsillo	ehl bvohl-<u>see</u>-yoh	the pocket
medir	meh-<u>deer</u>	to measure
la talla	lah <u>tah</u>-yah	the size
liso	<u>lee</u>-soh	plain; flat

Shopping for shirts

A word of wisdom: Men's shirts seem to come in the same sizes in Spanish-speaking countries as they do in the United States and Canada. But just in case, checking the fit is a good idea.

In some areas, people are smaller and sizes vary; the medium might be what you consider a small. Your best bet is to try on the shirt before you leave the store.

Talkin' the Talk

Here's how you might ask to try on pants:

Claudio:	**¿Puedo probarme este pantalón?**
	poo<u>eh</u>-doh proh-<u>bvahr</u>-meh <u>ehs</u>-teh pahn-tah-<u>lohn</u>
	May I try on these trousers?

Salesperson:	**Cómo no, por aquí.**
	<u>koh</u>-moh no pohr ah-<u>kee</u>
	Of course, this way.

Claudio:	**Me queda grande.**
	meh <u>keh</u>-dah <u>grahn</u>-deh
	They are too big. (Literally: It fits me large.)

Salesperson:	**Le busco otro.**
	leh <u>bvoos</u>-koh <u>oh</u>-troh
	I'll find you another.

Claudio:	**Este aprieta aquí.**
	<u>ehs</u>-teh ah-pree<u>eh</u>-tah ah-<u>kee</u>
	This one is tight here.

Salesperson:	**A ver este.**
	ah bvehr <u>ehs</u>-teh
	Let's see this one.

Claudio:	**¿Lo tiene en verde?**
	loh tee<u>eh</u>-neh ehn <u>bvehr</u>-deh
	Do you have it in green?

Salesperson:	**Este, ¿a ver?**
	<u>ehs</u>-teh ah bvehr
	This one, let's see?

Claudio:	**Queda muy bien.**
	<u>keh</u>-dah mooy bvee<u>ehn</u>
	It fits very well.

Words to Know

los pantalones	lohs pahn-tah-<u>loh</u>-nehs	the trousers
queda grande	keh-dah grahn-deh	the fit is big
queda bien	keh-dah bveeehn	the fit is right
probar	proh-bvahr	to try

Checking fibers and fabrics

When shopping, you may notice that poorer regions favor fabrics made with artificial fibers and that the prices for these fabrics are not lower than those of natural fibers. These terms help you ask about the fibers (or fabrics) of which the garments are made:

- ✔ **¿Este pantalón es de pura lana?** *(ehs-teh pahn-tah-lohn ehs de poo-rah lah-nah)* (Are these pants made of pure wool?)

- ✔ **No, es de lana con nylon.** *(noh ehs deh lah-nah kohn nahee-lohn)* (No, they are made of wool and nylon.)

- ✔ **¿La camisa es de puro algodón?** *(lah kah-mee-sah ehs deh poo-roh ahl-goh-dohn)* (Is the shirt made of pure cotton?)

- ✔ **No, es de algodón con poliéster.** *(noh, ehs deh ahl-goh-dohn ee poh-leeehs-tehr)* (No, it's made of cotton and polyester.)

- ✔ **¿Cuánto algodón tiene esta tela?** *(kooahn-toh ahl-goh-dohn teeeh-neh ehs-tah teh-lah?)* (How much cotton is there in this fabric?)

- ✔ **Tiene cuarenta por ciento.** *(teeeh-neh kooah-rehn-tah pohr seeehn-toh)* (It has forty percent.)

- ✔ **Busco ropa de fibras naturales.** *(bvoos-koh roh-pah deh fee-bvrahs nah-too-rah-lehs)* (I'm looking for natural fiber clothes.)

- ✔ **También tenemos.** *(tahm-bveeehn teh-neh-mohs)* (We have them also.)

Words to Know

pura	poo-rah	pure
la lana	lah lah-nah	the wool
el algodón	ehl ahl-goh-dohn	the cotton
la fibra	lah fee-bvrah	the fiber
por ciento	pohr seeehn-toh	percent; percentage

Wearing and Taking: The Verb Llevar

Whether you're wearing, tearing, or shopping, this is a great verb to have around.

In Spanish (to wear) and (to take with you) and (to keep track of) or (to keep count of) are the same verb — **llevar** (yeh-*bvahr*). Good news! This is a regular verb of the group ending in *-ar*; its root is *llev-* (yehbv-).

Another way to say *to wear* is **vestir** (bvehs-*teer*) (to dress), which comes from **vestido** (bves-*tee*-doh) (dress).

Conjugation	Pronunciation
yo llevo	yoh <u>yeh</u>-bvoh
tú llevas	too <u>yeh</u>-bvahs
él, ella, uno, usted lleva	ehl <u>eh</u>-yah <u>oo</u>-noh <u>oos</u>-tehd <u>yeh</u>-bvah
nosotros llevamos	noh-<u>soh</u>-trohs yeh-<u>bvah</u>-mohs
vosotros lleváis	bvoh-<u>soh</u>-trohs yeh-<u>bvaees</u>
ellos, ellas, ustedes llevan	<u>eh</u>-yohs <u>eh</u>-yahs oos-<u>teh</u>-dehs <u>yeh</u>-bvahn

Count on these examples to help you keep track of this dressing and tracking verb.

- ✔ **Me llevo esta camisa.** (meh <u>yeh</u>-bvoh <u>ehs</u>-tah kah-<u>mee</u>-sah) (I'll take this shirt.)

- ✔ **El vestido que llevas es bellísimo.** (ehl bvehs-<u>tee</u>-doh keh <u>yeh</u>-bvahs ehs bveh-<u>yee</u>-see-moh) (The dress you have on is very beautiful.)

- ✔ **Llevo un regalo para ti.** (<u>yeh</u>-bvoh ooh reh-<u>gah</u>-loh <u>pah</u>-rah tee) (I'm taking a present for you.)

- ✔ **Llevamos tres semanas sin vernos.** (yeh-<u>bvah</u>-mohs trehs seh-<u>mah</u>-nahs seen <u>bvehr</u>-nohs) (It's been [Literally: We are counting] three weeks without seeing each other.)

- ✔ **El lleva cuenta de cuántos vestidos compraste.** (ehl <u>yeh</u>-bvah koo<u>ehn</u>-tah deh koo<u>ahn</u>-tohs <u>bvehs</u>-tee-dohs kohm-<u>prahs</u>-teh) (He keeps track of the number of dresses you buy.)

- ✔ **La llevo.** (lah <u>yeh</u>-bvoh) (I'll take it.)

Talkin' the Talk

The skirt is the right color, so you want to try it on to be on the safe side before you make a final decision.

Salesperson: **Pase al probador, por favor.**
<u>pah</u>-seh ahl proh-bvah-<u>dohr</u> pohr fah-<u>bvohr</u>
Please go into the fitting room.

Silvia: **¿Dónde está?**
dohn-deh ehs-tah
Where is it?

Salesperson: **Por aquí.**
pohr ah-kee
This way.

¿Le quedó bien?
leh keh-doh bveeehn
Did it fit?

Silvia: **No, está muy apretada.**
noh, ehs-tah mooy ah-preh-tah-dah
No, it's very tight.

¿Puede traer una de talla más grande?
pooeh-deh trah-ehr oo-nah tah-yah mahs grahn-deh
Can you bring a larger size?

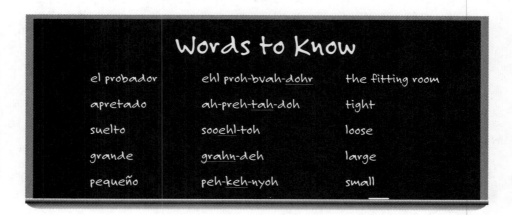

Words to Know		
el probador	ehl proh-bvah-dohr	the fitting room
apretado	ah-preh-tah-doh	tight
suelto	sooehl-toh	loose
grande	grahn-deh	large
pequeño	peh-keh-nyoh	small

Comparisons: Good, Better, Best, and More

When you compare one thing to another, you talk in comparatives and superlatives. In Spanish, most of the time you use the word **más** *(mahs)* (more) for comparisons and **el más** *(ehl mahs)*, which literally means (the most), for superlatives. An example is the word **grande** *(grahn-deh)*, which means (large) in English. **Más grande** *(mahs grahn-deh)* means (larger), and **el más grande** *(ehl mahs grahn-deh)* means (the largest).

In English, you usually change the word's ending; in Spanish, you just add **más** or **el más.** English has a similar system of adding comparatives and superlatives for longer words, such as *expensive,* where the comparative adds "more" before expensive, and the superlative adds "most."

Here are some examples of Spanish comparatives and superlatives:

- **grande** *(grahn-deh)* (big; large)
  más grande *(mahs grahn-deh)* (bigger; larger)
  el más grande *(ehl mahs grahn-deh)* (biggest; largest)

- **pequeño** *(peh-keh-nyoh)* (small)
  más pequeño *(mahs peh-keh-nyoh)* (smaller)
  el más pequeño *(ehl mahs peh-keh-nyoh)* (smallest)

- **chico** *(chee-koh)* (small; short; young)
  más chico *(mahs chee-koh)* (smaller; shorter; younger)
  el más chico *(ehl mahs chee-koh)* (smallest; shortest, youngest)

- **apretado** *(ah-preh-tah-doh)* (tight)
  más apretado *(mahs ah-preh-tah-doh)* (tighter)
  el más apretado *(ehl mahs ah-preh-tah-doh)* (tightest)

- **suelto** *(sooehl-toh)* (loose)
  más suelto *(mahs sooehl-toh)* (looser)
  el más suelto *(ehl mahs sooehl-toh)* (loosest)

- **caro** *(kah-roh)* (expensive)
  más caro *(mahs kah-roh)* (more expensive)
  el más caro *(ehl mahs kah-roh)* (most expensive)

- **barato** *(bvah-rah-toh)* (cheap)
  más barato *(mahs bvah-rah-toh)* (cheaper)
  el más barato *(ehl mahs bvah-rah-toh)* (cheapest)

Just as in English, a few exceptions exist, in which the comparative form does not require the word **más,** such as:

- **bueno** *(bvooeh-noh)* (good)
  mejor *(meh-Hohr)* (better)
  el mejor *(ehl meh-Hohr)* (best)

- **malo** *(mah-loh)* (bad)
  peor *(peh-ohr)* (worse)
  el peor *(ehl peh-ohr)* (worst)

Notice that the English meanings also are exceptions to the English rules for forming comparatives and superlatives.

When Superlatives Fail: Exaggerations

Spanish speakers love to exaggerate. What to non-Spanish speakers may seem an excessive way to talk, to the Spanish-speaking mind simply adds a bit more emphasis.

Exaggeration is something you see everywhere, even in classical Spanish poetry. For example, Francisco de Quevedo y Villegas *(frahn-sees-koh deh keh-bveh-doh ee bvee-yeh-gahs)*, the Spanish poet of the Golden Century (who lived from 1580-1645), says in his poem "A una nariz" *(ah oo-nah nah-rees)* (To a nose) to a person with a very large one:

"muchísima nariz" *(moo-chee-see-mah nah-reehs)* (a whole lotta nose)

So in Spanish, you can not only compare things, but you also have a way to express an exaggerated state of things.

To say that something is exaggeratedly this or that, you add **-ísimo** *(ee-see-moh)* or **-ísima** *(ee-see-mah)* to an adjective or an adverb. For example, to say that something good, **bueno** *(bvooeh-noh)*, is exaggeratedly so, you say **buenísimo** *(bvooeh-nee-see-moh)* (exceptionally good).

Here are some examples:

- ✔ **La película es buenísima.** *(lah peh-lee-koo-lah ehs bvooeh-nee-see-mah)* (The film is exceptionally good.)

- ✔ **La ciudad es grandísima.** *(lah seeoo-dahd ehs grahn-dee-see-mah grahn-dee-see-mah)* (The city is huge.)

- ✔ **Los perros son bravísimos.** *(los peh-rrohs sohn bvrah-bvee-see-mohs)* (The dogs are extremely fierce.)

- ✔ **El hotel es malísimo.** *(ehl oh-tehl ehs mah-lee-see-moh)* (The hotel is really bad.)

- ✔ **El postre está dulcísimo.** *(ehl pohs-treh ehs-tah dool-see-see-moh)* (The dessert is sickeningly sweet.)

- ✔ **Los colores son vivísimos.** *(losh koh-loh-rehs sohn bvee-bvee-see-mohs)* (The colors are exceedingly bright.)

- ✔ **El bus andaba lentísimo.** *(ehl bvoos ahn-dah-bvah lehn-tee-see-moh)* (The bus advanced extremely slowly.)

- ✔ **La tienda cobraba carísimo.** *(lah teeehn-dah koh-bvrah-bvah kah-ree-see-moh)* (The shop was exorbitantly expensive.)

Shopping for Finer Objects

You may want to shop in the specialized stores or galleries generally located on the more elegant boulevards, streets, and avenues in all Latin American countries. Seeking the finest artistic, cultural, or fashion items may include buying original art or silver in Lima, Peru (*lee*-mah peh-*roo*) and Mexico City, or shopping for paintings, sculpture, fine shoes, leather objects, and exquisite collectibles in Buenos Aires, Argentina (bvoo*eh*-nohs *ahee*-rehs ahr-Hehn-*tee*-nah).

For the shopping sophisticate

You can use these phrases when shopping at a specialized store or gallery:

- **Busco grabados de Rufino Tamayo.** (*bvoos*-koh grah-*bvah*-dohs deh roo-*fee*-noh tah-*mah*-yoh) (I'm looking for etchings by Rufino Tamayo.)

- **¿Tiene broches de plata?** (tee*eh*-neh *bvroh*-chehs deh *plah*-tah) (Do you have silver brooches?)

- **¿Cuánto cuesta el collar que tiene en la ventana?** (koo*ahn*-toh koo*ehs*-tah ehl koh-*yahr* keh tee*eh*-neh ehn la bvehn-*tah*-nah) (How much is the necklace you have in the window?)

- **¿Y la pintura?** (ee lah peen-*too*-rah) (And the painting?)

- **¿Vende perlas del sur de Chile?** (*bvehn*-deh *pehr*-lahs dehl soor deh *chee*-leh) (Do you sell pearls from the south of Chile?)

- **¿De quién es la escultura en la vitrina?** (deh kee*ehn* ehs lah ehs-kool-*too*-rah ehn lah bvee-*tree*-nah) (By whom is the sculpture in the display case?)

- **¿Lo embalamos y mandamos a su domicilio?** (loh ehm-bvah-*lah*-mohs ee mahn-*dah*-mohs a soo doh-mee-*see*-leeoh) (Shall we pack it and send it to your address?)

Words to Know		
el grabado	ehl grah-bvah-doh	the etching
la escultura	lah ehs-kool-too-rah	the sculpture
la pintura	lah peen-too-rah	the painting
el collar	ehl koh-yahr	the necklace
la perla	lah pehr-lah	the pearl

Shopping in Traditional Markets

You can find typical clothes and objects in the traditional markets, many of which are open every day and all year round, where bargaining and haggling are the norm. In these markets, you probably won't find any labels stating the prices, because the prices are not really fixed. (That's what the bargaining and haggling are all about.)

Typical market items: A treasure trove

As you travel around the market places of Latin America, you can end up with treasures such as these:

- ✔ **Un bol de madera tropical de Asunción, Paraguay** *(oon bvohl deh mah-deh-rah troh-pee-kahl deh ah-soon-seeohn pah-rah-gooahy)* (A bowl, made from tropical wood, from Asunción, Paraguay)

- ✔ **Una alfombra de lana de Otavalo, de Ecuador** *(oo-nah ahl-fohm-bvrah deh lah-nah deh oh-tah-bvah-loh eh-kooah-dohr)* (A rug made of wool from Otavalo, Ecuador)

- ✔ **Una tabla con jeroglíficos de la Isla de Pascua, Chile** *(oo-nah tah-bvlah kohn Heh-roh-glee-fee-kohs deh lah ees-lah deh pahs-kooah chee-leh)* (A wooden board covered with hieroglyphs, from Easter Island, Chile)

- ✔ **Una chaqueta hecha de tela de lana tejida a mano y bordada con seda, de Antigua, Guatemala** *(oo-nah chah-keh-tah eh-chah deh teh-lah deh lah-nah teh-Hee-dah ah mah-noh ee bvohr-dah-dah kohn seh-dah deh ahn-tee-gooah gooah-teh-mah-lah)* (A jacket, made of handwoven wool embroidered in silk, from Antigua, Guatemala)

In the markets, you find color in the merchandise, in the conversation, in the shopping style. You also find handcrafted goods, made in the manner of pre-industrial times where the human hand has left its mark unmatched in feeling by machine production. You find the informality that comes from the precariousness of open markets, and which also makes for displays of the goods in original ways — without display cases, and without marketing tricks.

Like the bazaars of *A Thousand and One Nights,* the markets of Otavalo *(oh-tah-bvah-loh),* Ecuador; Lima *(lee-mah),* Perú; Antigua *(ahn-tee-gooah)* in Guatemala; or Tlacolula *(tlah-koh-loo-lah)* in the State of Oaxaca *(oh-ah-Hah-kah)* in Mexico, are really magical fun places that put you in touch with life as it used to be and still is for many people in Latin America.

Words to Know

la alfombra	lah ahl-fohm-bvrah	rug
la bombilla	lah bvohm-bvee-yah	a tube, with filter, used to drink mate (mah-teh)
la olla	lah oh-yah	the pot
el barro	ehl bvah-rroh	the clay
rebajar	reh-bvah-Hahr	to bring the price down
el dibujo	ehl dee-bvoo-Hoh	the drawing; the pattern

Bargaining at a typical market

If you shop in traditional markets, getting there early is a good idea. Many merchants feel that they *must* make a first sale to kick off their day. If you find yourself in such a situation, you may notice that the merchant does not want you to leave without buying something, and is therefore more willing to reduce the price to make a sale, and you can end up with a bargain.

The following phrases help you when you need to haggle in the market place:

- ✔ **¿Cuánto cuesta?** *(koo_ahn_-toh koo_ehs_-tah)* (How much is it?)
- ✔ **¿Cuánto vale?** *(koo_ahn_-toh bv_ah_-leh)* (How much is it worth?)
- ✔ **¿A cuánto?** *(ah koo_ahn_-toh)* (How much?)
- ✔ **Es barato.** *(ehs bvah-_rah_-toh)* (It's cheap/inexpensive.)
- ✔ **Es caro.** *(ehs _kah_-roh)* (It's expensive.)

Use these phrases to provide emphasis. You won't be using these *all* the time, especially the second and third ones, yet they are fun to use and help you express a certain level of emotion:

- ✔ **¡Una ganga!** *(_oo_-nah _gahn_-gah)* (A bargain!)
- ✔ **¡Un robo!** *(oon _roh_-bvoh)* (A burglary!)
- ✔ **¡Un asalto!** *(oon ah-_sahl_-toh)* (A holdup!)

Advice for the bargainer

In a traditional market or on the streets, when you're offered something you're interested in and price is mentioned, offer half. Of course, this is really outrageous and the merchant reacts to that price with outrage. And thus a social game begins.

So after offering half, you get an answer from the merchant stating a sum slightly less than what was first asked for. At this point you *know* the game is on. So you offer a bit more than your first amount. And the game goes on until you *feel* or believe that the merchant will go no further and the price is what you can afford.

Bargaining like this is a very satisfying activity for the seller and can also be so for the buyer. You establish a certain relationship while you bargain that shows your stamina and that of the seller in addition to your ability to follow a certain rhythm in the operation.

Talkin' the Talk

Bargaining is sometimes a little difficult in a department store, but in traditional market places in Latin America, it is part of the deal. Listen to how Sylvia haggles over a nice rug that she's spotted at an outdoor market.

Sylvia: **Este tapete, ¿cuánto cuesta?**
ehs-teh tah-peh-teh kooahn-toh kooehs-tah
How much is this rug?

Merchant: **Quinientos pesos.**
kee-neeehn-tohs peh-sohs
Five hundred pesos.

Sylvia: **¿Tiene otros más baratos?**
teeeh-neh oh-trohs mahs bvah-rah-tohs
Do you have cheaper ones?

Merchant: **Tengo este, más pequeño.**
tehn-goh ehs-teh mahs peh-keh-nyoh
I have this smaller one.

Sylvia: **No me gusta el dibujo.**
noh meh goos-tah ehl dee-bvoo-Hoh
I don't like the pattern.

Merchant:	**Este en blanco y negro, a trescientos.**
	ehs-teh ehn bvlahn-koh ee neh-groh ah
	trehs-seeehn-tohs
	This black and white one, for three hundred.

Sylvia:	**Me gusta. ¿A doscientos?**
	meh goos-tah ah dohs-seeehn-tohs
	I like it. Two hundred?

Merchant:	**No puedo. Doscientos cincuenta. Ultimo precio.**
	noh pooeh-doh dohs-seeehn-tohs seen-kooehn-tah
	ool-tee-moh preh-seeoh
	I can't. Two hundred and fifty. Last price.

Sylvia:	**Bueno, me lo llevo.**
	bvooeh-noh meh loh yeh-bvoh
	Good. I'll take it.

Shopping for copper, glass, clay, and wood stuff

Latin American artisans are well known for their fine work in copper, glass, wood, textiles, and clay, and items made of these substances are highly sought after by collectors and lovers of their typical beauty.

Copper is beautiful and lasting but heavy to carry. However, you cannot resist these beautiful pieces . . . or the delicate glass . . . or the colorful but breakable clay pot. You see wooden spoons, and these intricately painted darling things are not so fragile as glass or clay, nor as heavy as the copper. What to buy?

These phrases can help you when you shop for these specialty items:

- ✔ **¿Dónde venden objetos de cobre?** (*dohn-deh bvehn-dehn ohbv-Heh-tohs deh koh-bvreh*) (Where do they sell copper objects?)

- ✔ **Busco objetos de vidrio.** (*bvoos-koh ohbv-Heh-tohs deh bvee-dreeoh*) (I'm looking for glass objects.)

- ✔ **Allí hay cerámica hecha a mano.** (*ah-kee ahy seh-rah-mee-kah eh-chah ah mah-noh*) (There are some hand-made ceramics.)

- ✔ **Estas ollas de barro sirven para cocinar.** (*ehs-tahs oh-yahs deh bvah-rroh seer-bvehn pah-rah koh-see-nahr*) (These clay pots are suitable for cooking.)

Words to Know

el cobre	ehl koh-bvreh	the copper
el vidrio	ehl bvee-dreeoh	the glass
soplar	soh-plahr	to blow
hecho a mano	eh-choh ah mah-noh	handmade
la cerámica	lah seh-rah-mee-kah	the ceramic

Shopping for embroidered clothes

Who has time to embroider any more? Well, in Latin America, you can find some wonders of embroidery skill. Here are some phrases that can help you make a good selection:

- ✔ **¡Qué bello este bordado!** *(keh bveh-yoh ehs-teh bvohr-dah-doh)* (What beautiful embroidery!)

- ✔ **¿Tiene blusitas para niña?** *(teeeh-neh bloo-see-tahs pah-rah nee-nyah)* (Do you have little blouses for a girl?)

- ✔ **¿Tiene vestidos para mujer?** *(teeeh-neh bvehs-tee-dohs pah-rah moo-Hehr)* (Do you have ladies' dresses?)

Shopping for baskets

Actually, you can pack everything you buy in one of those large, colorful baskets and then use them at home for storage and as decorative accents. Because baskets come in so many materials, shapes, and sizes and are generally quite long lasting, they make a beautiful addition to any home. The following sentences help you purchase baskets:

- ✔ **Estos son canastos de mimbre.** *(ehs-tohs sohn kah-nahs-tohs deh meem-bvreh)* (These are wicker baskets.)

- ✔ **¿Tiene canastos para la ropa?** *(teeeh-neh kah-nahs-tohs pah-rah lah roh-pah)* (Do you have laundry baskets?)

- ✔ **Estos canastos son de totora.** *(ehs-tohs kah-nahs-tohs sohn de toh-toh-rah)* (These baskets are made from a reed [found in the Andean Region].)

- ✔ **Estos canastos son de totomoztle.** *(ehs-tohs kah-nahs-tohs sohn deh toh-toh-mohs-tleh)* (These baskets are made from corn leaves. [Mexico])

If you need help with numbers and prices, see Chapter 5.

Fun & Games

Your boss just gave you a huge, unexpected raise. With money burning a hole in your pocket, you decide to go on a shopping spree. You're going to a department store and to the traditional market, allowing yourself five items each from several shops. Use the chart below to help you plan your attack.

		Item	*Material*	*Color*
Ropa	1.			
	2.			
	3.			
	4.			
	5.			
Objetos (de cobre, vidrio, o madera)	1.			
	2.			
	3.			
	4.			
	5.			
Canastos	1.			
	2.			
	3.			
	4.			
	5.			

Chapter 7

Going Out on the Town

....

In This Chapter

▶ Enjoying movies, art, theater, and other entertainment
▶ Identifying times of the day and days of the week

....

You have no chance of getting bored in Latin American circles. Be it music, movies, theater, or dance — you name it — you have much to see and experience.

Latinos love culture, and they rejoice in turning their cultural activities into social events — gathering with old friends and new arrivals for movies, concerts, the opera, or whatever. Latin American events combine color and costume, music and dance, artistry and passion. The people tend to be quite uninhibited and live life with great gusto. In fact, they invented the word *gusto*.

The larger cities of Latin America always have more to see than any one person can handle. And even in the smallest village, it's not uncommon for someone to decide to take a glass, call for a toast, and sing a song — just for the joy of living! Even children's birthday parties may have live music, and when important family events are celebrated, people dance and sing to the music of their local bands into the wee hours of the morning.

This chapter tells you what you need to know to enjoy yourself Latin-American style.

Timing Is Everything

Here are the days of the week in Spanish:

- **lunes** (*loo-nehs*) (Monday)
- **martes** (*mahr-tehs*) (Tuesday)
- **miércoles** (*meeehr-koh-lehs*) (Wednesday)

✔ **jueves** *(Hoo<u>eh</u>-bvehs)* (Thursday)

✔ **viernes** *(bvee<u>ehr</u>-nehs)* (Friday)

✔ **sábado** *(<u>sah</u>-bvah-doh)* (Saturday)

✔ **domingo** *(doh-<u>meen</u>-goh)* (Sunday)

Use the following phrases to practice the days of the week:

✔ **La clase va a ser el martes.** *(lah <u>klah</u>-seh bvah a sehr ehl <u>mahr</u>-tehs)* (The class will be held on Tuesday.)

✔ **No puedo ir hasta el miércoles.** *(noh poo<u>eh</u>-doh eer <u>ahs</u>-tah ehl mee<u>ehr</u>-koh-lehs)* (I can't go until Wednesday.)

✔ **Va a llegar el viernes.** *(bvah ah yeh-<u>gahr</u> ehl bvee<u>ehr</u>-nes)* (He's going to arrive on Friday.)

✔ **Me voy el domingo.** *(meh bvohy ehl doh-<u>meen</u>-goh)* (I'm leaving on Sunday.)

Sometimes, you also need to state the approximate time, as in the following phrases:

✔ **la semana entrante** *(lah seh-<u>mah</u>-nah ehn-<u>trahn</u>-teh)* (the next week [Literally: the week entering])

✔ **la semana próxima** *(lah seh-<u>mah</u>-nah <u>proh</u>-ksee-mah)* (next week)

✔ **la semana que viene** *(lah seh-<u>mah</u>-nah keh bvee<u>eh</u>-neh)* (next week [Literally: the week that comes])

✔ **Es mediodía.** *(ehs meh-deeoh-<u>deeah</u>)* (It's noon.)

✔ **Es medianoche.** *(ehs meh-deeah-<u>noh</u>-cheh)* (It's midnight.)

✔ **Es tarde.** *(ehs <u>tahr</u>-deh)* (It's late.)

✔ **Es temprano.** *(ehs tehm-<u>prah</u>-noh)* (It's early.)

✔ **Estoy atrasado.** *(<u>ehs</u>-tohy ah-trah-<u>sah</u>-doh)* (I'm late.)

These phrases can help you practice saying the days of the week and approximate times:

✔ **Es tarde; ya son las ocho.** *(ehs <u>tahr</u>-deh; yah sohn lahs <u>oh</u>-choh)* (It's late; it's already eight o'clock.)

✔ **A medianoche termina el baile.** *(ah meh-deeah-<u>noh</u>-cheh tehr-<u>mee</u>-nah ehl bvahee-leh)* (The dance ends at midnight.)

✔ **Estoy atrasado; ya es mediodía.** *(ehs-<u>tohy</u> ah-trah-<u>sah</u>-doh; yah ehs meh-deeoh-<u>deeah</u>)* (I'm late; it's already noon.)

> ✔ **Es el lunes, temprano en la mañana.** *(ehs ehl loo-nehs, tehm-prah-noh ehn lah mah-nyah-nah)* (It's on Monday, early in the morning.)

> ✔ **La semana entrante va a venir en avión.** *(lah seh-mah-nah ehn-trahn-teh bvah ah bveh-neer ehn ah-bveeohn)* (She/He'll come by air next week.)

> ✔ **La semana siguiente es buena fecha.** *(lah seh-mah-nah see-gheeehn teh ehs bvoo eh-nah feh-chah)* (The following week is a good date.)

See Chapter 15 if you need to know the months in the year; for help with numbers, see Chapter 5.

Having a Good Time

The pleasure that people take in cultural expression is universal. Everyone loves a good show. Everyone loves to sing (well, almost everyone) and hear others who do it well. Most people love to dance as well. In songs and in dance, people share a bit of themselves.

And nothing is better for your health than dancing and singing. Here are some phrases Spanish speakers use to express their culture:

> ✔ **¡Bailar y cantar!** *(bahee-lahr ee kahn-tahr)* (Dance and sing!)

> ✔ **¡Esta es para ti!** *(ehs-tah ehs pah-rah tee!)*
> (This one is for you! [from a Cuban song])

These phrases help you set the time and place when you're ready to go out on the town:

> ✔ **¿a qué hora?** *(ah keh oh-rah)* (at what time?)

> ✔ **¿cuándo comienza?** *(kooahn-doh koh-meeehn-sah)* (when does it start?)

> ✔ **¿hasta qué hora?** *(ahs-tah keh oh-rah)* (until what time?)

Social contacts are generally explored and expanded in cocktail parties in the United States and Canada. Cocktail parties exist in Spanish-speaking circles as well, but more often than not people get together during meals, or during dancing occasions, instead. And just like at cocktail parties, Latinos use their parties to meet and greet each other and to develop new social relationships.

Talkin' the Talk

When, where, and how long are party questions that need answers:

Consuelo:	**¿A qué hora comienza la fiesta?**
	ah keh <u>oh</u>-rah koh-mee<u>ehn</u>-sah la fee<u>ehs</u>-tah
	What time does the party start?
Raúl:	**A las diez de la noche.**
	ah lahs dee<u>ehs</u> deh lah <u>noh</u>-cheh
	Ten at night.
Consuelo:	**¿No será muy tarde?**
	noh seh-<u>rah</u> mooy <u>tahr</u>-deh
	Won't it be too late?
Raúl:	**No, ¡juntamos fuerzas durmiendo la siesta!**
	noh Hoon-<u>tah</u>-mohs foo<u>ehr</u>-sahs door-mee<u>ehn</u>-doh lah see<u>ehs</u>-tah
	No, we'll gather our energy sleeping during the siesta!
Consuelo:	**¿A qué hora acaba la fiesta?**
	ah keh <u>oh</u>-rah ah-<u>kah</u>-bvah lah fee<u>ehs</u>-tah
	What time will the party end?
Raúl:	**Dicen que dura hasta las dos de la mañana.**
	<u>dee</u>-sehn keh <u>doo</u>-rah <u>ahs</u>-tah lahs dohs deh lah mah-<u>nyah</u>-nah
	They say it lasts until two in the morning.
Consuelo:	**¿Hasta esa hora?**
	<u>ahs</u>-tah <u>eh</u>-sah <u>oh</u>-rah
	Until then?
Raúl:	**Sí, y luego vamos a tomar un buen chocolate.**
	see ee loo<u>eh</u>-goh <u>bvah</u>-mohs ah toh-<u>mahr</u> oon bvoo<u>ehn</u> choh-koh-<u>lah</u>-teh.
	Yes, and then we'll go to drink a good (cup of) chocolate.

Using the Inviting Verb Invitar

When you visit a Spanish-speaking country, you naturally are invited to many parties. And you may want to invite friends to your own parties as well. To do this, you need to be familiar with the verb "to invite," which in Spanish is

invitar *(een-bvee-tahr)*. Good news! **Invitar** is a regular verb of the *-ar* variety, as you can see from the table that follows. The root of this verb is ***invit-*** *(een-bveet-)*.

Conjugation	*Pronunciation*
yo invito	yoh een-<u>bvee</u>-toh
tú invitas	too een-<u>bvee</u>-tahs
él, ella, ello, uno, usted invita	ehl <u>eh</u>-yah <u>eh</u>-yoh <u>oo</u>-noh oos-<u>tehd</u> een-<u>bvee</u>-tah
nosotros invitamos	noh-<u>soh</u>-trohs een-bvee-<u>tah</u>-mohs
vosotros invitáis	bvoh-<u>soh</u>-trohs een-bvee-<u>tahees</u>
ellos, ellas, ustedes invitan	<u>eh</u>-yohs <u>eh</u>-yahs oos-<u>teh</u>-dehs een-<u>bvee</u>-than

Use the following phrases to help you give and receive invitations.

- **Te invito al teatro.** *(teh een-<u>bvee</u>-toh ahl teh-<u>ah</u>-troh)* (I invite you to the theater.)

- **Nos invitan al baile.** *(nohs een-<u>bvee</u>-tahn ahl <u>bvaee</u>-leh)* (We are invited to the dance.)

- **Ellos invitan a todos a la fiesta.** *(<u>eh</u>-yohs een-<u>bvee</u>-tahn ah <u>toh</u>-dohs la fee<u>ehs</u>-tah)* (They invite everybody to the fiesta.)

- **Tenemos que invitarlos a la casa.** *(teh-<u>neh</u>-mohs keh een-bvee-<u>tahr</u>-lohs ah la <u>kah</u>-sah)* (We have to invite them to our place.)

- **Voy a invitarlos al concierto.** *(bvohy ah een-bvee-<u>tahr</u>-lohs ahl kohn-see<u>ehr</u>-toh)* (I'm going to invite them to the concert.)

Notice the use of **al** *(ahl)* (to the) in phrases like **al teatro** and **al baile**. **Teatra** and **baile** are masculine words that would normally take the article **el**. But **A el**, formed when you add the preposition **a** *(ah)* (to) to the mix, sounds unpleasant to the Spanish ear. So Spanish joins the two words into **al**. That sounds much smoother, don't you think?

Talkin' the Talk

Rolando decides to invite his new co-worker Julieta to a party for two of their colleagues.

Rolando: **Te invito a una fiesta.**
   teh een-<u>bvee</u>-toh ah <u>oo</u>-nah fee<u>ehs</u>-tah
   I invite you to a party!

Julieta: **¿Cuándo?**
koo*ahn*-doh
When?

Rolando: **El sábado a las ocho de la noche.**
ehl *sah*-bvah-doh ah lahs *oh*-choh deh lah *noh*-che
Saturday, at 8 p.m. (Literally: Saturday, at eight in the night.)

Julieta: **Sí, puedo ir. ¿A qué viene la fiesta?**
see poo*eh*-doh eer ah keh bvee*eh*-neh lah fee*ehs*-tah
Yes, I can go. Why the party?

Rolando: **Mario y Lucy se van de viaje. Decidimos hacerles una fiesta informal.**
mah-reeoh ee *loo*-see seh bvahn deh bveeah-Heh ee deh-see-*dee*-mohs ah-*sehr*-lehs *oo*-nah fee*ehs*-tah een-fohr-*mahl*
Mario and Lucy are going on a trip. . . and we decided to give them an informal party.

Julieta: **Toda ocasión es buena para bailar. Voy con mucho gusto.**
toh-dah oh-kah-see*ohn* ehs bvoo*eh*-nah *pah*-rah bvahee-*lahr* bvohy kohn *moo*-choh *goos*-toh
Any occasion is good to dance. I'll go gladly.

Julieta wants to know more about the party this Saturday and asks Rolando about it.

Julieta: **¿Dónde va a ser la fiesta?**
dohn-deh bvah ah sehr lah fee*ehs*-tah
Where's the party going to be?

Rolando: **En el Mesón del Angel.**
ehn ehl meh-*sohn* dehl *ahn*-Hehl
At the Angel Meson.

Julieta: **¿Qué clase de bailes habrá?**
keh *klah*-seh deh *bvahee*-lehs ah-*bvrah*
What kind of dances will they have?

Rolando: **Habrá salsa, cumbia, un poco de todo. ¡Vamos hasta el reventón!**
ah-*bvrah* *sahl*-sah *koom*-bveeah oon *poh*-koh deh *toh*-doh *bvah*-mohs *ahs*-tah ehl reh-bvehn-*tohn*
They'll have salsa, cumbia, a bit of everything. It's going to be a riot! (Literally: We'll go until the blast!)

Speaking in idioms

In Spanish the word for "idiom" is **modismo** *(moh-dees-moh)*. An *idiom* is a phrase that cannot be translated literally. That is to say, translating it word-by-word doesn't give you the meaning it holds. So, when you translate idioms, you have to give an equivalent phrase. **¿A qué viene?** *(ah keh bveeeh-neh),* which literally translates as "what does it come for?," means

"what for," "why so," "what's the occasion," or simply "why," when it's used in relation to a thing or an event.

When used with a pronoun or a person, **¿A qué viene?** has the same meaning as its English translation: "What does he/she come for?"

Using the Dancing Verb: Bailar

Bailar *(bvahee-lahr)* (to dance) is a regularly beautiful verb, great to swing along to. The root of this verb is **bail-** *(bvahee-)* The conjugation of **bailar** in the present tense follows:

Conjugation	*Pronunciation*
yo bailo	yoh bvahee-loh
tú bailas	too bvahee-lahs
él, ella, ello, uno, usted baila	ehl eh-yah eh-yoh oo-noh oos-tehd bvahee-lah
nosotros bailamos	noh-soh-trohs bvahee-lah-mohs
vosotros bailáis	bvoh-soh-trohs bvahee-lahees
ellos, ellas, ustedes bailan	eh-yohs eh-yahs oos-teh-dehs bvahee-lahn

These phrases can help you when you want to dance:

- **La salsa es un baile nuevo.** *(lah sahl-sah ehs oon bvahee-leh nooeh-bvoh)* (The salsa is a new dance.)

- **La invito a bailar.** *(lah een-bvee-toh ah bvahee-lahr)* (I invite you [formal, female] to dance.)

- **Bailamos toda la noche.** *(bvahee-lah-mohs toh-dah lah noh-cheh)* (We danced all night.)

- **Bailan muy bien.** *(bvahee-lahn mooy bveeehn)* (They dance very well.)

- **Bailó hasta la mañana.** *(bvahee-loh ahs-tah lah mah-nyah-nah)* (He/she danced until morning.)

Words to Know

la cumbia	ah koom-bveea)	an African-American rhythm
el gusto	ehl goos-toh	the pleasure (Literally: the taste)
el mesón	ehl meh-sohn	old-style bar and restaurant
la ocasión	lah oh-kah-seeohn	the occasion
el reventón	ehl reh-bvehn-tohn	the riotous, noisy party
la salsa	lah sahl-sah	an African-Cuban dance and music rhythm (Literally: the sauce)
el viaje	ehl bveeah-Heh	the trip

Having a Good Time at Shows and Events

The types of events and shows available in Spanish-speaking America vary depending on where they happen. In villages or small towns, the events generally are related to celebrations of important dates, both private and public. Occasionally a traveling show or circus may pass through a town. Larger cities offer movies, theaters, opera, concerts, literary presentations and readings, and exhibition openings. Some neighborhoods have celebrations like the kind you see in the smaller towns.

Following are some phrases that can help when you're asked or you're asking to attend an event:

- **Voy a buscarte a las ocho.** *(bvohy a bvoos-kahr-teh ah lahs oh-choh)* (I'll pick you up at eight [Literally: I'll go search you at eight])

- **¡Qué pena, hoy no puedo!** *(keh peh-nah, ohy noh pooeh-doh)* (What a pity, today I can't!)

Talkin' the Talk

María José is trying to get tickets to see Julio Iglesias. He's been her favorite singer for many years:

María José: **Dos boletos para la matiné, por favor.**
                  dohs bvoh-leh-tohs pah-rah lah mah-tee-neh pohr fah-bvohr
                  Two tickets for the early show, please.

Booth attendant: **Los boletos para la matiné están agotados.**
                  lohs bvoh-leh-tohs pah-rah lah mah-tee-neh ehs-tahn ah-goh-tah-dohs
                  The tickets for the early show are sold out.

María José: **Dos boletos para la noche, entonces.**
                  dohs bvoh-leh-tohs pah-rah lah noh-cheh ehn-tohn sehs.
                  Two tickets for the night, then.

Talkin' the Talk

Imagine yourself in town with Catalina and Silverio just when a circus is playing:

Catalina: **¡Me dijeron que el circo es muy divertido!**
            meh dee-Heh-rohn keh ehl seer-koh ehs mooy dee-bvehr-tee-doh
            They tell me the circus is really fun!

Silverio: **¡Algo completamente nuevo!**
            ahl-goh kohm-pleh-tah-mehn-teh nooeh-bvoh
            Something completely new!

Catalina: **¿Qué tiene de nuevo?**
            keh teeeh-neh deh nooeh-bvoh
            What's new about it?

Silverio: **Es un circo con pura gente, no hay animales.**
            ehs oon seer-koh kohn poo-rah Hehn-teh noh ahy ah-nee-mah-lehs
            It's a circus with just people, no animals.

Catalina:	**¿Qué trae de especial?** *keh <u>trah</u>-eh deh ehs-peh-see<u>ahl</u>* What special things does it bring?
Silverio:	**Trae los mejores magos y payasos.** *<u>trah</u>-eh lohs meh-<u>Hoh</u>-rehs <u>mah</u>-gohs ee pah-<u>yah</u>-sohs* It brings the best magicians and clowns.
Catalina:	**¿Qué hacen los payasos?** *keh <u>ah</u>-sehn lohs pah-<u>yah</u>-sohs* What do the clowns do?
Silverio:	**Se especializan en bromas sobre políticos.** *seh ehs-peh-seeah-<u>lee</u>-sahn ehn <u>broh</u>-mahs <u>soh</u>-bvreh poh-<u>lee</u>-tee-kohs* They specialize in making fun of politicians.
Catalina:	**¿Y hay acróbatas?** *ee ahy ah-<u>kroh</u>-bvah-tahs* And are there acrobats?
Silverio:	**¡Unos campeones! ¡Vamos!** *<u>oo</u>-nohs kahm-peh-<u>oh</u>-nehs <u>bvah</u>-mohs* Real champions! Let's go!

Words to Know

agotados	ah-goh-<u>tah</u>-dohs	sold out (Literally: exhausted)
la broma	lah <u>broh</u>-mah	the joke
el campeón	ehl kahm-peh-<u>ohn</u>	the champion
divertido	dee-bvehr-<u>tee</u>-doh	amusing; funny
la gente	lah <u>Hehn</u>-teh	the people
la matiné	lah mah-tee-<u>neh</u>	the early show
pura	<u>poo</u>-rah	pure

At the cinema

Movies on television are fine, but they're even better in a well-equipped theater.

Latin America has produced rich and varied films. Unfortunately, too few make it into the theaters in the United States and Canada. A rare exception is **Como agua para chocolate** *(Like Water for Chocolate),* a Mexican film that had some success in the United States, and you do occasionally see films with some Latin connection, like *The House of the Spirits,* a movie based on Chilean author Isabelle Allende's book of the same name.

Several movies from Spain made it into U. S. and Canadian markets, especially those from the Spanish director Pedro Almodóvar, who won best director honors at the Cannes film festival in 1999.

Talkin' the Talk

Cristina is a new girl in town and Nemesio wants to spend some time with her and make a good impression. A movie buff, Nemesio has an idea:

Nemesio: **Si quieres, vamos al cine.**
see kee<u>eh</u>-rehs <u>bvah</u>-mohs ahl <u>see</u>-neh
If you want, we can go to the movies.

Cristina: **¿Hay muchos cines en esta ciudad?**
ahy <u>moo</u>-chohs <u>see</u>-nehs ehn <u>ehs</u>-tah seeoo-<u>dahd</u>
Are there many cinemas in this city?

Nemesio: **Sí, hay muchos cines.**
see ahy <u>moo</u>-chohs <u>see</u>-nehs
Yes, there are many cinemas.

Cristina: **¿Qué dan hoy?**
keh dahn ohy
What's playing today?

Nemesio: **Veamos la cartelera ¡Ah, mira, la version original de "Nosferatu"!**
bveh-<u>ah</u>-mohs lah kahr-teh-<u>leh</u>-rah ah mee-rah lah vehr-see<u>ohn</u> oh-ree-Hee-<u>nahl</u> deh nohs-feh-<u>rah</u>-too
Let's see the listings. Look! The original version of *Nosferatu!*

Cristina: **Esta película me gusta.**
ehs-*tah* peh-*lee*-koo-lah meh *goos*-tah
I like this film.

At the theater

Researchers have found that people learn more easily when new information is associated with emotions. And, because an opportunity to explore feelings is what lures people to the movies and the theater, they are perfect places to absorb a new language.

Talkin' the Talk

Going to the theater may involve a conversation similar to this one:

Diego: **¿Te gusta ir al teatro?**
the *goos*-tah eer ahl teh-*ah*-troh
Do you like going to the theater?

Gabriela: **Sí, ¡dan la obra de un dramaturgo de Chile!**
see dahn lah *oh*-bvrah deh oon drah-mah-*toor*-goh deh *chee*-leh
Yes, they're doing a piece by a Chilean playwright.

Diego: **Tuvo muy buena crítica.**
too-bvoh mooy bvoo*eh*-nah *kree*-tee-kah
It got very good reviews.

Gabriela: **Los actores son excelentes.**
lohs ahk-*toh*-rehs sohn eh-kseh-*lehn*-tehs
The actors are excellent.

Diego: **El teatro es bastante chico.**
ehl teh-*ah*-troh ehs bvahs-*tahn*-teh *chee*-koh
The theater is quite small.

Gabriela: **Tenemos que comprar los boletos pronto.**
teh-*neh*-mohs keh kohm-*prahr* lohs bvoh-*leh*-tohs *prohn*-toh
We have to buy the tickets soon.

Diego: **¿En qué fila te gusta ir?**
ehn keh *fee*-lah teh *goos*-tah
What row do you like to sit in?

Gabriela: **Para teatro prefiero estar bien adelante.**
pah-rah teh-ah-troh preh-feeeh-roh ehs-tahr bveeehn ah-deh-lahn-teh
For theater I prefer to be up front.

Diego: **Intentaré encontrar buenas butacas.**
een-tehn-tah-reh ehn-kohn-trahr bvooeh-nahs bvoo-tah-kahs
I'll try to find good seats.

Words to Know

el actor/la actriz	ehl ahk-tohr/lah ahk-trees	the actor/the actress
adelante	ah-deh-lahn-teh	in front; ahead
bastante	bvahs-tahn-teh	enough; quite
las butacas	lahs bvoo-tah-kahs	the seats
la fila	lah fee-lah	the row; the line; the line-up
la obra	lah oh-bvrah	the play (Literally: the work)
pronto	prohn-toh	soon

At art galleries and museums

Numerous exhibitions of works by Latin-American artists appear all the time, throughout the continent. Some exhibits take place in museums and public art galleries, others in private ones. Among the artists exhibited are some great names, people whose works sell for enormous amounts at art auctions. One such artist is Oswaldo Guayasamín, who created etchings. He was born in Ecuador in 1919 and died in 1999.

At the opera

The Italians came up with it, but opera is now enjoyed in every country. Going to the opera is always a special occasion. Most Spanish-American cities have important opera houses, witnessing to the strong interest city dwellers have for this musical spectacle, and have had for quite a long time.

Talkin' the Talk

In the following conversation, Reinaldo and Hortensia set a date to see an opera.

Reinaldo:	**Te invito a una ópera bufa.**
	teh een-bvee-toh ah oo-nah oh-peh-rah bvoo-fah
	I invite you to a comic opera.
Hortensia:	**¿Cuándo?**
	kooahn-doh
	When?
Reinaldo:	**Hoy. En el Teatro Esfinge. Tengo dos boletos.**
	ohy ehn ehl teh-ah-troh ehs-feen-Heh tehn-goh dohs bvoh-leh-tohs
	Today. At the Sphinx Theater. I have two tickets.
Hortensia:	**Me gusta la idea.**
	meh goos-tah lah ee-deh-ah
	I like the idea.
Reinaldo:	**Dicen que es un bello teatro.**
	dee-sehn keh ehs oon bveh-yoh teh-ah-troh
	They say it's a beautiful theater.
Hortensia:	**Sí, y tiene muy buena acústica.**
	see ee teeeh-neh mooy bvooeh-nah ah-koos-tee-kah
	Yes, and it has very good acoustics.
Reinaldo:	**Viene a cantar un tenor español.**
	bveeeh-neh a kahn-tahr oon teh-nohr ehs-pah-nyohl
	A Spanish tenor is coming to sing.

Words to Know

la acústica	lah ah-koos-tee-kah	the acoustics
bello	bveh-yoh	beautiful
bufa	bvoo-fah	comedy; mockery
el descubrimiento	ehl dehs-koo-bvree-meeehn-toh	the discovery
hoy	ohy	today

Using the Singing Verb: Cantar

Cantar *(kahn-tahr)* (to sing) is a regular verb, praise be, and its root is *cant-*
(kahnt). Its conjugation in the present tense follows:

Conjugation	*Pronunciation*
yo canto	yoh <u>kahn</u>-toh
tú cantas	too <u>kahn</u>-tahs
él, ella, ello, uno, usted canta	ehl <u>eh</u>-yah <u>eh</u>-yoh <u>oo</u>-noh oos-<u>tehd</u> <u>kahn</u>-tah
nosotros cantamos	noh-<u>soh</u>-trohs kahn-<u>tah</u>-mohs
vosotros cantáis	bvoh-<u>soh</u>-trohs kahn-<u>tah</u>ees
ellos, ellas, ustedes cantan	<u>eh</u>-yohs <u>eh</u>-yahs oos-<u>teh</u>-dehs <u>kahn</u>-than

Talkin' the Talk

What a great occasion! Your favorite singer comes to sing live and
in person.

Claudia: **¿Sabes si viene a cantar Julio Iglesias?**
*<u>sah</u>-bvehs see bvee<u>eh</u>-neh ah kahn-<u>tahr</u> <u>Hoo</u>-leeoh
ee-<u>gleh</u>-seeahs*
Do you know if Julio Iglesias is coming to sing?

Pedro: **Quizás. Lo anunciaron.**
kee-sahs loh ah-noon-seeah-rohn
Maybe. They advertised him.

Claudia: **Sí, pero espero que no va a cancelar.**
*see peh-roh ehs-peh-roh keh noh bvah ah
kahn-seh-lahr*
Yes, but I hope he's not going to cancel.

Talkin' the Talk

Sometimes you're lucky enough to know the people playing your
favorite music. In this case, Héctor and Eduardo are familiar with
the musicians giving the concert.

Héctor: **Sabes, mañana dan un concierto de violín con piano.**
*sah-bvehs mah-nyah-nah dahn oon kohn-seeehr-toh
de bvee-oh-leen kohn peeah-noh*
You know, tomorrow there's going to be a violin and
piano concert.

Eduardo: **¿Quiénes tocan?**
keeeh-nehs toh-kahn
Who's playing?

Héctor: **Nuestros amigos Luisa y Fernando.**
*nooehs-trohs ah-mee-gohs looee-sah ee
fehr-nahn-doh*
Our friends Luisa and Fernando.

Eduardo: **¿Cuál es el programa?**
kooahl ehs ehl proh-grah-mah
What's the program?

Héctor: **Un concierto de Alberto Ginastera y otro de Paul
Hindemith.**
*oon kohn-seeehr-toh de ahl-bvehr-toh
Hee-nahs-teh-rah ee oh-troh deh pahool
Heen-deh-meet*
A concert by Alberto Ginastera and another by Paul
Hindemith.

Eduardo: **¿Invitamos a María?**
een-bvee-tah-mohs ah mah-reeah
Shall we invite Maria?

Héctor:	**Claro, ella también toca el piano.**
	klah-roh eh-yah tahm-bveeehn toh-kah ehl
	peeah-noh
	Sure, she plays the piano, too.

Words to Know

anunciar	ah-noon-seeahr	to advertise; to announce
cancelar	kahn-seh-lahr	to cancel
juntas	Hoon-tahs	together (female)
libre	lee-bvreh	free of charge
la pena	(lah peh-nah)	sadness; in some countries, shame
el programa	ehl proh-grah-mah	the program
repetir	reh-peh-teer	to repeat

Talkin' the Talk

Book launchings call the public's attention to a new book. The book mentioned in this discussion is an art book by an author who is best known for his novels.

Leticia:	**En la biblioteca van a lanzar un libro.**
	ehn lah bveebv-leeoh-teh-kah bvahn ah lahn-sahr
	oon lee-bvroh
	The library is going to have a book launching.

Martín:	**¿Qué libro es?**
	keh lee-bvroh ehs
	What book is it?

Leticia:	**Es un libro de fotos de Juan Rulfo.**
	ehs oon lee-bvroh deh foh-tohs deh Hooahn rool-foh
	It's a book of photos by Juan Rulfo.

Martín:	**¿Cómo sabes?**
	koh-moh sah-bvehs
	How do you know?

Leticia:	**Lo ví en un cartel ayer.**
	loh bvee ehn oon kahr-tehl ah-yehr
	I saw it in a poster yesterday.

Martín:	**¿De quién son las fotos?**
	deh keeehn sohn lahs foh-tohs
	Who took the photos?

Leticia:	**Del mismo Rulfo.**
	dehl mees-moh rool-foh
	Rulfo himself.

Words to Know

la biblioteca	lah bvee-bvleeoh oh-teh-kah	the library
la cantante	lah kahn-tahn-teh	the singer (female)
el libro	ehl lee-bvroh	the book
maravilloso	mah-rah-bvee-yoh-soh	wonderful
la muestra	lah mooehs-trah	the show; the sampling
las piezas	lahs peeeh-sahs	the pieces (musical)
la vida	lah bvee-dah	the life

Fun & Games

• •

We have some good news and some bad news for you. The good news is that you and several of your friends are leaving next week for a whirlwind vacation. The bad news is that you have to plan fun, group activities — in Spanish — for the entire week. Use the chart below to help you plan your itinerary. For each day of the week, fill in what you'll do there and someone you might expect to meet. To keep your friends from complaining, try not to plan the same activity twice.

Day	What You'll Do There	Who You'll See
lunes	_____	_____
martes	_____	_____
miércoles	_____	_____
jueves	_____	_____
viernes	_____	_____
sábado	_____	_____
domingo	_____	_____

• •

Chapter 8

Enjoying Yourself: Recreation

. . . .

In This Chapter

▶ Walking around in the great outdoors

▶ Looking at what's out there: Animal and plant vocabulary

▶ Moving about: Sports and other interests

▶ Doing what you like to do

. . . .

*O*utdoor recreation is a big part of the Latin American lifestyle. You probably know many Spanish-speaking sports figures like Colombian Juan Montoya — number one on the CART auto-racing circuit in 1999 — and/or any of a number of baseball players, including the great Sammy Sosa.

Being outdoors can promote a quiet, contemplative feeling as you appreciate the beauty of nature, or it can energize you, inspiring you to action. This chapter deals with both the sporty and contemplative aspects of being outdoors.

The Good and the Bad of Going Outdoors

Spanish has two ways to express the idea of going outdoors:

✔ **al aire libre** *(ahl ahee-reh lee-bvreh)* (in the open air). You use this phrase when you're talking about going out to the street, garden, or taking a walk. It implies a feeling of openness and liberty.

✔ **a la intemperie** *(ah lah een-tehm-peh-reeeh)* (out of doors, exposed to the elements [Literally: in the unheated space]). This phrase implies that you are going to be without a roof nearby and therefore will be suffering or enjoying whatever weather you may find. It gives a feeling of exposure and less safety.

The following examples can help you determine which phrase to use:

- **Voy a nadar en una piscina al aire libre.** *(bvohy ah nah-dahr ehn oo-nah pee-see-nah ahl ahee-reh lee-bvreh)* (I'm going to swim in an outdoor pool.)
- **No dejes las plantas a la intemperie.** *(noh deh-Hehs lahs plahn-tahs ah lah een-tehm-peh-reeeh)* (Don't leave the plants out in the open.)

Typical Walking Phrases

In some places, **pasear** *(pah-seh-ahr)*, (to walk; to stroll) is a national sport. Here are some typical Spanish phrases about walking both far and near:

- **Salimos a dar un paseo.** *(sah-lee-mohs ah dahr oon pah-seh-oh)* (We go for a walk.)
- **Vivo en Los Angeles, aquí estoy de visita.** *(bvee-bvoh ehn lohs ahn-Heh-lehs ah-kee ehs-tohy deh vee-see-tah)* (I live in Los Angeles, I'm just visiting here.)

Talkin' the Talk

During a walk, Manuel and Jimena talk about what they like to do

Manuel:	**De todos los paseos me gusta más el de montaña.** *deh toh-dohs lohs pah-seh-ohs meh goos-tah mahs ehl deh mohn-tah-nyah* Of all kinds of walks, I prefer mountain ones.
Jimena:	**¿Eres alpinista?** *eh-rehs ahl-pee-nees-tah* Are you a climber?
Manuel:	**No, alpinista no, pero trepar me gusta.** *noh ahl-pee-nees-tah noh peh-roh treh-pahr meh goos-tah* No, not a climber, but I love to hike.

Trees and Plants

Walking about and enjoying the trees and plants go hand-in-hand. Following are some phrases you may use to describe such experiences:

✔ **Ayer paseamos en la Alameda.** *(ah-yehr pah-seh-ah-mohs ehn lah ah-lah-meh-dah)* (Yesterday we walked along the Poplar Grove.)

✔ **Hay robles y cipreses.** *(ahy roh-bvlehs ee see-preh-sehs)* (There are oaks and cypresses.)

✔ **Esa palmera da dátiles.** *(eh-sah pahl-meh-rah dah dah-tee-lehs)* (That palm [tree] yields dates.)

✔ **En Chile crecen muchos eucaliptus.** *(ehn chee-leh kreh-sehn moo-chohs ehoo-kah-leep-toos)* (Many eucaluptus [trees] grow in Chile.)

Checking Out the Animals

You're probably familiar with many of the animals common to both North and South America; in this section, we talk about animals more common to Mexico and South and Central America. The first breed that comes to mind is the **llama** *(yah-mah)*, and its cousins the **huanaco** *(ooah-nah-ko)* and **alpaca** *(ahl-pah-ka)*. You find these gentle creatures, from the same family as camels, mostly in the region around the Andes — from Colombia to Chile. **Llamas** and **alpacas** are highly domesticated, but **huanacos** are more likely to run around in the wild.

Pumas *(poo-mahs)* are South American mountain lions. They are very serious-minded, meat-eating predators. They are beautiful to behold in the zoo, but keep out of their way in the mountains. And you can find snakes — poisonous and otherwise — monkeys, insects, and birds of all kinds in the rain forests of Bolivia, Argentina, Paraguay, Ecuador, and Mexico. The Galapagos Islands of Ecuador are famous for their very unique fauna, first described by Charles Darwin, who actually conceived his theory of evolution while observing the turtles and birds that live there. Iguanas walk around freely in the south of Mexico — until someone puts them in the soup pot — and squirrels are everywhere.

These phrases get you started talking about animals while you observe them:

✔ **En el paseo ví muchas ardillas.** *(ehn ehl pah-seh-oh bvee moo-chahs ahr-dee-yahs)* (During the walk I saw many squirrels.)

✔ **Los tucanes están en la selva.** *(lohs too-kah-nehs ehs-tahn ehn lah sehl-bvah)* (The toucans are in the jungle.)

✔ **En la playa vemos gaviotas.** *(ehn lah plah-yah bveh-mohs gah-bveeoh-tahs)* (On the beach, we see seagulls.)

✔ **En el centro hay muchas palomas.** *(ehn ehl sehn-troh ahy moo-chahs pah-loh-mahs)* (Downtown has many pigeons.)

✔ **Los gorriones se ven en las ciudades.** *(lohs goh-rreeoh-nehs seh bvehn ehn lash seeoo-dah-dehs)* (The sparrows are seen in the cities.)

- ✔ **Voy a pasear los perros.** *(bvohy ah pah-seh-ahr lohs peh-rrohs)*
  (I'm going to walk the dogs.)

- ✔ **Van a una carrera de caballos.** *(bvahn ah oo-nah kah-rreh-rah deh kah-bvah-yohs)* (They're going to a horse race.)

- ✔ **La burra de mi vecino tuvo un burrito.** *(lah bvoo-rrah deh mee bveh-see-noh too-bvoh oon bvoo-rree-toh)*
  (My neighbor's jenny [female donkey] had a little donkey.)

- ✔ **Hay mapaches en casi todo el continente americano.**
  (ahy mah-pah-chehs ehn kah-see toh-doh ehl kohn-tee-nehn-teh ah-meh-ree-kah-noh) (Almost all of the American continents have raccoons.)

It would take whole books to talk about animals, but here are a few more examples:

- ✔ **El cerro estaba cubierto de mariposas.** *(ehl seh-rroh ehs-tah-bvah koo-bveeehr-toh deh mah-ree-poh-sahs)* (The hill was covered with butterflies.)

- ✔ **De paseo ví una manada de vacas.** *(deh pah-seh-oh bvee oo-nah mah-nah-dah deh bvah-kahs)* (While walking, I saw a herd of cows.)

- ✔ **Andamos con unas cabras.** *(ahn-dah-mohs kohn oo-nahs kah-bvrahs)* (We walk with some goats.)

- ✔ **Cuando pasé me perseguían unos gansos.** *(kooahn-doh pah-seh meh pehr-seh-gheeahn oo-nohs gahn-sohs)* (As I went by, the geese chased me.)

- ✔ **En el lago vimos patos silvestres.** *(ehn ehl lah-goh bvee-mohs pah-tohs seel-bvehs-trehs)* (We saw wild ducks in the lake.)

- ✔ **Una señora ¡paseaba un gato!** *(oo-nah seh-nyoh-rah pah-seh-ah-bvah oon gah-toh)* (A lady was walking a cat!)

- ✔ **La niña llevaba una iguana.** *(lah nee-nyah yeh-bvah-bvah oo-nah ee-gooah-nah)* (The girl was carrying an iguana.)

Words to Know

la burra	lah bvoo-rrah	the jenny; female burro
la iguana	lah ee-gooah-nah	large lizard, green, with yellow spots, native of Central and South America
el mapache	ehl mah-pah-cheh	the raccoon
el puma	ehl poo-mah	mountain lion
el tucán	ehl too-kahn	the toucan, a large, many colored, large-billed bird

Talkin' the Talk

The wonderful sport of horseback riding calls for some harmony between horse and rider and allows the rider to enjoy the landscape, as Mariana explains to Dora Luz.

Mariana: **Me encanta andar a caballo.**
meh ehn-kahn-tah ahn-dahr ah kah-bvah-yoh
I love riding a horse. [Literally: Riding a horse enchants (or delights) me.]

Dora Luz: **¿Te preparas para algún torneo?**
teh preh-pah-rahs pah-rah ahl-goon tohr-neh-oh
Are you preparing for a competition?

Mariana: **No, simplemente gozo el hecho de montar.**
noh seem-pleh-mehn-teh goh-soh ehl eh-choh deh mohn-tahr
No, I simply enjoy riding.

Dora Luz: **¿Tienes tu propio caballo?**
teeeh-nehs too proh-pee-oh kah-bvah-yoh
Do you have your own horse?

Mariana: **Sí, tengo una yegua. Se llama Lirio.**
see tehn-goh oo-nah yeh-gooah seh yah-mah lee-reeoh
Yes, I have a mare. Her name is Lirio [Lilly].

Dora Luz:	**Debe ser blanca.** *deh-bveh sehr <u>blahn</u>-kah* She must be white.
Mariana:	**Es blanca y tiene una mancha café en la frente.** *ehs <u>blahn</u>-kah ee tee<u>eh</u>-neh <u>oo</u>-nah <u>mahn</u>-chah kah-feh ehn lah <u>frehn</u>-teh* She's white and has a brown spot on her forehead.

Saying What You Like: The Verb Gustar

When you talk about liking something in Spanish, you use the reflexive verb form (see Chapter 16 for more information). The action, in this case, is **gustar** (*goos-<u>tahr</u>*) (to like; to enjoy).

Conjugation	Pronunciation
me gusta	meh <u>goos</u>-tah
te gusta	teh <u>goos</u>-tah
le gusta	leh <u>goos</u>-tah
nos gusta	nohs <u>goos</u>-tah
os gusta	ohs <u>goos</u>-tah
les gusta	lehs <u>goos</u>-tah

The following expressions can help you express what you like:

- **Me gusta pasear.** *(meh <u>goos</u>-tah pah-seh-<u>ahr</u>)* (I love to walk.)

- **Venga cuando guste.** *(<u>bvehn</u>-gah koo<u>ahn</u>-doh <u>goos</u>-teh)* (Come when you like.)

- **Le gusta jugar con el gato.** *(leh <u>goos</u>-tah Hoo-<u>gahr</u> kohn ehl <u>gah</u>-toh)* (She likes to play with the cat.)

- **¿Gustan comer algo?** *(<u>goos</u>-tahn koh-<u>mehr</u> <u>ahl</u>-goh)* (Would you like something to eat?)

Strolling Along: The Walking Verb, Pasear

The verb **pasear** *(pa-seh-<u>ahr</u>)*(to walk; to stroll) has many applications, and it's a regular verb. The root of this verb is **pase-** *(<u>pah</u>-seh)*. Here's how you conjugate its present tense:

Conjugation	*Pronunciation*
yo paseo	yoh pah-<u>seh</u>-oh
tú paseas	too pah-<u>seh</u>-ahs
él, ella, ello, uno, usted pasea	ehl, <u>eh</u>-yah, <u>eh</u>-yoh, <u>oo</u>-noh, oos-<u>tehd</u> pah-<u>seh</u>-ah
nosotros paseamos	noh-<u>soh</u>-trohs pah-seh-<u>ah</u>-mohs
vosotros paseáis	bvoh-<u>soh</u>-trohs pah-seh-<u>ah</u>ees
ellos ellas, ustedes pasean	<u>eh</u>-yohs, <u>eh</u>-yahs, oos-<u>teh</u>-dehs pah-<u>seh</u>-ahn

Take these phrases for a stroll:

- ✔ **La abuela pasea todas las tardes.** *(lah ah-bvoo<u>eh</u>-lah pah-<u>seh</u>-ah <u>toh</u>-dahs lahs <u>tahr</u>-dehs)* (Grandmother goes for walks every afternoon.)

- ✔ **¿Quieres pasear conmigo?** *(kee<u>eh</u>-rehs pah-seh-<u>ahr</u> kohn-<u>mee</u>-goh)* (Would you go on a walk with me?)

Words to Know

el caballo	ehl kah-<u>bvah</u>-yoh	the horse
encantar	ehn-kahn-<u>tahr</u>	to enchant; to delight
gozar	goh-<u>sahr</u>	to enjoy
la mancha	lah <u>mahn</u>-chah	the stain; the spot
preparar	preh-pah-<u>rahr</u>	to prepare
propio	<u>proh</u>-peeoh	[one's] own
torneo	tohr-<u>neh</u>-oh	competition; tournament
la yegua	lah <u>yeh</u>-gooah	the mare

Playing Ball Games

Team-sport activities often start with a ball, so when talking about ball games, you have to mention rubber.

The rubber tree is an American plant. (So is the tree we get chewing gum from!) You've heard about bubble gum and gumshoes (detectives with rubber-soled shoes). The word for all of these comes from **goma** *(goh-mah)*, which means "rubber." Other words for rubber are **caucho** *(kahoo-choh),* and, in Mexico, **hule** *(oo-leh).*

Why should you care about rubber? Because balls are made from it, and those balls bounce. From these bouncy balls, all ball games were created — some of which were played in America before America got its name. (Can you imagine tennis without a bouncing ball?)

Pre-Columbian games

Ball games were so important in pre-Columbian cultures that people built special playing courts. You can see these ball fields at many archeological sites in Mexico and Central America.

One such place is **Monte Albán** *(mohn-teh ahl-bvahn),* a city built on top of a mountain above present-day **Oaxaca** *(oh-ah-Hah-kah),* the capital of the state of the same name, in the south of Mexico. Seeing this ball court — and there are many others — you no longer wonder why basketball is such a popular sport in Mexico. Even the smallest village, in the most difficult terrain, has a basketball court, more often than not in front of the municipal building.

Also, a ball game called **chueca** *(chooeh-kah)* existed in Chile before the arrival of Caucasians. And **chueca** looked like field hockey. The **araucanos** *(ah-rahoo-kah-nohs),* members of an Indian nation in the south of Chile, hit the ball with a crooked stick. So the word for "crooked," in places like Chile and Mexico, is **chueco** *(chooeh-koh).*

The most popular ball game: Fútbol

Yes, **fútbol** *(foot-bvohl),* called "soccer" in North American English and *football* elsewhere, is the most popular game in Latin America. This game is the talk of taverns, bars, and living rooms, and its stars are national heroes. We dare say there is more talk about **fútbol** in Latin America than about anything else.

Talkin' the Talk

 Carla and Pedro talk shop about their favorite sport, soccer.

Pedro: **Me divierte ver jugar fútbol.**
meh dee-bvee<u>ehr</u>-teh bveh Hoo-<u>gahr</u> foot-<u>bvohl</u>
I enjoy watching soccer. [Literally: It amuses me to see soccer.]

Carla: **¿Adónde vas a verlo?**
ah-<u>dohn</u>-deh bvahs a <u>bvehr</u>-loh
Where do you go to watch it?

Pedro: **Voy al estadio de Boca Juniors.**
bvohy ahl ehs-<u>tah</u>-deeoh deh <u>bvoh</u>-kah <u>dyoo</u>-neeohrs
I go to the Boca Juniors stadium.

Carla: **¿Eres hincha del Boca?**
<u>eh</u>-rehs <u>een</u>-chah dehl <u>bvoh</u>-kah
Are you a Boca fan?

Pedro: **Sí, hace muchos años.**
see <u>ah</u>-seh <u>moo</u>-chohs <u>ah</u>-nyohs
Yes, for many years.

Carla: **¿Qué jugadores te gustan?**
keh Hoo-gah-<u>doh</u>-rehs teh <u>goos</u>-tahn
Which players do you like?

Pedro: **Siempre he preferido a los de la defensa.**
see<u>ehm</u>-preh eh preh-feh-<u>ree</u>-doh ah lohs deh lah deh-<u>fehn</u>-sah
I've always preferred those who play defense.

Carla: **¿Y no te gustan los centro delanteros?**
ee noh teh <u>goos</u>-tahn lohs <u>sehn</u>-troh deh-lahn-<u>teh</u>-rohs
You don't like the center forwards?

Pedro: **Sí, pero creo que la defensa tiene un rol muy especial.**
see <u>peh</u>-roh <u>kreh</u>-oh keh lah deh-<u>fehn</u>-sah tee<u>eh</u>-neh oon rohl mooy ehs-peh-see<u>ahl</u>
Yes, but I feel the defense has a very special role.

Words to Know

el arquero	ehl ahr-keh-roh	the goalkeeper [arco (ahr-koh) means "arch"]
la cancha	lah kahn-chah	the playing field
el defensa	ehl deh-fehn-sah	the defense
los delanteros	lohs deh-lahn-teh-rohs	the forwards
divertir	dee-bvehr-teer	to amuse
el equipo	ehl eh-kee-poh	the team
el estadio	ehl ehs-tah-deeoh)	the stadium
ganar	gah-nahr	to win
el gol	ehl gohl	the hit, goal
el hincha	ehl een-chah	the fan [hincha (een-chahr) means to inflate, to bloat]
el jugador	ehl Hoo-gah-dohr	the player
el rol	ehl rohl	the role
el sobrino	ehl soh-bree-noh	the nephew

Baseball's #2

El béisbol *(ehl bvehees-bvohl)* (baseball) is definitely the second most important ball game (after *fútbol*) in Mexico, Central America, and the Caribbean.

Talkin' the Talk

In the following conversation, Ernesto and Arnulfo, two avid fans, discuss a recent baseball game.

Ernesto:	**Ese tipo batea de maravilla.**	
	eh-seh tee-poh bvah-teh-ah deh mah-rah-bvee-yah	
	That guy's a wonder at bat.	

Arnulfo:	**E hizo una carrera estupenda.**
	eh ee-soh oo-nah kah-rreh-rah ehs-too-pehn-dah
	And he did a stupendous run.

Ernesto:	**No podía creer cuando llegó a la goma. . .**
	noh poh-deeah kreh-ehr kooahn-doh yeh-goh ah lah goh-mah
	I couldn't believe it when he made it to home plate. . .
	y eso que antes era un juego con once hits.
	ee eh-soh keh ahn-tehs eh-rah oon Hooeh-goh kohn ohn-seh Heets
	. . .and before that it was a game with 11 hits.

Arnulfo:	**El bateador merece un aplauso.**
	ehl bah-teh-ah-dohr meh-reh-seh oon ah-plahoo-soh
	The batter deserves applause.

Words to Know

batear	bvah-teh-ahr	to bat
la carrera	lah kah-rreh-rah	the run, the race
la goma	lah goh-mah	the home base [Literally: the rubber]

Tennis players star

Many Latin Americans are in the top ranks of professional tennis stars. For example, Marcelo Rios took the number one men's spot from Pete Sampras in 1998 (for a while, anyway).

Talkin' the Talk

In this conversation, Liliana and Enrique arrange to play a game of tennis.

Liliana:	**Mañana voy a jugar tenis.** *mah-nyah-nah bvohy a Hoo-gahr teh-nees* Tomorrow I'm going to play tennis.
Enrique:	**¿Juegas a menudo?** *Hooeh-gahs ah meh-noo-doh* Do you play often?
Liliana:	**Sí, practico todos los días.** *see prahk-tee-koh toh-dohs lohs deeahs* Yes, I practice every day.
Enrique:	**Yo me compré una raqueta especial.** *yoh meh kohm-preh oo-nah rah-keh-tah ehs-peh-seeahl* I bought a special racket.
Liliana:	**¡Hacemos un juego de dobles mixto!** *ah-seh-mohs oon Hooeh-goh deh doh-bvlehs meeks-tohs* We can play a game of mixed doubles!

Words to Know

juego	Hoo-eh-goh	the set
la pista	lah pees-tah	the court
la raqueta	lah rah-keh-tah	the racket

The Playing Verb: Jugar

GRAMMATICALLY SPEAKING

Jugar *(Hoo-gahr)* (to play) is a slightly irregular verb, but it's a very playful and useful one — definitely worth the effort.

Conjugation	Pronunciation
yo juego	yoh Hoo<u>eh</u>-goh
tú juegas	too Hoo<u>eh</u>-gahs
él, ella, ello, uno, usted juega	ehl, <u>eh</u>-yah, <u>eh</u>-yoh, <u>oo</u>-noh, oos-<u>tehd</u>, Hoo<u>eh</u>-gah
nosotros jugamos	noh-<u>soh</u>-trohs Hoo-<u>gah</u>-mohs
vosotros jugáis	bvoh-<u>soh</u>-trohs Hoo-<u>gah</u>-ees
ellos, ellas, ustedes juegan	<u>eh</u>-yohs, <u>eh</u>-yahs, oos-<u>teh</u>-dehs Hoo<u>eh</u>-gahn

It's always good to practice on your game a little. Following are some phrases that can help when you play:

- ✔ **¿Jugamos beisbol hoy?** *(Hoo-<u>gah</u>-mohs <u>bvehees</u>-bvohl ohy)* (Are we playing baseball today?)

- ✔ **Juega mejor que hace un mes.** *(Hoo<u>eh</u>-gah <u>meh</u>-Hohr keh <u>ah</u>-seh oon mehs)* ([He] plays better than a month ago.)

The Swimming Verb: Nadar

Water, water, everywhere — inviting you to jump right in. Before you do, you may want to know how to conjugate **nadar** *(nah-<u>dahr</u>)* (to swim). It's easy. It's a regular verb and its root is **nad-** *(nahd)*

Conjugation	Pronunciation
yo nado	yoh <u>nah</u>-doh
tú nadas	too <u>nah</u>-dahs
él, ella, ello, uno, usted nada	ehl, <u>eh</u>-yah, <u>eh</u>-yoh, <u>oo</u>-noh, oos-<u>tehd</u>, <u>nah</u>-dah
nosotros nadamos	noh-<u>soh</u>-trohs nah-<u>dah</u>-mohs
vosotros nadáis	bvoh-<u>soh</u>-trohs nah-<u>dahees</u>
ellos, ellas, ustedes nadan	eh-yohs, <u>eh</u>-yahs, oos-<u>teh</u>-dehs <u>nah</u>-dahn

Okay. Maybe you don't want to get wet right now. How about practicing your swimming here, for just a couple of laps?

- ✔ **Carlos nada como un pez.** *(<u>kahr</u>-lohs <u>nah</u>-dah <u>koh</u>-moh oon pehs)* (Carlos swims like a fish.)

- ✔ **Yo no sé nadar.** *(yoh noh seh nah-<u>dahr</u>)* (I can't swim.)

Swimming pun

This pun is based on the double play of the words **nada** (_nah_-dah) and **traje** (_trah_-Heh). **Nada** means both the third person of the verb **nadar** (nah-_dahr_) (to swim) and "nothing." And **traje** can be the past tense of the verb **traer** (trah-_ehr_) (to bring) and also means "suit."

¿No nada nada? (noh _nah_-dah nah-dah) ([Literally: nothing] You are not swimming at all?)

No traje traje. (noh _trah_-Heh _trah_-Heh.) (I didn't bring [my] swimsuit.)

Talkin' the Talk

María Luisa likes to swim, and she would like to compete against Alvaro. But first she needs to find out how good a swimmer he is:

María Luisa: **¿Cuándo vas a nadar?**
koo<u>ahn</u>-doh bvahs ah <u>nah</u>-dahr
When do you go swimming?

Alvaro: **Los martes y los viernes.**
lohs <u>mahr</u>-tehs ee lohs bvee<u>ehr</u>-nehs
Tuesdays and Fridays.

María Luisa: **¿Qué estilo nadas?**
keh ehs-<u>tee</u>-loh <u>nah</u>-dahs
What style do you swim?

Alvaro: **Nado principalmente pecho.**
<u>nah</u>-doh preen-see-pahl-<u>mehn</u>-teh <u>peh</u>-choh
I swim mainly breaststroke.

María Luisa: **¿Sabes nadar crol?**
<u>sah</u>-bvehs nah-<u>dahr</u> krohl
Do you know how to swim the crawl?

Alvaro: **Sí, y también de espalda.**
see ee tahm-bvee<u>ehn</u> deh ehs-<u>pahl</u>-dah
Yes, and also the backstroke.

María Luisa: **¿Cuánto nadas?**
koo<u>ahn</u>-toh <u>nah</u>-dahs
How much do you swim?

Alvaro: **Nado un kilómetro cada vez.**
<u>nah</u>-doh oon kee-<u>loh</u>-meh-troh <u>kah</u>-dah bvehs
I swim one kilometer each time.

Maria Louisa: **¡Que bien!**
(keh bvehn)
Very good!

Words to Know

el estilo	ehl ehs-<u>tee</u>-loh	the style
el estilo crol	ehl ehs-<u>tee</u>-loh krohl	crawl stroke
el estilo espalda	ehl ehs-<u>tee</u>-loh ehs-<u>pahl</u>-dah	the backstroke
el estilo pecho	ehl ehs-<u>tee</u>-loh <u>peh</u>-choh	the breaststroke

Talkin' the Talk

Fernando and Matías are discussing their friend Agustín, who is training for the Tour de France bicycle race.

Fernando: **Agustín practica el ciclismo.**
ah-goos-<u>teen</u> prahk-<u>tee</u>-kah ehl seek-<u>lees</u>-moh
Agustín does cycling.

Matías: **¿Tiene una bicicleta de montaña?**
tee<u>eh</u>-neh <u>oo</u>-nah bvee-seek-<u>leh</u>-tah deh mohn-<u>tah</u>-nyah
Does he have a mountain bike?

Fernando: **No, usa una bicicleta de carrera.**
noh <u>oo</u>-sah <u>oo</u>-nah bvee-seek-<u>leh</u>-tah deh kah-<u>rreh</u>-rah
No, he uses a racing bike.

Matías: **¿Participa en concursos?**
pahr-tee-<u>see</u>-pah ehn kohn-<u>koor</u>-sohs
Does he participate in competitions?

Fernando: **Sí, la semana pasada estuvo en una carrera.**
see lah seh-<u>mah</u>-nah pah-<u>sah</u>-dah ehs-<u>too</u>-bvoh ehn <u>oo</u>-nah kah-<u>rreh</u>-rah
Yes, last week he was in a race.

Matías: **¿Qué posición obtuvo?**
keh poh-see-see<u>ohn</u> ohb-<u>too</u>-bvoh
How did he place?

Fernando: **Llegó segundo.**
yeh-<u>goh</u> seh-<u>goon</u>-doh
He came in second.

Words to Know

la bicicleta	lah bvee-see-kleh-tah	the bicycle
de carrera	deh kah-rreh-rah	racing [kind]
la carrera	lah kah-rreh-rah	the race
el ciclismo	ehl see-klees-moh	cycling
la montaña	lah mohn-tah-nyah	mountain

Playing Chess in Spain

Chess can be a fascinating game to watch or play. It has been popular in Spain since the Arab invasion of 711 A.D. In fact, some of the terms used in chess come from a combination of Arabic and Spanish words. Checkmate, for example, is derived from the Arabic word **sheik** *(sheek)* (king) and from the Spanish word **matar** *(mah <u>tahr</u>)* (to kill). That's why you say checkmate when the king is captured at the end of the game.

Talkin' the Talk

In this conversation, Gabriel and Cornelia discuss a chess tournament in Spain:

Gabriel:	**A mí me gusta el deporte de los reyes.**
	ah mee meh <u>goos</u>-tah ehl deh-<u>pohr</u>-teh deh lohs <u>reh</u>-yehs
	I like the sport of kings.

Cornelia:	**¿También juegas ajedrez?**
	tahm-bvee<u>ehn</u> Hoo<u>eh</u>-gahs ah-Heh-<u>dreth</u>
	Do you also play chess?

Gabriel:	**Sí, ayer estuve en una competencia.**
	see ah-<u>yehr</u> ehs-<u>too</u>-bveh ehn <u>oo</u>-nah kohm-peh-<u>tehn</u>-theeah
	Yes, yesterday I was in a contest.

Cornelia:	**¿Quién ganó?**
	keeehn gah-<u>noh</u>
	Who won?

Gabriel:	**Pedro. Dió jaquemate en sólo diez movidas.**
	<u>peh</u>-droh deeoh Hah-keh-<u>mah</u>-teh ehn <u>soh</u>-loh deeeth moh-<u>bvee</u>-dahs
	Pedro. He checkmated [his opponent] in only ten moves.

Words to Know

el ajedrez	ehl ah-Heh-<u>drehs</u>	chess
el jaquemate	ehl Hah-keh-<u>mahteh</u>	checkmate

The Reading Verb: Leer

Reading is a pleasure, a joy and often a wonder. Here is the verb that helps you talk about reading in Spanish: **leer** *(leh-<u>ehr</u>)*(to read.)

Conjugation	Pronunciation
yo leo	yoh <u>leh</u>-oh
tú lees	too <u>leh</u>-ehs
él, ella, ello, uno, usted lee	ehl, <u>eh</u>-yah, <u>eh</u>-yoh, <u>oo</u>-noh, oos-<u>tehd</u>, <u>leh</u>-eh
nosotros leemos	noh-<u>soh</u>-trohs leh-<u>eh</u>-mohs
vosotros leéis	bvoh-<u>soh</u>-trohs leh-<u>eh</u>ees
ellos, ellas, ustedes leen	<u>eh</u>-yohs, <u>eh</u>-yahs, oos-<u>teh</u>-dehs <u>leh</u>-ehn

Obviously, you're a great reader. Why not practice your speaking by using this reading verb:

✔ **Felipe lee todo el día.** *(feh-<u>lee</u>-peh <u>leh</u>-eh <u>toh</u>-doh ehl deeah)* (Felipe reads all day long.)

✔ **A mí me gusta leer revistas.** *(ah mee meh <u>goos</u>-tah <u>leh</u>-ehr reh-<u>bvees</u>-tahs)* (I like to read magazines.)

Talkin' the Talk

Marisa and Aurelia are discussing reading material.

Marisa: **¿Qué vas a leer?**
keh bvahs ah leh-<u>ehr</u>
What are you going to read?

Aurelia: **Yo traje una novela.**
yoh <u>trah</u>-Heh <u>oo</u>-nah noh-<u>bveh</u>-lah
I brought a novel.

Marisa: **Estoy entusiasta de una biografía.**
ehs-<u>toy</u> ehn-too-see<u>ahs</u>-tah deh <u>oo</u>-nah bveeoh-grah-<u>fee</u>ah
I am enthusiastic about a biography.

Aurelia: **Hablando de biografía. . .**
ah-<u>bvlahn</u>-doh deh bveeoh-grah-<u>fee</u>ah
Speaking of biography. . .

¿. . .supiste que va a salir un libro sobre Vallejo?
. . .soo-<u>pees</u>-teh keh bvah ah sah-<u>leer</u> oon <u>lee</u>-bvroh <u>soh</u>-bvreh bvah-<u>yeh</u>-Hoh
. . .did you know that there's going to be a book about Vallejo?

Marisa:	**¿Quién, el poeta peruano?**
	keeehn ehl poh-eh-tah peh-rooah-noh
	Who, the Peruvian poet?

Aurelia:	**Sí, dicen que va a ser excepcional.**
	see dee-sehn keh bvah ah sehr eh-ksehp-seeoh-nahl
	Yes, they say it's going to be exceptional.

The Writing Verb: Escribir

The writing verb **escribir** *(ehs-kree-bveer)* (to write) is a regular one. Its root is **escrib-** *(ehs-kreebv)*. Here's how you conjugate its present tense:

Conjugation	*Pronunciation*
yo escribo	yoh ehs-kree-bvoh
tú escribes	too ehs-kree-bvehs
él, ella, ello, uno, usted escribe	ehl, eh-yah, eh-yoh, oo-noh, oos-tehd, ehs-kree-bveh
nosotros escribimos	noh-soh-trohs ehs-kree-bvee-mohs
vosotros escribís	bvoh-soh-trohs ehs-kree-bvees
ellos, ellas, ustedes escriben	eh-yohs, eh-yahs, oos-teh-dehs ehs-kree-bvehn

Use these phrases to practice talking about writing:

✔ **Mi madre escribe poemas.** *(mee mah-dreh ehs-kree-bveh poh-eh-mahs)* (My mother writes poems.)

✔ **Tú siempre escribes en tu diario.** *(too seeehm-preh ehs-kree-bvehs ehn too deeah-reeoh)* (You always write in your journal.)

Talkin' the Talk

While on vacation, Catalina is coming indoors from the outdoors to write her father, as she explains to Eduardo.

Catalina:	**Le escribí a mi padre.**
	leh ehs-kree-bvee ah mee pah-dreh
	I wrote my father.

Eduardo:	**¿Le escribes regularmente?**
	leh ehs-kree-bvehs reh-goo-lahr-mehn-teh
	Do you write him regularly?

Catalina:	**Sí, por lo menos una vez a la semana.**
	see pohr loh <u>meh</u>-nohs <u>oo</u>-nah bves ah lah seh-<u>mah</u>-nah
	Yes, at least once a week.

Eduardo:	**¿Escribiste alguna carta hoy?**
	ehs-kree-<u>bvees</u>-teh ahl-<u>goo</u>-nah <u>kahr</u>-tah ohy
	Did you write a letter today?

Catalina:	**Voy a terminar de escribir una.**
	bvohy ah tehr-mee-<u>nahr</u> deh ehs-kree-<u>bveer</u> <u>oo</u>-nah
	I'm going to finish writing one.

Words to Know

la biografía	lah bveeoh-grah-<u>feeah</u>	the biography
la carta	lah <u>kahr</u>-tah	the letter
la novela	lah noh-<u>bveh</u>-lah	the novel
el poeta	ehl poh-<u>eh</u>-tah	the poet

Fun & Games

Here's your chance to let your animal magnetism show through. Match the Spanish animals on the left with their English counterparts on the right.

ardilla	butterfly
caballo	cat
cabra	cow
gansos	dog
gato	geese
gaviota	goat
gorrión	horse
mapache	mare
mariposa	raccoon
perro	seagull
vaca	sparrow
yegua	squirrel

Chapter 9

Talking on the Phone

- -

In This Chapter

▶ Conversing by phone

▶ Using the alphabet

▶ Making reservations and appointments

▶ Understanding simple past tense

- -

*T*alking on the phone, arranging things over the phone, even having a social life on the phone, are activities that people in the United States and Canada often take for granted.

In the United States and Canada, you can get and place phone calls quite easily, with practically no delay. This is not the case everywhere in Latin America. In larger cities, a good deal of business is done on the phone, and people use it frequently. But in smaller places, where getting a phone can take years and costs heaps of money, people aren't used to relying on them. In those places, you use the phone mostly to set up appointments, and then you conduct your business in person.

If you travel to a Spanish-American country, you may notice that some places still primarily have rotary dial phones instead of TouchTone ones. Nevertheless, talking on the phone hasn't changed much in the last half century, and this chapter gives you a pretty accurate idea of what you may say and hear, no matter what kind of phone you use.

Opening Lines

So you punch in or dial a phone number — then what?

▬ Argentinians say **¡Holá!** (oh*lah*).

▬ Chileans say **¡Aló!** (ah-*loh*).

▬ Mexicans say **¡Bueno!** (bvoo*eh*-noh).

▬ In Spain, you hear **¡Sí!**

These words all mean (Hello!). Most Spanish-speaking countries use **aló**, in the Chilean way.

These phrases come in very handy when you use the phone:

- ✔ **llamar por teléfono** *(yah-mahr pohr teh-leh-foh-noh)* (make a phone call)
- ✔ **marcar el número** *(mahr-kahr ehl noo-meh-roh)* (dial/punch in the number)
- ✔ **colgar** *(kohl-gahr)* (hang up)
- ✔ **la línea está libre** *(lah lee-neah ehs-tah lee-bvreh)* (the line is open)
- ✔ **la línea está ocupada** *(lah lee-neh-ah ehs-tah oh-koo-pah-dah)* (the line is busy)
- ✔ **el teléfono no responde** *(ehl teh-leh-foh-noh noh rehs-pohn-deh)* (there's no answer)

Words to Know

llamar	yah-mahr	to call
marcar	mahr-kahr	to mark; to dial; to punch in the number
el número	ehl noo-meh-roh	the number
colgar	kohl-gahr	to hang; to hang up
la línea	lah lee-neh-ah	the line
libre	lee-bvreh	free
ocupada	oh-koo-pah-dah	busy (female)
responder	rehs-pohn-dehr	to answer

Dealing with "Porridge" (When You Can't Make Out the Words)

When learning a language, you may find that some people you talk to speak too fast for you. You can't make out the words; everything seems mushy, like porridge. On the phone, fast talking is even more of a problem. You don't see the person, so you can't get the gist of the communication from body language or facial expressions.

Don't be too hard on yourself. Gently insist that the other person repeat the sentence more clearly. You're not being rude in the least; you simply didn't get the whole message, so you're asking for a repeat. No harm there.

The person you're talking to may have similar difficulties, even if the language is his own, so please be just as patient with him as you'd like him to be with you.

Talkin' the Talk

Take a look at these handy phrases, which you can use when the conversation turns to "porridge":

Clarisa: **¡Bueno! ¿Hablo con Juanita?**
bvooeh-noh ah-bvloh kohn Hooah-nee-tah
Hello! Am I speaking to Juanita?

Voice on other side: **Mzfg utrc eeruet.**
(Not intelligible.)

Clarisa: **Perdone, no le escucho.**
pehr-doh-neh noh leh ehs-koo-choh
Excuse me, I can't hear you.

Voice on other side: **N st mmet o st.**
(Not intelligible.)

Clarisa: **Está muy mala la línea, ¿lo repite por favor?**
ehs-tah mooy mah-lah lah lee-neh-ah loh reh-pee-teh pohr fah-bvohr
The line is very bad, will you please repeat what you said?

Voice on other side: **En este momento no está.**
ehn ehs-teh moh-mehn-toh noh ehs-tah
She's not here at the moment.

Clarisa: **Llamo más tarde, gracias.**
yah-moh mahs tahr-deh grah-seeahs
I'll call later, thanks.

Words to Know

hablar	ah-bvlahr	to talk
escuchar	ehs-koo-chahr	to listen; to hear
más tarde	mahs tahr-deh	later
en la tarde	ehn lah tahr-deh	in the afternoon

The word **tarde** (_tahr-deh),_ without the article **la**, means (late). But when you hear the article **la** (the) in front of it, as in **la tarde**, you know that the speaker is talking about (the afternoon).

A Word about "Spelling Out"

Because English spelling is erratic, you may automatically spell out your name or other information you give out. Spanish has more regular spelling rules, however, so generally no one will ask to have a Spanish name like Rodríguez spelled out — the spelling is obvious. As a result, many Spanish speakers aren't used to spelling out information or taking down information that is being spelled out. Therefore, if asked to spell your name, try to do so veeeery slooowly so that people can absorb the unusual situation.

Talkin' the Talk

Use this conversation to help you practice spelling out names. (Chapter 1 has the complete Spanish alphabet, so head that way if you need it.)

Sheryl Lyons: **Quisiera dejar un mensaje.**
kee-see_eh_-rah deh-_Hahr_ oon mehn-_sah_-Heh
I would like to leave a message.

El mensaje es que la señora Lyons va a llegar hoy a las cinco de la tarde.
ehl mehn-_sah_-Heh ehs keh lah seh-_nyoh_-rah _lahee_-ohns bvah ah yeh-_gahr_ ohy ah lahs _seen_-koh deh lah _tahr_-deh
The message is that Mrs. Lyons will arrive today at five in the afternoon.

Voice: **¿Me puede repetir su apellido, por favor?**
meh poo<u>eh</u>-deh reh-peh-<u>teer</u> soo ah-peh-<u>yee</u>-doh pohr fah-<u>bvohr</u>
Can you repeat your last name, please?

Sheryl Lyons: **Me llamo Lyons.**
meh <u>yah</u>-moh Lyons
My name is Lyons.

Voice: **¿Cómo se escribe?**
koh-moh seh ehs-<u>kree</u>-bveh
How do you spell it?

Sheryl Lyons: **Ele, i griega, o, ene, ese.**
<u>eh</u>-leh ee gree<u>eh</u>-gah oh <u>eh</u>-neh <u>eh</u>-seh
L-Y-O-N-S.

Voice: **Ah, Lyons. Gracias. ¿Cómo es su nombre?**
ah <u>lee</u>-ohns <u>grah</u>-see-ahs <u>koh</u>-moh ehs soo <u>nohm</u>-bvreh
Ah, Lyons, thank you. What's your first name?

Sheryl Lyons: **Es Sheryl. Ese, hache, e, ere, i griega, ele.**
ehs Sheryl <u>eh</u>-seh <u>ah</u>-cheh eh <u>eh</u>-reh ee gree<u>eh</u>-gah <u>eh</u>-leh
It's Sheryl. S-H-E-R-Y-L.

Voice: **Ah, Sheryl, gracias. Diré que llamó la señora Sheryl Lyons, y va a llegar a las cinco de la tarde.**
ah <u>cheh</u>-reel <u>grah</u>-seeahs dee-<u>reh</u> keh yah-<u>moh</u> lah seh-<u>nyoh</u>-rah <u>cheh</u>-reel <u>lee</u>-ohns ee keh bvah a yeh-<u>gahr</u> ah lahs <u>seen</u>-koh deh lah <u>tahr</u>-deh
Ah, Sheryl, thanks. I'll say Mrs. Sheryl Lyons phoned, and that she'll arrive at five p.m.

For days, hours, months, and other date and calendar words, refer to Chapter 15. For numbers, refer to Chapter 5. In some countries, calling long-distance can cost twice as much as the same call in the United States or Canada. If you travel in Spanish-speaking America, remember that collect calls can save you quite a bit of money.

Talkin' the Talk

 Lucy wants to make a collect call to her parents because she's short on change.

Lucy:	**¡Bueno!, operadora, quisiera hacer una llamada por cobrar.** *bvooeh-noh oh-peh-rah-doh-rah kee-seeeh-rah ah-sehr oo-nah lyah-mah-dah pohr koh-bvrahr* Hello, operator, I'd like to make a collect call.
Operator:	**¿A qué número?** *ah keh noo-meh-roh* To what number?
Lucy:	**Al 4372-2351.** *ahl kooah-troh trehs seeeh-teh dohs dohs trehs seen-koh oo-noh* To 4372-2351.
Operator:	**¿Y el código del área?** *ee ehl koh-dee-goh dehl ah-reh-ah* And the area code?
Lucy:	**El 11.** *ehl ohn-seh* 11.
Operator:	**¿Cómo se llama usted?** *koh-moh seh yah-mah oos-tehd* What's your name?
Lucy:	**Lucy Sánchez.** Lucy Sánchez.
Operator:	**Muy bien, un momento . . . .** *mooy bveeehn oon moh-mehn-toh* Very well, one moment. . . .
Operator:	**La línea no responde. Llame más tarde, por favor.** *lah lee-neh-ah noh rehs-pohn-deh yah-meh mahs tahr-deh pohr fah-bvohr* The line doesn't answer. Call later, please.

Talkin' the Talk

Here's how you might discuss your weekend activities with a friend:

Jorge: **Hola Felipe, ¿cómo te fue en el fin de semana?**
          *oh-lah feh-lee-peh koh-moh teh fooeh ehn ehl feen
          deh seh-mah-nah*
          Hello, Felipe, how was your weekend?

Felipe: **Ahora, pienso que muy bien. Ayer todavía no sabía.**
          *ah-oh-rah peeehn-soh keh mooy bveeehn ah-yehr
          toh-dah-bveeah noh sah-bveeah*
          Now, I think it went very well. Yesterday I didn't
          know yet.

Jorge: **¿No sabías qué?**
          noh sah-bveeahs keh
          You didn't know what?

Felipe: **Quién era la persona que encontré en el club.**
          *keeehn eh-rah lah pehr-soh-nah keh ehn-kohn-treh
          ehn ehl kloobv*
          Who the person is that I had met at the club.

Jorge: **¿Y quién es?**
          ee keeehn ehs
          And who is he?

Felipe: **Gonzalo Ramírez, el director del diario.**
          *gohn-sah-loh rah-mee-rehs ehl dee-rehk-tohr dehl
          deeah-reeoh*
          Gonzalo Ramírez, the manager of the newspaper.

Jorge: **¿Qué dijo?**
          keh dee-Hoh
          What did he say?

Felipe:	**Que iba a dejar el diario.**
	keh ee-bvah ah deh-Hahr ehl deeah-reeoh
	That he's going to leave the newspaper.

Jorge:	**¿Quién va a reemplazarlo?**
	keeehn bvah a rehm-plah-sahr-loh
	Who will replace him?

Felipe:	**Me dijo que me recomendaría, y hoy me llamaron para una entrevista.**
	meh dee-Hoh keh meh reh-koh-mehn-dah-reeah ee ohy meh yah-mah-rohn pah-rah oo-nah ehn-treh-bvees-tah
	He said he would recommend me, and today they called me for an interview.

Jorge:	**¡Muy buena noticia!**
	mooy bvooeh-nah noh-tee-seeah
	Very good news!

Words to Know

el fin de semana	ehl feen deh seh-mah-nah	the weekend
pensar	pehn-sahr	to think
ahora	ah-oh-rah	now
ayer	ah-yehr	yesterday
hoy	ohy	today
el diario	ehl deeah-reeoh	the newspaper
jugar	Hoo-gahr	to play
preguntar	preh-goon-tahr	to ask (a question)

Calling: Llamar

The verb **llamar** *(yah-mahr)* means "to call." So then why is that verb in Chapter 3, which covers names? Because when asked for their names, Spanish speakers respond with **me llamo** *(meh yah-moh),* which literally means, "I call myself" or "I give myself the name."

In this section, however, we talk about calling as a way of trying to reach someone with words and messages. We also talk about calling someone on the phone. **Llamar** also means "to phone."

Here are some examples:

- **Mañana te llamo por teléfono.** *(mah-nyah-nah teh yah-moh pohr teh-leh-foh-noh)* (Tomorrow, I'll call you.)

- **Hoy no nos llamó nadie.** *(ohy noh nohs yah-moh nah-deeeh)* (Nobody called us today.)

- **Ella llama a su madre todos los días.** *(eh-yah yah-mah ah soo mah-dreh toh-dohs lohs deeahs)* (She phones her mother every day.)

- **Llamamos para saber el horario.** *(yah-mah-mohs pah-rah sah-bvehr ehl oh-rah-reeoh)* (We're calling to ask about the schedule.)

See Chapter 3 for more about the verb llamar.

Phone-y Verbs: To Call, to Leave, and to Listen and Hear

What do these *phoneful* verbs have in common? Good news, all three are regular verbs, belonging to the **-ar** *(ahr)* group. If you take off the **-ar,** you get the root of each verb. And, when you conjugate **llamar** *(yah-marh)*(to call), **dejar** *(deh-Har)* (to leave), and **escuchar** *(ehs-koo-char)* (to listen; to hear), the words end the same way for each pronoun. So, if we give you the conjugation for **llamar**, you can also conjugate **dejar** and **escuchar**.

Conjugation	Pronunciation
yo llamo	yoh yah-moh
tú llamas	too yah-mahs
él, ella, ello, uno, usted llama	ehl eh yah eh-yoh oo-noh oos-tehd yah-mah

Conjugation	Pronunciation
nosotros llamamos	noh-<u>soh</u>-trohs-yah-<u>mah</u>-mohs
vosotros llamáis	bvoh-<u>soh</u>-trohs yah-<u>mah</u>-ees
ellos llaman	<u>eh</u>-yohs <u>yah</u>-mahn

Don't forget to try your own conjugation. Check the verb tables in the back of this book if you're stumped.

Using the Simple Past Tense

This section tells you about the past tenses of the three verbs in the previous section: **llamar, dejar,** and **escuchar.** Because they are all regular verbs ending in **-ar,** you add the same letters to each pronoun.

You called? The past tense of llamar

Use the root of **llamar** *(yah-<u>mahr</u>),* which is **llam-,** to conjugate for the past tense.

Conjugation	Pronunciation
yo llamé	yoh yah-<u>meh</u>
tú llamaste	too yah-<u>mahs</u>-teh
él, ella, ello, uno, usted llamó	ehl <u>eh</u>-yah <u>eh</u>-yoh <u>oo</u>-noh oos-<u>tehd</u> yah-<u>moh</u>
nosotros llamamos	noh-<u>soh</u>-trohs yah-<u>mah</u>-mohs
vosotros llamásteis	bvoh-<u>soh</u>-trohs yah-<u>mahs</u>-tehees
ellos, ellas, ustedes llamaron	<u>eh</u>-yohs <u>eh</u>-yahs oos-<u>teh</u>-dehs yah-<u>mah</u>-rohn

If you missed a call, you may hear the following:

✔ **Te llamaron por teléfono.** *(teh yah-<u>mah</u>-rohn pohr teh-<u>leh</u>-foh-noh)* (You had a phone call.)

✔ **Le llamé ayer.** *(leh yah-<u>meh</u> ah-<u>yehr</u>)* (I called you [formal] yesterday.)

✔ **Ayer no me llamaste.** *(ah-yehr noh meh yah-mahs-teh)* (Yesterday you [informal] didn't call me.)

✔ **Cuando te llamé me colgaron.** *(kooahn-doh teh yah-meh meh kohl-gah-rohn)* (When I called you [informal], they hung up on me.) (Literally: they hung me up)

✔ **Si hoy me llamaste, no me enteré.** *(see ohy meh yah-mahs-teh noh meh ehn-teh-reh)* (If you called me today, I didn't know about it.)

Did you leave a message? The past tense of dejar

Here is the past tense of **dejar** *(deh-Hahr)*, that "leaving and allowing" verb. The root is **dej-** *(dehH)*.

Conjugation	*Pronunciation*
yo dejé	yoh deh-Heh
tú dejaste	too deh-Hahs-teh
él, ella, ello, uno, usted dejó	ehl eh-yah eh-yoh oo-noh oos-tehd deh-Hoh
nosotros dejamos	noh-soh-trohs deh-Hah-mohs
vosotros dejásteis	bvoh-soh-trohs deh-Hahs-tehees
ellos, ellas, ustedes dejaron	eh-yohs eh-yahs oos-teh-dehs deh-Hah-rohn

These examples use forms of the verb **dejar:**

✔ **Te dejé un recado.** *(teh deh-Heh oon reh-kah-doh)* (I left you a message.)

✔ **¿Dejaste un mensaje largo?** *(deh-Hahs-teh oon mehn-sah-Heh lahr-goh)* (Did you [informal] leave a long message?)

✔ **El mensaje que dejaron es breve.** *(ehl mehn-sah-Heh keh deh-Hah-rohn ehs bvreh-bveh)* (The message they left is brief.)

✔ **Dejamos tres mensajes.** *(deh-Hah-mohs trehs mehn-sah-Hehs)* (We left three messages.)

✔ **Dejó el número de teléfono.** *(deh-Hoh ehl noo-meh-roh deh teh-leh-foh-noh)* (She left the telephone number.)

Have you heard? The past tense of escuchar

In the case of the verb **escuchar** (*ehs-koo-chahr*)(to listen), the conjugation is very similar to the previous two verbs as they are all regular verbs with **-ar** endings. For **escuchar**, the root is **escuch-** (*ehs-kooch*).

Conjugation	Pronunciation
yo escuché	yoh ehs-koo-cheh
tú escuchaste	too ehs-koo-chahs-teh
él, ella, ello, uno, usted escuchó	ehl eh-yah eh-yoh oo-noh oos-tehd ehs-koo-choh
nosotros escuchamos	noh-soh-trohs ehs-koo-chah-mohs
vosotros escuchásteis	bvoh-soh-trohs ehs-koo-chahs-tehees
ellos, ellas, ustedes escucharon	eh-yohs eh-yahs oos-teh-dehs ehs-koo-chah-rohn

Test your hearing-verb abilities with the following phrases:

✔ **Aló, ¿me escuchaste, Juan?** (*ah-loh me ehs-koo-chahs-teh Hooahn*)
(Hello, did you hear me, Juan?)

✔ **No te escuché nada.** (*noh teh ehs-koo-cheh nah-dah*)
(I didn't hear anything.)

✔ **¿Así escuchó bien?** (*ah-see ehs-koo-choh bveeehn*)
(Did she hear well this way?)

✔ **Así te escuchamos un poco mejor.** (*ah-see teh ehs-koo-chah-mohs oon poh-koh meh-Hohr*) (This way we heard you [informal] a little better.)

✔ **Así escucharon muy bien.** (*ah-see ehs-koo-chah-rohn mooy bveeehn*)
(This way they heard very well.)

A popular book title that uses the verb **llamar** is Jack London's *The Call of the Wild,* which in Spanish reads ***El llamado de la selva*** (*ehl yah-mah-doh deh lah sehl-bvah*).

Fun & Games

Throughout this book, we show you how to conjugate regular Spanish verbs, mostly in Chapter 2. You start with the root of the verb and add the same endings corresponding to the pronouns for each verb in that class: All regular -**ar** verbs conjugate the same way, as do all -**er** and -**ir** verbs.

This section asks you to complete the missing conjugation segments of the verb **dejar.** You can follow in the tracks of the verb *llamar,* which we conjugate for you earlier in the chapter. The root of **llamar** is ***llam-*** *(yahm-);* the root of **dejar** *(deh-Hahr)* (to leave; to allow) is ***dej-*** *(dehH-).*

Are you ready to fly solo? C'mon, fill in the gaps! Go for it!

yo dej _____	*yoh <u>deh</u>-Hoh*	I leave
tú dej _____	*too <u>deh</u>-Hahs*	you leave
él dej _____	*ehl <u>deh</u>-Hah*	he leaves
nosotros dej _____	*noh-<u>soh</u>-trohs deh-<u>Hah</u>-mohs*	we leave
vosotros dej _____	*bvoh-<u>soh</u>-trohs deh-<u>Hahees</u>*	you leave
ellos dej _____	*<u>eh</u>-yohs deh-<u>Hahn</u>*	they leave

You made it! For more practice, try another one. Here, the verb is **escuchar** *(ehs-koo-chahr)* (to listen; to hear). The root is ***escuch-*** *(ehs-kooch-).*

yo escuch _____	*yoh ehs-<u>koo</u>-choh*	I listen; I hear
tú escuch _____	*too ehs-<u>koo</u>-chahs*	you listen; you hear
ella escuch _____	*<u>eh</u>-yah ehs-<u>koo</u>-chah*	she listens; she hears
nosotros escuch _____	*noh-<u>soh</u>-trohs ehs-koo-<u>chah</u>-mohs*	we listen; we hear
vosotros escuch _____	*bvoh-<u>soh</u>-trohs ehs-koo-<u>chahees</u>*	you listen; you hear
ellos escuch _____	*<u>eh</u>-yohs ehs-<u>koo</u>-chahn*	they listen; they hear

Chapter 10

At the Office and Around the House

*L*atin American architecture provides very beautiful working and living environments. This chapter explores both work-related and home-related Spanish vocabulary.

Buildings Small and Tall

In larger Latin American cities, people often live and work in high-rise buildings and office towers, just like in New York or Chicago. In smaller cities or towns, the workplace may be built around an open-air courtyard filled with flowers or fountains — one of the benefits of living in a warm climate. But no matter what the climate, the size of the city decides the style of the building.

Here are some words and phrases that you can use to describe buildings:

✔ **edificio de oficinas** *(eh-dee-fee-seeoh deh oh-fee-see-nahs)* (office building)

✔ **edificio de apartamentos** *(eh-dee-fee-seeoh deh ah-pahr-tah-mehn-tohs)* (apartment building)

✔ **edificio de muchos pisos** *(eh-dee-fee-seeoh deh moo-chohs pee-sohs)* (building with many floors; high-rise)

✔ **edificio alto** *(eh-dee-fee-seeoh ahl-toh)* (tall building; high-rise)

✔ **edificio de torre** *(eh-dee-fee-seeoh deh toh-rreh)* (a tower building)

✔ **edificio de una planta** *(eh-dee-fee-seeoh deh oo-nah plahn-tah)* (one-story building)

How big is this building?

Practice the building terms with the following phrases:

- **El edificio de Correos tiene siete pisos.** *(ehl eh-dee-fee-seeoh deh koh-rreh-ohs tee-eh-neh see-eh-teh pee-sohs)* (The Postal building is seven stories high.)

- **La Torre del Banco tiene cincuenta y cinco pisos.** *(lah toh-rreh dehl bvahn-koh teeeh-neh seen-kooehn-tah ee seen-koh pee-sohs)* (The Bank Tower is 55 stories high.)

- **La oficina está en un edificio de dos pisos.** *(lah oh-fee-see-nah ehs-tah ehn oon eh-dee-fee-seeoh deh dohs pee-sohs)* (The office is in a two-story building.)

- **Busco el edificio de oficinas fiscales.** *(bvoos-koh ehl eh-dee-fee-seeoh deh oh-fee-see-nahs fees-kah-lehs)* (I'm looking for the building of public revenues.)

- **Vamos a un edificio muy alto.** *(bvah-mohs a oon eh-dee-fee-seeoh mooy ahl-toh)* (We're going to a very tall building.)

- **En ese edificio sólo hay oficinas.** *(ehn eh-seh eh-dee-fee-seeoh soh-loh ahy oh-fee-see-nahs)* (This building only has offices.)

- **Tres plantas de ese edificio son de la compañía.** *(trehs plahn-tahs deh eh-seh eh-dee-fee-seeoh sohn deh lah kohm-pah-nyeeah)* (Three floors in that building belong to the company.)

Which floor comes first?

In some places, the first floor that you count in a building is at street level. Some cities, however, refer to the street level floor as **planta baja** *(plahn-tah bvah-Hah)* (ground floor [Literally: low floor]), and the first floor is the one immediately above it. Keep this information in mind when you try to find a specific address.

Words to Know

el edificio	ehl eh-dee-fee-seeoh	the building
el piso	ehl pee-soh	the floor
la planta baja	lah plahn-tah bvah-Hah	the floor at ground level
alto	ahl-toh	tall; high

At work

Conversations about jobs, workplaces, and offices don't differ much from one country to another. Here are some terms that will help you talk about life on the job:

- ✔ **el empleo** *(ehl ehm-pleh-oh)* (the job; employment)
- ✔ **presentarse** *(preh-sehn-tahr-seh)* (to go to be present at some place; to introduce oneself)
- ✔ **la entrevista** *(lah ehn-treh-bvees-tah)* (the interview)
- ✔ **el personal** *(ehl pehr-soh-nahl)* (the staff; the personnel)
- ✔ **el ascensor** *(ehl ah-sehn-sohr)* (the elevator)
- ✔ **el pasillo** *(ehl pah-see-yoh)* (the corridor; the aisle)
- ✔ **la cita** *(lah see-tah)* (the appointment; the date [as in going on a date with someone])
- ✔ **la secretaria** *(lah seh-kreh-tah-reeah)* (the female secretary)
- ✔ **el secretario** *(ehl seh-kreh-tah-reeoh)* (the male secretary)
- ✔ **gerencial** *(Heh-rehn-see-ahl)* (managerial)
- ✔ **antes** *(ahn-tehs)* (before)
- ✔ **la carta** *(lah kahr-tah)* (the letter)
- ✔ **la recomendación** *(lah reh-koh-mehn-dah-see-ohn)* (the recommendation)

Talkin' the Talk

Inés has been transferred to her company's Mexico City office. She wants to transfer to a new department. Here's how she describes her experience.

Manager:	**¿Tiene experiencia con computadoras?** *teeeh-neh ehks-peh-reeehn-seeah kohn kom-poo-tah-doh-rahs* Do you have experience with computers?
Inés:	**Sí tengo cinco años de experiencia.** *see tehn-goh seen-koh ah-nyos deh ehks-peh-ree-ehn-seealh* Yes, I have five years' experience.
Manager:	**¿Qué trabajo ha hecho con computadoras?** *keh trah-bvah-Hoh ah eh-choh kohn kohm-poo-tah-doh-rahs* What work did you do with computers?
Inés:	**He trabajado en captura de datos y también en procesar textos.** *eh trah-bvah-Hah-doh ehn kahp-too-rah de dah-tohs ee tahm-bveeehn ehn proh-seh-sahr tehks-tohs* I've done data processing, as well as word processing.
Manager:	**¿Le ha tocado hacer diseño?** *leh ah toh-kah-doh ah-sehr dee-seh-nyoh* Have you done any design?
Inés:	**Sí, el año pasado hice un curso especial.** *see ehl ah-nyoh pah-sah-doh ee-seh oon koor-soh ehs-peh-seeahl* Yes, last year I took a special course.
Manager:	**¿Maneja usted el correo electrónico?** *mah-neh-Hah oos-tehd ehl koh-rreh-oh eh-lehk-troh-nee-koh* Do you handle e-mail?
Inés:	**Sí. También manejo otros programas. Mi anterior jefe era diseñador de programas.** *see tahm-bveeehn mah-neh-Hoh oh-trohs proh-grah-mahs mee ahn-teh-ree-ohr Heh-feh eh-rah dee-seh-nyah-dohr deh proh-grah-mahs* Yes, and also other programs. My previous boss was a programmer.

Words to Know

la computadora	lah kohm-poo-tah-_doh_-rah	the computer
la captura	lah kahp-_too_-rah	the capture (in computer speak: processing)
los textos	lohs _teks_-tohs	the texts (in computer speak: words)
el diseño	ehl dee-_seh_-nyoh	the design
el curso	ehl _koor_-soh	the course
manejar	mah-neh-_Hahr_	to handle; to drive (a car)
programar	proh-grah-_mahr_	to program; to make software
el programa	ehl proh-_grah_-mah	the software

Talkin' the Talk

No business is safe from meetings. Here, Sr. Alvarez, the CEO of the company, and his assistant Julia try to quickly set up a meeting to discuss new developments.

Sr. Alvarez: **Quiero organizar una reunión para el miércoles. Quiero que esté todo el personal de gerencia.**
keee_eh_-roh ohr-gah-nee-_sahr_ _oo_-nah rehoo-nee_ohn_ _pah_-rah ehl meee_ehr_-koh-lehs keee_eh_-roh keh ehs-_teh_ _toh_-doh ehl pehr-soh-_nahl_ deh Heh-_rehn_-seeah
I want to arrange a meeting for Wednesday with all the managerial staff.

Julia: **Usted tiene disponible dos horas en la tarde.**
oos-_tehd_ teee_eh_-neh dees-poh-_nee_-bvleh dohs _oh_-rahs ehn lah _tahr_-deh
You have two hours available in the afternoon.

Sr. Alvarez:	**Bien. Póngala en la sala de conferencias.**
	bveeehn pohn-gah-lah ehn lah sah-lah deh kohn-feh-rehn-seeahs
	Good. Put it into the conference room.
Julia:	**El miércoles, de cuatro a seis de la tarde en la sala de conferencias.**
	ehl meeehr-koh-lehs deh kooah-troh ah sehees deh lah tahr-deh ehn lah sah-lah deh kohn-feh-rehn-seeas
	Wednesday, from four to six p.m. in the conference room.
Sr. Alvarez:	**Avise por fax a mi socio, por favor y recuérdeme el día antes.**
	ah-bvee-seh pohr fahks ah mee soh-seeoh pohr fah-bvohr ee reh-koo-ehr-deh-meh ehl deeah ahn-tehs
	Please let my partner know, via fax, and remind me the day before.
Julia:	**Sin falta.**
	seen fahl-tah
	Without fail.

CULTURAL WISDOM

A proverb: Let them eat cake

Here are some Spanish proverbs for your amusement. These may be similar to some proverbs you already know.

✔ **A falta de pan buenas son las tortas.** (*ah fahl-tah deh pahn bvooeh-nahs sohn lahs tohr-tahs*) (Literally: If there's no bread, cake will do.)

This translation works everywhere, except in Mexico, where **torta** is the word for sandwich in a bun. In Mexico the proverb goes:

✔ **A falta de pan, tortillas.** (*ah fahl-tah deh pahn, torh-tee-yahs*) (Literally: If there's no cake, tortillas [maize flatbread] will do.)

In both cases, the English proverb equivalent is: Half a loaf is better than none.

Another Spanish proverb conveys the same message:

✔ **Más vale pájaro en mano, que cien volando.** (*mahs bvah-leh pah-Hah-roh ehn mah-noh keh seeehn bvoh-lahn-doh* (Literally: A bird in hand is worth more than one hundred flying.)

The English equivalent is: A bird in hand is worth two in the bush. (The Spanish version is more emphatic — Spanish speakers love drama.)

Words to Know

el archivo	ehl ahr-_chee_-bvoh	the file
la base de datos	lah _bvah_-seh de _dah_-tohs	the data base
imprimir	eem-pree-_meer_	to print
teclear	tehk-leh-ahr	to type
el teclado	ehl tehk-_lah_-doh	the keyboard
enviar	ehn-bveeahr	to send
quedarse	keh-_dahr_-seh	to stay
el compromiso	ehl kohm-proh-_mee_-soh	the commitment; the engagement; plans
el informe	ehl een-_fohr_-meh	the report
junto	Hoon-toh	together

Talkin' the Talk

The meeting time arrives. All the managers — male and female — are together. (The plural for mixed company in Spanish is in the male form.)

CEO: **Señores, ante todo agradezco su presencia. Estamos aquí por un asunto de importancia. Estamos considerando este contrato.**
seh-_nyoh_-rehs _ahn_-teh _toh_-doh ah-grah-_dehs_-koh soo preh-_sehn_-seeah ehs-_tah_-mohs ah-_kee_-pohr oon ah-_soon_-toh deh eem-pohr-_tahn_-seeah ehs-_tah_-mohs kohn-see-deh-_rahn_-doh _ehs_-teh kohn-_trah_-toh
Ladies and gentlemen, I first want to thank you for coming. We're here for an important matter: We're considering this contract.

Ingeniero Gutiérrez: **¿Señor Presidente, se ha firmado algo ya?**
seh-nyohr preh-see-dehn-teh seh ah
feer-mah-doh ahl-goh yah
Mr. President, has anything been signed yet?

CEO: **No, no hemos firmado nada. Quiero consultar con ustedes primero y también quiero
consultar con nuestros abogados.**
*noh noh eh-mohs feer-mah-doh nah-dah
keeeh-roh kohn-sool-tahr kohn oos-teh-dehs
pree-meh-roh ee tahm-bveeehn keeeh-roh
kohn-sool-tahr kohn nooehs-trohs ah-bvoh-
gah-dohs*
No, we haven't signed anything. I want to
consult with you first, and I also want to consult with our lawyers.

CEO: **Señorita Julia, tome nota para las actas de la
reunión.**
*seh-nyoh-ree-tah Hoo-leeah toh-meh
noh-tah pah-rah lahs ahk-tahs deh lah
rehoo-neeohn*
Miss Julia, take minutes of the meeting.

Julia Fernández: **Lo tengo grabado.**
loh tehn-goh grah-bvah-doh
I've taped it.

Words to Know

el asunto	ehl ah-soon-toh	the matter
firmar	feer-mahr	to sign
consultar	koh-sool-tahr	to consult
el abogado	ehl ah-bvoh-gah-doh	the lawyer
grabar	grah-bvahr	to tape

Some Typical Phrases or Idioms: Asunto

The following phrases include the word **asunto** *(ah-soon-toh)* (matter; business; that which concerns you). In some parts of South America, **asunto** can replace the phrase "what for."

✔ **Estoy hablando de asuntos de negocios.** *(ehs-tohy ah-bvlahn-doh deh ah-soon-tohs deh neh-goh-seeohs)* (I'm talking about business matters.)

✔ **¡No es asunto tuyo!** *(noh ehs ah-soon-toh too-yoh)* (It's none of your business!)

✔ **¡Si pelean, les quito la pelota y asunto concluído!** *(see peh-leh-ahn lehs kee-toh lah peh-loh-tah ee ah-soon-toh kohn-klooee-doh)* (If you fight, I'll take the ball away, and that's the end of that!)

✔ **¿A asunto de qué le dijiste?** *(ah ah-soon-toh deh keh leh dee-Hees-teh)* (Why'd you tell him?)

In Chapter 5 you find the conjugation of the verb **tomar** *(toh-mahr)* (to take). You can also use **tomar** as a drinking verb, meaning "to drink." However, it's primary meaning is "to take," as when the chief executive urges the secretary to take notes.

Using Emplear: The Hiring Verb

Emplear *(ehm-pleh-ahr)* (to employ; to hire; to use) is a multifaceted verb. This regular verb uses the root **emple-** *(ehm-pleh)*. Here's how you conjugate **emplear:**

Conjugation	Pronunciation
yo empleo	yoh ehm-pleh-oh
tú empleas	too ehm-pleh-ahs
él, ella, ello, uno, usted emplea	ehl eh-yah eh-yoh oo-noh oos-tehd ehm-pleh-ah
nosotros empleamos	noh-soh-trohs ehm-pleh-ah-mohs
vosotros empleáis	bvoh-soh-trohs ehm-pleh-ah-ees
ellos, ellas, ustedes emplean	eh-yohs eh-yahs oos-teh-dehs ehm-leh-ahn

Here are some phrases to help you practice using **emplear:**

✔ **La fábrica emplea cincuenta operarios.** *(lah fah-bvree-kah ehm-pleh-ah seen-kooehn-tah oh-peh-rah-reeohs)* (The factory employs 50 workers.)

- **Nosotros empleamos dos horas en el trabajo.** *(noh-soh-trohs ehm-pleh-ah-mohs dohs oh-rahs ehn ehl trah-bvah-Hoh)* (It took us two hours to do the work.)

- **Van a emplearlos en un taller.** *(bvahn ah ehm-pleh-ahr-lohs ehn oon tah-yehr)* (They're going to hire them in a [work]shop.)

- **Esa computadora se emplea para diseñar.** *(eh-sah kohm-poo-tah-doh-rah seh ehm-pleh-ah pah-rah dee-seh-nyahr)* (That computer is used for design work.)

- **Queremos emplear personas responsables.** *(keh-reh-mohs ehm-pleh-ahr pehr-soh-nahs rehs-pohn-sah-bvlehs)* (We want to employ responsible people.)

- **Emplean sólo personas de confianza.** *(ehm-pleh-ahn soh-loh pehr-soh-nahs deh kohn-feeahn-sah)* (They only employ dependable people.)

- **La emplean porque es persona con quien se puede contar.** *(lah ehm-pleh-ahn pohr-keh ehs pehr-soh-nah kohn keeehn seh pooeh-deh kohn-tahr)* (They employ her because they can count on her.)

Talkin' the Talk

Workers sometimes find their jobs through hearsay. In the following dialog, several positions are open in a furniture factory:

Catalina: **En esa fábrica emplean gente.**
ehn eh-sah fah-bvree-kah ehm-pleh-ahn Hehn-teh
That factory is hiring.

Baltasar: **¿Qué producen allí?**
keh proh-doo-sehn ahee
What do they make there?

Catalina: **Es una fábrica de muebles.**
ehs oo-nah fah-bvree-kah deh mooeh-bvlehs
It's a furniture factory.

Baltasar: **¿Qué empleos ofrecen?**
keh ehm-pleh-ohs oh-freh-sehn
What jobs do they have open?

Catalina: **Hay un empleo de oficina y otro en la planta.**
ahy oon ehm-pleh-oh deh oh-fee-see-nah ee oh-troh ehn lah plahn-tah
There's an office job and another in the shop.

Baltasar: **El de la planta me interesa. Yo tengo experiencia de tornero.**
ehl deh lah <u>plahn</u>-tah meh een-teh-<u>reh</u>-sah yoh tehn-goh ehks-peh-ree<u>ehn</u>-seeah deh tohr-<u>neh</u>-roh
I'm interested in the one in the plant. I have experience operating a lathe.

Catalina: **¿Por qué no pides información?**
pohr keh noh <u>pee</u>-dehs een-fohr-mah-see-<u>ohn</u>
Why don't you ask for information?

Baltasar: **Allá voy.**
ah-<u>yah</u> bvohy
I'm on my way.

Words to Know

la fábrica	lah <u>fah</u>-bvree-kah	the factory
producir	proh-doo-<u>seer</u>	to produce; to make
el mueble	ehl moo<u>eh</u>-bvleh	the furniture (Literally: the movable)
el empleo	ehl ehm-<u>pleh</u>-oh	the employment; the job
la planta	lah <u>plahn</u>-tah	the plant (as in a factory)
interesar	een-the-reh-<u>sahr</u>	to interest
pedir	peh-<u>deer</u>	to ask for
ofrecer	oh-freh-<u>sehr</u>	to offer

Hacer: The Doing, Making Verb

Like most of the verbs that you have to use frequently, **hacer** *(ah-<u>sehr</u>)* (to do; to make) is a very irregular verb, changing its root from pronoun to pronoun and from tense to tense.

Hacer's root, **hac-** transforms and deforms itself within the first person singular. Here's how you conjugate **hacer** in the present tense:

Conjugation	*Pronunciation*
yo hago	yoh <u>ah</u>-goh
tú haces	too <u>ah</u>-sehs
él, ella, ello, uno, usted hace	ehl <u>eh</u>-yah <u>eh</u>-yoh <u>oo</u>-noh, oos-<u>tehd</u> <u>ah</u>-seh
nosotros hacemos	noh-<u>soh</u>-trohs ah-<u>seh</u>-mohs
vosotros hacéis	bvoh-<u>soh</u>-trohs hah-<u>seh</u>ees
ellos, ellas, ustedes hacen	<u>eh</u>-yohs <u>eh</u>-yahs oos-<u>teh</u>-dehs <u>ah</u>-sehn

Here are some phrases you can use to practice the verb **hacer:**

- **Carlos hace muebles.** *(<u>kahr</u>-lohs <u>ah</u>-seh moo<u>eh</u>-bvlehs)* (Carlos makes furniture.)

- **Nosotros hacemos nuestro pan.** *(noh-<u>soh</u>-trohs ah-<u>seh</u>-mohs noo<u>ehs</u>-troh pahn)* (We make our own bread.)

- **Todos hacen cola.** *(<u>toh</u>-dohs <u>ah</u>-sehn <u>koh</u>-lah)* (They all line up. [Literally: They all make a tail.])

- **Tú haces mucha comida.** *(too <u>ah</u>-sehs <u>moo</u>-chah koh-<u>mee</u>-dah)* (You make a lot of food.)

- **No tiene nada que hacer.** *(noh tee<u>eh</u>-neh <u>nah</u>-dah keh <u>ah</u>-sehr)* (He has nothing to do.)

- **No hacemos nada malo.** *(noh ah-<u>seh</u>-mohs <u>nah</u>-dah <u>mah</u>-loh)* (We're doing no harm [Literally: bad].)

- **Ignacio hace casas de adobe.** *(eeg-<u>nah</u>-seeoh <u>ah</u>-seh <u>kah</u>-sahs deh ah-<u>doh</u>-bveh)* (Ignacio makes adobe houses.)

- **Rosa María hace bellos jardines.** *(<u>roh</u>-sah mah-<u>reeah</u> <u>ah</u>-seh <u>bveh</u>-yohs Har-<u>dee</u>-nehs)* (Rosa María makes beautiful gardens.)

Speaking of Houses . . .

La casa *(lah <u>kah</u>-sah)* (the house): These words express in Spanish what you call home in English. **La casa** can also express the building in which you make your home.

The Spanish word **el hogar** *(ehl-oh-gahr)* (the home) is closest in meaning to "the hearth" in English. **El hogar** invokes the fire in a shelter where warmth and food are offered. **El hogar** is a place of warmth during the cold days, a place to stay dry during rain and snow, a place of repose when you're tired, a place of joy during the many happy events of your life.

Use the following phrases to discuss your house and home:

- ✔ **Hogar dulce hogar.** *(oh-gahr dool-seh oh-gahr)* (Home sweet home.)

- ✔ **Especialidad de la casa.** *(ehs-peh-seeah-lee-dahd deh lah kah-sah)* (Specialty of the house.)

- ✔ **Un error grande como una casa.** *(oon eh-rrohr grahn-deh koh-moh oo-nah kah-sah)* (An immense mistake. [Literally: A mistake the size of a house.])

- ✔ **Anda como Pedro por su casa.** *(ahn-dah koh-moh peh-droh pohr soo kah-sah)* (Acts like he owns the place. [Literally: Goes about like Pedro in his house.])

- ✔ **Mudarse de casa.** *(moo-dahr-seh deh kah-sah)* (To move. [Literally: To change houses.])

Some rental wisdom

Almost everyone must search for a new home sooner or later. And with the world rapidly becoming one global village, you may find yourself living in a Spanish-speaking country some day (or in some close-by neighborhood in the States where many Spanish-speaking people live). This section covers the ins and outs of searching for a new place to live.

Find out from friends or people from whom you're not renting the rules for rentals in the country that you're going to stay. For example, in most Latin American countries, rental does not include appliances, unless you rent a fully furnished house or apartment. Likewise, heating, water supply, and so on aren't always included in the cost of rent.

Therefore, when you rent, you need to think about the added cost of hooking up utilities. (In most places electricity is expensive, so you cook and heat your water with gas.)

Because water isn't drinkable everywhere, you're not always going to be able to use the water from the tap for drinking and cooking. Therefore, you also need to consider that you may have to buy your drinking water, generally in large (20-liter/5-gallon) bottles. Although bottled water isn't a great expense, you must consider the cost of buying your drinking water with the price of rent.

In countries where the currency isn't stable, you may have difficulty negotiating a lease that lasts more than six months, unless the lease is for commercial use.

More likely than not, you're going to begin living on your own in a rented property, which can include several different kinds of housing. Use the following phrases to help you with your search:

- **edificio de apartamentos** *(eh-dee-fee-seeoh deh ah-pahr-tah-mehn-tohs)* (apartment building)

- **casa de una planta** *(kah-sah deh oo-nah plahn-tah)* (one-story house)

- **casa de dos pisos** *(kah-sah deh dohs pee-sohs)* (two-story house)

- **casa adosada** *(kah-sah ah-doh-sah-dah)* (semi-detached house [meaning one of its walls touches the wall of the neighboring house])

- **casa residencial** *(kah-sah reh-see-dehn-seeahl)* (residence; house used for residential purposes)

- **apartamento en arriendo** *(ah-pahr-tah-mehn-toh ehn ah-rreeehn-doh)* (apartment for rent)

- **apartamento en régimen de propiedad horizontal** *(ah-pahr-tah-mehn-toh ehn reh-Hee-mehn deh proh-peeeh-dahd oh-ree-sohn-tahl)* (condominium) Literally, this phrase means an apartment that is governed by a set of rules related to horizontal — meaning on the ground — real estate.

Rental offices are very useful. They can cost a little, but they also save a great deal of footwork. Knowing your needs, rental offices can recommend spaces that fit your requirements. Use the following phrases to convey the urgency of your need for a dwelling to call your own:

- **Sin falta necesito un apartamento.** *(seen fahl-tah neh-seh-see-toh oon ah-pahr-tah-mehn-toh)* (I absolutely [literally: without fail] need an apartment.)

- **Es urgente encontrar un apartamento.** *(ehs oor-Hehn-teh ehn-kohn-trahr oon ah-pahr-tah-mehn-toh)* (We must find an apartment urgently.)

- **Como tenemos niños, debemos encontrar una casa.** *(koh-moh teh-neh-mohs nee-nyohs deh-bveh-mohs ehn-kohn-trahr oo-nah kah-sah)* (Because we have children, we must find a house.)

- **Hay que preguntar a los amigos.** *(ahy keh preh-goon-tahr ah lohs ah-mee-gohs)* (We must ask our friends [to help us find a place].)

- **Hay que ver los avisos del diario.** *(ahy keh bvehr lohs ah-bvee-sohs dehl deeah-reeoh)* (We must look at the ads in the papers.)

If you plan to buy a house or land, make sure that you first find out what kind of legal steps are necessary to give you ownership. The rules for house or land ownership vary from country to country and from year to year. Some countries welcome foreign buyers, but others resist them. A notary public is probably your best source for this kind of information.

Words to Know

falta	fahl-tah	lack of something
urgente	oor-Hehn-teh	urgent
encontrar	ehn-kohn-trahr	to find

Talkin' the Talk

Jeff and Lydia have been hired as consultants to a company in Bolivia, and they need to find an apartment fast. They're interested in an apartment they found in an ad in the paper, and they're ready to check it out:

Jeff and Lydia: **Vimos su aviso en el diario y llamamos por el apartamento. ¿Está disponible aún?**
bvee-mohs soo ah-bvee-soh ehn ehl deeah-reeoh ee yah-mah-mos pohr ehl ah-pahr-tah-mehn-toh ehs-tah dees-poh-nee-bleh ahoon
We saw your ad in the paper, and we're calling about the apartment. Is it still available?

Margarita: **No, ya se ocupó.**
noh, yah seh oh-koo-poh
No, it's already taken.

Jeff and Lydia: **Ah, qué lástima, gracias.**
ah keh lahs-tee-mah, grah-seeahs
Oh, that's a shame. Thank you.

Margarita: **Les recomiendo ese otro apartamento.**
lehs reh-koh-mee<u>ehn</u>-doh <u>eh</u>-seh <u>oh</u>-tro
ah-pahr-tah-<u>mehn</u>-toh
I recommend the other apartment.

Jeff and Lydia: **¿Cuándo podemos verlo?**
koo<u>ahn</u>-doh poh-<u>deh</u>-mohs <u>bvehr</u>-loh
When can we see it?

Margarita: **Mañana en la tarde se desocupa. Luego se va a pintar. El martes pueden verlo.**
mah-<u>nyah</u>-nah ehn lah <u>tahr</u>-deh seh
dehs-oh-<u>koo</u>-pah loo<u>eh</u>-goh seh bvah ah peen-<u>tahr</u>
ehl <u>mahr</u>-tehs poo<u>eh</u>-dehn <u>bvehr</u>-loh
It will be vacant tomorrow afternoon. Then it will be painted. You can see it on Tuesday.

CULTURAL WISDOM

Whose house?

In Mexico, many natives use the phrase **la casa de usted** *(lah <u>kah</u>-sah deh oos-<u>tehd</u>)*, which literally translates to "your house" or "your home." However, Mexicans use this phrase to express the generous implication that the house of the person speaking is also the house of the person invited. This phrase leads to lots of funny confusions. Susana, one of the authors, tells the following story:

When I first received an invitation in Mexico to visit someone, I was invited to dinner in the following manner:

La espero a comer en la casa de usted. *(lah ehs-<u>peh</u>-roh ah koh-<u>mehr</u> ehn lah <u>kah</u>-sah*

deh oos-<u>tehd</u>) (Literally: I'm expecting you [formal] to dinner at your house.)

My first and rather alarmed understanding of the invitation was that somehow, the person expected to have the meal in my house, with me as the chef. However, the invitation meant no such thing. I learned this the hard way though, because as I was waiting for my friend to come to the dinner I managed to improvise, she phoned to tell me she was still waiting for me, as the invitation was to *her* house. By using **la casa de usted**, she wanted me to feel as though I were in my own home.

Words to Know

disponible	dees-poh-<u>nee</u>-bvleh	available
ocupar	oh-koo-<u>pahr</u>	to take up; to occupy
desocupar	dehs-oh-koo-<u>pahr</u>	to vacate
lástima	<u>lahs</u>-tee-mah	pity; shame
pintar	peen-<u>tahr</u>	to paint

Talkin' the Talk

In the following dialog, Liliana and Juan are looking at an apartment that they know is vacant.

Liliana y Juan: **Venimos a ver el apartamento.**
bveh-<u>nee</u>-mohs ah bvehr ehl ah-pahr-tah-<u>mehn</u>-toh
We came to see the apartment.

Lupe: **Aquí está.**
ah-<u>kee</u> ehs-<u>tah</u>
Here it is.

Liliana y Juan: **¿Cuánto cuesta?**
koo<u>ahn</u>-toh koo<u>ehs</u>-tah
How much does it cost?

Lupe: **Cinco mil pesos al mes.**
<u>seen</u>-koh meel <u>peh</u>-sohs ahl mehs
Five thousand pesos a month.

Liliana y Juan: **¿El gas y el agua están incluídos en el arriendo?**
ehl gahs ee ehl <u>ah</u>-gooah ehs-<u>tahn</u>
een-kloo<u>ee</u>-dohs ehn ehl ah-rree<u>ehn</u>-doh
Are gas and water included in the rent?

Lupe:	**No, el gas y el agua lo pagan ustedes. Aquí están los medidores.**
	noh ehl gahs ee ehl ah-gooah loh pah-gahn oos-teh-dehs ah-kee ehs-tahn lohs meh-dee-doh-rehs
	No, you pay the gas and water. Here are the meters.
Liliana y Juan:	**¿Se necesita hacer un depósito?**
	Se neh-seh-see-tah ah-sehr oon deh-poh-see-toh
	Do we have to give you a down payment?
Lupe:	**Sí, necesito un depósito de cinco mil pesos, más el primer mes.**
	see neh-seh-see-toh oon deh-poh-see-toh deh seen-koh meel peh-sohs, mahs ehl pree-mehr mehs
	Yes, I need a down payment of five thousand pesos and the first month's rent.
Liliana y Juan:	**Vamos a pensarlo, mañana volvemos.**
	bvah-mohs ah pehn-sahr-loh mah-nyah-nah bvohl-bveh-mohs
	We're going to think about it. We'll come back tomorrow.

CULTURAL WISDOM

Four house-related proverbs

Though proverbs often contain wisdom, some of them can be fun as well. Here are four house-related proverbs that you may enjoy:

✔ **Echar la casa por la ventana.** *(eh-chahr lah kah-sah pohr lah bvehn-tah-nah)* (Literally: To throw the house out the window.) Use this proverb to express that you're doing things in a big way — when you're preparing a superb party, for example.

✔ **Empezar la casa por el tejado.** *(ehm-peh-sahr lah kah-sah pohr ehl teh-Hah-doh)* (Literally: To start the house at the roof.) The English equivalent of this proverb is: To put the cart before the horse.

✔ **En casa de herrero, cuchillo de palo.** *(ehn kah-sah deh eh-rreh-roh koo-chee-yoh de pah-loh)* (Literally: In the blacksmith's house, a knife of wood.) The English equivalent of this proverb is: The shoemaker's son always goes barefoot.

✔ **A quien se muda, Dios lo ayuda.** *(ah keeehn seh moo-dah deeohs loh ah-yoo-dah)* (God helps those who move.) If you've ever moved from one house to another, you can probably appreciate this one!

Some Variations on the Renting Verb

Spanish has two words that mean "to rent": **rentar** *(rehn-tahr)*, which is used in Mexico, and **arrendar** *(ah-rrehn-dahr)*, which is used mostly everywhere else. Following are examples of both:

✔ **Aquí se rentan carros.** *(ah-kee seh rehn-tahn kah-rrohs)*
   (They rent cars here [Mexico].)

✔ **Aquí se arriendan autos.** *(ah-kee seh ah-rreeehn-dahn ahoo-tohs)*
   (They rent cars here. [Most of the rest of Spanish-speaking America.])

✔ **Necesito rentar una casa.** *(neh-seh-see-toh rehn-tahr oo-nah kah-sah)*
   (I need to rent a house.)

✔ **Aquí arriendan apartamentos.** *(ah-kee ah-rreeehn-dahn ah-pahr-tah-mehn-tohs)* (They rent apartments here.)

✔ **Emilia arrienda una casa.** *(eh-meh-leeah ah-rreeehn-dah oo-nah kah-sah)*
   (Emilia rents a house.)

Arrendar *(ah-rrehn-dahr)* (to rent) is an irregular verb. However, **arrendar** is very useful when you're looking for a dwelling or car to loan or rent. Use the following conjugation to help you rent a dwelling, car, and so on:

Conjugation	Pronunciation
yo arriendo	yoh ah-rreeehn-doh
tú arriendas	too ah-rreeehn-dahs
él, ella, ello, uno, usted arrienda	ehl eh-yah eh-yoh oo-noh oos-tehd ah-rreeehn-dah
nosotros arrendamos	noh-soh-trohs ah-rrehn-dah-mohs
vosotros arrendáis	bvoh-soh-trohs ah-rrehn-dahees
ellos, ellas, ustedes arriendan	eh-yohs eh-yahs oos-teh-dehs ah-rreeehn-dahn

Here are some phrases to use when practicing **arrendar**:

✔ **Mi tía arrienda su casa.** *(mee tee-ah ah-rreeehn-dah soo kah-sah)*
   (My aunt rents her house.)

✔ **Julio y María arriendan un apartamento.** *(Hoo-leeoh ee mah-reeah ah-rreeehn dahn oon ah-pahr-tah-mehn-toh)* (Julio and María rent an apartment.)

✔ **Voy a arrendar un auto.** *(bvohy ah ah-rehn-dahr oon ahoo-toh)*
   (I'm going to rent a car.)

✔ **Tú arriendas en una zona cara.** *(too ah-rree<u>ehn</u>-dahs ehn <u>oo</u>-nah <u>soh</u>-nah <u>kah</u>-rah)* (You rent in an expensive area.)

✔ **Nosotros arrendamos un cuarto.** *(noh-<u>soh</u>-trohs ah-rrehn-<u>dah</u>-mohs oon koo<u>ahr</u>-toh)* (We rent a room.)

Talkin' the Talk

You can also go to a rental office to look for furnished apartments. Use the following dialog as a guideline for the conversation you may have with the rental office employee. Conrado is looking for an apartment in a high-rise building.

Conrado:	**Busco un apartamento amueblado.** *<u>bvoos</u>-koh oon-ah-pahr-tah-<u>mehn</u>-toh ah-mooeh-<u>bvlah</u>-doh* I'm looking for a furnished apartment.
Rental agent:	**Tenemos uno en el noveno piso.** *teh-<u>neh</u>-mohs <u>oo</u>-noh ehn ehl noh-<u>bveh</u>-noh <u>pee</u>-soh* We have one on the ninth floor.
Conrado:	**¿Está disponible?** *ehs-<u>tah</u> dees-poh-<u>nee</u>-bvleh* Is it available?
Rental agent:	**Sí, se limpió bien y está disponible.** *see seh leem-pee <u>oh</u> bveeehn ee ehs-<u>tah</u> dees-poh-<u>nee</u>-bvleh* Yes, it's been cleaned well and is available.
Conrado:	**Me gusta; lo voy a tomar.** *meh <u>goos</u>-tah loh bvohy ah <u>toh</u>-mahr* I like it; I'll take it.

GRAMMATICALLY SPEAKING

Three for one

Spanish has three words for "room." You can take your pick from any of them:

✔ **la habitación** *(lah ah-bvee-tah-see<u>ohn</u>)*

✔ **la pieza** *(la pee<u>eh</u>-sah)*

✔ **el cuarto** *(ehl koo<u>ahr</u>-toh)*

Words to Know

el depósito	ehl deh-<u>poh</u>-see-toh	the deposit
reembolsar	reh-ehm-bvol-<u>sahr</u>	to refund
incluido	een-kloo<u>ee</u>-doh	included
pagar	<u>pah</u>-gahr	to pay
amueblado	ah-mooeh-<u>bvlah</u>-doh	furnished
limpiar	leem-pee<u>ahr</u>	to clean

Talkin' the Talk

Instead of renting an apartment, you may want to rent a house. Although renting a house may be a bit costlier and take more work, it's worth the trouble. Here, Victoria is discussing a house rental in Chile.

Victoria: **Esta casa ¿cuántos baños tiene?**
<u>ehs</u>-tah <u>kah</u>-sah koo<u>ahn</u>-tohs <u>bvah</u>-nyohs tee<u>eh</u>-neh
How many bathrooms does this house have?

Owner: **Hay dos baños: el baño principal y el baño del servicio**
ahy dohs <u>bvah</u>-nyohs ehl <u>bvah</u>-nyoh preen-see-<u>pahl</u>
ee ehl <u>bvah</u>-nyoh dehl sehr-<u>bvee</u>-seeoh
There are two bathrooms: the main bathroom and the servant's bathroom.

Victoria: **¿Dónde está la cocina?**
<u>dohn</u>-deh ehs-<u>tah</u> lah koh-<u>see</u>-nah
Where's the kitchen?

Owner: **Por aquí.**
pohr ah-<u>kee</u>
This way.

Victoria: **¿Hay cocina a gas o eléctrica?**
ahy koh-<u>see</u>-nah ah gahs oh eh-<u>lehk</u>-tree-kah
Is there a gas or electric stove?

Owner: **No, la cocina la debe instalar usted.**
*noh lah koh-<u>see</u>-nah lah <u>deh</u>-beh eens-tah-<u>lahr</u>
oos-<u>tehd</u>*
No, you have to have the stove put in.

Victoria: **¿Cuántas habitaciones hay?**
koo<u>ahn</u>-tahs ah-bvee-tah-see<u>oh</u>-nehs ahy
How many rooms are there?

Owner: **Está el living, el comedor, un dormitorio y la pieza del
servicio.**
*ehs-<u>tah</u> ehl <u>lee</u>-bveeng ehl koh-meh-<u>dohr</u> oon
dohr-mee-<u>toh</u>-reeoh ee lah peee<u>eh</u>-sah dehl
sehr-<u>bvee</u>-seeoh*
There's the living room, the dining room, one bedroom, and the servant's room.

Words to Know

la cocina	lah koh-<u>see</u>-nah	the stove; the kitchen
la habitación	lah ah-bvee-tah -<u>seeohn</u>	the room
el living	ehl <u>lee</u>-bveeng	the living room (in Chile)
el comedor	ehl koh-meh-<u>dohr</u>	the dining room
el dormitorio	ehl dohr-mee-<u>toh</u>-reeoh	the bedroom (in Chile and Argentina)
la recámara	lah reh-<u>kah</u>-mah-rah	the bedroom (in Mexico)
la sala	lah <u>sah</u>-lah	the living room
el refrigerador	ehl reh-free-Heh-rah-<u>dohr</u>	the refrigerator

Words to Know

la piscina	lah pees-<u>see</u>-nah	the swimming pool
pavimentado	pah-bvee-mehn-<u>tah</u>-doh	paved
la sombra	lah <u>sohm</u>-brah	the shade; the shadow

Talkin' the Talk

 Sonia is showing Juan her new house. Juan is especially impressed by the garden.

Juan Ignacio: **Lo bello de aquí es el jardín.**
loh <u>bveh</u>-yoh deh ah-<u>kee</u> ehs ehl Hahr-<u>deen</u>
The beauty here is the garden.

Sonia: **Sí, los jardines agregan mucho a una casa.**
see lohs Hahr-<u>dee</u>-nehs ah-<u>greh</u>-gahn <u>moo</u>-choh ah <u>oo</u>-nah <u>kah</u>-sah
Yes, gardens add a lot to a house.

Juan Ignacio: **Este jardín está muy bien diseñado.**
<u>ehs</u>-teh Hahr-<u>deen</u> ehs-<u>tah</u> mooy bveeehn dee-seh-<u>nyah</u>-doh
This garden is very well designed.

Sonia: **Al fondo del jardín hay una piscina. Está pavimentado alrededor de la piscina.**
ahl <u>fohn</u>-doh dehl Hahr-<u>deen</u> ahy <u>oo</u>-nah pees-<u>see</u>-nah ehs-<u>tah</u> pah-bvee-mehn-tah-doh ahl-reh-deh-<u>dohr</u> deh lah pees-<u>see</u>-nah
At the back of the garden there's a swimming pool. It's paved around the swimming pool.

Juan Ignacio: **El pasto del jardín está bien cuidado.**
ehl <u>pahs</u>-toh dehl Hahr-<u>deen</u> ehs-<u>tah</u> bveeehn kooee-<u>dah</u>-doh
The garden is well tended.

Sonia: **Las flores son todas tropicales.**
lahs <u>floh</u>-rehs sohn <u>toh</u>-dahs troh-pee-<u>kah</u>-lehs
All the flowers are tropical.

Juan Ignacio: **Hay árboles que dan buena sombra.**
ahy <u>ahr</u>-bvoh-lehs keh dahn bvoo<u>eh</u>-nah <u>sohm</u>-bvrah
There are good shade trees.

Words to Know

el tamaño	ehl tah-<u>mah</u>-nyoh	the size
el ascensor	ehl ah-sehn-<u>sohr</u>	the elevator
la vista	lah <u>bvees</u>-tah	the view
los baños	lohs <u>bvah</u>-nyohs	the bathrooms
medio baño	<u>meh</u>-deeoh <u>bvah</u>-nyoh	half-bathroom (a bathroom with no shower or tub)
la cocina	lah koh-<u>see</u>-nah	the kitchen
la estufa	lah ehs-<u>too</u>-fah	the stove (in Mexico)
la calefacción	lah kah-leh-fahk-<u>seeohn</u>	the heating

Fun & Games

Fernando, Claudia, and their dog, Perro, have just moved into the house you see below. A solid line points to various rooms or items in the home. Please provide the Spanish word for those items. (If you really want to challenge yourself, look at the mini–dictionary or elsewhere in this book, and try to name several other items in the home as well.)

Part III
Spanish on the Go

The 5th Wave
By Rich Tennant

"I just think if we're going to be in a foreign country, we should know their units of measurement better. By the way, how's your Espresso Grande?"

In this part . . .

This part gives you the tools you need to take your Spanish on the road, whether it's to a local Spanish restaurant or to a museum in Mexico. This part is devoted to the traveler in you, helping you to survive the Customs process, check into hotels, nab a taxi, exchange dollars for pesos, and have a great time doing it. Sprinkled throughout are cultural tidbits that introduce you to people, places, and things that are important in Spanish-speaking cultures.

Chapter 11

Money, Money, Money

- -

- -

*Y*ou worked hard, you paid your dues, you made that money. But you didn't go through all that effort just for the money. You worked for the money because it gives you the means to get what you need and to do what you wish.

All of your frustrations in accessing your money have to do with the fact that, without money, you cannot provide for a need or a wish. When you are away from home, you especially want to avoid this kind of frustration. In this chapter, you discover all the money-handling knowledge you need in all those Spanish-speaking places you plan to visit.

You probably made your money in dollars (U.S. or Canadian). If you're traveling in Latin America, you may feel that you should not and cannot use your dollars the way you would at home. This is not completely true, as this chapter shows, and financial transactions are quite a lot easier than you may suppose. That's good news!

You can think about money as fun — when you have it — and as a problem — when you lose it. We talk about the losing bit in Chapter 16, so we'll try to roll out the red carpet treatment here for the fun part.

Salary, a word you know in English, is **salario** *(sah-lah-reeoh)* in Spanish and comes from the word **sal** *(sahl)* (salt). In the times of the Romans, some people were paid for their work with salt — valuable because you can't live without it.

Because you must carry some cash, here are a few cash-carrying terms:

✔ **dinero en efectivo** *(dee-neh-roh ehn eh-fehk-tee-bvoh)* (money in cash)

✔ **en billetes** *(ehn bvee-yeh-tehs)* (in bills)

- ✔ **en monedas** *(ehn moh-neh-dahs)* (in coins)

- ✔ **una moneda de oro** *(oo-nah moh-neh-dah deh oh-roh)* (a gold coin)

- ✔ **la moneda de plata** *(lah moh-neh-dah deh plah-tah)* (the silver coin)

The following little cash-carrying phrases also may come in handy:

- ✔ **¿Traes algún dinero?** *(trah-ehs ahl-goon dee-neh-roh)*
  (Do you have any money?)

- ✔ **¿Tienes dinero en efectivo?** *(teeeh-nehs dee-neh-roh ehn eh-fehk-tee-bvoh)* (Do you have cash?)

- ✔ **¿Tiene una moneda de cincuenta centavos?**
  (teeeh-neh oo-nah moh-neh-dah deh seen-kooehn-tah sehn-tah-bvohs)
  (Do you have a fifty-cent coin?)

- ✔ **No tenemos monedas.** *(noh teh-neh-mohs moh-neh-dahs)*
  (We have no coins.)

- ✔ **Necesitan dos monedas de diez centavos.**
  (neh-seh-see-tahn dohs moh-neh-dahs deh deeehs sehn-tah-bvohs)
  (They need two ten-cent coins.)

- ✔ **Pagamos con dos billetes de veinte pesos.**
  (pah-gah-mohs kohn dohs bvee-yeh-tehs deh bveheen-teh peh-sohs)
  (We paid with two twenty-peso bills.)

- ✔ **Aquí tiene un billete de cien colones.**
  (ah-kee teeeh-neh oon bvee-yeh-teh deh seeehn koh-loh-nehs)
  (Here you have a hundred colon bill.)

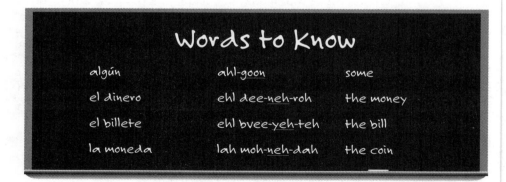

Words to Know

algún	ahl-goon	some
el dinero	ehl dee-neh-roh	the money
el billete	ehl bvee-yeh-teh	the bill
la moneda	lah moh-neh-dah	the coin

Using the ATM

When they're in working order, those bank machines known as ATMs (automated teller machines) can be a great way to handle your money. And more than 90 percent of the time, they do work very well.

ATM machines are now available in cities and at resorts almost all over the world. ATM machines are the simplest and most discreet way to access your funds.

You can use your banking card and your credit card at the ATM. Simply go to the machine, punch in your personal identification number (PIN), get cash in the local currency, and on you go.

The exchange rate you get at the ATM is definitely the most favorable, because it's bank exchange — between the other bank and yours — which is better than what you get at other currency-exchanging outlets.

On some occasions, the ATM may not work or may be out of cash. Or it can happen that the computer systems of the banks involved cannot communicate (talk about not understanding a language!). When those situations happen, you can access your money only by using your credit card. These are also times when your traveler's checks come in handy.

I've seen ATMs that flash their signals in both Spanish and English. Just in case yours doesn't have the English display, here are the sentences you see in the order in which they appear:

- **Introduzca su tarjeta por favor.** *(een-troh-doos-kah soo tahr-Heh-tah pohr-fah-bvohr)* (Insert your card please.)

- **Por favor teclee su número confidencial.** *(pohr fah-bvohr teh-kleh-eh soo noo-meh-roh kohn-fee-dehn-seeahl)* (Please type your PIN.)

At this point, you have to press the button that reads: **Continuar** *(kohn-tee-nooahr)* (Continue; keep going.) After you press the button, the following choices appear:

- **Retiro en efectivo** *(reh-tee-roh ehn eh-fehk-tee-bvoh)* (Cash withdrawal)

  If you choose cash withdrawal, these other choices come up:

  - **Tarjeta de crédito** *(tahr-Heh-tah deh kreh-dee-toh)* (Credit card)
  - **Cuenta de cheques** *(kooehn-tah deh cheh-kehs)* (Checking account)
  - **Débito/inversiones** *(deh-bvee-toh/een-bvehr-seeoh-nehs)* (Debit/investments)

- **Consulta de saldo** *(kohn-sool-tah deh sahl-doh)* (Checking your balance)

If you're slow about pressing those buttons, these signs came up:

- **¿Requiere más tiempo?** *(reh-kee<u>eh</u>-reh mahs tee<u>ehm</u>-poh?):* Do you need more time?
- **Sí/No** *(see/noh)* (Yes/No)

If you press yes, you go back to the previous screen. When this happens, choose **cuenta de cheques** *(koo<u>ehn</u>-tah deh <u>cheh</u>-kehs),* which gives you choices for cash:

- **100, 200, 300, 400, 500, 1000, 1500**
- **¿Otra cantidad?** *(<u>oh</u>-trah kahn-tee-<u>dahd</u>)* (Another amount?)

Press the key for the desired amount, and your money comes out. Then the following messages come up:

- **Entregado** *(ehn-treh-<u>gah</u>-doh)* (Delivered)
- **Saldo** *(<u>sahl</u>-doh):* (Balance)
- **Por favor tome su dinero** *(pohr fah-<u>bvohr</u> <u>toh</u>-meh soo dee-<u>neh</u>-roh)* (Please take your money)

 Keep all the receipts that ATMs deliver. If you get no receipt or if your trip to the ATM was unsuccessful, be sure to write down the place, time, and date. When you arrive home, check everything against your bank statement. Also, be sure to check that no amount was debited to you on those occasions when you received no money from the ATM machine. Follow your bank's procedures if you see any discrepancies.

Words to Know

introducir	een-troh-doo-<u>seer</u>	insert
retiro	reh-<u>tee</u>-roh	withdrawal
saldo	<u>sahl</u>-doh	balance
cuenta	koo<u>ehn</u>-tah	account
débito	<u>deh</u>-bvee-toh	debit
cantidad	kahn-tee-<u>dahd</u>	quantity; amount
entregar	ehn-treh-<u>gahr</u>	to deliver

Using Your Credit Card

Credit cards are a safe, clean way of handling your money. Paying with your credit card has many advantages. One of them is that you don't have to carry cash; another is that your expenses are registered in your account. Plus, you always have a valid receipt. Problems arise only when you go to a place that does not take credit cards or that doesn't take the one you have.

Be aware that places that take credit cards are a bit pricier than the ones that don't. You can eat at restaurants that don't take credit cards and have excellent food and service for a lot less money.

Talkin' the Talk

 In this dialog, Juan wants to pay for his purchase in a store. Here's how he finds out whether the store accepts his credit card.

Juan: **¿Aceptan tarjetas de crédito?**
ah-_sehp_-tahn tahr-_Heh_-tahs deh _kreh_-dee-toh
Do you take credit cards?

Storekeeper: **Con mucho gusto.**
kohn _moo_-choh _goos_-toh
With pleasure.

Juan: **Aquí tiene mi tarjeta.**
ah-_kee_ tee_eh_-neh mee tahr-_Heh_-tah
Here is my card.

Storekeeper: **Un momento, ya vuelvo con su recibo**
oon moh-_mehn_-toh, yah bvoo_ehl_-bvoh kohn soo reh-_see_-bvoh
One moment, I'm coming back with your receipt.

Firme aquí, por favor.
feer-meh ah-_kee_, pohr fah-_bvohr_
Sign here, please.

Aquí tiene su tarjeta y su recibo. Gracias.
ah-_kee_ tee_eh_-neh soo tahr-_Heh_-tah ee soo reh-_see_-bvoh _grah_-seeahs
Here's your card and your receipt. Thank you.

Words to Know

servir	sehr-bveer	to serve; to be of service
la tarjeta	lah tahr-Heh-tah	the card
el recibo	ehl reh-see-bvoh	the receipt
firmar	feer-mahr	to sign
la autorización	lah ahoo-toh-ree-sah-seeohn	the authorization
la ventanilla	lah bvehn-tah-nee-yah	the little window
la identificación	lah ee-dehn-tee-fee-kah-seeohn	the identification

Banking with your credit card at an ATM in Latin America isn't very different from the banking you do at home with your bank card. But if you want to get some cash directly from a bank with your credit card, you need to know a little bit of Spanish.

Getting cash with your credit card can take a little while because the bank must check to see whether the money you request is available. If the bank does not have a direct electronic line to your credit card company, it has to phone the company directly to get authorization. This process takes a bit of time, so be patient.

Using Travelers' Checks

Travelers' checks are another safe way to carry your money. One inconvenience of traveler's checks is that you need to find the right place to cash them. Banks do, and many money exchange places do as well. The better hotels also take travelers' checks.

Less expensive hotels, restaurants, and most stores do not take traveler's checks. Try to exchange them before you go on your forays, and take just moderate amounts of cash with you.

Talkin' the Talk

 In the following dialog, Ana Maria is at a bank to cash in some travelers' checks.

Ana María: **¿A cuánto el dólar de cheque de viajero?**
ah kooahn-toh ehl doh-lahr deh cheh-keh deh bveeah-Heh-roh
What's the exchange per dollar for traveler's checks?

Cashier: **A nueve sesenta.**
ah nooeh-bveh seh-sehn-tah
At nine sixty.

Ana María: **Quiero cambiar estos cheques de viajero.**
keeeh-roh kahm-bveeahr ehs-tohs cheh-kehs deh bveeah-Heh-roh
I want to cash these travelers' checks

Cashier: **¿Tiene sus documentos, por favor?**
teeeh-neh soos doh-koo-mehn-tohs pohr fah-bvohr
Do you have your identification please?

Ana María: **Mi pasaporte.**
mee pah-sah-pohr-teh
My passport.

Cashier: **Muy bien. Ahora puede firmar sus cheques.**
mooy bveeehn ah-oh-rah pooeh-deh feer-mahr soos cheh-kehs
Very good. Now you may sign your checks.

Words to Know

el viajero	ehl bveeah-<u>Heh</u>-roh	the traveler
a cuánto	ah koo-ahn-toh	for how much
cambiar	kahm-bvee-ahr	to change
el mostrador the	ehl mohs-trah-dohr	the counter (literally: place where you show)
los documentos	lohs doh-koo-mehn-tohs	identification (literally: documents)

Using the Verb Cambiar (To Exchange)

In Spanish, to change and to exchange are expressed with the same verb, **cambiar** *(kahm-bvee-<u>ahr</u>)* (to change, to exchange). It is the verb for doing both. **Cambiar** is a regular verb, and its root is **cambi-** *(kahm-bvee)*. Here's how you conjugate its present tense:

Conjugation	*Pronunciation*
yo cambio	yoh <u>kahm</u>-bveeoh
tú cambias	too <u>kahm</u>-bveeahs
él, ella, ello, uno, usted cambia	ehl, <u>eh</u>-yah, <u>eh</u>-yoh, <u>oo</u>-noh, oos-<u>tehd</u> <u>kahm</u>-bveeah
nosotros cambiamos	noh-<u>soh</u>-trohs kahm-bvee<u>ah</u>-mohs
vosotros cambiáis	bvoh-<u>soh</u>-trohs kahm-bvee<u>ah</u>ees
ellos, ellas, ustedes cambian	eh-yohs, <u>eh</u>-yahs, oos-<u>teh</u>-dehs <u>kahm</u>-bveeahn

Try the following phrases to practice using **cambiar:**

- ✔ **En esa ventanilla cambian monedas.** *(ehn <u>eh</u>-sah bvehn-tah-<u>nee</u>-yah <u>kahm</u>-bveeahn moh-<u>neh</u>-dahs)* (At that window, they change coins.)

- ✔ **Quiero cambiar bolívares por dólares.**
  (kee<u>eh</u>-roh kahm-bvee<u>ahr</u> bvoh-<u>lee</u>-bvah-rehs pohr <u>doh</u>-lah-rehs)
  (I want to exchange bolivars for dollars.)

✔ **La casa de cambio te puede cambiar tus dólares.** *(lah kah-sah deh kahm-bveeoh teh pooeh-deh kahm-bveeahr toos doh-lah-rehs)* (The exchange bureau can exchange your dollars.)

✔ **En el banco cambian dólares.** *(ehn ehl bvahn-koh kahm-bveeahn doh-lah-rehs)* (At the bank you can exchange [your dollars].)

✔ **Es muy alta la comisión con que cambian.** *(ehs mooy ahl-tah la koh-mee-seeohn kohn keh kahm-bveeahn)* (The commission they charge for the exchange is too high.)

The person who lends or exchanges money is called **el cambista** *(ehl kahm-bvees-tah)* (money changer).

Exchanging Your Dollars for the Local Currency

Each country has its own currency. When you travel, you need to use the local currency to make your transactions. Don't use your dollars to buy goods or services because the exchange won't be advantageous.

When you want to exchange your dollars for the local currency, take a look at the signs telling you how much you'll get for your dollar. At stores, restaurants, and such, the amount of local money you get for your dollar is less than what exchange bureaus or banks give you. So your purchase may be more expensive than if you pay in local money.

Banks and exchange bureaus charge a fee for their services; the fee is reflected in the way they chart their prices. Check those charts first. In some areas, the banks might be more expensive than the exchange bureaus because they charge some extra amount or commission; in other areas, this situation might be reversed. In any case you will see signs stating, for example:

Dollar USA   Buy 9.70   Sell 9.80

What this means is that the company or banks buys your dollars for 9.70 of the local currency. And if you want to buy dollars, they'll charge you 9.80. So they are making ten cents of their currency on every dollar they handle.

The exchange bureaus give you formal receipts, just as banks do; these receipts are the proofs of purchase that you need when you discover that something is amiss with your money. So instead of exchanging your money on the street, look for the sign that says **cambio** *(kahm-bveeoh)* (exchange).

These phrases come in handy when exchanging money:

- ✔ **¿Dónde puedo cambiar dólares?** *(dohn-deh pooeh-doh kahm-bveeahr doh-lah-rehs)* (Where can I exchange dollars?)

- ✔ **Una cuadra a la derecha hay una agencia.** *(oo-nah kooah-drah ah lah deh-reh-chah ahy oo-nah ah-Hehn-seeah)* (One block to the right, there's an exchange bureau.)

- ✔ **Dónde encuentro una casa de cambio?** *(dohn-deh ehn-kooehn-troh oo-nah kah-sah deh kahm-bveeoh)* (Where can I find a place to exchange money?)

Words to Know

la cuadra	lah kooah-drah	the block
derecha	deh-reh-chah	right
la agencia	ah-Hehn-seeah	the agency
encontrar	ehn-kohn-trahr	to find

Talkin' the Talk

In this conversation, José Manuel exchanges some currency:

José Manuel: **¿A cuánto está el dólar americano?**
*ah kooahn-toh ehs-tah ehl doh-lahr
ah-meh-ree-kah-noh*
What's the exchange for the U.S. dollar?

Bureau attendant: **¿A la compra o a la venta?**
ah lah kohm-prah oh ah lah bvehn-tah
Buying or selling?

José Manuel: **A la venta.**
ah lah bvehn-tah
Selling.

Bureau attendant: **A nueve ochenta.**
ah nooeh-bveh oh-chehn-tah
At nine eighty.

José Manuel:	**¿Y a la compra?**
	ee ah lah <u>kohm</u>-prah
	And buying?

Bureau attendant:	**A nueve setenta.**
	ah noo<u>eh</u>-bveh seh-<u>tehn</u>-tah
	At nine seventy.

José Manuel:	**¿Me cambia cien, por favor?**
	meh <u>kahm</u>-bveeah see<u>eh</u>n poh fah-<u>bvohr</u>
	Will you exchange me one hundred, please?

Bureau attendant:	**Cómo no, aquí tiene el recibo, aquí el dinero.**
	<u>koh</u>-moh noh, ah-kee-tee<u>eh</u>-neh ehl reh-<u>see</u>-bvoh ah-kee ehl dee-<u>neh</u>-roh
	Sure, here's the receipt, here's the money.

Currency Wise: Impressing Friends with Latin American Currencies

How can you impress your friends? Just ask them things like, "What is the name of the currency in Ecuador?"

Take a look at the following list and then amaze your friends. Here are the names of many currencies:

- ✔ **La moneda de Argentina es el peso.** *(lah moh-<u>neh</u>-dah deh ahr-Hehn-<u>tee</u>-nah ehs ehl <u>peh</u>-soh)* (The currency of Argentina is the peso.)

- ✔ **En Bolivia se usa el peso boliviano.** *(ehn bvoh-<u>lee</u>-bveeah seh <u>oo</u>-sah ehl <u>peh</u>-soh bvoh-lee-bvee<u>ah</u>-noh)* (In Bolivia they use the Bolivian peso.)

- ✔ **La moneda de Colombia también se llama peso.** *(lah moh-<u>neh</u>-dah deh koh-<u>lohm</u>-bveeah tahm-bvee<u>ehn</u> seh <u>yah</u>-mah <u>peh</u>-soh)* (The currency of Colombia is also called peso.)

- ✔ **En Chile pagan sus cuentas con pesos chilenos.** *(ehn <u>chee</u>-leh <u>pah</u>-gahn soos koo<u>eh</u>-tahns kohn <u>peh</u>-sohs chee-<u>leh</u>-nohs)* (In Chile they pay their bills with Chilean pesos.)

- ✔ **En Costa Rica la moneda que usan se llama colón.** *(ehn <u>kohs</u>-tah <u>ree</u>-kah lah moh-<u>neh</u>-dah keh <u>oo</u>-sahn seh <u>yah</u>-mah koh-<u>lohn</u>)* (In Costa Rica the currency they use is called the colón.)

- ✔ **La moneda de Cuba sigue siendo el peso.** *(lah moh-<u>neh</u>-dah deh <u>koo</u>-bvah <u>see</u>-gheh see<u>eh</u>n-doh ehl <u>peh</u>-soh)* (The Cuban currency is still the peso.)

✔ **En Ecuador la moneda que se usa se llama sucre.** *(ehn eh-kooah-dohr lah-moh-neh-dah keh seh oo-sah seh yah-mah soo-kreh)* (In Ecuador the currency in use is called the Sucre.)

✔ **La moneda de El Salvador, como la de Costa Rica, se llama colón.** *(lah moh-neh-dah deh ehl sahl-bvah-dohr koh-moh lah deh kohs-tah ree-kah seh yah-mah koh-lohn)* (El Salvador's currency, like that of Costa Rica, is called the colón.)

✔ **Guatemala tiene la moneda con el bello nombre: Quetzal.** *(gooah-teh-mah-lah teeeh-neh lah moh-neh-dah kohn ehl bveh-yoh nohm-bvreh keh-tsahl)* (Guatemala has a currency with a beautiful name: Quetzal.)

✔ **Honduras usa una moneda de nombre extraño: Lempira.** *(ohn-doo-rahs oo-sah oo-nah moh-neh-dah deh nohm-bvreh ehks-trah-nyoh lehm-pee-rah)* (Honduras uses a currency with a strange name: Lempira.)

✔ **En México se usa el peso.** *(ehn meh-Hee-koh seh oo-sah ehl peh-soh)* (In Mexico they use the peso.)

✔ **En Nicaragua se paga con córdobas.** *(ehn nee-kah-rah-gooah seh pah-gah kohn kohr-doh-bvahs)* (In Nicaragua you pay with córdobas.)

✔ **En Panama se paga con balboas.** *(ehn pah-nah-mah seh pah-gah kohn bvahl-bvoh-ahs)* (In Panama you pay with balboas.)

✔ **Puerto Rico usa el dólar Americano.** *(pooehr-toh ree-koh oo-sah ehl doh-lahr ah-meh-ree-kah-noh)* (Puerto Rico uses the U.S. dollar.)

✔ **El Guaraní es la moneda del Paraguay.** *(ehl gooah-rah-nee ehs lah moh-neh-dah dehl pah-rah-gooahy)* (The guaraní is the Paraguayan currency.)

✔ **En Perú compré con soles.** *(ehn peh-roo kohm-preh kohn soh-lehs)* (In Peru I purchased with sols.)

✔ **El peso pasa por la República Dominicana.** *(ehl peh-soh pah-sah pohr lah reh-poo-bvlee-kah doh-mee-nee-kah-nah)* (The Peso is used throughout the Dominican Republic.)

✔ **En Uruguay se compra la leche con pesos.** *(ehn oo-roo-gooahy seh kohm-prah lah leh-cheh kohn peh-sohs)* (In Uruguay you buy milk with pesos.)

✔ **En Venezuela se ganan el pan en bolivares.** *(ehn bveh-neh-sooeh-lah seh gah-nahn ehl pahn ehn bvoh-lee-bvah-rehs)* (In Venezuela they make their dough [*Literally:* they earn their bread] with bolivars.)

✔ **En España se usa la peseta.** *(ehn ehs-pah-nyah seh oo-sah lah peh-seh-tah)* (In Spain they use the peseta.)

CULTURAL WISDOM

What's in a name?

The names of currencies tell some tales, revealing things like weight measures and history. So to further impress your friends, here is some wisdom about where currency names come from.

Peso *(peh-soh),* means "weight." It relates to the original gold-coin currency, which actually weighed **un peso,** or one weight.

Bolívar *(boh-lee-bvahr)* comes from Simón Bolívar *(see-mohn bvoh-lee-bvahr),* who was born in what is today Venezuela. He was a great general, winning independence from Spain for Venezuela, Colombia, and other South American countries. Incidentally, Bolivia, the country, takes its name from Simón Bolívar.

Sucre *(soo-kreh)* takes its name from Antonio José de Sucre *(ahn-toh-neeoh Hoh-seh deh soo-kreh),* also from Venezuela. He liberated Ecuador and Peru from Spanish rule and became president of Bolivia. He was a close collaborator of Bolívar's.

Balboa *(bvahl-bvoh-ah)* comes from Vasco Núñez deh Balboa *(bvahs-koh noo-nyes deh bvahl-bvoh-ah),* who crossed the mosquito-infested lowlands of what is now Honduras and Panama. He discovered the ocean he named **Pacific.**

Guaraní *(gooah-rah-nee),* the coin, is also the name of both a people and the language they speak. In pre-Columbian times, **los guaraníes** *(lohs gooah-rah-neeehs)* navigated the rivers from Paraguay deep into the Amazon.

Sol *(sohl),* literally meaning sun, is the name of the Peruvian currency that honors Inti, the Incan god of the sun.

Colón *(koh-lohn),* the currency of Costa Rica and El Salvador, is the Spanish form of Columbus, the person considered the discoverer of the Americas.

Quetzal *(keh-tsahl)* is the name of a wondrous bird with vividly green feathers much appreciated by the discerning Maya and Aztec monarchs of old.

Lempira *(lehm-pee-rah)* is the name of a Honduran chief who fought the invading Spaniards. The region in western Honduras, where opal mines are found, also bears his name.

Córdoba *(kohr-doh-bvah)* is a beautiful city in Spain. The homesick Spaniards, like some homesick English, named many places after the cities they were missing. Many cities in Latin America are called **Córdoba.** And the word is also used to designate the currency of Nicaragua.

FUN & GAMES

• •

A quick-change artist (aren't we punny?) has rearranged the letters in several Spanish words below. Unscramble the words and then match them with their English translation.

al promca	account
al tanev	balance
cibore	bills
damones	cash
dolsa	coins
entuac	credit card
ernoid	money
jetarat ed drotice	PIN number
le canob	receipt
ne votecife	the bank
romeun fendicclaon	the purchase
sibellet	the sale
tireor	withdrawal

• •

Chapter 12

¿Dónde Está? (Where Is It?): Asking Directions

"*L*et's go" is your motto for walking about, riding about, or finding places to go. But where you should go requires asking an important question. In Spanish, that question is ¿**dónde?** (_dohn-deh_) (where).

¿Dónde? The Question for Going Places:

Consider the question:

¿**A dónde ir?** (_ah dohn-deh eer?_) (Where are you going?)

Where is one of the big questions, the wandering question, the question that answers your need to experience places that can give you a sense of wonder, a sense of the new.

Where is the question of movement, *where* concerns displacement, *where* is what you ask when you seek the unknown other place, the place where desire takes you.

Where is the question that makes searchers and explorers conquer our planet and unravel its mysteries. For example, the question, "Where do I go for pepper?" has led seafarers to travel around Africa, cross the oceans, and discover the American continent. Likewise, the question, "Where do these people come from?" is the question that creates new connections between nations.

Of course, most times asking *where* simply helps you find what you are looking for, and takes you to a place quite ordinary but most necessary. Where would we be without *where?* The following sections help you practice using *where* in Spanish-speaking countries.

¿Adónde Vamos? Where Do We Go?

In Chapter 3, you find out about the Spanish verb that you most often associate with the question **¿dónde?** *(dohn-deh)* (where). Because looking for directions is a sign of movement, and because most of us consider moving a nonpermanent state of being, **dónde** is associated with **estar** *(ehs-tahr)*, the verb that means "to be" in a temporary state.

Sample the following sentences that use *¿dónde?* and *estar*:

- ✔ **¿Dónde está el Museo de Larco?** *(donh-deh ehs-tah ehl moo-seh-oh deh lahr-koh* (Where is the Larco Museum?)

- ✔ **¿Dónde estamos ahora?** *(dohn-deh ehs-tah-mohs ah-oh-rah)* (Where are we now?)

- ✔ **¿Dónde está el Hotel del Camino?** *(dohn-deh ehs-tah ehl oh-tehl dehl kah-mee-noh)* (Where is the Hotel del Camino?)

- ✔ **¿Dónde estuviste anoche?** *(dohn-deh ehs-too-bvees-teh ah-noh-cheh)* (Where were you last night?)

And here is a sentence for the person who wants to know everything:

¡Quiero saber el cómo, el cuándo, y el dónde! *(keeeh-roh sah-bvehr ehl koh-moh ehl kooahn-doh ee ehl dohn-deh)* (I want to know the how, the when, and the where!)

You can use another line to express your determination to find that special place:

¡Dondequiera que esté, lo encontraremos! *(donh-deh-keeeh-rah keh ehs-teh, loh ehn-kohn-trah-reh-mohs)* (Wherever it is, we'll find it!)

Where in Your Body: Orienting Space to Your Person

You can identify the space around your body in six ways:

✔ **delante** *(deh-lahn-teh)* (in front)

- **Paula camina delante de Clara.** *(pahoo-lah kah-mee-nah deh-lahn-teh deh klah-rah)* (Paula walks in front of Clara.)

✔ **detrás** *(deh-trahs)* (behind)

- **Clara va detrás de Paula.** *(klah-rah bvah deh-trahs deh pahoo-lah)* (Clara goes behind Paula.)

✔ **a la derecha** *(ah-lah deh-reh-chah)* (to the right)

- **A la derecha de Paula está Felipe.** *(ah lah deh-reh-chah deh pahoo-lah ehs-tah feh-lee-peh)* (To the right of Paula is Felipe.)

✔ **a la izquierda** *(ah lah ees-keeehr-dah)* (to the left)

- **José se pone a la izquierda de Clara.** *(Hoh-seh seh poh-neh ah lah ees-keeehr-dah deh klah-rah)* (José gets [Literally: he puts himself] to the left of Clara.)

✔ **debajo** *(deh-bvah-Hoh)* (beneath; under)

- **Hay pasto debajo de los pies de José.** *(ahy pahs-toh deh-bvah-Hoh deh lohs peeehs deh Hoh-seh)* (There's grass under Jose's feet.)

✔ **encima** *(ehn-see-mah)* (above)

- **La rama está encima de la cabeza de Paula.** *(lah rah-mah ehs-tah ehn-seez-mah deh lah kah-bveh-sah deh pahoo-lah)* (The branch is above Paula's head.)

Before you go any further, you need to understand the distinction between two very similar words: **derecho** *(deh-reh-choh)* (straight) and **derecha** *(deh-reh-chah)* (right).

What was that, you say? Look again. The only difference between the words is that one word ends in *o* and the other in *a,* and the meaning is no longer the same!

✔ **derecho** *(deh-reh-choh)* (straight; straight ahead)

- **Siga derecho por esta calle.** *(see-gah deh-reh-choh pohr ehs-tah kah-yeh)* (Keep going straight on this street.)

✔ **derecha** *(deh-reh-chah)* (right)

- **En la esquina doble a la derecha.** *(ehn lah ehs-kee-nah doh-bvleh ah lah deh-reh-chah)* (At the corner turn to the right.)

Talkin' the Talk

After checking in at her hotel, Catalina asks the hotel receptionist for directions to the restaurant and the pool.

Catalina: **¿Dónde está el restaurante?**
<u>dohn</u>-deh ehs-<u>tah</u> ehl rehs-tahoo-<u>rahn</u>-teh
Where's the restaurant?

Receptionist: **Está arriba, en el segundo piso.**
ehs-<u>tah</u> ah-<u>rree</u>-bvah ehn ehl seh-<u>goon</u>-doh <u>pee</u>-soh
It's upstairs, on the second floor.

Catalina: **¿En qué piso está la piscina?**
ehn keh <u>pee</u>-soh ehs-<u>tah</u> lah pee-<u>see</u>-na
On what floor is the pool?

Receptionist: **Está en el quinto piso . . .**
ehs-<u>tah</u> ehn ehl <u>keen</u>-toh <u>pee</u>-soh . . .
It's on the fifth floor

Puede tomar el ascensor.
poo<u>eh</u>-deh toh-<u>mahr</u> ehl ah-sehn-<u>sohr</u>
You may take the elevator.

Catalina: **¿Y cómo llego al ascensor?**
ee <u>koh</u>-moh <u>yeh</u>-goh ahl ah-sehn-<u>sohr</u>
How do I get to the elevator?

Receptionist **El ascensor está ahí, a la izquierda.**
ehl ah-sehn-<u>sohr</u> ehs-<u>tah</u> ah-<u>kee</u> ah lah
ees-kee<u>ehr</u>-dah
The elevator is here, to the left.

Understanding Spatial Directions

We use words to tell where people or things are in relation to other people and things. You can use these terms to describe the relationships.

- **al lado** (*ahl <u>lah</u>-doh*) (beside, next to, at the side of)
- **al frente** (*ahl <u>frehn</u>-teh*) (in front of)
- **dentro** (*<u>dehn</u>-troh*) (inside)

- **adentro** *(ah-dehn-troh)* (inside; because **dentro** also means "inside," **adentro** may express movement, as when someone or something moves toward an interior)
- **fuera** *(fooeh-rah)* (outside)
- **afuera** *(ah-fooeh-rah)* (outside; can express movement, as in the case of **adentro** — the fourth bullet point in this list)
- **bajo** *(bvah-Hoh)* (under; below)
- **debajo** *(deh-bvah-Hoh)* (underneath)
- **arriba** *(ah-ree-bvah)* (above)

Practicing these directions comes in handy. The sentences that follow use spatial-direction terms:

- **La pastelería está al lado del banco.** *(lah-pahs-teh-leh-reeah ehs-tah ahl lah-doh dehl bvahn-koh)* (The pastry shop is next to the bank.)
- **Al frente del banco hay una zapatería.** *(ahl frehn-teh dehl bvahn-koh ahy oo-nah sah-pah-teh-reeah)* (In front of the bank there is a shoe store.)
- **Las mesas del café están afuera.** *(lahs meh-sahs dehl kah-feh ehs-tahn ah-fooeh-rah)* (The tables of the cafe are outside.)
- **Cuando llueve ponen las mesas adentro.** *(kooahn-doh yooeh-bveh poh-nehn lahs meh-sahs ah-dehn-troh)* (When it rains they put the tables inside.)
- **Arriba hay cielo despejado.** *(ah-ree-bvah ahy see-eh-loh dehs-peh-Hah-doh)* (Above, the sky is clear.)
- **Hay agua bajo los pies de Carlos.** *(ahy ah-gooah bvah-Hoh lohs peeehs de kahr-lohs)* (There's water under Carlos's feet.)
- **Debajo de la calle corre el tren subterráneo.** *(deh-bvah-Hoh deh lah kah-yeh koh-rreh ehl trehn soobv-teh-rrah-neh-oh)* (The subway runs under the street.)
- **Este ascensor va arriba.** *(ehs-teh ah-sehn-sohr bvah ah-rree-bvah)* This elevator goes up.)
- **Hay un gato dentro de la caja.** *(ahy oon gah-toh dehn-troh deh lah kah-Hah)* (There's a cat inside the box.)

Words to Know

encontrar	ehn-kohn-trahr	to find
la rama	lah rah-mah	the branch
el pasto	ehl pahs-toh	the grass
la esquina	lah ehs-kee-nah	the corner
despejado	dehs-peh-Hah-doh	uncluttered; clear
correr	koh-rrehr	to run
la caja	lah kah-Hah	the box
lejano	leh-Hah-noh	distant; far

Mapping the Place

Maps are your keys to your getting around. The first thing you should ask for at your car rental office, or the first thing to buy on arrival in a city, is a map. You can get around more easily if you find your way on a map or if someone can show you on the map how to get to the place you are looking for.

Some directions are used throughout the world to explain how to get somewhere or find something by using the points on a compass. The following terms help you specify north from south and east from west:

- ✔ **el norte** *(ehl nohr-teh)* (the north)
- ✔ **el sur** *(ehl soor)* (the south)
- ✔ **el este** *(ehl ehs-teh)* (the east)
- ✔ **el oriente** *(ehl oh-reeehn-teh)* (the east [Literally: where the sun originates])
- ✔ **el oeste** *(ehl oh-ehs-teh)* (the west)
- ✔ **el poniente** *(ehl poh-neeehn-teh)* (the west [Literally: where the sun sets])

Here are some "mapping" phrases to practice:

- **La avenida Venus está al este de aquí.** (*lah ah-bveh-nee-dah bveh-noos ehs-tah ahl ehs-teh deh ah-kee*) (Venus Avenue is east of here.)

- **Al oeste se encuentra la calle Las Violetas.** (*ahl oh-ehs-teh seh ehn-kooehn-trah lah kah-yeh lahs bveeoh-leh-tahs*) (To the west is Violetas street.)

- **El parque está al norte.** (*ehl pahr-keh ehs-tah ahl nohr-teh*) (The park is at the north.)

- **Al sur se va hacia el río.** (*ahl soor seh bvah ah-see-ah ehl reeoh*) (To the south, is [Literally: one goes toward] the river.)

- **El oriente es donde el sol se levanta.** (*ehl oh-reeehn-teh ehs dohn-deh ehl sohl seh leh-bvahn-tah*) (The east is where the sun rises.)

- **El poniente es donde el sol se pone.** (*ehl poh-neeehn-teh ehs dohn-deh ehl sohl seh poh-neh*) (The west is where the sun sets.)

- **Jordania está en el Cercano Oriente.** (*Hohr-dah-neeah ehs-tah ehn ehl sehr-kah-noh oh-reeehn-teh*) (Jordan is in the Near East.)

- **China está en el Lejano Oriente.** (*chee-nah ehs-tah ehn ehl leh-Hah-noh oh-reeehn-teh*) (China is in the Far East.)

- **América está al oriente del Océano Pacífico.** (*ah-meh-ree-kah ehs-tah ahl oh-reeehn-teh dehl oh-seh-ah-noh pah-see-fee-koh*) (America is east of the Pacific Ocean.)

- **Asia está al poniente del océano.** (*ah-seeah ehs-tah ahl poh-neeehn-teh dehl oh-seh-ah-noh*) (Asia is west of the ocean.)

The following phrases are helpful when asking or giving general directions:

- **la calle** (*lah kah-yeh*) (the street)

- **la avenida** (*lah ah-bveh-nee-dah*) (the avenue)

- **el bulevar** (*ehl bvoo-leh-bvahr*) (the boulevard)

- **el río** (*ehl ree-oh*) (the river)

- **la plaza** (*lah plah-sah*) (the square)

- **el parque** (*ehl pahr-keh*) (the park)

- **el jardín** (*ehl Hahr-deen*) (the garden; sometimes a small park)

- **el barrio** (*ehl bvah-rreeoh*) (the neighborhood)

- **izquierda** (*ees-keeehr-dah*) (left)

- **derecha** (*deh-reh-chah*) (right)

- **derecho** (*deh-reh-choh*) (straight)

- **doblar** *(doh-bvlahr)* (to turn)
- **seguir** *(seh-gheer)* (to keep going)
- **la cuadra** *(lah kooah-drah)* (the block)
- **la manzana** *(lah mahn-sah-nah)* (the block)

Asking for directions is always a bit problematic. The people who answer your questions know the city and the answers seem so obvious to them! So to keep you going and to sharpen your ear, here are some phrases to practice.

- **En el barrio hay una avenida ancha.** *(ehn ehl bvah-rreeoh ahy oo-nah ah-bveh-nee-dah ahn-chah)* (In the neighborhood, there is a wide avenue.)
- **Nuestra calle va de norte a sur.** *(nooehs-trah kah-yeh bvah deh nohr-teh ah soor)* (Our street runs north-south.)
- **Mi tía vive en la Cerrada del Olivo.** *(mee teeah bvee-bveh ehn lah seh-rrah-dah dehl oh-lee-bvoh)* (My aunt lives at the Cerrada [street with no exit] del Olivo [olive tree].)
- **Junto al río hay un gran parque.** *(Hoon-toh ahl reeoh ahy oon grahn pahr-keh)* (On the river side there is a large park.)
- **La plaza está en el centro de la ciudad.** *(lah plah-sah ehs-tah ehn ehl sehn-troh deh lah seeoo-dahd)* (The square is in the center of the city.)
- **En el jardín hay juegos para niños.** *(ehn ehl Hahr-deen ahy Hooeh-gohs pah-rah nee-nyohs)* (In the small park, they have a children's playground.)
- **El Zócalo de México es una plaza enorme.** *(ehl soh-kah-loh deh meh-Hee-koh ehs oo-nah plah-sah eh-nohr-meh)* (The Zocalo in Mexico is an immense square.)
- **Esa avenida se llama La Alameda.** *(eh-sah ah-bveh-nee-dah seh yah-mah lah ah-lah-meh-dah)* (The name of that avenue is La Alameda [Poplar Grove].)

Talkin' the Talk

Ana Luisa is an artist who's anxious to visit the Graphics Museum. She plans to walk there from her hotel so she can avoid the heavy traffic.

Ana Luisa: **Disculpe, ¿cómo llego al Museo de la Estampa?**
dees-kool-peh koh-moh yeh-goh ahl moo-seh-oh deh lah ehs-tahm-pah
Excuse me, how do I get to the Graphics Museum?

Receptionist: **Muy fácil. Está muy cerca.**
mooy *fah*-seel esh-*tah* mooy *sehr*-kah
Very easy. It's very close.

Receptionist: **Sale del hotel.**
sah-leh dehl *oh*-tehl
You go out of the hotel.

Ana Luisa: **¿Dónde está la salida?**
dohn-deh ehs-*tah* lah sah-*lee*-dah
Where is the exit?

Receptionist: **La salida está a la derecha.**
lah sah-*lee*-dah ehs-*tah* ah lah deh-*reh*-chah
The exit is to the right.

Al salir va hacia la izquierda
ahl sah-*leer* bvah *ah*-seeah lah ees-kee*ehr*-dah
As you get out, you go to the left

camina hasta la segunda calle
kah-*mee*-nah *ahs*-tah lah seh-*goon*-dah *kah*-yeh
walk to the second street

da vuelta a la derecha, una cuadra
dah bvoo*ehl*-tah ah lah deh-*reh*-chah oo-nah
koo*ah*-drah
turn to the right, go one block

y llega al museo.
ee *yeh*-gah ahl moo-*seh*-oh
and you arrive at the museum.

Ana Luisa: **Gracias por su ayuda.**
grah-seeahs pohr soo ah-*yoo*-dah
Thanks for your help.

The Verb that Takes You Up: Subir

The following mini-table shows you how to conjugate the present tense of the verb **subir** *(soo-bveer)* (to go up; to ascend) — a very useful regular verb when you want to go up! I like the way it sounds, too. Its root is **sub-** *(soobv)*.

Conjugation	Pronunciation
yo sub**o**	yoh <u>soo</u>-bvoh
tú sub**es**	too <u>soo</u>-bvehs
él, ella, ello, uno, usted sub**e**	ehl, <u>eh</u>-yah, <u>eh</u>-yoh, <u>oo</u>-noh, oos-<u>tehd</u> <u>soo</u>-bveh
nosotros sub**imos**	noh-soh-trohs soo-<u>bvee</u>-mohs
vosotros sub**ís**	bvoh-<u>soh</u>-trohs soo-<u>bvees</u>
ellos, ellas, ustedes sub**en**	<u>eh</u>-yohs, <u>eh</u>-yahs, oos-<u>teh</u>-dehs <u>soo</u>-bvehn

Practicing verb conjugations is essential; that way, they soon become second nature. But until they do become second nature, here are some phrases to help you:

- **Suben por esa escalera.** *(<u>soo</u>-bvehn pohr <u>eh</u>-sah ehs-kah-<u>leh</u>-rah)* (They go up the stairs.)

- **Subes por esa calle, a la izquierda.** *(<u>soo</u>-bvehs pohr eh-sah <u>kah</u>-yeh, ah lah ees-kee<u>ehr</u>-dah)* (You go up on that street, to the left.)

- **Nosotros vamos a subir con ustedes.** *(noh-<u>soh</u>-trohs <u>bvah</u>-mohs ah soo-<u>bveer</u> kohn oos-<u>teh</u>-dehs)* (We're going to go up with you.)

- **El ascensor de la derecha sube.** *(ehl ah-sehn-<u>sohr</u> deh lah deh-<u>reh</u>-chah <u>soo</u>-bveh)* (The elevator to the right goes up.)

- **Yo subo allí todos los días.** *(yoh <u>soo</u>-bvoh ah-<u>yee</u> <u>toh</u>-dohs lohs deeahs)* (I go up there every day.)

The Verb that Goes Down: Bajar

What goes up, must come down, right? The "descending" verb is **bajar** *(bvah-<u>Hahr</u>)* (to go down.)

Bajar is a regular verb and its root is **baj-** *(bvahH)*. Here's how you conjugate **bajar** in the present tense:

Conjugation	Pronunciation
yo baj**o**	yoh <u>bvah</u> Hoh
tú baj**as**	too <u>bvah</u>-Hahs
él, ella, ello, uno, usted baj**a**	ehl, <u>eh</u>-yah, <u>eh</u>-yoh, <u>oo</u>-noh, oos-<u>tehd</u>, <u>bvah</u>-Hah
nosotros baj**amos**	noh-<u>soh</u>-trohs bvah-<u>Hah</u>-mohs
vosotros baj**áis**	bvoh-<u>soh</u>-trohs bvah-<u>Hah</u>ees
ellos, ellas, ustedes baj**an**	<u>eh</u>-yohs, <u>eh</u>-yahs, oos-<u>teh</u>-dehs <u>bvah</u>-Hahn

When you need to go down; right down you go! Practice, practice, practice!

- ✔ **Ella baja por la escalera.** *(eh-yah bvah-Hah pohr lah ehs-kah-leh-rah)* (She goes down the stairs.)

- ✔ **Bajamos por esta calle.** *(bvah-Hah-mohs pohr ehs-tah kah-yeh)* (We go down this street.)

- ✔ **Tú bajas del auto con el perro.** *(too bvah-Hahs dehl ahoo-toh kohn ehl peh-rroh)* (You leave [literally go down] the car with the dog.)

- ✔ **Dicen que ya van a bajar.** *(dee-sehn keh bvahn a bvah-Hahr)* (They say they are going to go down [to the lobby or some other lower area].)

- ✔ **Yo bajo de noche.** *(yoh bvah-Hoh deh noh-cheh)* (I go down by night.)

Here and There and Everywhere

An old saying has the confused person never knowing whether he's here or there. In Spanish, whether you're here or there doesn't matter — just choose the word you like, and end the confusion.

In Spanish, you can indicate *here* and *there* in two ways. Native Spanish speakers interchange *here* and *there* often, with no distinction between the two words. Here and there are adverbs; they always work in the vicinity of a verb and words that talk about space.

- ✔ **allá** *(ah-yah)* (there)

- ✔ **allí** *(ah-yee)* (there)

- ✔ **acá** *(ah-kah)* (here)

- ✔ **aquí** *(ah-kee)* (here)

To show that it makes no difference whether you use one of these pairs of words or the other, the following sentences enable you to practice situations in which you may use *here* or *there*:

- ✔ **Allí, en la esquina, está el banco.** *(ah-yee ehn lah ehs-kee-nah ehs-tah ehl bvan-koh)* (There, on the corner, is the bank.)

- ✔ **Allá van los turistas.** *(ah-yah bvahn lohs too-rees-tahs)* (There go the tourists.)

- ✔ **Aquí se come muy bien.** *(ah-kee seh koh-meh mooy bveehn)* (Here one eats very well.)

- ✔ **Acá está el museo.** *(ah-kah ehs-tah ehl moo-seh-oh)* (Here is the museum.)

- ✔ **¡Ven acá!** *(bvehn ah-kah)* (Come here!)

- ✔ **¡Corre allá!** *(koh-rreh ah-yah)* (Run there!)

Sometimes you talk about no-places and all-places: nowhere and everywhere, along with anywhere. You can use the following phrases to express the idea of all places or no particular places in Spanish:

- ✔ **en todas partes** *(ehn toh-dahs pahr-tehs)* (everywhere)
- ✔ **en ninguna parte** *(ehn neen-goo-nah pahr-teh)* (nowhere, anywhere)

The following sentences can help you practice using these phrases:

- ✔ **En todas partes hay gente simpática.** *(ehn toh-dahs pahr-tehs ahy Hehn-teh seem-pah-tee-kah)* (There are nice people everywhere.)
- ✔ **Busqué mis llaves por todas partes.** *(bvoos-keh mees yah-bvehs pohr toh-dahs pahr-tehs)* (I searched for my keys everywhere.)
- ✔ **En ninguna parte encuentro mis llaves.** *(ehn neen-goo-nah pahr-teh ehn-kooehn-troh mees yah-bvehs)* (I cannot find my keys anywhere.)
- ✔ **Mira por todas partes cuando busca algo.** *(mee-rah pohr toh-dahs pahr-tehs kooahn-doh bvoos-kah ahl-goh)* (He/she looks everywhere when searching for something.

Ordinal Numbers: The Big Countdown

You may identify what you did during the day by reciting what you did first, second, third, and so on. Those very words *first, second,* and *third* are ordinal numbers. They are different from *one, two* and *three;* they tell you order and sequence.

When given directions, you hear a lot of phrases describing things like the *third* block to the left or the *fourth* floor. So ordinal numbers are extremely useful. Here are the first ten:

- ✔ **primero** *(pree-meh-roh)* (first)
- ✔ **segundo** *(seh-goon-doh)* (second)
- ✔ **tercero** *(tehr-seh-roh)* (third)
- ✔ **cuarto** *(kooahr-toh)* (fourth)
- ✔ **quinto** *(keen-toh)* (fifth)
- ✔ **sexto** *(sehks-toh)* (sixth)
- ✔ **séptimo** *(sehp-tee-moh)* (seventh)
- ✔ **octavo** *(ohk-tah-bvoh)* (eighth)
- ✔ **noveno** *(noh-bveh-noh)* (ninth)
- ✔ **décimo** *(deh-see-moh)* (tenth)

Here are some phrases to help you practice using ordinal numbers:

- **Vivo en el octavo piso.** (*bvee-bvoh ehn ehl ohk-tah-bvoh pee-soh*) (I live on the eighth floor.)

- **En la tercera calle hay un museo.** (*ehn lah tehr-seh-rah kah-yeh ahy oon moo-seh-oh*) (At the third street there is a museum.)

- **Este es el cuarto cine que veo aquí.** (*ehs-teh ehs ehl kooahr-toh see-neh keh bveh-oh ah-kee*) (This is the fourth cinema I've seen here.)

- **En el primer piso hay una florería.** (*ehn ehl pree-mehr pee-soh ahy oo-nah floh-reh-reeah*) (On the first floor there is a flower shop.)

- **Voy a bajar al segundo piso.** (*bvohy ah bvah-Hahr ahl seh-goon-doh pee-soh*) (I'm going down to the second floor.)

- **La terraza está en el décimonoveno piso.** (*lah teh-rrah-sah ehs-tah ehn ehl deh-see-moh-noh-bveh-noh pee-soh*) (The terrace is on the nineteenth floor.)

Talkin' the Talk

Here's Ana Louisa, who just bought some postcards at a newsstand. But she also needs some stamps. She asks the newsstand attendant for directions to the post office.

Ana Luisa:	**¿Me puede decir dónde está la Oficina de Correos?**
	meh pooeh-deh deh-seer dohn-deh ehs-tah lah oh-fee-see-nah deh koh-rreh-ohs
	Can you tell me where the Post Office is?

Newsstand attendant:	**Está a tres cuadras.**
	ehs-tah a trehs kooah-drahs
	It's three blocks from here.
	Va derecho hasta la Catedral
	bvah deh-reh-choh ahs-tah lah kah-teh-drahl
	You go straight to the Cathedral
	sigue derecho al lado de la Catedral
	see-gheh deh-reh-choh ahl lah-doh deh lah kah-teh-drahl
	keep going straight on the side of the Cathedral

cruza la plaza, siempre derecho
kroo-sah lah plah-sah seeehm-preh
deh-reh-choh
cross the square, always straight ahead

y llega a la Oficina de Correos.
ee yeh-gah ah lah oh-fee-see-nah deh
koh-rreh-ohs
and you get to the Post Office.

Ana Luisa: **Muy gentil, muchas gracias.**
mooy Hehn-teel moo-chahs grah-seeahs
Very kind, thank you very much.

Cerca and Lejos: How Far Should You Go?

In this section, you can explore the words **cerca** (_sehr-kah_) (near; close) and **lejos** (_leh-Hohs_) (far). Use these two words when you want to discuss how great the distance, and the possible size of the effort, required to arrive at a specific place.

Talkin the Talk

Ines is deciding how to spend her day. Should she attend the cinema, visit a museum, or do both? First, she needs to find out how near these places are to her and to each other.

Ines: **¿Está lejos el cine Las Flores?**
ehs-tah leh-Hohs ehl see-neh lahs floh-rehs
Is the Las Flores cinema far?

Martine: **No está muy cerca . . .**
noh ehs-tah mooy sehr-kah . . .
No, it's quite near . . .

. . . a sólo dos cuadras.
ah soh-loh dohs kooah-drahs
. . . only two blocks away.

Ines: **¿Y el Teatro Bolívar?**
ee ehl teh-ah-troh bvoh-lee-bvahr
And the Bolivar Theater?

Martine: **El teatro Bolívar sí está lejos . . .**
            ehl teh-ah-troh bvoh-lee-bvahr see ehs-tah leh-Hohs
            The Bolivar Theater is really far . . .

            tiene que tomar el subte.
            teeeh-neh keh toh-mahr ehl soobv-teh
            you have to take the subway.

Words to Know

la calle	lah kah-yeh	the street
la avenida	lah ah-bveh-nee-dah	the avenue
el bulevar	ehl bvoo-leh-bvahr	the boulevard
el barrio	ehl bvah-rreeoh	the neighborhood
doblar	doh-bvlahr	to turn
seguir	seh-gheer	to keep going
la cuadra	lah kooah-drah	the block

Felipe and Bárbara Rodriguez, who speak very little English, are coming to your birthday party. You sent directions to everyone along with their invitations, but they were in English. Bárbara has asked you to translate your directions for them:

Go to the square. _____

Go around the corner. _____

Go straight to Alabaster Ave. _____

Turn left. _____

Go north to Camisa St. _____

Turn right. _____

Go two more blocks and turn left on Reina Blvd. _____

My house is behind Santa Clara church. _____

Chapter 13

Checking into a Hotel

- -

In This Chapter

▶ Checking into a hotel

▶ Using the verbs **despertar** and **dormir**

▶ Understanding possessive pronouns

- -

*L*atin American hotels are often places of special pleasures. In warmer places, they have lots of open areas such as balconies, courtyards, and patios. More often than not, these open areas are filled with flowers, exotic plants and trees, and, in some cases, even birds. This chapter gives you all the information you need to check into a hotel anywhere in Spanish-speaking America.

Check Out the Hotel Before You Check in

By the time you get to your hotel, you're likely to be tired from your travels. However, even tired as you are, seeing the rooms before you check in is a good idea. Checking out the hotel's rooms before you check in is an even better idea if you're coming to a city or town where the tastes and levels of cleanliness may differ from your own — especially when the hotel is less than four stars. The advantage of such hotels is that they are much less expensive than the ones you book beforehand.

Size up the following:

✔ **The inside of the closets**

✔ **The bathroom:** Does it really have hot water, and does the toilet flush properly?

✔ **The windows:** Where do they open to?

In addition, finding a place to park your car, if you have one, before you check in to your hotel is especially important when you visit places like the beautiful colonial downtown areas of Latin American cities. More often than not, a hotel attendant is at the door to help you, taking care of your vehicle while you go inside.

Knowing the following phrases before you arrive at your hotel can make getting a room much easier.

- **con baño** *(kohn bvah-nyoh)* (with bathroom)

- **con agua caliente** *(kohn ah-gooah kah-leeehn-teh)* (with hot water)

- **sólo con agua fría** *(soh-loh kohn ah-gooah free-ah)* (with cold water only)

- **a la calle** *(ah lah kah-yeh)* (opening to the street)

- **al interior** *(ahl een-teh-reeohr)* (opening to the interior)

- **la piscina** *(lah pee-see-nah)* (the swimming pool) — in Mexico, use **la alberca** *(lah ahl-bvehr-kah)* instead

Sometimes Spanish has two words for the same thing. For example, **la habitación** *(lah ah-bvee-tah-seeohn)* and **el cuarto** *(ehl kooahr-toh)* both mean "the room." In those instances, we give you both words. When a word is used more in one country than in others, we tell you so in the brackets.

Talkin' the Talk

Anita knows that finding a place to park her car is important when visiting places like the beautiful colonial downtown areas of Latin American cities, where few parking spaces are available except at the large hotels.

Anita Smith: **Buenas tardes, ¿tiene estacionamiento para mi auto?**
bvoo-eh-nahs tahr-dehs teeeh-neh
ehs-tah-seeoh-nah-meeehn-toh pah-rah mee ahoo-toh
Good afternoon, do you have parking for my car?

Receptionist: **Sí. Hay estacionamiento. Está en el portón al lado de este. Ya van a abrirle.**
see ahy ehs-tah-seeoh-nah-meeehn-toh ehs-tah ehn ehl pohr-tohn ahl lah-doh deh ehs-teh yah bvahn ah ah-bvreer-leh
Yes, there's parking. It's at the large door, next to this one. They're going to open it for you now.

Anita Smith: **Gracias. Espero afuera.**
grah-seeahs ehs-peh-roh ah-fooeh-rah
Thanks. I'll wait outside.

Words to Know

la cuadra	lah koo<u>ah</u>-drah	the block
el estacionamiento	ehl ehs-tah-seeoh-nah-mee-<u>ehn</u>-toh	the parking
el portón	ehl pohr-<u>tohn</u>	the [large] door; doorway
abrir	ah-<u>bvreer</u>	to open
esperar	ehs-peh-<u>rahr</u>	to wait

Check out the dialog about table reservations in Chapter 5. Change the words of the dialog from tables to rooms and the remaining conversation stays much the same.

Talkin' the Talk

Anita has just arrived in town, and she's at the front desk of a large hotel. She asks for a room for the night.

Anita Smith: **Necesito una habitación, con baño.**
neh-seh-<u>see</u>-toh <u>oo</u>-nah ah-bvee-tah-see<u>ohn</u> kohn <u>bvah</u>-nyoh
I need a room, with bath.

Receptionist: **¿Le gusta hacia la calle o hacia el patio?**
leh <u>goos</u>-tah <u>ah</u>-seeah lah <u>kah</u>-yeh oh <u>ah</u>-seeah ehl <u>pah</u>-teeoh
Do you prefer a room facing the street or the patio?

Anita Smith: **Prefiero hacia el patio.**
preh-fee<u>eh</u>-roh <u>ah</u>-seeah ehl <u>pah</u>-teeoh
I prefer it toward the patio.

Receptionist:	**Las del patio son muy tranquilas. Las habitaciones hacia el patio cuestan cuarenta pesos, sin desayuno.** *lahs dehl pah-teeoh sohn mooy trahn-kee-lahs lahs ah-bvee-tah-seeoh-nehs ah-seeah ehl pah-teeoh kooehs-tahn kooah-rehn-tah peh-sohs seen deh-sah-yoo-noh* The patio rooms are very quiet. The rooms facing the patio cost forty pesos, without breakfast.
Anita Smith:	**En el primer piso?** *ehn ehl pree-mehr pee-soh* On the first floor?
Receptionist:	**No, las del segundo piso. Las del primero son a cincuenta pesos.** *noh lahs dehl seh-goon-doh pee-soh lahs dehl pree-meh-roh sohn a seen-kooehn-tah peh-sohs* No, the second floor ones. The first floor rooms are priced at fifty pesos.
Anita Smith:	**Prefiero una en el primer piso.** *preh-feeeh-roh oo-nah ehn ehl pree-mehr pee-soh* I prefer one on the first floor.
Receptionist:	**Muy bien, señora.** *mooy bveeehn sey-nyoh-rah* Very well.

Words to Know

doble	doh-bvleh	double
el baño	ehl bvah-nyoh	the bath; the bathroom
hacia	ah-seeah	toward
tranquila	trahn-kee-lah	quiet
primer; primero	pree-mehr; pree-meh-roh	first
el piso	ehl pee-soh	the floor
preferir	preh-feh-reer	to prefer

Talkin' the Talk

Hotels can have diverse accommodations. You often have a choice of which you'd prefer. The receptionist checks with Anita to see what type of room she likes.

Receptionist: **¿Prefiere con cama matrimonial o con dos camas?**
preh-feeeh-reh kohn kah-mah
mah-tree-moh-neeahl oh kohn dohs kah-mahs
Do you prefer a double bed or two beds?

Anita Smith: **Prefiero con dos camas.**
preh-feeeh-roh kohn dohs kah-mahs
I prefer two beds.

Receptionist: **Tengo disponible en el primer piso la habitación número ciento diecinueve. Quiere verla?**
tehn-goh dees-poh-nee-bvleh ehn ehl pree-mehr
pee-soh lah ah-bvee-tah-seeohn noo-meh-roh
seeehn-toh-deeeh-see-nooeh-bveh keeeh-reh
bvehr-lah

Room 119 is available on the first floor. Do you want to see it?

Anita Smith: **Sí, quiero verla.**
see keeeh-roh bvehr-lah
Yes, I want to see it.

Receptionist: **Pedro, acompañe a la señora a la habitación ciento diecinueve. Aquí está la llave.**
peh-droh ah-kohm-pah-nyeh ah lah seh-nyoh-rah ah lah ah-bvee-tah-seeohn seeehn-toh-deeeh-see-nooeh-bveh. ah-kee ehs-tah lah yah-bveh
Pedro, take the lady to room 119. Here's the key.

Words to Know

la cama	lah kah-mah	the bed
matrimonial	mah-tree-moh-neeahl	double (Literally: for married people)
disponible	dees-poh-nee-bvleh	available
ver	bvehr	to see
acompañar	ah-kohm-pah-nyahr	to go with; to accompany
la llave	lah yah-bveh	the key

Talkin' the Talk

Anita wants to be able to relax in her room. A bubble bath sounds good. But first, she needs to make sure that it has a private bath and a tub. Otherwise, she may need to change her plans.

Pedro: **La ciento diecinueve está en el segundo patio. Es una habitación preciosa.**
lah seeehn-toh-deeeh-see-nooeh-bveh ehs-tah ehn ehl seh-goon-doh pah-teeoh ehs oo-nah ah-bvee-tah-seeohn preh-seeoh-sah
One-nineteen is on the second patio. It's a gorgeous room.

Anita Smith: **¿Tiene baño?**
                 tee<u>eh</u>-neh <u>bvah</u>-nyoh
                 Does it have a [private] bath?

Pedro: **Sí. Pase, por aquí está el baño.**
                 see <u>pah</u>-seh pohr ah-<u>kee</u> ehs-<u>tah</u> ehl <u>bvah</u>-nyoh
                 Yes. The bathroom is this way.

Anita Smith: **¿El baño no tiene tina?**
                 ehl <u>bvah</u>-nyoh noh tee<u>eh</u>-neh <u>tee</u>-nah
                 The bathroom doesn't have a bathtub?

Pedro: **No. Como hace calor, aquí la gente prefiere ducharse.**
                 noh <u>koh</u>-moh <u>ah</u>-seh kah-<u>lohr</u> ah-<u>kee</u> lah <u>Hen</u>-teh preh-fee<u>eh</u>-reh doo-<u>chahr</u>-seh
                 No. Because it's hot, people here prefer to shower.

Anita Smith: **¿Hay agua caliente?**
                 ahy <u>ah</u>-gooah kah-lee<u>ehn</u>-teh
                 Is there hot water?

Pedro: **Sí, hay agua caliente y fría todo el día.**
                 see ahy <u>ah</u>-gooah kah-lee<u>ehn</u>-teh ee free<u>ah</u> <u>toh</u>-doh ehl dee<u>ah</u>
                 Yes, there is hot and cold water all day long.

Words to Know

preciosa	preh-<u>seeoh</u>-sah	gorgeous; beautiful; lovely
la tina	lah <u>tee</u>-nah	the tub
ducharse	doo-<u>chahr</u>-seh	to take a shower
caliente	kah-lee<u>ehn</u>-teh	hot
fría	<u>free</u>ah	cold (female)

Talkin' the Talk

Anita is resigned to doing without her bubble bath; she'll watch TV to relax instead. Of course, if she doesn't check to make sure that the room has a TV, she may have to change her plans again.

Anita Smith: **¿La habitación tiene televisión?**
lah ah-bvee-tah-seeohn teeeh-neh teh-leh-bvee-seeohn
Does the room have TV?

Pedro: **Sí, tiene un excelente televisor. Está dentro de este mueble. Aquí está el control automático.**
see teeeh-neh oon ehks-seh-lehn-teh teh-leh-bvee-sohr ehs-tah dehn-troh dehl mooeh-bvleh ah-kee ehs-tah ehl kohn-trohl ahoo-toh-mah-tee-koh
Yes, it has an excellent TV. It's inside this cabinet. Here's the automatic control.

Anita Smith: **¿Se puede ver canales en inglés?**
seh pooeh-deh bvehr kah-nah-lehs ehn een-glehs
Can you get channels in English?

Pedro: **Sí, hay muchos canales en inglés y también en español.**
see ahy moo-chohs kah-nah-lehs ehn een-glehs ee tahm-bveeehn ehn ehs-pah-nyohl
Yes, there are many channels in English and also in Spanish.

Words to Know

la ventana	lah bvehn-tah-nah	the window
abrir	ah-bvreer	to open
el mueble	ehl mooeh-bvleh	the cabinet
el canal	ehl kah-nahl	the channel

Talkin' the Talk

Anita likes the hotel. She has to give up her bubble bath, but there's plenty on TV and the room is really nice. Now she needs to take care of the arrangements and check in.

Anita Smith: **Me gusta la habitación ciento diecinueve. La voy a tomar.**
meh goos-tah lah ah-bvee-tah-seeohn seeehn-toh-deeeh-see-nooeh-bveh lah bvohy ah toh-mahr
I like room 119. I'm going to take it.

Receptionist: **¿Cuántos días desea quedarse?**
koo-ahn-tohs deeahs deh-seh-ah keh-dahr-seh
How many days do you want to stay?

Anita Smith: **Me quedo por tres dias.**
meh keh-doh pohr trehs deeahs
I'm staying three days.

Receptionist: **Haga el favor de registrarse. El desayuno no está incluído en el precio. ¿Va a hacer un depósito por la primera noche?**
ah-gah ehl fah-bvohr deh reh-Hees-trahr-she ehl deh-sah-yoo-noh noh ehs-tah een-klooee-doh ehn ehl preh-seeoh bvah ah ah-sehr oon deh-poh-see-toh pohr lah pree-meh-rah noh-cheh
Please check in. Breakfast is not included in the price. Are you going to make a deposit for the first night?

Anita Smith: **Sí, lo voy a hacer. ¿Con tarjeta o efectivo?**
see loh bvohy ah ah-sehr kohn tahr-Heh-tah oh eh-fehk-tee-bvoh
Yes, I'll make it. Cash or credit card?

Receptionist: **Como usted guste.**
koh-moh oos-tehd goos-teh
Whichever you like.

Anita Smith: **¿Me pueden despertar a las siete de la mañana?**
meh pooeh-dehn dehs-pehr-tahr ah lahs seeeh-teh deh lah mah-nyah-nah
Can you wake me at seven in the morning?

Receptionist: **Como no. Que pase buenas noches.**
    koh-moh noh keh pah-seh bvooeh-nahs noh-chehs
    Of course. Have a good night.

Words to Know

cuánto	kooahn-toh	how much
quedarse	keh-dahr-seh	to stay
registrarse	reh-Hees-trahr-seh	to check in
incluído	een-klooee-doh	includede
precio	ehl preh-seeoh	the price

Registering and Checking Out the Water

Here are some terms to know when filling out your hotel registration form:

- **dirección permanente** *(dee-rehk-see-ohn pehr-mah-nehn-teh)* (permanent address)

- **calle, ciudad, estado, o provincia** *(kah-yeh seeoo-dahd ehs-tah-doh oh proh-bveen-seeah)* (street, city, state, or province)

- **país, código postal, teléfono** *(pahees koh-dee-goh pohs-tahl teh-leh-foh-noh)* (country, postal code, telephone)

- **número de su pasaporte** *(noo-meh-roh deh soo pah-sah-pohr-teh)* (your passport number)

- **si viene con vehículo . . .** *(see bveeeh-neh ehn bvehee-koo-loh)* If coming by vehicle . . .

- **número de placa de matrícula** *(noo-meh-roh deh plah-kah deh mah-tree-koo-lah)* (plate number)

- **fecha en que vence** *(feh-chah ehn keh bvehn-seh)* (expiration date)

Words to Know

llenar	yeh-<u>nahr</u>	to fill in
la ciudad	lah seeoo-<u>dahd</u>	the city
el estado	ehl ehs-<u>tah</u>-doh	the state
la provincia	lah proh-<u>bveen</u>-seeah	the province
el código postal	ehl <u>koh</u>-dee-goh pohs-<u>tahl</u>	the postal code [ZIP code]
el vehículo	ehl bvehee-<u>koo</u>-loh	the vehicle
la placa	lah <u>plah</u>-kah	the license plate
vencer	bvehn-<u>sehr</u>	to expire

When you visit any foreign country, always ask whether the water is safe to drink. You can never take the safety of your water for granted. Here are some phrases that will help you determine how safe the water is:

- ✔ **¿Es potable el agua del hotel?** *(ehs poh-<u>tah</u>-bleh ehl <u>ah</u>-gooah dehl <u>oh</u>-tehl)* (Is the hotel's water drinkable?)

- ✔ **Sí, y también tenemos agua embotellada.** *(see ee tahm-bvee<u>ehn</u> teh-<u>neh</u>-mohs <u>ah</u>-gooah ehm-bvoh-teh-<u>yah</u>-dah)* (Yes, and we also have bottled water.)

- ✔ **¿Dónde encuentro el agua?** *(<u>dohn</u>-deh ehn-koo<u>ehn</u>-troh ehl <u>ah</u>-gooah)* (Where do I find the water?)

- ✔ **Las botellas están en su habitación.** *(lahs bvoh-<u>teh</u>-yahs ehs-<u>tahn</u> ehn soo ah-bvee-tah-see<u>ohn</u>)* (The bottles are in your room.)

Words to Know

la tarjeta	lah tahr-<u>Heh</u>-tah	the card
el efectivo	ehl eh-fehk-<u>tee</u>-bvoh	cash
la maleta	lah mah-<u>leh</u>-tah	the luggage; the suitcase
potable	poh-tah-bvleh	drinkable
embotellada	ehm-bvoh-teh-<u>yah</u>-dah	bottled
despertar	dehs-pehr-<u>tahr</u>	to awaken

Although the water may taste different in various regions of the United States and Canada, the water won't make you sick if you happen to swallow some of it when taking a shower or brushing your teeth. However, some countries don't treat their water to remove harmful bacteria as thoroughly as do the United States and Canada. Therefore, you need to keep your mouth shut when showering, which may be hard to do at first. Keeping your mouth shut is important because that way you can better control what kind of water gets into your stomach.

Dormir: The Sleeping Verb

After a long day, the sweet hour when you can finally rest and go to sleep comes. In Spanish, **dormir** *(dohr-<u>meer</u>)* (to sleep) is a bit irregular, much like a really tired person.

In the following conjugation of the present tense of **dormir**, notice the differences between the singular and plural first person verb forms.

Conjugation	Pronunciation
yo duerm**o**	yoh doo<u>ehr</u>-moh
tú duerm**es**	too doo<u>ehr</u>-mehs
él, ella, ello, uno, usted duerme	ehl <u>eh</u>-yah <u>eh</u>-yoh <u>oo</u>-noh oos-<u>tehd</u> doo<u>ehr</u>-meh
nosotros dorm**imos**	noh-<u>soh</u>-trohs dohr-<u>mee</u>-mohs
vosotros dorm**ís**	bvoh-<u>soh</u>-trohs dohr-<u>mees</u>
ellos, ellas, ustedes duerm**en**	<u>eh</u>-yohs <u>eh</u>-yahs oos-<u>teh</u>-dehs doo<u>ehr</u>-mehn

Here are some phrases to help you practice using **dormir**:

- ✔ **Yo duermo todos los días ocho horas.** *(yoh doo<u>ehr</u>-moh <u>toh</u>-dohs lohs deeahs <u>oh</u>-choh <u>oh</u>-rahs)* (I sleep eight hours every day.)

- ✔ **Camilo duerme en su cama.** *(kah-<u>mee</u>-loh doo<u>ehr</u>-meh ehn soo <u>kah</u>-mah)* (Camilo sleeps in his bed.)

- ✔ **Dormimos en nuestra casa.** *(dohr-<u>mee</u>-mohs ehn noo<u>ehs</u>-trah <u>kah</u>-sah)* (We sleep in our home.)

- ✔ **Los invitados duermen en tu recámara.** *(lohs een-bvee-<u>tah</u>-dohs doo<u>ehr</u>-mehn ehn too reh-<u>kah</u>-mah-rah)* (The guests sleep in your bedroom. [Mexico])

- ✔ **En mi cama duermen dos gatos.** *(ehn mee <u>kah</u>-mah doo<u>ehr</u>-mehn dohs <u>gah</u>-tohs)* (Two cats sleep in my bed.)

- ✔ **Tú duermes con un osito.** *(too doo<u>ehr</u>-mehs kohn oon oh-<u>see</u>-toh)* (You sleep with a little [teddy] bear.)

- ✔ **Los pájaros también duermen.** *(lohs <u>pah</u>-Hah-rohs tahm-bvee<u>ehn</u> doo<u>ehr</u>-mehn)* (The birds also sleep.)

Using Despertar: The Waking Up Verb

You use the verb **despertar** *(dehs-pehr-<u>tahr</u>)* (to awaken) after a good night's sleep. You can tell that this verb is irregular when you see that the root of the verb in the first person singular is different from that of the first person plural.

Conjugation	Pronunciation
yo despiert**o**	yoh dehs-pee<u>ehr</u>-toh
tú despiert**as**	too dehs-pee<u>ehr</u>-tahs
él, ella, ello, uno, usted despiert**a**	ehl <u>eh</u>-yah <u>eh</u>-yoh <u>oo</u>-noh oos-<u>tehd</u> dehs-pee<u>ehr</u>-tah
nosotros despert**amos**	noh-<u>soh</u>-trohs dehs-pehr-<u>tah</u>-mohs
vosotros despert**áis**	bvoh-<u>soh</u>-trohs dehs-pehr-<u>tahees</u>
ellos, ellas, ustedes despiert**an**	<u>eh</u>-yohs <u>eh</u>-yahs oos-<u>teh</u>-dehs dehs-pee<u>ehr</u>-tahn

You understand the previous conjugations, but you say, "I either wake up or I don't." How can I practice using this verb? The following examples show you how to start practicing:

- ✔ **Yo despierto temprano en la mañana.** *(yoh dehs-pee<u>ehr</u>-toh tehm-<u>prah</u>-noh ehn lah mah-<u>nyah</u>-nah)* (I wake up early in the morning.)

- ✔ **Ustedes despiertan juntos.** *(<u>oos</u>-teh-dehs dehs-pee<u>ehr</u>-tahn <u>Hoon</u>-tohs)* (You [formal] wake up together.)

- ✔ **Ellos no despiertan de noche.** *(<u>eh</u>-yohs noh dehs-pee<u>ehr</u>-tahn deh <u>noh</u>-cheh)* (They don't wake up at night.)

- ✔ **Despierta con el canto de los pájaros.** *(dehs-pee<u>ehr</u>-tah kohn ehl <u>kahn</u>-toh deh lohs pah-<u>Hah</u>-rohs)* (He awakens with the birds' singing.)

Las mañanitas

In Mexico, someone might sing (with a band) morning songs under the window of the person that he or she wants to wake up and serenade. **Mañanita** *(mah-nyah-<u>nee</u>-tah)* is the Spanish word for this kind of song. In fact, every child knows a **mañanita** sung specially for birthdays, and more for the celebrations of the names of saints who coincide with people's birthdays.

Being Possessive

In Spanish, you can use the words that signal possession in singular or plural form, depending on the number of things to which you refer. For example, you say **mi llave** *(mee yah-bveh)* (my key), if you refer to one. More often than not, however, you'll say **mis llaves** *(mees yah-bvehs)* (my keys), because you likely possess more than one key.

You follow the same rules when you say **esta llave es mía** *(ehs-tah yah-bveh ehs meeah)* (this key is mine), or, in the case of several, **estas llaves son mías** *(ehs-tahs yah-bvehs sohn meeas)* (these keys are mine).

Notice that because **llave** is feminine, you use **mía,** the female-gender possessive. This rule sounds more complicated than it actually is. Just use the number (singular or plural) and the gender (male of female) of the things you talk about.

Possessive adjectives

The following list shows you all the possibilities of possessive adjectives:

- ✔ **mi/mis** *(mee/mees)* (my)
- ✔ **tú/tus** *(too/toos)* (your)
- ✔ **su/sus** *(soo/soos)* (his, her, its)
- ✔ **nuestro/nuestros** *(nooehs-troh/nooehs-trohs)* (our [when the possessed person, animal, or object is masculine])
- ✔ **nuestra/nuestras** *(nooehs-trah/nooehs-trahs)* (our [when the possessed person, animal, or object is feminine])
- ✔ **vuestro/vuestros** *(bvooehs-troh/bvooehs-trohs)* (your [when the possessed person, animal, or object is masculine])
- ✔ **vuestra/vuestras** *(bvooehs-trah/bvooehs-trahs)* (your [when the possessed person or animal or object is feminine])
- ✔ **su/sus** *(soo/soos)* (their)

Here are some examples of how to use possessive adjectives:

- ✔ **Esta es mi habitación.** *(ehs-tah ehs mee ah-bvee-tah-see<u>ohn</u>)* (This is my room.)

- ✔ **Tus llaves están en la mesa.** *(toos <u>yah</u>-bvehs ehs-<u>tahn</u> ehn lah <u>meh</u>-sah)* (Your keys are on the table.)

- ✔ **Sus llaves se las llevó la camarera.** *(soos <u>yah</u>-bvehs seh lahs yeh-<u>bvoh</u> lah kah-mah-<u>reh</u>-rah)* (The maid took his keys.)

- ✔ **Ese es nuestro hotel.** *(<u>eh</u>-seh ehs noo<u>ehs</u>-troh <u>oh</u>-tehl)* (That is our hotel.)

- ✔ **Vinieron en su auto.** *(bvee-nee<u>eh</u>-rohn ehn soo <u>ahoo</u>-toh)* (They came in their car.)

- ✔ **Tus toallas están secas.** *(toos toh-<u>ah</u>-yahs ehs-<u>tahn</u> <u>seh</u>-kahs)* (Your towels are dry.)

- ✔ **Esas son mis maletas.** *(<u>eh</u>-sahs sohn mees mah-<u>leh</u>-tahs)* (Those are my suitcases.)

- ✔ **Nuestras sábanas están limpias.** *(noo<u>ehs</u>-trahs <u>sah</u>-bvah-nahs ehs-<u>tahn</u> <u>leem</u>-peeahs)* (Our sheets are clean.)

- ✔ **Mis zapatos están en el auto.** *(mees sah-<u>pah</u>-tohs ehs-<u>tahn</u> ehn ehl <u>ahoo</u>-toh)* (My shoes are in the car.)

- ✔ **Tu pasaporte está en la recepción.** *(too pah-sah-<u>pohr</u>-teh <u>ehs</u>-tah ehn lah reh-sehp-see<u>ohn</u>)* (Your passport is at the reception [desk].)

Possessive pronouns

The following list shows you the basic possessive pronouns:

- ✔ **el mío/los míos** *(ehl <u>mee</u>oh/lohs <u>mee</u>ohs)* (mine [when the possessed person, animal, or object is masculine])

- ✔ **la mía/las mías** *(lah <u>mee</u>ah/lahs <u>mee</u>ahs)* (mine [when the possessed person, animal, or object is feminine])

- ✔ **el tuyo/los tuyos** *(ehl <u>too</u>-yoh/lohs <u>too</u>-yohs)* (yours [when the possessed person, animal, or object is masculine])

- ✔ **la tuya/las tuyas** *(lah <u>too</u>-yah/lahs <u>too</u>-yahs)* (yours [when the possessed person, animal, or object is feminine)

- ✔ **el suyo/los suyos** *(ehl <u>soo</u>-yoh/lohs <u>soo</u>-yohs)* (his, hers, its [when the possessed person, animal, or object is masculine])

✔ **la suya/las suyas** *(lah soo-yah/lahs soo-yahs)* (his, hers, its [when the possessed person, animal, or object is feminine])

✔ **el nuestro/los nuestros** *(ehl nooehs-troh/lohs nooehs-trohs)* (ours [when the possessed person, animal, or object is masculine])

✔ **la nuestra/las nuestras** *(lah nooehs-trah/lahs nooehs-trahs)* (ours [when the possessed person, animal, or object is feminine])

✔ **el vuestro/los vuestros** *(ehl bvooehs-troh/lohs bvooehs-trohs)* (yours [when the possessed person, animal, or object is masculine])

✔ **la vuestra/las vuestras** *(lah bvooehs-trah/lahs bvooehs-trahs)* (yours [when the possessed person, animal, or object is feminine])

✔ **el suyo/los suyos** *(ehl soo-yoh/lohs soo-yohs)* (theirs [when the possessed person, animal, or object is masculine])

✔ **la suya/las suyas** *(lah soo-yah/lahs soo-yahs)* (theirs [when the possessed person, animal, or object is feminine])

Here are some examples of possessive pronouns for you to practice:

✔ **La cama esa es mía.** *(lah kah-mah eh-sah ehs meeah)* (That bed is mine.)

✔ **Las camas que están en el otro cuarto son suyas.** *(lahs kah-mahs que ehs-tahn ehn ehl oh-troh kooahr-toh sohn soo-yahs)* (The beds in the other room are yours [formal plural].)

✔ **Esa maleta es la tuya.** *(eh-sah mah-leh-tah ehs lah too-yah)* (That suitcase is yours.)

✔ **Ese otro hotel es el suyo.** *(eh-seh oh-troh oh-tehl ehs ehl soo-yoh)* (That other hotel is yours [formal].)

✔ **Esos pasaportes son los nuestros.** *(eh-sohs pah-sah-pohr-tehs sohn lohs nooehs-trohs)* (Those passports are ours.)

✔ **La maleta que es tuya está en la recepción.** *(lah mah-leh-tah keh ehs too-yah ehs-tah ehn lah reh-sehp-seeohn)* (Your suitcase is at the reception desk.)

✔ **Los calcetines son míos.** *(lohs kahl-seh-tee-nehs sohn meeohs)* (The socks are mine.)

✔ **Ese vaso es suyo.** *(eh-seh bvah-soh ehs soo-yoh)* (That glass is hers.)

✔ **La cuenta del restaurante es nuestra.** *(lah kooehn-tah dehl rehs-tahoo-rahn-teh ehs nooehs-trah)* (The restaurant bill is ours.)

✔ **Son suyas las almohadas.** *(sohn soo-yahs lahs ahl-moh-ah-dahs)* (The pillows are his.)

Fun & Games

The following word search contains several Spanish words that we introduced in this chapter. The English translation is listed below. Find the Spanish equivalent and circle it. (See Appendix D for the answer key.)

Word Search

R	Y	L	D	N	E	I	R	F	B	D
O	A	O	T	N	A	U	C	A	I	E
D	C	M	P	G	M	K	Ñ	R	Q	R
I	V	A	A	C	Y	O	E	O	U	I
U	C	V	L	C	X	C	W	I	E	R
L	U	L	W	I	C	M	F	C	D	E
C	H	F	A	I	E	Z	O	E	A	F
N	E	I	O	M	M	N	H	R	R	E
I	R	N	Z	L	B	G	T	P	S	R
F	N	I	A	T	P	A	C	E	E	P
I	C	X	E	S	R	A	H	C	U	D

address	hot	to prefer
bathroom	how much	to stay
bed	included	to take a shower
cold	price	

Chapter 14

Getting Around: Planes, Trains, Taxis, and More

Getting where you want to go is generally your first concern. However, as you travel around a Spanish-speaking country or try to help Spanish speakers navigate your own neighborhood, you're going to encounter all kinds of situations. This chapter gives you an idea of what to expect and tells you how to deal with the various circumstances that may arise.

Getting Around

After you fly in, the airport personnel can help you get where you're going. While your luggage is being unloaded, you first go to the section where your identity papers will be checked. Here are some phrases that you may hear during this process:

▶ **Pase a Migración.** (*pah-seh a mee-grah-see<u>ohn</u>*) (Go to Migration.)

▶ **Pase a Inmigración.** (*pah-seh a een-mee-grah-see<u>ohn</u>*) (Go to Immigration.)

▶ **Pase por aquí con su pasaporte en la mano.** (*pah-seh pohr ah-<u>kee</u> kohn soo pah-sah-<u>pohr</u>-teh ehn lah <u>mah</u>-noh*) (Go this way with your passport in your hand.)

While waiting in line at the Immigration office, you can get ready to answer some of these questions that the officer may ask you:

- ✔ **¿Me permite su pasaporte?** *(meh pehr-mee-teh soo pah-sah-pohr-the)* (May I have your passport?)

- ✔ **¿De dónde viene?** *(deh dohn-deh bveeeh-neh)* (Where do you come from?)

- ✔ **¿En qué vuelo llegó?** *(ehn keh bvooeh-loh yeh-goh)* (What flight did you come on?)

- ✔ **¿A dónde va?** *(ah dohn-deh bvah)* (Where are you going?)

- ✔ **¿Cuánto tiempo quiere quedarse en el país?** *(kooahn-toh teeehm-poh keeeh-reh keh-dahr-seh ehn ehl pahees)* (How long do you want to stay in the country?)

- ✔ **¿Cuánto dinero trae consigo?** *(kooahn-toh dee-neh-roh traheh kohn-see-goh)* (How much money do you have with you?)

- ✔ **¡Que tenga una estadía feliz!** *(keh tehn-gah oo-nah ehs-tah-deeah feh-lees)* (Have a happy stay!)

- ✔ **¡Que lo pase muy bien!** *(keh loh pah-seh mooy bveeehn)* (Have a good time!)

- ✔ **Pase a la Aduana, por favor.** *(pah -seh ahl lah ah-dooah-nah pohr fah-bvohr)* (Go to Customs, please.)

Words to Know

Migración	mee-grah-seeohn	Migration
Inmigración	een-mee-grah-seeohn	Immigration
el documento	ehl doh-koo-mehn-toh	the document; the paper
el pasaporte	ehl pah-sah-pohr-teh	the passport
quedar	keh-dahr	to stay
el dinero	ehl dee-neh-roh	the money
la estadía	lah ehs-tah-deeah	the stay

Finding the train station

If you're looking for the train station. Here are some phrases that can help:

- ✔ **¿Dónde está la estación del tren?** (*dohn-deh ehs-tah lah ehs-tah-seeohn-dehl trehn*) (Where's the train station?)

- ✔ **¿Cómo llego a la Estación Central?** (*koh-moh yeh-goh ah lah ehs-tah-seeohn sehn-trahl*) (How do I get to the Central Station?)

- ✔ **Lléveme por favor a la estación del tren.** (*yeh-bveh-meh pohr fah-bvohr ah lah ehs-tah-seeohn dehl trehn*) (Please take me to the station.)

Talkin' the Talk

Sonia has decided to travel to La Paz, in Bolivia. She's at the train station and wants to buy her ticket.

Sonia:	**Un boleto para La Paz, por favor.** *oon bvoh-leh-toh pah-rah lah pahs pohr fah-bvohr* One ticket for La Paz, please.
Window Attendant:	**¿Primera, segunda o tercera clase?** *pree-meh-rah she-goohn-dah oh tehr-seh-rah klah-she* First, second, or third class?
Sonia:	**Primera clase, por favor.** *pree-meh-rah klah-she pohr fah-bvohr* First class, please.
Window Attendant:	**Son quinientos pesos, por favor.** *sohn kee-neeehn-tohs peh-sohs pohr fah-bvohr* That's 500 pesos, please.
Sonia:	**Aquí los tiene. ¿A qué hora sale el tren?** *ah-kee lohs teeeh-neh ah keh oh-rah sah-leh ehl trehn* Here [is the money]. What time does the train leave?
Window Attendant:	**Sale diez minutos atrasado, a las 12:15.** *sah-leh deeehs mee-noo-tohs ah-trah-sah-doh ah lahs doh-seh keen-seh* It leaves ten minutes late, at 12:15.
Sonia:	**¿De qué andén sale?**

deh keh ahn-dehn sah-leh
What platform does it leave from?

Window Attendant:	**Del andén número dos.** *dehl ahn-dehn noo-meh-roh dohs* From Platform Two.
Sonia:	**Muchas gracias, señor.** *moo-chahs grah-seeahs she-nyor* Thank you very much, Sir.
Window Attendant:	**De nada. ¡Que tenga un buen viaje!** *deh nah-dah keh tehn-gah oon bvooehn* *bveeah-Heh* You're welcome. Have a good trip!

Checking your documents on the train

As you are traveling on the train between two countries, the ticket collector comes at some moment and says such things as

- ✔ **¿Me permiten sus pasaportes por favor?** *(meh pehr-mee-tehn soos pah-sah-pohr-tehs pohr fah-bvohr)* (May I have your passports, please?)

- ✔ **Me llevo sus pasaportes un rato.** *(meh yeh-bvoh soos pah-sah-pohr-tehs oon rah-toh)* (I'll take your passports for a while.)

- ✔ **Aquí tienen de vuelta sus pasaportes.** *(ah-kee teeeh-nehn deh bvooehl-tah soos pah-sah-pohr-tehs)* (Here are your passports back.)

- ✔ **Aquí tienen sus formularios de Aduana.** *(ah-kee teeeh-nehn soos fohr-moo-lah-reeohs deh ah-dooah-nah)* (Here are your Customs forms.)

- ✔ **Llenen por favor el cuestionario.** *(yeh-nehn pohr fah-bvohr ehl kooehs-teeoh-nah-reeoh)* (Please fill in the questions.)

- ✔ **Al llegar llévelo a la Aduana.** *(ahl yeh-gahr yeh-bveh-loh ah lah ah-dooah-nah)* (When you arrive, take it to Customs.)

Words to Know

la estación	lah ehs-tah-seeohn	the station
el tren	ehl trehn	the train
el boleto	ehl bvoh-leh-toh	the ticket
primera clase	pree-meh-rah klah-seh	first class
el asiento	ehl ah-seeehn-toh	the seat
el formulario	ehl fohr-moo-lah-reeoh	the form
el cuestionario	ehl kooehs-teeoh-nah-reeoh	the form; questionnaire

Dealing with the Customs Office

When you buy your tickets, ask about the Customs regulations for your destination. Take care not to carry any items that may be prohibited by law.

Each country has its own rules. Your travel agency or the consulate of the country you are visiting can give you all the Customs-related information you need without any charge. Customs officers in the countries that you're likely to visit are more often than not concerned with things like cigarettes, alcoholic beverages, weapons, electrical equipment, and antique art of national interest.

Declare (write on the form or verbally acknowledge) anything you have that may be subject to duties or may be suspect in any way. In most cases, for example, when things are for your personal use, you can take them into the country without paying duties. The Customs officials ultimately decide whether you owe any duties.

Here are some phrases to know when dealing with Customs:

✔ **¿Este objeto paga derechos?** (*ehs-teh ohbv-Heh-toh pah-gah deh-reh-chohs*) (Does one pay duties on this item? [Literally: Does this object pay duties?])

✔ **¿Cuánto se paga en derechos por este objeto?** *(kooahn-toh se pah-gah ehn deh-reh-chohs pohr ehs-teh ohbv-Heh toh)* (How much duties does one pay for this thing [object]?)

✔ **Debe pagar impuestos.** *(deh-bveh pah-gahr eem-pooehs-tohs)* (You have to pay duty.)

✔ **Está libre de impuestos.** *(ehs-tah lee-bvreh de eem-pooehs-tohs)* (It's duty free.)

Remember, the Customs officer is not out to get you. He's simply being paid to see that people don't bring unwanted or illegal items into the country.

Never joke around with a Customs officer. He also has to control his sense of humor. He's there for serious business.

Talkin' the Talk

Here, Juan Carlos meets with a Customs officer.

Customs officer: **¿Tiene algo que declarar?**
teeeh-neh ahl-goh keh deh-klah-rahr
Do you have anything to declare?

Juan Carlos: **No, no tengo nada que declarar.**
noh noh tehn-goh nah-dah keh deh-klah-rahr
No, I have nothing to declare.

Customs officer: **¿Trae algún material explosivo?**
trah-eh ahl-goon mah-teh-reeahl ehks-ploh-see-bvoh
Do you have anything explosive? [Literally: Do you bring...]

¿Trae alguna bebida alcohólica?
trah-eh ahl-goo-nah bveh-bvee-dah ahl-koh-oh-lee-kah
Do you have any alcoholic beverages?

¿Trae algún aparato eléctrico?
trah-eh ahl-goon ah-pah-rah-toh eh-lehk-tree-koh
Do you have any electrical devices?

Juan Carlos: **Sólo para mi uso personal.**
soh-loh pah-rah mee oo-soh pehr-soh-nahl
Only for my personal use.

Customs Officer:	**Muy bien, pase. Que disfrute su estadía.**
	mooy bveeehn pah-seh. keh dees-froo-teh soo ehs-tah-deeah
	Very good, go [this way]. Enjoy your stay.

Registering cameras, computers, and other equipment

Some countries may require that you register the serial numbers of your camera, video camera, or computer. Come to think of it, you also benefit from having that registration paper and knowing what you brought with you into the country.

Generally, you — and only you — have to take the registered objects out with you when you leave the country. At that time, you have to show the registration documents that you got when you arrived. This is also good — you do want to keep your goodies, don't you?

The idea behind registration is that the Customs people don't want you to sell (or otherwise give away) or leave your dutiable objects in the country you are visiting. For obvious reasons, they don't want their citizens to access goods that have no duty paid on them.

Here are some phrases you may need to know when registering your electrical equipment:

- ✔ **Por favor llene este formulario.** *(pohr fah-bvohr yeh-neh ehs-teh foh-moo-lah-reeoh)* (Please fill in this form.)

- ✔ **¿Cuáles son las máquinas que hay que registrar?** *(kooah-lehs sohn lahs mah-kee-nahs keh ahy keh reh-Hees-trahr)* (Which electrical devices do we have to register?)

- ✔ **Al salir del país debe presentar este formulario.** *(ahl sah-leer dehl paheehs deh-bveh preh-sehn-tahr ehs-teh fohr-moo-lah-reeoh)* (When you exit the country, you must show this form.)

- ✔ **Puede pasar hacia la salida.** *(pooeh-deh pah-sahr ah-seeah lah sah-lee-dah)* (You may proceed to the exit.)

Talkin' the Talk

The Customs officer needs to see the contents of Peter's luggage.

Customs officer: **Necesitamos revisar sus maletas.**
neh-seh-see-tah-mohs reh-bvee-sahr soos mah-leh-tahs
We need to see your suitcases.

¿Cúantas piezas tiene?
kooahn-tahs peeeh-sahs teeeh-neh
How many pieces do you have?

Peter Woolrich: **Tengo dos maletas.**
tehn-go dohs mah-leh-tahs
I have two suitcases.

Customs officer: **Póngalas aquí por favor.**
pohn-gah-lahs ah-kee pohr fah-bvohr
Put them here please.

Peter Woolrich: **Aquí están.**
ah-kee ehs-tahn
Here they are.

Customs officer: **Por favor abra esta maleta.**
pohr fah-bvohr ah-bvrah ehs-tah mah-leh-tah
Please open this suitcase.

Peter Woolrich: **En seguida.**
enh seh-ghee-da
Right away.

Customs officer: **¿Esto qué es?**
ehs-toh keh ehs
What's this?

Peter Woolrich: **Es mi máquina de afeitar eléctrica.**
ehs mee mah-kee-nah deh ah-fehee-tahr eh-lehk-tree-kah
It's my electric razor.

Customs officer: **¿Trae alguna cámara fotográfica?**
teeeh-neh ahlgoo-nah kah-mah-rah foh-toh-grah-fee-kah
Do you have a camera?

¿Tiene cámara de video?
teeeh-neh kah-mah-rah deh bvee-deh-oh
Do you have a video camera?

Peter Woolrich:	**Aquí lo tengo.**	
	ah-kee loh tehn-goh	
	Here [I have it].	
Customs officer:	**¿Trae computadora portátil?**	
	tra-eh kohm-poo-tah-doh-rah pohr-tah-teel	
	Did you bring a laptop computer?	
Peter Woolrich:	**Aquí está.**	
	ah-kee ehs-tah	
	Here it is.	
Customs officer:	**Por favor pase a registrarlos en la oficina "A."**	
	porh fah-bvohr pah-seh ah reh-Hees-trahr-lohs ehn la oh-fee-see-nah ah	
	Please go register them [your equipment] at the "A" office.	

Words to Know

la aduana	lah ah-dooah-nah	Customs
el aparato	ehl ah-pah-rah-toh	the machine; the appliance
uso personal	oo-soh pehr-soh-nahl	personal use
revisar	reh-bvee-sahr	to go through
las maletas	lahs mah-leh-tahs	the suitcases
abrir	ah-bvreer	to open
afeitar	ah-fehee-tahr	to shave
la cámara de video	lah kah-mah-rah deh bvee-deh-oh	the video camera
la computadora portátil	lah kohm-poo-tah-doh-rah pohr-tah-teel	the laptop computer
salir	sah-leer	to exit; to get out

Using the Verb Traer (to Bring)

A useful, albeit irregular, verb is **traer** (*trah-ehr*) (to bring). You are always bringing something, and someone often brings things to you. For example, you bring a camera to photograph your vacation; at the restaurant, a waiter brings you your food and drink. Yes, **traer** is definitely useful. Here's how you use it:

Conjugation	Pronunciation
yo traig**o**	yoh trahee-goh
tú tra**es**	too trah-ehs
él, ella, ello, uno, usted tra**e**	ehl, eh-yah, eh-yoh, oo-noh oos-tehd trah-eh
nosotros tra**emos**	noh-soh-trohs trah-eh-mohs
vosotros tra**éis**	bvoh-soh-trohs trah-ehees
ellos, ellas, ustedes tra**en**	eh-yohs eh-yahs oos-teh-dehs trah-ehn

Practicing the bringing verb

It's always good to practice the verb to which you are just introduced. Here are some phrases for you to try:

- ✔ **Traigo una cámara.** (*trahee-goh oo-nah kah-mah-rah*) (I bring a camera.)

- ✔ **¿Traes las fotos?** (*trah-ehs lahs foh-tohs*) (Are you bringing the photos?)

- ✔ **Lo que traemos no es problema.** (*loh keh trah-eh-mohs noh ehs proh-bvleh-mah*) (There's no problem with what we are bringing.)

- ✔ **Traen cosas de uso personal.** (*trah-ehn koh-sahs deh oo-soh pehr-soh-nahl*) (They bring things for their personal use.)

Getting a Taxi, Bus, or Car Rental

Whether you came by plane or train, you're going to leave the station and search for a taxi, a bus, or the car rental office. At some airports, you pay the taxi before taking it. This way, the company can guarantee that you're taking a taxi they know to a destination they know.

These phrases help you make the arrangements you need:

- ✔ **¿Dónde encuentro un taxi?** (*dohn-deh ehn-kooehn-troh oon tah-ksee*) (Where do I find a taxi?)

- ✔ **¿Hay paraderos de taxis?** (*ahy pah-rah-deh-rohs deh tah-ksees*) (Is there a taxi stop?)

- ✔ **¿Se paga aquí el taxi?** (*seh pah-gah ah-kee ehl tah-ksee*) (Do I pay the taxi here?)

- ✔ **No. El taxi se paga al llegar a su destino.** (*noh ehl tah-ksee seh pah-gah ahl yeh-gahr ah soo dehs-tee-noh*) (No. You pay the taxi when you arrive to your destination.)

Talkin' the Talk

 Teresa had just hailed a taxi to get to a hotel someone had recommended to her and had written the address on a card.

Teresa: **Voy al hotel Las Américas.**
bvoy ahl oh-tehl lahs ah-meh-ree-kahs
I'm going to the Las Américas hotel.

Taxi driver: **¿En qué calle está?**
ehn keh kah-yeh ehs-tah
On what street is it?

Teresa: **Está en Junín 228.**
ehs-tah ehn Hoo-neen dohs-seeehn-tohs bveheen-tee-oh-choh
It's on Junin 228.

Taxi driver: **A ver la tarjeta? . . .**
ah bvehr lah tahr-Heh-tah
Can I see the card?

Ah, ya sé. Vamos.
ah yah seh bvah-mohs
Ah, I know. Here we go.

Getting the bus to take you there

Here are some phrases that are useful to know when you need to take a bus from the airport or train station:

- ✔ **¿Hay paraderos de buses?** (*ahy pah-rah-deh-rohs deh bvoo-sehs*) (Is there a bus stop?)

✔ **¿Hay buses para ir al centro?** *(ahy bvoo-sehs pah-rah eer ahl sehn-troh)* (Are there buses for downtown?)

✔ **¿Se compran los boletos antes?** *(seh kohm-prahn lohs bvoh-leh-tohs ahn-tehs)* (Do I buy the tickets beforehand?)

Talkin' the Talk

Juanita is tired from her flight and can't find a taxi. She spots a bus. Is it going where she needs to go? Will she have to walk far with her luggage? Here's how she finds out:

Juanita:	**¿Este bus va al centro?** *ehs-teh bvoos bvah ahl sehn-troh* Is this bus going downtown?
Bus driver:	**¿A qué calle va?** *ah keh kah-yeh bvah* What street are you going to?
Juanita:	**Avenida Pilcomayo.** *ah-bveh-nee-dah peel-koh-mah-yoh* Pilcomayo Avenue.
Bus driver:	**Sí le dejo cerca. Suba.** *see, leh deh-Hoh sehr-kah. soo-bvah* Yes, I'll leave you close. Come on up.

Words to Know

el paradero	ehl pah-rah-deh-roh	the stop
se paga	seh pah-gah	one pays
la calle	lah kah-yeh	the street
el bus	ehl bvoos	the bus
cerca	sehr-kah	close by

Driving Concerns

Fortunately, when you drive in any country in Latin America where Spanish is spoken, the rules of the road are very similar to those you already know.

If you plan to rent a car during your trip, try to find out whether arranging the rental from your home base, before you go, has any advantages for you. Generally it *is* cheaper.

Driver's licenses

Some countries, such as Mexico, accept your valid driver's license from your home country. Other countries may require an International Driver's License. You can get one from the American and Canadian automobile drivers' associations, whether or not you are a member. The association itself can tell you which countries require an International Driver's License.

Road signs

Most road signs in Latin America are based on symbols rather than words. This system makes them very easy to understand, no matter what language you speak. In fact, most driving signs have become quite universal; they are much the same everywhere:

- ✔ A *do not enter* sign is a circle in a red field, crossed by a diagonal line.

- ✔ A stop sign is always an octagonal red field with black borders. Inside is a word such as **pare** *(pah-reh)* (stop) or **alto** *(ahl-toh)* (stop), instead of the English word "stop."

- ✔ On the highway, left turns and right turns are indicated with signs that have a diamond shape with an arrow bent in the direction of the turn. A turn sign with a diagonal across it means *no turn*.

Ask at the car rental office whether you should expect any road signs that you don't understand.

Whether at the airport or on the street, these two questions can come in handy when you need to find transportation:

- ✔ **¿Dónde arriendan autos?** *(dohn-deh ah-rreeehn-dahn ahoo-tohs)* (Where do they rent cars?)

- ✔ **¿Hay oficina de renta de autos?** *(ahy oh-fee-see-nah deh rehn-tah deh ahoo-tohs)* (Is there a car rental office?)

Talkin' the Talk

At the car rental office, Samuel gets information about differences in road signs between the area he's used to driving in and the one he's about to explore.

Samuel Thompson:	**¿La señalización es igual que en Estados Unidos?** *lah seh-nyah-lee-sah-see__ohn__ ehs ee-goo__ahl__ keh ehn ehs-__tah__-dohs oo-__nee__-dohs* Are the road signs the same as in the United States?
Rental office attendant:	**Son muy parecidos. Aquí tiene ejemplos.** *sohn mooy pah-reh-__see__-dohs ah-__kee__ tee__eh__-neh eh-__Hehm__-plohs* They are very similar [to those of the U.S.]. Here you can see some examples.
Samuel Thompson:	**¿Como son los reglamentos de tráfico?** *__koh__-moh sohn lohs reh-glah-__mehn__-tohs deh __trah__-fee koh* What are the traffic rules like?
Rental office attendant:	**Son los mismos reglamentos que usa en su país.** *sohn lohs __mees__-mohs reh-glah-__mehn__-tohs keh __oo__-sah soo pahees* They are the same as the ones in your country.
Samuel Thompson:	**¿Se puede doblar a la derecha con luz roja?** *seh poo__eh__-deh __doh__-bvlahr ah lah deh-__reh__-chah kohn loos __roh__-Hah* Can you turn right on a red light?
Rental office attendant:	**Sí, se puede.** *see seh poo__eh__-deh* Yes, you can.

TIP

About those kilometers

Did you know that a mile is 1.6 kilometers? You probably have other things to worry about. Well, we had to learn the miles thing, because everywhere else that we've lived uses kilometers. We learned to use miles with no trouble, so you can surely use kilometers.

Just remember that whatever the number getting there from here is, it will be always the same *distance*. Doesn't that sound funny? It helped us! Remember, you don't travel any farther going 1.6 kilometers than 1 mile; they're the same. (Just between us *For Dummies* book lovers, this is not a serious concern.)

Here are some more things that you can think about when trying to figure out how far there was from here: 30 miles is 50 kilometers. (So 50kph is 30mph, right?) Also, 50 miles is 80 kilometers. Finally, 60 miles is 96 kilometers — but you can think of it as *close* to 100.

And to end your problems in conversion, your rental car shows *kilometers* on the dashboard! And the signs are in *kilometers!* So just go with the flow.

Renting a Car

Now you come to the nitty gritty of trying to rent a car. Here are some things you can say when inquiring about a rental car:

- ✔ **Quiero arrendar un auto.** *(keeeh-roh ah-rrehn-dahr oon ahoo-toh)* (I want to rent a car.)

- ✔ **Me puede dar la lista de precios?** *(meh pooeh-deh dahr lah lees-tah deh preh-seeohs)* (Can you give me the price list?)

- ✔ **¿Cuánto cuesta al día?** *(kooahn-toh kooehs-tah ahl deeah)* (How much is it per day?)

- ✔ **¿Cuánto cuesta por semana?** *(kooahn-toh kooehs-tah pohr seh-mah-nah)* (How much is it per week?)

- ✔ **¿Cuántos kilómetros puedo andar?** *(kooahn-tohs kee-loh-meh-trohs pooeh-doh ahn-dahr)* (How many kilometers may I go?)

- ✔ **¿Cuántos kilómetros por litro da este auto?** *(kooahn-tohs kee-loh-meh-trohs pohr lee-tro dah ehs-teh ahoo-toh)* (How many kilometers per liter does this car make?)

- ✔ **¿Cuánto cuesta el seguro?** *(kooahn-toh kooehs-tah ehl seh-goo-roh)* (How much is the insurance?)

- ✔ **¿Tiene mapas de la región?** *(teeeh-neh mah-pahs deh lah reh-Heeohn)* (Do you have maps of the region?)

> ✔ **¿Dónde está la rueda de repuesto?** (_dohn_-deh ehs-_tah_ lah roo_eh_-dah deh reh-_pooehs_-toh) (Where's the spare tire?)

> ✔ **¿Dónde tengo que devolver el auto?** (_dohn_-deh _tehn_-goh keh deh-bvohl-_bvehr_ ehl _ahoo_-toh) (Where do I have to return the car?)

Questions about driving

You also want to know about the car you are renting, and the driving conditions in the area you're visiting. These phrases will help you get the information you need:

> ✔ **¿El auto es estándar o automático?** (ehl _ahoo_-toh ehs ehs-_tahn_-dahr oh ahoo-toh-_mah_-tee-koh) (Is the car standard or automatic?)

> ✔ **¿Es difícil manejar por aquí?** (ehs dee-_fee_-seel mah-neh-_Hahr_ pohr ah-_kee_) (Is it hard to drive around here?)

> ✔ **Hay que tener mucha prudencia.** (ahy keh teh-_nehr_ _moo_-chah proo-_dehn_-seeah) (You have to be very prudent/careful.)

> ✔ **¿Habrá mucho tráfico en la mañana?** (ah-_bvrah_ moo-choh _trah_-fee-koh ehn lah mah-_nyah_-nah) (Will there be much traffic in the morning?)

> ✔ **¿Cuál es la mejor hora para salir de la ciudad?** (kooahl ehs lah meh-_Hohr_ oh-rah _pah_-rah sah-_leer_ deh lah seeoo-_dahd_) (Which is the best time to get out of the city?)

Questions about the road

The people at the car rental office may know something about the roads that you are about to explore. Here are some questions and answers you may get while the agent and you are looking at a map:

> ✔ **¿Están pavimentados los caminos?** (ehs-_tahn_ pah-bvee-mehn-_tah_-dohs lohs kah-_mee_-nohs) (Are the roads paved?)

> ✔ **No todos. Estos son de tierra.** (noh _toh_-dohs _ehs_-tohs sohn deh tee_eh_-rrah) (Not all of them. These are dirt roads.)

> ✔ **No todos. Estos son de terracería.** (noh _toh_-dohs _ehs_-tohs sohn deh teh-rrah-seh-_reeah_) (Not all of them. These are dirt roads.) [Mexico].

> ✔ **Esos caminos tienen muchos baches.** (_eh_-sohs kah-_mee_-nohs tee_eh_-nehn _moo_-chohs _bvah_-chehs) (Those roads have a lot of potholes.)

> ✔ **Estos caminos están excelentes.** (_eh_-sohs _kah_-mee-nohs sohn ehk-seh-_lehn_-tehs) (Those roads are excellent.)

> ✔ **Hay autopista.** *(ahy ahoo-toh-pees-tah)* (There's a freeway.)
>
> ✔ **Son caminos de cuotas.** *(sohn kah-mee-nohs deh koooh-tahs.)* (They are toll roads.) [Mexico]
>
> ✔ **Son caminos de peaje.** *(sohn kah-mee-nohs deh peh-ah-Heh)* (They are toll roads.)

Words to Know

arriendan	ah-rreeehn-dahn	they rent
renta	rehn-tah	rental
el camino	ehl kah-mee-noh	the road
el pavimento	ehl pah-bvee-mehn-toh	the pavement
de tierra	deh teeeh-rrah	dirt [road]
de terracería	teh-rrah-seh-reeah	dirt [road]
la autopista	lah ahoo-toh-pees-tah	the freeway
la cuota	lah koooh-tah	the toll [Mexico]
el peaje	ehl peh-ah-Heh	the toll
manejar	mah-neh-Hahr	to drive
los reglamentos	lohs rehg-lah-mehn-tohs	the rules
doblar	doh-bvlahr	to turn
salir	sah-leer	to exit

Scheduling Issues: Running Late, Early, or On Time

No matter what mode of transportation you are using, it's helpful to know what kind of schedule you're on and whether you will be able to reach your destination on time. The following list contains phrases to know when you want to schedule something and need to know how well the timing is being met:

✔ **a la hora** *(ah lah oh-rah)* (on time)

✔ **anda atrasado** *(ahn-dah ah-trah-sah-doh)* ([it] is running late)

✔ **viene adelantado** *(bveeeh-neh ah-deh-lahn-tah-doh)* ([it] is coming early)

✔ **el horario** *(ehl oh-rah-reeoh)* (the schedule)

✔ **es temprano** *(ehs tehm-prah-noh)* (it's early) [time]

✔ **es tarde** *(ehs tahr-deh)* (it's late) [time]

✔ **la tarde** *(lah tahr-deh)* (the afternoon)

The word **tarde** *(tahr-deh)* has different meanings depending on whether you use the article. Chapter 2 discusses when to use the article.

Sometimes the posted or printed schedule for a bus, train, or plane is not up-to-date and you may need to ask someone about it. Here are some responses you may hear where scheduling phrases come into play:

✔ **Hay que esperar, está atrasado.** *(ahy keh ehs-peh-rahr ehs-tah ah-trah-sah-doh)* (One has to wait; it's late.)

✔ **El vuelo llegó adelantado.** *(ehl bvooeh-loh yeh-goh ah-deh-lahn-tah-doh)* (The flight came in late.)

✔ **El reloj está adelantado.** *(ehl reh-lohH ehs-tah ah-deh-lahn-tah-doh)* (The clock is slow.)

✔ **El bus va adelantado.** *(ehl bvoos bvah ah-deh-lahn-tah-doh)* (The bus goes early.)

✔ **El tren va a llegar a la hora.** *(ehl trehn bvah ah yeh-gahr ah lah oh-rah)* (The train will arrive on time.)

✔ **Esperan porque va a llegar tarde.** *(ehs-peh-rahn pohr-keh bvah a yeh-gahr tahr-deh)* (They're waiting because it will arrive late.)

✔ **El bus viene a la hora.** *(ehl bvoos bveeeh-neh ah lah oh-rah)* (The bus comes on time.)

Talkin' the Talk

Scheduling information is most important when you are trying to catch a flight. Susana tries to pick up a schedule at the last minute but hasn't time to read it, so she asks for help from the airline information attendant:

Susana: **Necesito el horario de los vuelos.**
neh-seh-see-toh ehl oh-rah-reeoh deh lohs bvooeh-lohs
I need the flight schedule.

Information attendant:	**Aquí hay uno.** *ah-kee ahy oo-noh* Here's one.
Susana:	**¿A qué hora sale el avión para Mendoza?** *ah keh oh-rah sah-leh ehl ah-bveeohn pah-rah mehn-doh-sah* When does the plane for Mendoza leave?
Information attendant:	**Según el horario sale a las tres de la tarde.** *seh-goon ehl oh-rah-reeoh sah-leh ah lahs trehs deh lah tahr-deh* According to schedule, it leaves at 3:00 in the afternoon.
Susana:	**Me tengo que apurar, estoy atrasada.** *meh tehn-goh keh ah-poo-rahr, ehs-tohy ah-trah-sah-dah* I have to hurry; I'm late.
Information attendant:	**Todavía no sale, va atrasado.** *toh-dah-bveeah noh sah leh bvah ah-trah-sah-doh* It doesn't leave yet; it's running [going] late.

The Outgoing Verb: Salir

GRAMMATICALLY SPEAKING

Salir *(sah-leer)* (to go out) is an irregular verb that has many different uses. Here are just a few of the uses of this outgoing verb:

- ✔ **¿De dónde sale el tranvía a Callao?** *(deh dohn-deh sah-leh ehl trahn-bveeah ah kah-yah-oh)* (Where does the Callao street car leave from?)

- ✔ **¿Cada cuánto sale el bus?** *(kah-dah kooahn-toh sah-leh ehl bvoos)* (How often does the bus leave?)

- ✔ **Salimos a andar en trolebús.** *(sah-lee-mohs ah ahn-dahr ehn troh-leh-bvoos)* (We went out to ride around in the trolleybus.)

✔ **Ellos salen de la estación del tren.** (*<u>eh</u>-yohs <u>sah</u>-lehn deh lah ehs-tah-see<u>ohn</u> dehl trehn*) (They are going out of the station.)

✔ **Vamos a salir en la calle Oro.** (*<u>bvah</u>-mohs ah sah-<u>leer</u> ehn lah <u>kah</u>-yeh <u>oh</u>-roh*) (We'll come out at Oro street.)

Here's how you conjugate **salir** in the present tense:

Conjugation	Pronunciation
yo salgo	yoh <u>sahl</u>-goh
tú sales	too <u>sah</u>-lehs
él, ella, ello, uno, usted sale	ehl, <u>eh</u>-yah, <u>eh</u>-yoh, <u>oo</u>-noh, oos-<u>tehd</u>, <u>sah</u>-leh
nosotros salimos	noh-<u>soh</u>-trohs sah-<u>lee</u>-mohs
vosotros salís	bvoh-<u>soh</u>-trohs sah-<u>lees</u>
ellos, ellas, ustedes salen	<u>eh</u>-yohs, <u>eh</u>-yahs, oos-<u>teh</u>-dehs <u>sah</u>-lehn

Using the Waiting Verb: Esperar

Esperar (*ehs-<u>pehr</u>-ahr*) is the verb of hoping and waiting — maybe you're waiting because you are hoping. In any case, **esperar** is a regular verb, easy to handle, as shown in the following conjugation in the present tense. The root of this verb is **esper-** (*ehs-<u>pehr</u>*); this is the part of the verb to which you add the various endings.

Conjugation	Pronunciation
yo espero	yoh ehs-<u>peh</u>-roh
tú esperas	too ehs-<u>peh</u>-rahs
él, ella, ello, uno, usted espera	ehl, <u>eh</u>-yah, <u>eh</u>-yoh, <u>oo</u>-noh, oos-<u>tehd</u>, ehs-<u>peh</u>-rah
nosotros esperamos	noh-<u>soh</u>-trohs ehs-peh-<u>rah</u>-mohs
vosotros esperáis	bvoh-<u>soh</u>-trohs ehs-peh-<u>rahees</u>
ellos, ellas, ustedes esperan	<u>eh</u>-yohs, <u>eh</u>-yahs, oos-<u>teh</u>-dehs ehs-<u>peh</u>-rahn

Practicing the waiting verb

Esperar que (*ehs-peh-<u>rahr</u> keh*) is hoping. **Esperar** plain and simple is waiting. Here are some phrases to practice:

✔ **Espero que le guste mi auto.** (*ehs-<u>peh</u>-roh keh leh <u>goos</u>-teh mee <u>ahoo</u>-toh*) (I hope you'll like my car.)

- **Esperamos en la cola.** *(ehs-peh-rah-mohs ehn lah koh-lah)* (We are waiting in the lineup.)

- **Espero que venga el taxi.** *(ehs-peh-roh keh bvehn-gah ehl tah-ksee)* (I hope the taxi will come.)

- **Espero el taxi.** *(ehs-peh-roh ehl tah-ksee)* (I'm waiting for the taxi.)

- **No esperamos más el bus.** *(noh ehs-peh-rah-mohs mahs ehl bvoos)* (We won't wait for the bus any longer.)

- **Deben esperar el avión.** *(deh-bvehn ehs-peh-rahr ehl ah-bveeohn)* (They must wait for the plane.)

- **Espera el camión de Insurgentes.** *(ehs-peh-rah ehl kah-meeohn deh een-soor-Hehn-tehs)* (He waits for the Insurgentes bus. [Mexico])

Getting around in the City

Getting around in a city can be fun but also confusing. Fortunately, many people are willing to give directions. Just ask, and you'll get answers. Most people love to help.

The places we're talking about in this section are in Buenos Aires.

- **En esta ciudad hay buses y trolebuses.** *(ehn ehs-tah seeoo-dahd ahy bvoo-sehs ee troh-leh-bvoo-sehs)* (In this city there are buses and trolley-buses.)

- **En Buenos Aires hay trenes subterráneos.** *(ehn bvooeh-nohs ahee-rehs ahy treh-nehs soob-teh-rrah-neh-ohs)* (There are subways in Buenos Aires.)

- **El mapa del subte está en la estación.** *(ehl mah-pah dehl soob-teh ehs-tah ehn lah ehs-tah-seeohn)* (The subway map is in the station.)

- **Sale en la estación de Callao.** *(sah-leh ehn lah ehs-tah-seeohn deh kah-yah-oh)* (You go out at Callao station.)

- **¿Aquí para el bus de Palermo?** *(ah-kee pah-rah ehl bvoos deh pah-lehr-moh)* (Does the Palermo bus stop here?)

- **¿Este bus va por Rivadavia?** *(ehs-teh bvoos bvah pohr ree-bvah-dah-bveeah)* (Does this bus go on Rivadavia?)

- **Hay que hacer cola.** *(ahy keh ah-sehr koh-lah)* (You have to line up.)

- **¿Qué bus tomo para Caballito?** *(keh bvoos toh-moh pah-rah kah-bvah-yee-toh)* (What bus do I take for Caballito?)

- **¿El cuarenta me deja en Rivadavia con La Rural?** *(ehl kooah-rehn-tah meh deh-Hah ehn ree-bvah-dah-bveeah kohn lah roo-rahl)* (Does [bus] number 40 leave me at Rivadavia and La Rural?)

Words to Know

la cola	lah koh-lah	the line [literally: the tail]
el camión	ehl kah-meeohn	the bus [in Mexico]
el trolebús	ehl troh-leh-bvoos	the trolley bus
el trolley	ehl troh-ley	the trolley bus
la micro	lah mee-kroh	the bus [in Chile]

Fun and Games

Anytime you travel to a new place, you're going to have loads of questions. This game provides you with the start of common questions. Unscramble the Spanish words and then circle their English translations in the word find. Or find the English and then unscramble the Spanish. It's your book and your game, so don't let us dictate the rules!

¿omóc egoll a . . . ?　　　　_____

¿mevaéll orp ravof a . . . ?　　_____

¿dedón eáts . . . ?　　　　　_____

¿a nóded av?　　　　　　　_____

¿a équ hoar?　　　　　　　_____

¿sote uéq se?　　　　　　　_____

¿denód countreen . . . ?　　　_____

¿nucoát catsue?　　　　　　_____

See Appendix D for the answer key. And don't forget to turn the page for the word jumble!

Chapter 15
Planning a Trip

* *

* *

This chapter will move you! No, you won't end up tear-soaked. Rather, you find out about moving to new worlds, new experiences, and moving out of your daily chores. It's about moving into vacation, onto beaches and mountains, into different climates. Get moving to see things still unseen, to experience the inexperienced. It's adventure time.

In Latin America you can go to many very diverse places. Almost all have one thing in common, though: They speak this wonderful language called Spanish. (In Brazil, people speak a close cousin, Portuguese, and some Caribbean countries include non-Spanish speakers, as well.)

For half the year, the climates in the United States and Canada are cold. Many folks who live there like to head to the sunny valleys and glittering beaches of Latin America to warm their bones. Latin America has plenty of sun-filled sites from which to choose.

You may also be interested in visiting places where you can explore the cultures of the peoples who were living in Spanish-speaking America before the arrival of the Spaniards and who still live there and influence its culture.

Spain itself is a wonderful country, well worth a visit. May through October are the best times to go. Much of Spain is very hot and dry, but the northern third is comfortable and the beaches are superb. Avoid Madrid in July and August; the Spaniards do.

When you go to Latin America, you experience a civilization that is mainly the result of the mixing of peoples and cultures from four continents: the Americas, Europe, and Africa.

The balancing of these mixtures varies. In some places, such as in the southeast of Mexico or much of Bolivia and Peru, the aboriginal Indian heritage prevails. In countries like Argentina or Uruguay, European cultures are more evident. But wherever you go, in Latin America or sunny Spain, you will find something that is unique, something special to take home in your hands, and in your heart as well.

Making Travel Plans

One thing you already know: Whatever your choices or your desires, you can find them in Latin America, in the Spanish-speaking countries, among the Spanish-speaking peoples. Right?

- ✔ **Looking for beaches?** You can find dozens of wonderful beaches everywhere, except in Bolivia and Paraguay.

- ✔ **Looking for waterfalls?** Head for **El Salto del Angel** (*ehl <u>sahl</u>-toh dehl ahn-Hehl*) (The Angel's Leap), the highest in the world, in Venezuela. Or the most spectacular one, **Las Cataratas del Iguazú** (*lahs kah-tah-<u>rah</u>-tahs dehl ee-gooah-<u>sooh</u>*) (The Iguazú Falls), in Argentina, on the border with Brazil and Paraguay.

- ✔ **Looking for lakes?** Consider Lake Titicaca between Peru and Bolivia or tour the lakes connecting the southern regions of Chile and Argentina.

- ✔ **On an ecological excursion?** Try the forests of Honduras, Venezuela, Colombia, Bolivia, Peru, Guatemala, or Costa Rica.

- ✔ **Discovering ancient civilizations?** There are literally hundreds of places in Mexico, Guatemala, Colombia, Peru, Paraguay, and Spain.

If shopping is your heart's desire, put on some comfortable shoes and check out these tips:

- ✔ **Looking for fine porcelain?** Head for Spain.

- ✔ **Shopping for leather goods?** Argentina and Mexico are prime locations.

- ✔ **Looking for silverware?** Try Mexico or Peru.

For more about preparing for shopping trips, see Chapter 6.

Planning for the Weather

The *Southern Cone* is the name of the area in which Chile, Argentina, and Uruguay are located. The name of the area comes from the fact that on the map it looks like an ice cream cone. The best time to visit is between spring and fall, between September and March.

One special characteristic of the western part of South America is the chain of mountains called the **Andes** (*ahn-dehs*). Only the Himalayas have altitudes that can compare to this chain. On the border between Chile and Argentina there is a peak called **Aconcagua** (*ah-kohn-kah-gooah*) that rises over 21,000 feet. Many other peaks and volcanoes between its segments in Colombia and the south of Chile come close to that size also. Mountains like these are inconceivable to those who haven't lived under them. Some cloud formations in the Rockies spark memories of the peaks that I used to see in Chile.

Of course, the temperatures on top of these mountains are very low — eternal ice covers them. Oxygen also gets scarce. And down in the valleys, the temperatures rise and fall according to the latitudes, in the same way that it is cooler in the valleys of the Yukon than those of southern California.

In the tropics, in countries like Peru, Bolivia, Ecuador, Colombia, Venezuela, Guatemala, and Mexico, the temperatures change mostly due to the altitude of the places you visit.

From northern Peru to the central parts of Mexico, you have mainly two seasons: **La Seca** (*lah seh-kah*) (the dry season) from November to May; and **la de Las Lluvias** (*lah deh lahs yoo-bveeahs*) (the rainy season) when on the coasts you may have hurricanes.

In the rainy season in these regions, it can rain quite forcefully, sometimes for longer periods, even days. But the air is nicely warm.

In the dry season, you have sunny, very bright days in almost all areas (with the exception of places like the Peruvian capital city of Lima that stays under a protective layer of clouds many months of the year. This comes handy when you want to get out of the sun.)

In Spain, you don't have a rainy season and a dry season, you have rainy and dry areas. The northern third is rainy with comfortable temperatures. The rest of Spain, except for the coasts, is very hot and dry, with deep blue skies and a rich and varied history.

Talkin' the Talk

Juan decides to take a bus to a Chilean beach. But first he needs some information.

Juan: **¿A qué hora parte el bus para Pichidangui?**
ah keh oh-rah pahr-teh ehl bvoos pah-rah pee-chee-dahn-ghee
At what time goes the bus for Pichidangui?

Attendant: **A las diez de la mañana y a las diez de la noche.**
ah lahs deeehs deh lah mah-<u>nyah</u>-nah ee ah lahs deees deh lah <u>noh</u>-cheh
At ten in the morning and ten at night.

Juan: **Ah, hay un bus de día y otro de noche.**
ah, ahy oon bvoos deh deeah ee <u>oh</u>-troh de <u>noh</u>-cheh
Ah, there is a bus in daytime and another at night.

¿Hay bus todos los días?
ahy bvoos <u>toh</u>-dohs lohs deeahs
Is there a bus every day?

Attendant: **Los buses a Pichidangui van los lunes, miércoles y viernes.**
lohs <u>bvoo</u>-sehs ah pee-chee-<u>dahn</u>-gee bvahn lohs <u>loo</u>-nehs, mee<u>ehr</u>-koh-lehs y bvee<u>ehr</u>-nehs
The Pichidangui buses go on Mondays, Wednesdays, and Fridays.

Timing your trip: pick a month

Whether you prefer the warmth of the dry season or the drama of the wet season, you need to know the months of the year to help you plan your trip. (Note that in Spanish, the names of the months do not begin with a capital letter, as they do in English.)

- **enero** *(eh-<u>neh</u>-roh)* (January)
- **febrero** *(feh-<u>bvreh</u>-roh)* (February)
- **marzo** *(<u>mahr</u>-soh)* (March)
- **abril** *(ah-<u>bvreel</u>)* (April)
- **mayo** *(<u>mah</u>-yoh)* (May)
- **junio** *(<u>Hoo</u>-neeoh)* (June)
- **julio** *(<u>Hoo</u>-leeoh)* (July)
- **agosto** *(ah-<u>gohs</u>-toh)* (August)
- **septiembre** *(sehp-tee<u>ehm</u>-breh)* (September)
- **octubre** *(ohk-<u>too</u>-bvreh)* (October)
- **noviembre** *(noh-bvee<u>ehm</u>-breh)* (November)
- **diciembre** *(dee-see<u>ehm</u>-breh)* (December)

Take a look at the following examples to help you practice using dates for your trip:

- **En enero voy a ir a Colombia.** *(ehn eh-neh-roh bvoy ah eer a koh-lohm-bveeah)* (In January, I'm going to go to Colombia.)

- **Vuelvo de España en marzo.** *(bvoo ehl-bvoh de ehs-pah-nyah ehn mahr-soh)* (I return from Spain in March.)

- **El viaje es de julio a diciembre.** *(ehl bveeah-Heh ehs deh Hoo-leeoh ah dee-seeehm-bvreh)* (The trip is from July to December.)

- **La estación de lluvias es de mayo a noviembre.** *(lah ehs-tah-seeohn deh yoo-bveeahs ehs deh mah-yoh ah noh-bveeehm-bvreh)* (The rainy season is from May to November.)

Talkin' the Talk

 Sergio wants to fly from Mexico City to Cancún. He goes to a travel agency to book his flight.

Sergio: **Buenos días.**
bvooeh-nohs deeahs
Good morning.

Travel agent: **Buenos días, señor. ¿En qué le puedo servir?**
bvooeh-nohs deeahs seh-nyohr ehn keh leh pooeh-doh sehr-bveer
Good morning, sir. How may I

Sergio: **Necesito un boleta para Cancún.**
neh-seh-see-to oon bvoh-leh-tah pah-rah kahn-koon
I need a ticket for Cancún.

Travel agent: **¿En qué día le acomoda?**
ehn keh deeah leh ah-koh-moh dah
What day works for you?

Sergio: **El viernes en la mañana.**
ehl bveeehr-nehs ehn lah mah-nyah-nah
Friday morning.

Travel agent: **Hay un vuelo a las ocho.**
ahy oon bvooeh-loh ah lahs oh-choh
There's a flight at eight.

Sergio: **¿Un poco más tarde?**
oon poh-koh mahs tahr-deh
A little later?

Travel agent: **Sí, hay otro a las nueve.**
see, ahy oh-troh ah lahs nooeh-bveh
Yes, there's another one at nine.

Sergio: **Tomo ese.**
toh-moh eh-seh
We'll take that one.

Travel agent: **¿Hasta qué día?**
ahs-tah keh deeah
Until what day?

Sergio: **Hasta el domingo en la tarde.**
ahs-tah ehl doh-meen-goh ehn lah tahr-deh
Until Sunday afternoon.

Travel agent: **Hay un vuelo a las siete de la tarde.**
*ahy oon bvooeh-loh ah lahs seeeh-teh deh lah
tahr-deh*
There's a flight at seven in the afternoon.

Sergio: **Es buena hora. Hágame las reservaciones.**
*ehs bvooeh-nah oh-rah ah-gah-meh lahs
reh-sehr-bvah-seeoh-nehs*
It's a good time. Book me that flight.

Travel agent: **Aquí tiene, señor. El vuelo sale de México a las 9 de la
mañana. Tienen que estar en el aeropuerto una hora
antes.**
*ah-kee teeeh-neh seh-nyor
el bvooeh-loh sah-leh deh meh-Hee-koh ah lahs
nooeh-bveh deh lah mah-nyah-nah teeeh-nehn keh
ehs-tahr ehn ehl ah-eh-roh-pooehr-toh oo-nah oh-rah
ahn-tehs*
Here are the tickets. Your departure time will be 9
a.m. You have to be at the airport an hour ahead of
time.

Mastering Visas and Passports

To enter another country you need to go through some formalities. The
requirements to enter each country can vary. My advice is to check with a
travel agent or the consulate of the destination country to determine the documents and medical requirements (like shots) that you need in order to
enter. Often, travel agents can make the necessary arrangements.

Always carry your passport, whether or not you need to; you may want to go
beyond your original destination. A passport is an important document to
have when dealing with banking or emergencies.

When you're required to have a visa, you must have a passport. The passport is where your visa (a permit to visit a country) is stamped. Some countries do not require visas.

You can find more money-handling wisdom in Chapter 11.

Talkin' the Talk

The following dialog is meant for citizens of both Canada and the United States who wish to go to a Mexican destination.

Patricia, a Canadian, has some questions about traveling to Mexico.

Patricia:

¿Es éste el Consulado de México?
ehs ehs-teh ehs ehl kohn-soo-lah-doh deh meh-Hee-koh
Is this the Mexican Consulate?

Consulate attendant:

Sí, ¿en qué le puedo servir?
see, ehn keh leh pooeh-doh sehr-bveer
Yes, how can I help you?

Patricia:

¿Necesito una visa para ir a México?
neh-seh-see-toh oo-nah bvee-sah pah-rah eer ah meh-Hee-koh
Do I need a visa to go to Mexico?

Consulate attendant:

Depende. ¿Es ciudadano de Estados Unidos o de Canadá?
deh-pehn-deh ehs seeoo-dah-dah-noh deh ehs-tah-dohs oo-nee-dohs oh deh kah-nah-dah
That depends. Are you a citizen of the United States or Canada?

Patricia:

Soy canadiense.
sohy kah-nah-deeehn-seh
I'm Canadian.

Consulate attendant:

¿Por cuánto tiempo va?
pohr kooahn-toh teeehm-poh bvah
How long will you be there?

Patricia:

De noviembre a marzo.
deh noh-bveeehm-breh ah mahr-soh
From November to March.

Consulate attendant:	**Son cinco meses. ¿Va como turista?** *sohn seen-koh meh-sehs bvah koh-moh* *too-rees-tah* That's five months. Are you going as a tourist?
Patricia:	**Sí.** *see* Yes.
Consulate attendant:	**Va a necesitar visa de turista.** *bvah ah neh-seh-see-tahr bvee-sah deh* *too-rees-tah* You will need a tourist visa.
Patricia:	**¿Tengo que venir aquí por una visa?** *tehn-goh keh bveh-neer ah-kee pohr oo-* *nah bvee-sah* Do I have to come here for a visa?
Consulate attendant:	**No.**

Phrases to Know

la hora de despegue	lah oh-rah dehl dehs-peh-geh	The take-off time
la fecha de llegada	lah feh-chah deh yeh-gah-dah	The arrival date
la fecha de partida	lah feh-chah deh pahr-tee-dah	The departure date
boleto de ida	bvoh-leh-toh deh ee-dah	One way ticket (Literally: Ticket to go)
boleto de vuelta	bvoh-leh-toh deh bvooehl-tah	Return ticket
boleto de ida y vuelta	bvoh-leh-toh deh ee-dah ee bvooehl-tah	Round trip ticket (Literally: Ticket to go and return)
vuelo directo	bvooeh-loh dee-rehk-toh	Direct flight
vuelo con escalas	bvooeh-loh kohn ehs-kah-lahs	Flight with stopovers

Talkin' the Talk

John Raymond needs to cancel a trip.

John Raymond: **Señorita, ¿me ayuda por favor?**
seh-nyoh-ree-tah meh ah-yoo-dah pohr fah-bvohr
Miss, can you help me, please?

Travel agent: **Sí, ¿en qué puedo servirle?**
see ehn keh pooeh-doh sehr-bveer-leh
Yes, what can I do for you?

John Raymond: **Quisiera cancelar un viaje a Cartagena.**
kee-seeeh-rah kahn-seh-lahr oon bveeah-Heh ah kahr-tah-Heh-nah
I would like to cancel a trip to Cartagena.

Travel agent: **¿Cuándo iba a viajar?**
kooahn-doh ee-bvah ah bveeah-Hahr
When were you going?

John Raymond: **El lunes próximo.**
ehl loo-nehs proh-ksee-moh
Next Monday.

Travel agent: **¿A qué nombre está la reservación?**
ah keh nohm-bvreh ehs-tah lah reh-sehr-bvah-seeohn
Under what name is the booking?

John Raymond: **A nombre de John Raymond.**
ah nohm-bvreh deh John Raymond
In the name of John Raymond.

Travel agent: **Ah, bien, ya lo cancelé. ¿Algo más?**
ah bveeehn, yah loh kahn-seh-leh ahl-goh mahs
Ah, good, I canceled it. Anything else?

John Raymond: **No, eso es todo, gracias.**
noh eh-soh ehs toh-doh, grah-seeahs
No, that's all, thank you.

Using the Verb to Go: Ir

Ir *(eer)* (to go) is a very irregular verb — so much so that you have to take it on faith from me that the following table shows the present tense conjugation of the verb. You can't tell just by looking at it.

Conjugation	Pronunciation
yo voy	yoh bvohy
tú vas	too bvahs
él, ella, ello, uno, usted va	ehl, <u>eh</u>-yah, <u>eh</u>-yoh, <u>oo</u>-noh, oos-<u>tehd</u>, bvah
nosotros vamos	noh-<u>soh</u>-trohs <u>bvah</u>-mohs
vosotros váis	bvoh-<u>soh</u>-trohs <u>bvahees</u>
ellos, ellas, ustedes van	<u>eh</u>-yohs, <u>eh</u>-yahs, oos-<u>teh</u>-dehs bvahn

Traveling into the simple future: ir a viajar

The verb **ir** *(eer)* (go), like the English verb *to go,* can be used to make a kind of future tense called the *simple future.* It's like saying, "I'm *going to travel.*" In Spanish, that phrase is **voy a viajar** *(bvohy ah bveeah-<u>Hahr</u>)*. So what follows is an example of the use of the verb **ir** with the infinitive of **viajar** *(bveeah-<u>Hahr</u>)*, to tell about the simple future of the traveling verb.

Word	Pronunciation
yo voy a viajar	yoh bvoy ah bveeah-<u>Hahr</u>
tú vas a viajar	too bvahs ah bveeah-<u>Hahr</u>
él, ella, ello, uno, usted va a viajar	ehl, <u>eh</u>-yah, <u>eh</u>-yoh, <u>oo</u>-noh, oos-<u>tehd</u>, bvah a bveeah-<u>Hahr</u>
nosotros vamos a viajar	noh-<u>soh</u>-trohs <u>bvah</u>-mohs ah bveeah-<u>Hahr</u>
vosotros váis a viajar	bvoh-<u>soh</u>-trohs bvahees ah bveeah-<u>Hahr</u>
ellos, ellas, ustedes van a viajar	<u>eh</u>-yohs, <u>eh</u>-yahs, oos-<u>teh</u>-dehs bvahn a bveeah-<u>Hahr</u>

Practice using the future tense of **ir a viajar**. It's quite fun, so check it out:

- ✔ **Voy a viajar en avión.** *(bvoy a bveeah-<u>Hahr</u> ehn ah-bvee<u>ohn</u>)* (I'm going to travel by air.)

- ✔ **Ellos van a viajar en autobús.** *(<u>eh</u>-yohs bvahn ah bveeah-<u>Hahr</u> ehn ahoo-toh-<u>bvoos</u>)* (They are going to travel by bus.)

✔ **Vamos a viajar en tren.** (*bvah-mohs ah bveeah-Hahr ehn trehn*) (We will be traveling by rail.)

✔ **Tú vas a ir en avión.** (*too bvahs a eer ehn ah-bveeohn*) (You're going to go by plane.)

✔ **Voy a ir a comer.** (*bvohy ah eer ah koh-mehr*) (I'm going to go to eat.)

✔ **Todos nos vamos a divertir.** (*toh-dohs nohs bvah-mohs ah dee-bvehr-teer*) (We are all going to have fun.)

✔ **Va a llegar cansado.** (*bvah ah yeh-gahr kahn-sah-doh*) (He will be tired when he arrives.)

✔ **Va a querer volver.** (*bvah ah keh-rehr bvohl-bvehr*) (He will want to return.)

✔ **Nosotros vamos a llevar las maletas.** (*noh-soh-trohs bvah-mohs ah yeh-bvahr lahs mah-leh-tahs*) (We are going to carry the luggage.)

Scheduling hours and minutes

Whether it's the past, present, or future, you're talking about *time*. And when you talk about time, you need to know about minutes and hours. Here you go! Right on time!

✔ **Voy a las diez de la mañana.** (*bvohy ah lahs deeehs deh lah mah-nyah-nah*) (I'm going at ten o'clock in the morning.)

✔ **Llega a las nueve de la noche.** (*yeh-gah ah lahs nooeh-bveh deh lah noh-cheh*) (He arrives at nine o'clock in the evening.)

✔ **Son las veinte y treinta horas.** (*sohn lahs bveheen-teh ee treheen-tah oh-rahs*) (It's 8:30 p.m. [Literally: It's twenty and thirty hours.])

✔ **Son las ocho cuarenta y cinco.** (*sohn lahs oh-choh kooah-rehn-tah ee seen-koh*) (It's 8:45.)

✔ **Vengo a la una y cuarto.** (*bvehn-goh ah lah oo-nah ee kooahr-toh*) (I'm coming at a quarter past one.)

✔ **Un cuarto para las dos llovió.** (*oon kooahr-toh pah-rah lahs dohs yoh-bveeoh*) (It rained at a quarter to two.)

✔ **Son diez para las once.** (*sohn deeehs pah-rah lahs ohn-seh.*) (It's ten to eleven.)

Head over to the end of Chapter 5 for more about numbers. In the meantime, continue to practice your scheduling phrases with the following:

✔ **¿Qué hora es?** (*keh oh-rah ehs*) (What time is it?)

✔ **Un minuto, por favor.** (*oon mee-noo-toh, pohr fah-bvohr*) (One minute, please.)

✔ **Un segundo, por favor.** (*ooh seh-<u>goon</u>-doh, pohr fah-<u>bvohr</u>*) (One second, please.)

✔ **Un momento por favor.** (*oon moh-<u>mehn</u>-toh pohr fah-<u>bvoh</u>*) (One moment, please.)

Words to Know

la hora	lah <u>oh</u>-rah	the hour
el minuto	ehl mee-<u>noo</u>-toh	the minute
el segundo	ehl seh-<u>goon</u>-doh	the second
el cuarto	ehl <u>kooahr</u>-toh	the quarter
el medio	ehl <u>meh</u>-deeoh	the half
la tarde	lah <u>tahr</u>-deh	the afternoon
la noche	lah <u>noh</u>-cheh	the night

Packing: Less Is More

You're planning what to take with you.

When visiting colonial monuments such as churches, plan to wear skirts, dresses, or long trousers. Shorts are great on the beach, but in cities you will look more in style with longer wear.

Latins are a bit more formal than people in the United States and pay a good deal of attention to beautiful clothing. You will feel better walking on the city streets if you also have something nice to wear.

Talkin' the Talk

 Gabriela and Tomás are talking about what to pack for their upcoming trip. Listen as they discuss what they will need.

Gabriela: **Falta hacer las maletas.**
<u>fahl</u>-tah <u>ah</u>-sehr lahs mah-<u>leh</u>-tahs
We still have to pack the luggage.

Tomás:	**Mejor es llevar un piyama.**
	meh-Hohr ehs yeh-bvahr oon pee-yah-mah
	It's better to take pajamas.
	Y un pulóver, por si hace fresco.
	ee oon pool-oh-bvehr pohr see ah-seh frehs-koh
	And a pullover, in case it's cool.
Gabriela:	**Llevo ropa liviana de algodón.**
	yeh-bvoh roh-pah lee-bveeah-nah deh ahl-goh-dohn
	I'm taking light, cotton clothes.
Tomás:	**Aquí está el traje de baño.**
	ah-kee ehs-tah ehl trah-Heh deh bvah-nyoh
	Here is the swimsuit.
Gabriela:	**Llevo zapatos para la playa.**
	yeh-bvoh sah-pah-tohs pah-rah lah plah-yah
	I'm taking shoes for the beach.
Tomás:	**Estos zapatos son para la ciudad.**
	ehs-tohs sah-pah-tohs soh pah-rah lah seeoo-dahd
	These shoes are for the city.
Gabriela:	**También llevo un vestido liviano.**
	tahm-bveeehn yeh-bvoh oon bvehs-tee-doh lee-bveeah-noh
	I'm also taking a light dress.
Tomás:	**Aquí están mis zapatos cómodos.**
	ah-kee ehs-tahn mees sah-pah-tohs koh-moh-dohs
	Here are my comfortable shoes.
Gabriela:	**Tenemos tres maletas y un bolso marinero.**
	teh-neh-mohs trehs mah-leh-tahs ee oon bvohl-soh mah-ree-neh-roh
	We have three suitcases and one duffel bag [Argentina].

Taking Along Your Computer

For those hours between activities, you might decide to do something on your laptop computer. Work never stops, not even when you're on vacation. Here are some phrases that can help when talking about your laptop:

- **Voy a llevar conmigo la computadora portátil.** *(bvohy ah yeh-bvahr kohn-mee-goh lah kohm-poo-tah-doh-rah pohr-tah-teel)* (I'll take the laptop computer.)

- **No te olvides las baterías.** *(noh teh ohl-bvee-dehs lahs bah-teh-reeahs)* (Don't forget the batteries.)

- **Vas a llevar el adaptador de corriente.** *(bvahs a yeh-bvahr ehl ah-dahp-tah-dohr deh koh-rreeehn-teh)* (You will take the voltage adapter.)

- **Necesitamos el adaptador para cargar la batería.** *(neh-seh-see-tah-mohs ehl ah-dahp-tah-dohr pah-rah kahr-gahr la bah-teh-reeah)* (We need the adapter to charge the battery.)

Words to Know

la computadora portátil	lah kohm-poo-tah-doh-rah pohr-tah teel	laptop computer
la batería	lah bah-teh-reeah	battery
la corriente	lah koh-rreeehn-teh	current
cargar	kahr-gahr	to charge

Talkin the Talk

The trip is over and these friends are talking about how it was. You can practice with them.

Daniel: **¿Cómo estuvo tu viaje?**
koh-moh ehs-too-bvoh too bveeah-Heh
How was your trip?

Agustín: **¡Fabuloso!**
fah-bvoo-loh-soh
Fabulous!

Daniel: **¿Adónde estuviste?**
ah-dohn-deh ehs-too-bvees-teh
Where were you?

Agustín:	**Estuve en Puerto Escondido.**
	ehs-<u>too</u>-bveh ehn poo<u>ehr</u>-toh ehs-kohn-<u>dee</u>-doh
	I was in Puerto Escondido.

Daniel:	**¿Cómo fuiste?**
	<u>koh</u>-moh foo<u>ees</u>-teh
	How did you go?

Agustín:	**Fui en avión y volví en autobús.**
	fooee ehn ah-bvee<u>ohn</u> ee bvohl-<u>bvee</u> ehn
	ahoo-toh-<u>bvoos</u>
	I went by plane and returned by bus.

Daniel:	**¿Cuánto demora el avión?**
	koo<u>ahn</u>-toh deh-<u>moh</u>-rah ehl ah-bvee<u>ohn</u>
	How long does the plane take?

Agustín:	**Quince minutos.**
	<u>keen</u>-seh mee-<u>noo</u>-tohs
	Fifteen minutes.

Daniel:	**¿Y el autobús?**
	ee ehl ahoo-toh-<u>bvoos</u>
	And the bus?

Agustín:	**Seis horas.**
	sehees <u>oh</u>-rahs
	Six hours.

Fun & Games

Choosing the month that you're going to travel is the first part of planning any vacation. The illustration below shows each of the four seasons. Each of the twelve months is scrambled below. Unscramble the month and then write it in the blank next to the appropriate season. (Remember, the names of the months aren't capitalized in Spanish.)

beefror	biomnerve
breedicim	goosta
joinu	libra
oneer	oyam
permbitees	rozam
tubecor	ujoil

Chapter 16

Help! Handling Emergencies

*B*e prepared. That's the Boy Scout motto, and it's not a bad idea for any situation. You should always be prepared for emergencies, especially in areas whose residents don't speak your native language. The language difference can complicate the emergency if no one can understand you, or if you don't understand what is being said.

This chapter looks at two main areas where you may experience an emergency. The first part of the chapter looks at health concerns — breaking an arm or experiencing stomach flu; the second part deals with "legal" emergencies — car accidents and other law infractions that may require the help of your consulate or a lawyer. But before you start preparing for these emergencies, you need to know a few important words that will quickly get you the help you need.

Shouting for Help

You may find yourself in a situation where you need to cry for help. Thumbing through your dictionary is not going to be quick enough, so you may want to memorize these words. You can use the first two interchangeably.

Following are basic distress-signaling words:

- **¡Socorro!** *(soh-koh-rroh)* (Help!)
- **¡Auxilio!** *(ahoo-ksee-leeoh)* (Help!)
- **¡Ayúdeme!** *(ah-yoo-deh-meh)* (Help me!)
- **¡Incendio!** *(een-sehn-deeoh)* (Fire!)
- **¡Inundación!** *(ee-noon-dah-seeohn)* (Flood!)
- **¡Temblor!** *(tehm-bvlohr)* (Earth tremor!)
- **¡Terremoto!** *(teh-rreh-moh-toh)* (Earthquake!)
- **¡Maremoto!** *(mah-reh-moh-toh)* (Tidal wave!)

You can help speed up your request by using one of these two words:

- **¡Rápido!** *(rah-pee-doh)* (Quick!)
- **¡Apúrense!** *(ah-poo-rehn-seh)* (Hurry!)

CULTURAL WISDOM

When the pot falls

You see a flower pot falling from a balcony while someone is passing by. What do you shout? All Spanish speakers, with the exception of Mexicans, react to:

- **¡Cuidado!** *(kooee-dah-doh)* (Watch out!) (Literally: Care!)

When the flower pot is falling in Mexico, however, you have to say:

- **¡Aguas!** *(ah-gooahs)* (Watch out!) (Literally: Waters!)

This habit most likely comes from the times when drains were nonexistent, so people in colonial cities simply tossed their dirty water out the second floor window. They shouted "¡Aguas!" to warn passersby that dirty water was coming their way. Eventually, the habit of shouting **"aguas"** extended to all danger.

Handling Health Problems

When an illness or an accident jeopardizes your health, losing your head is a common and understandable reaction. We try to guide you through these potential problems in a calm and prudent manner.

In our experience, most native Spanish speakers are caring, gentle people who are tolerant of faulty pronunciation and very ready to help a foreigner. In fact, they may even be overly helpful, leaving you with the difficult task of being firm and level-headed about your needs without damaging their feelings and being negative about their good will.

Here are some sentences to help you be just as caring and kind, but at the same time firm with your refusal for help, when you don't want any. Suppose the person trying to be helpful says things like:

- ✔ **¡Pobrecito!, ¿le ayudo?** *(poh-breh-see-toh leh ah-yoo-doh)* (Poor little you [male], can I help you?)

- ✔ **¡Vengan todos, a ayudar!** *(bvehn-gahn toh-dohs ah ah-yoo-dar)* (Come, everybody, let's help him!)

In which case, you can answer with things like:

- ✔ **Por favor, estoy bien, no me ayude.** *(pohr fah-bvohr ehs-tohy bvee-en noh meh ah-yoo-deh)* (Please, I'm fine, don't help me.)

- ✔ **Muchas gracias, le agradezco, prefiero estar solo.** *(moo-chahs grah-seeahs leh ah-grah-dehs-koh preh-feeeh-roh ehs-tahr soh-loh)* (Thank you very much, I prefer to be alone.)

- ✔ **Estoy muy bien, gracias, no necesito ayuda.** *(ehs-tohy mooy bveeehn grah-seeahs noh neh-seh-see-toh ah-yoo-dah)* (I'm fine, thanks, I don't need help.)

- ✔ **Usted es muy gentil, gracias, no me ayude, por favor.** *(oos-tehd ehs mooy Hehn-teel grah-seeahs noh meh ah-yoo-deh pohr fah-bvohr)* You are very kind, thanks, don't help me, please.)

- ✔ **Ustedes son muy amables, pero estoy bien.** *(oos-teh-dehs sohn mooy ah-mah-bvlehs peh-roh ehs-tohy bveeehn)* (You [formal, plural] are very kind, but I'm fine.)

If you ask for a doctor who speaks English, and you're introduced to one, try to make sure that the doctor's English is better than your Spanish before you get involved with him or her. If you're having trouble being understood in English or Spanish, ask for another doctor whose language skills more nearly match your own.

Remember that if you have to speak in Spanish to the Spanish-speaking person you are addressing, things will go better if you speak s-l-o-w-l-y. Another thing to keep in mind is that in an emergency generally the best part of people comes to the fore. Don't worry about money when those about you want to help. There will be time for that when you have recovered, or are out of the mess. Also, let people help you if at all possible; that makes *them* feel good. As to procedures relating to emergency rooms or hospitals, let those things work themselves out, and simply be a patient patient. Remember that all those concerned are doing the best they can. Finally, keep in mind that procedures can vary from place to place in relation to the availability of people and equipment.

If you get sick while travelling, ask for advice at your hotel's reception desk.

Helping out: Using ayudar (to help)

The verb **ayudar** *(ah-yoo-dahr)* (to help), is, as you would expect, a very helpful word to know. It's a regular verb of the *-ar* variety, so it's very easy to conjugate. Here it is in the present tense:

Conjugation	Pronunciation
yo ayudo	yoh ah-<u>yoo</u>-doh
tú ayudas	too ah-<u>yoo</u>-dahs
él, ella, ello, uno, usted, ayuda	ehl <u>eh</u>-yah <u>eh</u>-yoh <u>oo</u>-noh oos-<u>tehd</u> ah-<u>yoo</u>-dah
nosotros ayudamos	noh-<u>soh</u>-trohs ah-yoo-<u>dah</u>-mohs
vosotros ayudáis	bvoh-<u>soh</u>-trohs ah-yoo-<u>dahees</u>
ellos, ellas, ustedes ayudan	<u>eh</u>-yos <u>eh</u>-yas oos-<u>teh</u>-dehs ah-<u>yoo</u>-dahn

What follows are phrases that are helpful in cases when you're talking to people you haven't met — like a doctor, or some passerby. We also give you phrases for situations when those around you are closely related to you, or when they are children.

We begin with some phrases you can use when you want to be formally helpful. The formal way of speech is more normal to use both on your part and on the part of those who are helping. It shows respect on your part to the doctor, for example, and on his part to you. Neither of you have an intimate or informal relationship:

- **¿Le ayudo?** *(leh ah-<u>yoo</u>-doh)* (Can I help you?)

- **Sí, ayúdame a pedir una ambulancia.** *(see ah-<u>yoo</u>-deh-meh ah peh-<u>deer</u> <u>oo</u>-nah ahm-bvoo-<u>lahn</u>-seeah)* (Yes, help me get an ambulance.)

✔ **Espere. Le van a ayudar a cargar al herido.** *(ehs-peh-reh leh bvahn ah ah-yoo-dahr ah kahr-gahr ahl eh-ree-doh)* (Wait. They'll help you carry the injured person.)

✔ **Usted ayude al enfermo a bajar de la camilla.** *(oos-tehd ah-yoo-deh ahl ehn-fehr-moh ah bvah-Hahr deh lah kah-mee-yah)* (You go help the sick person get off the stretcher.)

✔ **¡Apúrese!** *(ah-poo-reh-seh)* (Hurry up!)

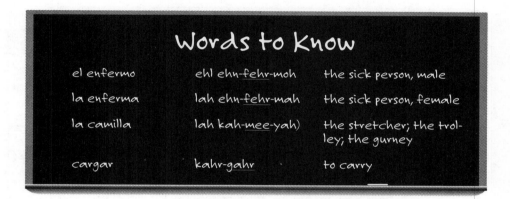

Words to Know

el enfermo	ehl ehn-fehr-moh	the sick person, male
la enferma	lah ehn-fehr-mah	the sick person, female
la camilla	lah kah-mee-yah)	the stretcher; the trolley; the gurney
cargar	kahr-gahr	to carry

The following phrases are for informal situations. Remember, informality is appropriate when you talk to a child, or if the person helping you is someone you know or who is close to you.

✔ **¿Te ayudo?** *(teh ah-yoo-doh)* (Can I help you?)

✔ **Sí, ayúdame.** *(see ah-yoo-dah-meh)* (Yes, help me.)

✔ **Te busco un médico.** *(teh bvoos-koh oon meh-dee-koh)* (I'll get a doctor for you.)

✔ **¡Apúrate!** *(ah-poo-rah-teh)* (Hurry up!)

✔ **¡Sujétame!** *(soo-Heh-tah-meh)* (Hold onto me!)

Reflex action: Helping yourself with pronouns

The pronouns you use when you talk about someone to whom something happened are *reflexive* pronouns, and Spanish uses them quite often — much more so than in English. Table 16-1 shows you which pronoun to use when the person the pronoun represents is the object of the action.

Table 16-1	Reflexive Pronouns
Pronoun	*Translation*
me *(meh)*	me
te *(teh)*	you
le *(leh)*	him, her, you (formal, singular)
nos *(nohs)*	us
os *(ohs)*	you
les *(lehs)*	them, you (formal, plural)

So how and when do you use these pronouns? Hang in there! Help is on its way!

In English you say "his leg hurts." In Spanish, you say **le duele la pierna** *(leh-doo<u>eh</u>-leh lah pee<u>ehr</u>-nah)* (Literally: him hurts the leg). The difference between the two is that in English, the leg is supposed to feel the pain (leg is the subject); in Spanish, it is the owner of the leg who feels the pain. And because both the leg and the pain belong to the same person, in Spanish the pain goes back to "him" — the owner of the leg and of the pain — which in Spanish is indicated by **le** *(leh).* So the verb, which expresses an action, is actually reflected back onto the person, not the leg; it is the person who is hurt by virtue of owning the leg. **Le** is the object of the action. And **le** is a pronoun — a reflexive pronoun.

Painful phrases for when it hurts

When you're hurt, you want to be able to tell people about it so that they can help ease your pain. The following sentences tell you how to talk about pain — and, just as carrying an umbrella can prevent rain, perhaps practicing talking about pain can prevent you from getting hurt (in Spanish, anyway)!

- **Me duele la espalda.** *(meh doo<u>eh</u>-leh lah ehs-<u>pahl</u>-dah)* (My back hurts.)

- **¿Le duele la cabeza?** *(leh doo<u>eh</u>-leh lah kah-<u>bveh</u>-sah)* (Does your head hurt? [single, formal])

- **Les duele todo.** *(lehs doo<u>eh</u>-leh <u>toh</u>-doh)* (They hurt all over.)

- **Nos duelen las manos.** *(nohs doo<u>eh</u>-lehn lahs <u>mah</u>-nohs)* (Our hands hurt.)

- **¿Te duele aquí?** *(teh doo<u>eh</u>-leh ah-<u>kee</u>)* (Does it hurt you [singular, informal] here?)

Talkin' the Talk

After a collision, Nancy is taken to a hospital and is being looked after to see whether she's broken anything.

Doctor: **¿Tiene dolor en la pierna?**
tee-eh-neh doh-lohr ehn lah pee-ehr-nah
Does your leg hurt? [Literally: Do you have any pain in the leg?]

Nancy: **Sí doctor, ¡duele mucho!**
see dohk-tohr dooeh-leh moo-choh
Yes, doctor, it hurts a lot!

Doctor: **Vamos a sacarle rayos X.**
bvah-mohs ah sah-kahr-leh rah-yohs eh-kees
We'll take an X ray.

X ray technician: **Aquí, súbanla a la mesa.**
ah-kee, soo-bvahn-lah ah lah meh-sah
Here, get her on the table.

No se mueva por favor.
noh seh mooeh-bvah pohr fah-bvor
Don't move, please.

Doctor: **Ya está la radiografía.**
yah ehs-tah lah rah-deeoh-grah-feeah
The X ray picture is ready.

Aquí tiene la fractura.
ah-kee teeeh-neh lah frahk-too-rah
We have a fracture here.

Vamos a tener que enyesar su pierna.
bvah-mohs ah teh-nehr keh ehn-yeh-sahr soo peeehr-nah
We have to put your leg in a cast.

Le voy a dar un analgésico.
leh bvohy a dahr oon ah-nahl-Heh-see-koh
I'll give you a pain killer.

Words to Know

el médico	meh-dee-koh	the doctor
la pierna	lah peeehr-nah	the leg
la fractura	lah frahk-too-rah	the fracture (medical term for broken bone)
la radiografía	lah rah-deeoh-grah-feeah	the X ray picture
el yeso	ehl yeh-soh	the plaster (either in casts or walls)
enyesar	ehn-yeh-sahr	to set in a cast
el analgésico	ehl ah-nahl-geh-see-koh	the pain killer

Getting help for a bleeding wound

Following are some examples of how to get medical help for someone who's bleeding:

- ¡Hay una emergencia! *(ahy oo-nah eh-mehr-Hehn-see-ah)* (There's an emergency!)

- ¡Traigan un médico! *(trahee-gahn oon meh-dee-koh)* (Bring a doctor!)

- ¡Traigan una ambulancia! *(trahee-gahn oo-nah ahm-bvoo-lahn-seeah)* (Bring an ambulance!)

- Lo más rápido posible. *(loh mahs rah-pee-doh poh-see-bleh)* (As fast as possible.)

- Tiene un corte. *(teeeh-neh oon kohr-teh)* (You [formal] have a cut.)

- Necesita puntos. *(neh-seh-see-tah poon-tohs)* (You [formal] need stitches.)

Words to Know

la cabeza	lah kah-_bveh_-sah	the head
la emergencia	lah eh-mehr-_Hehn_-seeah	the emergency
el corte	ehl _kohr_-teh	the cut
los puntos	lohs _poon_-tohs	the stitches [surgical]

Closing the wound

If you ever need to get stitches, here are some useful phrases:

- **Me duele mucho.** *(meh doo-_eh_-leh _moo_-choh)* (It hurts me a lot.)

- **Le vamos a poner anestesia local**. *(leh _bvah_-mohs a poh-_nehr_ ah-nehs-_teh_-seeah loh-_kahl_)* (We'll use local anesthesia.)

- **Ya se pasó el dolor.** *(yah seh _pah_-soh ehl doh-_lohr_)* (The pain is gone.)

Words to Know

la anestesia	lah ah-nehs-_teh_-seeah	the anesthesia
sangrar	_sahn_-grahr	to bleed
la herida	lah eh-_ree_-dah	the wound
el dolor	ehl doh-_lohr_	the pain

Telling where it hurts

Here, we give you several phrases that may be useful in telling someone where you hurt. (Later, we provide some vocabulary words that may also come handy.)

⮕ **Me sangra la nariz.** *(meh <u>sahn</u>-grah lah nah-<u>rees</u>)* (My nose is bleeding.)

⮕ **No puedo ver.** *(noh poo<u>eh</u>-doh bvehr)* (I can't see.)

⮕ **Me entró algo en el ojo.** *(meh ehn-<u>troh</u> <u>ahl</u>-goh ehn ehl <u>oh</u>-Hoh)* (Something got into my eye.)

⮕ **Me torcí el tobillo.** *(meh tohr-<u>see</u> ehl toh-<u>bvee</u>-yoh)* (I twisted my ankle.)

⮕ **Se quebró el brazo derecho.** *(seh keh-<u>broh</u> ehl <u>bvrah</u>-soh deh-<u>reh</u>-choh)* (He broke his right arm.)

⮕ **La herida está en el antebrazo.** *(lah eh-<u>ree</u>-dah ehs-<u>tah</u> ehn ehl ahn-teh-<u>bvrah</u>-soh)* (The wound is on the forearm.)

⮕ **Le duele la muñeca izquierda.** *(leh doo<u>eh</u>-leh lah moo-<u>nyeh</u>-kah ees-kee<u>ehr</u>-dah)* (Her left wrist hurts.)

⮕ **Se cortó el dedo índice.** *(seh kohr-<u>toh</u> ehl <u>deh</u>-doh <u>een</u>-dee-seh)* (He cut his index finger.)

⮕ **Se torció el cuello.** *(seh tohr-see<u>oh</u> ehl koo<u>eh</u>-yoh)* (She twisted her neck.)

⮕ **Ahora ya no sale sangre.** *(ah-<u>oh</u>-rah yah noh <u>sah</u>-leh <u>sahn</u>-greh)* (It stopped bleeding. [Literally: Now there is no more blood coming out.])

⮕ **Usted tiene la presión muy alta.** *(oos-<u>tehd</u> tee<u>eh</u>-neh lah preh-see<u>ohn</u> mooy <u>ahl</u>-ta)* (You have very high blood pressure.)

⮕ **He sentido náuseas.** *(eh sehn-<u>tee</u>-doh <u>nah</u>oo-seh-ahs)* (I felt nauseated.)

Talkin' the Talk

Julia just can't get rid of her headache, and she decides to see her doctor. She's at her doctor's office, talking to the receptionist.

Julia: **¿Está el doctor Díaz?**
ehs-<u>tah</u> ehl dohk-<u>tohr</u> <u>dee</u>eahs
Is Dr. Díaz in?

Receptionist: **Sí, está. ¿Tiene cita?**
see ehs-<u>tah</u> tee<u>eh</u>-neh <u>see</u>-tah
Yes, he's in. Do you have an appointment?

Julia: **No tengo cita, pero necesito verle.**
noh <u>tehn</u>-goh <u>see</u>-tah <u>peh</u>-roh neh-seh-<u>see</u>-toh <u>bvehr</u>-leh
I don't have an appointment, but I need to see him.

Tengo mucho dolor de cabeza.
<u>Tehn</u>-goh <u>moo</u>-cho doh-<u>lohr</u> deh kah-<u>bveh</u>-sah
I have a bad headache.

Receptionist: **Muy bien, ¿cómo se llama?**
mooy bveeehn, koh-moh seh-yah-mah
Very well, what's your name?

Julia: **Soy Julia Frank.**
sohy Hoo-leeah frahnk
I'm Julia Frank.

Receptionist: **Un momento, por favor. Tome asiento en la sala de espera.**
oon moh-mehn-toh, pohr fah-bvohr toh-meh ah-see ehn-toh ehn lah sah-lah deh ehs-peh-rah
One moment, please. Please take a seat in the waiting room.

Talkin' the Talk

 After waiting a few minutes, Julia is ushered into the doctor's office and begins to explain her symptoms.

Julia: **Me duele la cabeza.**
meh dooeh-leh lah kah-bveh-sah
My head hurts.

Dr. Díaz: **¿Desde cuándo?**
dehs-deh kooahn-doh
Since when?

Julia: **Desde ayer. Me golpeé la cabeza.**
dehs-deh ah-yehr meh gohl-peh-eh lah kah-bveh-sah
Since yesterday. I banged my head.

Dr. Díaz: **¿Cómo se golpeó?**
koh-moh seh gohl-peh-oh
How did you bang [your head]?

Julia: **Me caí en la calle.**
meh-kah-ee ehn lah kah-lyeh
I fell on the street.

Dr. Díaz: **Tiene mareos?**
tee-eh-neh mah-reh-ohs
Do you get dizzy?

Julia:	**Sí, tengo mareos.**
	see <u>tehn</u>-goh mah-<u>reh</u>-ohs
	Yes, I get dizzy.
Dr. Díaz:	**Vamos a tenerle en observación durante dos días.**
	<u>vah</u>-mohs ah teh-<u>nehr</u>-leh ehn
	ohbv-sehr-bvah-see<u>ohn</u> doo-<u>rahn</u>-teh dohs deeahs
	We'll keep you under observation for two days.

Words to Know

la cita	lah <u>see</u>-tah	the appointment
ver	bvehr	to see
golpear	gohl-peh-<u>ahr</u>	to hit; to bang
el mareo	ehl mah-<u>reh</u>-oh	the dizziness
la observación	lah obv-sehr-bvah-see<u>ohn</u>	the observation

Describing symptoms

Table 16-2 lists common terms for medical problems and body parts that you may need to know when visiting the doctor.

Table 16-2	Helpful Words in a Medical Emergency	
Spanish	**Pronunciation**	**English**
Head and Neck Words		
el ojo	*ehl <u>oh</u>-Hoh*	the eye
la boca	*lah <u>bvoh</u>-kah*	the mouth
la lengua	*lah <u>lehn</u>-gooah*	the tongue
la oreja	*lah oh-<u>reh</u>-Hah*	the ear
la nariz	*lah nah-<u>rees</u>*	the nose

Spanish	Pronunciation	English
el rostro	*ehl <u>rohs</u>-troh*	the face
la barba	*lah <u>bvahr</u>-bvah*	the beard
el bigote	*el bvee-<u>goh</u>-teh*	the whiskers; moustache
el cuello	ehl koo<u>eh</u>-yoh	the neck
las amígdalas	*ahs ah-<u>meeg</u>-dah-lahs*	the tonsil
Torso Words		
el hombro	*ehl <u>ohm</u>-broh*	the shoulder
el corazón	*ehl koh-rah-<u>sohn</u>*	the heart
el pulmón	*el pool-<u>mohn</u>*	the lung
el estómago	*ehl ehs-<u>toh</u>-mah-goh*	the stomach
el intestino	*ehl een-tehs-<u>tee</u>-noh*	the bowel; intestine; gut
el hígado	*ehl <u>ee</u>-gah-doh*	the liver
el riñón	*ehl ree-<u>nyohn</u>*	the kidney
Arm and Hand Words		
el brazo	*ehl <u>bvrah</u>-soh*	the arm
el antebrazo	*ehl ahn-teh-<u>bvrah</u>-soh*	the forearm
la muñeca	*lah moo-<u>nyeh</u>-kah*	the wrist
la mano	*lah <u>mah</u>-noh*	the hand
el dedo	*ehl <u>deh</u>-doh*	the finger
el pulgar	*ehl pool-<u>gahr</u>*	the thumb
el dedo índice	*ehl <u>deh</u>-doh <u>een</u>-dee-seh*	the forefinger
el dedo del medio	*ehl <u>deh</u>-doh dehl <u>meh</u>-deeoh*	the middle finger
el dedo anular	*ehl <u>deh</u>-doh ah-noo-<u>lahr</u>*	the ring finger
el dedo meñique	*ehl <u>deh</u>-doh meh-<u>nyee</u>-keh*	the little finger
Leg and Foot Words		
el muslo	*ehl <u>moos</u>-loh*	the thigh
la pierna	*lah pee<u>ehr</u>-nah*	the leg
el pie	*ehl pee<u>eh</u>*	the foot

(continued)

Table 16-2 (continued)

Spanish	Pronunciation	English
el dedo del pie	*ehl deh-doh dehl peeeh*	the toe
el tobillo	*ehl toh-bvee-yoh*	the ankle
la pantorrilla	*lah pahn-toh-rree-yah*	the calf
la planta del pie	*lah plahn-tah dehl peeeh*	the sole of the foot
General Health Words		
la salud	*sah-lood*	the health
sano	*sah-noh*	healthy
enfermo	*ehn-fehr-moh*	sick
derecho	*deh-reh-choh*	right
izquierdo	*ees-keeeehr-doh*	left
la cirugía	*lah see-roo-Heeah*	the surgery
la herida	*lah eh-ree-dah*	the wound
la orina	*lah oh-ree-nah*	the urine
la sangre	*lah sahn-greh*	the blood
la presión sanguínea	*lah preh-seeohn sahn-ghee-neh-ah*	the blood pressure
el estornudo	*ehl ehs-tohr-noo-doh*	the sneeze
la náusea	*lah nahoo-seh-ah*	the nausea; sickness
el estreñimiento	*ehl ehs-treh-nyee-meeehn-toh*	the constipation
la evacuación	*lah eh-bvah-kooah-seeohn*	the bowel movement (Literally: evacuation)
la receta	*lah reh-seh-tah*	the prescription
la medicina	*lah meh-dee-see-nah*	the medication; the medicine
la farmacia	*lah fahr-mah-seeah*	the pharmacy
el jarabe	*ehl Hah-rah-bveh*	the syrup; the elixir

When you sneeze among native Spanish-speakers, you never get a chance to excuse yourself. The moment you sneeze, someone immediately says: ¡Salud! *(sah-lood)* (Health!) And you immediately answer: **¡Gracias!** *(grah-seeahs)*.

Braving the dentist

If you have a dental problem while you're in a Spanish-speaking country, you'll probably discover that dental care is a lot less expensive in Spanish-speaking America than it is in English-speaking America. Part of the reason may be that dental offices in Mexico, Central, South, and Latin America aren't as jazzy as they usually are in the United Stataes and Canada; just be sure to find a dentist with the proper equipment to take care of your problem.

You may find the following phrases helpful when you go to a Spanish-speaking dentist:

✔ **Necesito un dentista.** *(neh-seh-see-toh oon dehn-tees-tah)* (I need a dentist.)

✔ **¿Me puede recomendar un dentista?** *(meh pooeh-deh reh-koh-mehn-dahr oon dehn-tees-tah)* (Can you recommend a dentist?)

✔ **Doctor me duele el diente.** *(dohk-ohr meh dooeh-leh ehl deeehn-teh)* (Doctor, I have a toothache.)

✔ **Tiene una caries.** *(tee-eh-neh oo-nah kah-reeehs)* (You have a cavity.)

✔ **Quebré una muela.** *(keh-breh oo-nah mooeh-lah)* (I broke a molar.)

✔ **Le pondré anestesia.** *(leh pohn-dreh ah-nehs-teh-seeah)* (I'll give you anesthesia.)

✔ **Le taparé la caries.** *(leh tah-pah-reh lah kah-reeehs)* (I can fill the cavity.)

✔ **Le sacaré la muela.** *(leh sah-kah-reh lah mooeh-lah)* (I'll [have to] pull the molar out.)

✔ **Le pondré un puente.** *(leh-pohn-dreh oon pooehn-teh)* (I'll put in a bridge.)

✔ **Le pondré una corona.** *(leh-pohn-dreh oo-nah koh-roh-nah)* (I'll put on a crown.)

Words to Know

el diente	ehl deeehn-teh	the tooth
la muela	lah mooeh-lah	the molar
la caries	lah kah-reeehs	the cavity
el dentista	ehl dehn-tees-tah	the dentist
dolor de muelas	doh-lohr deh mooeh-lahs	toothache

Insuring that you get reimbursed

If you need to visit a dentist, or any other professional, while you're traveling, be sure you get a receipt to give to your insurance carrier at home. The following phrases are useful in dealing with insurance questions:

- ✔ **¿Tiene seguro dental?** *(tee<u>eh</u>-neh seh-<u>goo</u>-roh dehn-<u>tahl</u>)* (Do you have dental insurance?)

- ✔ **¿Tiene seguro de salud?** *(tee<u>eh</u>-neh seh-<u>goo</u>-roh deh sah-<u>lood</u>)* (Do you have health insurance?)

- ✔ **¿Me puede dar un recibo para el seguro?** *(meh poo<u>eh</u>-deh dahr ooh reh-<u>see</u>-bvoh <u>pah</u>-rah ehl seh-<u>goo</u>-roh)* (Can you give me a receipt for my insurance?)

Getting Help with Legal Problems

Most people obey the laws and usually don't engage in activities that involve the police or other aspects of the legal system. But accidents happen, and it is possible to break a law that you know nothing about. If that is the case, you need help from your consulate or a lawyer to make sure that your rights are protected.

If you have legal dealings in a Spanish-speaking country, take into account that the legal system is likely to be completely different from the one you're familiar with, and the laws of the country you're in override the laws of the country you hold citizenship in. Be aware, too, that the philosophy behind the legal system applies to many of the institutions you may encounter. Probably the most important difference is that, in the United States and Canada, you are innocent until proven guilty, whereas in all Latin American countries, you're guilty until proven innocent.

In an emergency of any kind, but particularly in a situation involving legal officials, try to be patient, and above all, firm. Keep in mind that, just as you are unfamiliar with the practices and procedures of a foreign system, the officers and administrators of that system are unaware of your legal expectations.

If you get involved in a Spanish-speaking country's legal system, try to get someone from your consulate to help you handle the situation — he or she will take your interests much more to heart than a local lawyer or the local police. In fact, after you set the dates for a visit to a Spanish-American area, find out where your country's closest consulate is — and when you arrive, register there in case you need emergency assistance.

You may also ask when you arrive:

- ✔ **¿Hay aquí un Consulado de Estados Unidos?** *(ahy ah-kee oon kohn-soo-lah-doh deh ehs-tah-dohs oo-nee-dohs)* (Is there an American consulate here?)

- ✔ **¿Hay un abogado que hable inglés?** *(ahy oon ah-bvoh-gah-doh keh ah-bvleh een-glehs)* (Is there a lawyer who speaks English?)

If Spanish is not your first language, and you're in a Spanish-speaking area, ask for a lawyer who speaks English and make sure the lawyer's English is better than your Spanish before you get involved with him or her. Don't accept just anyone. If you have trouble making yourself understood, get another lawyer.

Talkin' the Talk

It is most unlikely that you'll be involved in a situation like Silverio's, but we want to cover all your bases, and just in case, these few sentences may be useful.

Police officer: **Usted va detenido.**
oos-tehd bvah deh-teh-nee-doh
You're under arrest.

Silverio: **¿Por qué?**
pohr keh
Why?

Police officer: **Está circulando ebrio.**
ehs-tah seer-koo-lahn-doh eh-bvreeoh
For impaired driving.

Silverio: **Oficial, yo no tomo alcohol.**
oh-fee-see-ahl yoh noy toh-moh ahl-koh-ohl
Officer, I don't drink alcohol.

Police officer: **Vamos a la comisaría.**
bvah-mohs ah lah koh-mee-sah-reeah
We're going to the police station.

Silverio: **Creo que usted se equivoca.**
kreoh keh oos-ehd seh eh-kee-bvoh-kah
I believe you are mistaken.

Police officer: **Va preso conmigo.**
bvah preh-soh kohn-mee-goh
Come with me. (Literally: You go prisoner with me.)

Silverio:	**Quiero hablar con un abogado** *keeeh-roh ah-bvlahr kohn oon ah-bvoh-gah-doh* I want to talk to a lawyer
	Quiero hablar con mi cónsul *keeeh-roh ah-bvlahr kohn mee kohn-sool* I want to talk to my consulate
	Quiero hablar por teléfono. *keeeh-roh ah-bvlahr pohr teh-leh-foh-noh* I want to talk on the phone.

Stick 'em up: Words when robbed

If someone robs you while you're in a Spanish-speaking area, you can attract the help you need by using these phrases.

- ✔ **¡Un robo!** *(oon roh-bvoh)* (A burglary!)
- ✔ **¡Un asalto!** *(oon ah-sahl-toh)* (A holdup!)
- ✔ **¡Atrápenlo!** *(ah-trah-pehn-loh)* (Catch him!)
- ✔ **¡Policía!** *(poh-lee-seeah)* (Police!)

We hope you never need to use them, but if you're ever robbed or attacked in a Spanish-speaking area, these phrases are important to know:

- ✔ **¡Llamen a la policía!** *(yah-mehn ah lah poh-lee-seeah)* (Call the police!)
- ✔ **¡Me robó la billetera!** *(meh roh-bvoh lah bvee-yeh-teh-rah)* ([She/he] stole my wallet!)
- ✔ **Haga una denuncia a la policía.** *(ah-gah oo-nah deh-noon-seeah ah la poh-lee-seeah)* (Report it to the police. [Literally: Make an accusation to the police.])

Reporting to the police

If you do have an unpleasant encounter with a thief, here are some words that can be helpful in describing the culprit to the police:

- ✔ **Era un hombre bajo, corpulento.** *(eh-rah oon ohm-bvreh bvah-Hoh kohr-poo-lehn-toh)* (He was a short man, heavyset.)
- ✔ **Tenía cabello oscuro y barba.** *(teh-neeah kah-bveh-yoh ohs-koo-roh ee bvahr-bvah)* (He had dark hair and a beard.)

✔ **Vestía pantalón de mezclilla, y camisa blanca.** *(bvehs-teeah pahn-tah-lohn deh mehs-klee-yah ee kah-mee-sah bvlahn-kah)* (He wore jeans, and a white shirt.)

✔ **Tendrá unos cuarenta años.** *(tehn-drah oo-nohs kooah-rehn-tah ah-nyos)* (He's around forty.)

✔ **Iba con una mujer delgada.** *(ee-bvah kohn oo-nah moo-Hehr dehl-gah-dah)* (He was with a thin woman.)

✔ **Era alta, rubia, de ojos claros.** *(eh-rah ahl-tah roo-bveeah deh oh-Hohs klah-rohs)* (She was tall, blond, light colored eyes.)

Words to Know

atacar	ah-tah-kahr	to attack
robar	roh-bvahr	to steal; to rob
oscuro	ohs-koo-roh	dark
claro	klah-roh	light
la billetera	lah bvee-yeh-teh-rah	the wallet
la tarjeta de crédito	lah tahr-Heh-tah deh kreh-dee-toh	the credit card
la denuncia	lah deh-noon-seeah	the report

Talkin' the Talk

Crash! bang! A collision. Julieta doesn't need it, but here she is. What does she do?

Julieta: **¡Rápido, vengan!**
rah-pee-doh bven-gahn
Quickly, come here!

Passerby: **Hubo un choque.**
oo-bvoh oon choh-keh
There was a collision.

Julieta:	**Paré porque cambió la luz.**	
	pah-reh pohr-keh kahm-bveeoh lah loos	
	I stopped because the light changed.	

Police officer:	**¿A qué velocidad iba?**	
	ah keh bveh-loh-see-dahd ee-bvah	
	How fast were you going?	

Julieta:	**Iba lento, a menos de cuarenta kilómetros.**	
	ee-bvah lehn-toh ah meh-nohs deh kooah-rehn-tah kee-loh-meh-trohs	
	I was going slowly, less than 40 kilometers.	

Police officer:	**¿Tiene usted seguro para el auto?**	
	teeeh-neh oos-tehd seh-goo-roh pah-rah ehl ahoo-toh	
	Do you have car insurance?	

Julieta:	**Sí, quiero avisar a mi compañía de seguros.**	
	see, keeeh-roh ah-bvee-sahr ah mee kohm-pah-nyeeah deh seh-goo-rohs	
	Yes, I want to notify my insurance company.	

Words to Know

el choque	ehl choh-keh	the crash
la velocidad	lah-bveh-loh-see-dahd	the speed
despacio	dehs-pah-seeoh	slow
rápido	rah-pee-doh	fast
romper	rohm-pehr	to break

Talkin' the Talk

Julieta and Jorge's car dies on their way to work. They're lucky enough to find a mechanic who tries to figure out what's wrong.

Julieta: **Necesito ayuda. Mi auto no funciona.**
           neh-seh-see-toh ah-yoo-dah mee ahoo-toh noh foon-seeoh-nah
           I need help. My car doesn't work.

Jorge: **Buscamos un mecánico.**
           bvoos-kah-mohs oon meh-kah-nee-koh
           We're looking for a mechanic.

Nino: **Yo soy mecánico.**
           yoh sohy meh-kah-nee-koh
           I'm a mechanic.

Jorge: **Hasta ahora estuvo bien y ahora no parte.**
           ahs-tah ah-oh-rah ehs-too-bvoh bveeehn ee ah-oh-rah noh pahr-teh
           Until now it was fine, and now it won't start.

Nino: **Vamos a revisar la batería y las bujías también.**
           bvah-mohs ah reh-bvee-sahr lah bvah-teh-reeah ee lahs bvoo-Heeahs tahm-bveeehn
           We'll check the battery and the spark plugs too.

Words to Know

el mecánico	ehl meh-kah-nee-koh	the mechanic
partir	pahr-teer	to start
el motor	ehl moh-tohr	the engine
revisar	reh-bvee-sahr	to check
la batería	lah bvah-teh-reeah	the battery
las bujías	lah bvoo-Heeahs	the spark plugs

Using the Searching Verb: Buscar

Buscar *(bvoos-kahr)* is a much-used regular verb with a number of meanings: to look for, to try to find, or to search for.

Conjugation	Pronunciation
yo busc**o**	yoh <u>bvoos</u>-koh
tú busc**as**	too <u>bvoos</u>-kahs
él, ella, ello, uno, usted busc**a**	ehl <u>eh</u>-yah <u>eh</u>-yoh <u>oo</u>-noh oos-<u>tehd</u> <u>bvoos</u>-kah
nosotros busc**amos**	noh-<u>soh</u>-trohs bvoos-<u>kah</u>-mohs
vosotros busc**áis**	bvoh-<u>soh</u>-trohs bvoos-<u>kah</u>ees
ellos, ellas busc**an**	<u>eh</u>-yohs <u>eh</u>-yahs <u>bvoos</u>-kahn

Practice using **buscar** with these phrases:

- ✔ **Buscan un mecánico.** *(<u>bvoos</u>-kahn oon meh-<u>kah</u>-nee-koh)* They're looking for a mechanic.

- ✔ **Ellos buscan un médico.** *(<u>eh</u>-yohs <u>bvoos</u>-kahn oon <u>meh</u>-dee-koh)* They are looking for a doctor.

- ✔ **Buscas un lugar donde descansar**. *(<u>bvoos</u>-kahs oon <u>loo</u>-gahr <u>dohn</u>-deh dehs-kahn-<u>sahr</u>)* (You are looking for a place where you can rest.)

- ✔ **Ya no busca, encontró un abogado.** *(yah noh <u>bvoos</u>-kah ehn-kohn-<u>troh</u> oon ah-bvoh-<u>gah</u>-doh)* She isn't searching any more, she found a lawyer.

- ✔ **Buscan un espacio y no encuentran**. *(<u>bvoos</u>-kahn oon ehs-<u>pah</u>-seeoh ee noh ehn-koo<u>ehn</u>-trahn)* They are looking for a space and cannot find one.

Fun & Games

Alberto doesn't know it yet, but he's going to have an accident on that surfboard of his. You see, he invited you to join him on vacation, and then he decided to take up surfing to impress a girl. The thing is, Alberto is not nearly as good a surfer as he thinks he is, and he's going to knock himself out. Good friend that you are, you're going to accompany Alberto to the doctor and explain what happened. Fill in all of Alberto's body parts (in Spanish) on the illustration below. That way, you can refer to the picture if you happen to get flustered at the sight of blood. (Oh, and don't worry, Alberto will be fine — just a few bumps and bruises, and some sorely wounded pride.)

Part IV
The Part of Tens

The 5th Wave   By Rich Tennant

"I called ahead and told Morris I'd love to have flautas for dinner tonight, so we'll see how he did."

In this part . . .

If you're looking for small, easily digestible pieces of information about Spanish, this part is for you. Here, you can find ten ways to speak Spanish quickly, ten useful Spanish expressions to know, and ten celebrations worth joining.

Chapter 17

Ten Ways to Speak Spanish Quickly

In this Chapter
- ► Acquiring Spanish via travel
- ► Adding Spanish to your repertoire through media
- ► Making a game of Spanish vocabulary

*Y*ou know the best way to thread a needle, drive a nail into wood, or type a letter. Just as you can acquire these skills in many ways, so can you acquire the Spanish language. The following suggestions are great ways for you to add this beautiful language to your life.

Go to Spanish-Speaking Places

This information probably comes as no surprise, but the absolute best way, by far, to learn Spanish, is to be in an environment where everybody speaks the language and no one speaks yours.

Finding this sort of environment is pretty simple if you can afford to travel. Consider submerging yourself in the language by giving yourself a Spanish-speaking vacation. With Spanish-speaking places appearing just as you come across the southern border of the United States, travel by car, bus, or plane is generally inexpensive.

Investigate Your Neighborhood

You may be able to find Spanish-speaking people in your own neighborhood or town. And among these people, you may find some who are willing to spend a few hours a week with you, doing everyday activities. You may join one of their clubs or their voluntary work. This way, you will be able to reach children, who can be great teachers, and you might also participate in parties, outings, and a playful life.

Listen to Radio and TV

Because so many people in North, Central, and South America speak Spanish, you may be lucky enough to find a radio station or a TV channel in your area that offers Spanish programming. By listening to and watching these programs, you add new vocabulary, gain an understanding of the body language and idioms of Spanish-speaking people, and gain insight into their idea of fun.

Rent a Movie

Video centers in your area may offer films in Spanish. (These films come from any of the countries listed in Appendix D.) To get the effect of being in a Spanish-speaking country, choose a film that has no dubbing or subtitles. You'll be amazed at how much you understand even the first time you see the movie, but the good thing about video is that you can play the film as many times as your whim and time allow.

Check Out Your Library

Your local library may house books, tapes, and other things about Spanish and Spanish-speaking countries. Every bit of information you get counts in building up your mental Spanish library. Here are some things you are looking for

- Atlases and maps of Spanish-speaking North, Central, and South American countries
- Travel guides and books that describe Spanish-speaking areas
- Novels by authors that describe Spanish places. Most of these are translations of texts by authors from countries that speak Spanish, but others are written in English.

You can also find access to the Internet through your library's computer. On the Internet you will find an enormous amount of information and fun things related to Spanish-speaking places.

Read the Liner Notes

The liner notes you find in CDs and cassette tapes often have the song lyrics printed on them. Try buying albums by your favorite Spanish singers and then check the liner notes. Eventually, liner notes or not, you're bound to find yourself singing along — in Spanish!

Create a Game (Secret or Not)

You can make up games of your own (see the sidebar "Susana's Secret Game" for an example of one of the author's creations). For example, you may decide to make a game of learning a sentence a day:

1. **Put the sentence with little stickers on your refrigerator, next to your phone, on your bathroom mirror, or other places you choose.**

2. **Every time you open the refrigerator, you read and repeat the sentence aloud.**

   Likewise when you hang up your phone, when you look into your mirror, or when you go to all those other places where the sentence awaits you.

Use your imagination and have fun!

Susana's Secret Game

As a teenager, I had to learn three languages. Ashamed of my clumsiness, I invented my Secret Game. In the game, I simply inserted any word or phrase I had grasped in the language I was learning into sentences and thoughts I had in my head. You can also try this game.

Here's how you play: Imagine any situation you like, as though you're telling a story, explaining an event, or describing a dream. In your own mind, try to do so in Spanish. For any word you don't know in Spanish, insert the English word instead.

At first, you'll have many English words with only a sprinkling of Spanish. But as you go on — in even a few days — the number of Spanish words will increase.

I used to like this game very much because nobody noticed whether I left something out or made some mistake. I didn't use dictionaries and I didn't have the opportunity to tune into foreign radio or TV, but slowly a new world opened up in my mind and I became fluent in English, Spanish, and French.

Use Stickers

On little stickers, write the Spanish word for all the things in one room of your house. Put each sticker on the correct item. Say the Spanish word aloud every time you use the object. As you feel comfortable with the words, remove the stickers, but continue saying the name aloud. If you forget the name, replace the sticker. When the majority of stickers are gone, move to another room.

Say It Again, Sam

You hear a Spanish phrase in a film, you sing a line in Spanish of a song, you catch a Spanish sentence in an ad. These are treasures, and your goal is to use and polish them all the time. Several times a day, repeat those words and phrases aloud. So that you know what you are repeating, you may consult a dictionary, which could be the very one in the Appendix of this book. Soon, the treasure is yours to keep.

Take a Spanish Class

Berlitz, our partner for this book and world leader in teaching languages, offers Spanish courses for all levels. You can attend a group class or learn one-on-one. In fact, you'll find a coupon for a free lesson in the back of this book. Try it out!

Chapter 18

Ten Favorite Spanish Expressions

● ●

In This Chapter
▶ Terms that show you're in the know
▶ Phrases you hear all the time among Spanish speakers

● ●

This chapter gives you almost a dozen phrases or words that Spanish speakers use all the time in the way they greet and deal with each other.

¿Qué tal?

You use the greeting **"¿Qué tal?"** *(keh tahl)* (How are things?) when meeting someone you already know. This phrase (we introduce it in Chapter 3) is easy to pronounce and immediately gives the impression of someone speaking the language fluently.

¿Quiubo?

"¿Quiubo?" *(kee̲oo-boh?)* (What's up?) is very similar in its effect to **"¿Qué tal?"**, but it's even more colloquial. You only use this phrase, which is common in Chile and a few other countries, with someone you know well and with whom you have an informal relationship.

"¿Quiubo?" is a compression of the phrase **"¿qué hubo?"** *(keh o̲o-bvoh)*, meaning "What happened?" To really sound like an insider, let **"¿Quiubo?"** just flow out of your mouth, as though you were saying *queue-boh.* (We also mention this greeting in Chapters 1 and 3.)

¿Qué pasó?

In Mexico you frequently hear **"¿Qué pasó?"** *(keh pah-<u>soh</u>)* (What's up? [Literally: What happened?])

This phrase may seem funny to you at first. Someone sees another person and cries out **"¿Qué pasó?"** as though they've been separated just before some big event and now want to know what happened. That's what the phrase means, but its use is much broader.

Even people who barely know each other and haven't seen one another for ages can use this greeting. In any case, when *you* use it in Mexico do so with someone you've seen at least once before. You'll sound like you've been there forever. (We mention this greeting in Chapters 1 and 3.)

¿Cómo van las cosas?

"¿Cómo van las cosas?" *(<u>koh</u>-moh bvahn lahs <u>koh</u>-sahs)* (How are things going?) Well-educated people use this very gentle greeting to express concern. People also use this phrase in cases where they've met the other person before.

"¿Cómo van las cosas?" is more appropriate than **"¿Quiubo?"** or **"¿Qué pasó?"** when greeting someone who is older than you or someone to whom you want to show your respect. (We discuss this phrase in Chapter 3.)

¡Del uno!

"¡Del uno!" *(dehl <u>oo</u>-noh)* (First rate!). This phrase (see Chapter 1) is common in Chile, but you may hear it in other places as well. Its meaning is clear, even if you haven't heard it before. A little ditty goes with this:

"¿Cómo estamos?," dijo Ramos. *(<u>koh</u>-moh ehs-<u>tah</u>-mohs <u>dee</u>-Hoh <u>rah</u>-mohs)* ("How are things? [Literally: How are we?]" said Ramos.)

"¡Del uno!," dijo Aceituno. *(dehl <u>oo</u>-noh <u>dee</u>-Hoh ah-sehee-<u>too</u>-noh)* ("First rate!" said Aceituno.)

Ramos and Aceituno are just family names used to call out the rhyme. You'll sound like one of the bunch with this one.

¿Cuánto cuesta?

"**¿Cuánto cuesta?**" *(kooahn-toh kooehs-tah)* (How much does it cost?) You ask this question when you're shopping and need to know the price. (See Chapter 6 for some examples.)

¿A cuánto?

"**¿A cuánto?**" *(ah-kooahn-toh)* (How much?) is very similar to "**¿Cuánto cuesta?**" except that this phrase may imply that you're asking the price of several things grouped together, as in "**¿A cuánto la docena?**" *(ah-kooahn-toh lah doh-seh-nah)* (How much for the dozen?). You'll seem like an expert shopper when you use this one. (See Chapter 6 for an example of this phrase.)

¡Un asalto!

You may think that exclaiming "**¡Un asalto!**" *(oon ah-sahl-toh)* (A holdup!) in the midst of bargaining for a lower price is hyping things up a bit. However, adding hype to your speech can be useful — at least the vendor knows that you're familiar with this phrase that shows your indignation.

This phrase is also useful when you really *are* indignant. (See Chapters 6 and 16 for more on this expression.)

¡Una ganga!

Vendors often use the phrase "**¡Una ganga!**" *(oo-nah gahn-gah)* (A bargain!) when trying to sell you an item. You can show your familiarity with the language when you use this expression to boast about a really good buy.

¡Buen provecho!

¡Buen provecho! *(bvooehn proh-bveh-choh!)* ("Enjoy your meal!" or *"Bon appetit!"* [Literally: Good profit!])

Imagine that you're sitting at the table, soup spoon in hand, ready to begin your meal and about to dip it into a cup of steaming soup. In order to sound like a native, you want to say — at this exact moment — **"¡Buen provecho!"** before someone else does.

"¡Buen provecho!" is also the right thing to say when you set a tray of food in front of your guests. (Refer to Chapter 5 to see this phrase in usage.)

¡Salud!

"¡Salud!" (sah-_lood_) (Health!) has two usages:

✔ You use this word when giving a toast as a way to say "Cheers!"

✔ You use this word after someone sneezes — it's the Spanish equivalent of "Bless you," to which you answer, **"¡Gracias!"**

(See Chapters 5 and 16 for more information.)

¡Buen viaje!

You hear the phrase **"¡Buen viaje!"** (bvooehn _bveeah-Heh_) (Have a good trip!) all around you in train stations, airports, and bus terminals. Use this expression when you want to wish those you care for a safe trip. (See Chapter 15 for more information.)

If you are reading this book as part of your preparation for travel, then we would like to say **"¡Buen viaje!"** to you.

Chapter 19

Ten Holidays to Remember

● ●

In This Chapter

▶ **Año Nuevo** (New Year's Eve)

▶ **La Fiesta de Reyes** (The Day of the Three Kings)

▶ **Paradura del Niño** (Searching for the Child)

▶ **Carnaval La Diablada and Morenada de Oruro** (Carnival)

▶ **Viernes Santo** (Good Friday)

▶ **Día de la Madre** (Mother's Day)

▶ **Nuestra Señora de Aiquina** (Our Lady of Aiquina)

▶ **Nuestro Señor de los Milagros** (Our Miraculous Lord)

▶ **Día de los Muertos** (Day of the Dead)

▶ **Día de Santiago** (St. James's Day)

● ●

Spanish speaking countries celebrate many holidays and feasts that have their origin in Christian religion and mythology. These Christian myths, together with those of pre-Columbian times and the ones brought from Africa, are the origin of the new and peculiar ones that have shaped what nowadays make the great holidays. People celebrate these with gusto and enthusiasm as this chapter shows.

Año Nuevo

Throughout the Spanish-speaking world, people celebrate the **Fiesta de Año Nuevo** (*feeehs-tah deh ah-nyoh nooeh-bvoh*) (New Year's Eve Party). Wherever you go during the night of December 31, and into the morning of January 1, parties and revelers surround you, helping you cheer in the New Year in Spanish. People sing and shout **¡Salud!, ¡Feliz Año Nuevo!** (*sah-lood feh-lees ah-nyoh nooeh-bvoh*) (Cheers!, Happy New Year!).

There are few details that distinguish the New Year's Eve celebrations from those of the United States or Canada. At one place in Mexico I was invited to celebrate eating grapes. I was given 12 grapes, which I was supposed to eat as the clock chimed 12 times. Much hugging and rejoicing followed, and we danced and played games until the wee hours. The games we played were of the social kind, with all ages participating. In one of the games, each of us had to open a gift wrapped box that was chosen randomly and then put on the garment or object it contained. We had a roaring good time with this game.

La Fiesta de Reyes

In Spain and most of Latin America, children get their holiday presents on January 6, which is **La Fiesta de Reyes** *(lah fee-ehs-tah deh reh-yehs)* (The Kings' Holiday). *Note:* In Spain, this holiday is called **la epifanía** *(lah eh-pee-fah-neeah)* (the epiphany). January 6th celebrates the Three Kings' visit to Bethlehem. Because the Kings brought presents to the infant Jesus, children participate in the celebration by getting their own presents. All business and normal endeavors stop and families spend the holiday with their children. It's good to be a child at the time of Reyes. Adults don't get gifts.

Paradura del Niño

In many parts of Spanish-speaking America, the fun times surrounding the birth of Jesus start at Christmas and don't end until the beginning of February.

In the Andean Region of Venezuela people have a special way of enjoying this time by celebrating **La Paradura, Robo, y Búsqueda del Niño** *(lah pah-rah-doo-rah roh-bvoh ee-bvoos-keh-dah dehl-nee-nyoh)* (The Hosting, Stealing, and Searching for the Child). The figure of Jesus as a Child is "stolen" from the manger representation in someone's house, instigating a search. Of course the person "stealing" the Child is some neighbor and the place the Child is hidden in is a secret, the same way hide and seek is played. The neighbor or family member that finds the Child has to host a party on February 2nd, on the **Fiesta de la Candelaria** *(fee-ehs-tah deh lah kahn-deh-lah-reeah)* (Candelmas) also called **Fiesta de la Purificación** *(fee-ehs-tah deh lah poo-ree-fee-kah-seeohn)* (The Feast of Purification). So the search and the finding are moments of rejoicing in which children and adults take part. The person that has to run with the costs of the party is the most surprised of all, and generally takes the news with laughter and the secret purpose of hiding the Child in someone else's house the following year, because the party is supposed to be a supper with chocolate and typical Venezuelan Andean food for all those who have participated in the "searching" for and "finding" the Child — a potentially big affair.

Carnaval

Countless places in the Spanish-speaking world— from **Oruro** *(oh-roo-roh)* in Bolivia and **Cartagena** *(kahr-tah-Heh-nah)* in Colombia, on to **Veracruz** *(bveh-rah-kroos)* in Mexico and **Ciudad Real** *(thiu-dahd reh-ahl)* and **Santa Cruz de Tenerife** *(teh-neh-ree-feh)* in Spain — celebrate **Carnaval** *(kahr-nah-bvahl)* (Shrovetide, or Mardi Gras) just before the arrival of Lent. **Carnaval** is a feast of dancing, singing, and excess before the time of moderation and fasting.

Lent begins on Ash Wednesday, which falls exactly forty days before Easter Sunday. Because Easter falls on different dates, Ash Wednesday does as well, but always sometime between the beginning of February and the beginning of March. **Carnaval** activities come into full swing and frenzy on the Saturday, Sunday, Monday, and Shrove Tuesday that precede Ash Wednesday.

Traditionally **Carnaval** was the name of the period of **diversiones** *(dee-bvehr-seeoh-nehs)* (fun) between January 6, **La Fiesta de Reyes** *(lah feeehs-tah deh reh-yehs)* (The Kings' Holiday) and **Miércoles de Ceniza** *(mee-ehr-koh-lehs deh seh-nee-sah)* (Ash Wednesday).

One truly special **Carnaval** event is known in South America as **La Diablada de Oruro** *(lah deeah-bvlah-dah deh oh-roo-roh)*. **Oruro** is a fascinating city on a high plateau in Peru, surrounded by mountains that used to have working tin mines.

During both Saturday and Sunday, a very long **recorrido** *(reh-koh-ree-doh)* (procession) with many **conjuntos** *(kohn-Hoon-tohs)* (groups) pass one after the other into and out of the church where they worship **La Virgen del Socavón** *(lah bveer-Hehn dehl soh-kah-bvohn)* (The Virgin of the Shaft or Tunnel.)

Huge multitudes gather to see this procession. Fantastic masks and outfits captivate and give flight to the imagination. This is definitely one of the most spectacular and unbelievably colorful carnivals in the world.

Viernes Santo

Viernes Santo *(bveeehr-nehs sahn-toh)* is Good Friday. On this day many Spanish-speaking communities in Latin America and Spain display exceptional ceremonies and events. This remembrance of the crucifixion of Jesus is accompanied in some places by real enactments of the event. Whole communities will represent — like one large play, in which all participate — the Biblical story. One person is chosen to take the part of Jesus and is "crucified," while other village actors recite the New Testament texts. Those who act out this drama prepare for months and sometimes years ahead of time and do it out of religious fervor. Thousands of villagers and visitors see these enactments each year.

Día de la Madre

Mother's Day, **Día de la Madre** *(deeah deh lah mah-dreh)* isn't celebrated any-where quite like the way it's celebrated in Mexico on May 10. People travel thousands of miles to come home, because on this day they *must* be there.

Nothing is more sacred to Mexicans than their mothers and they show it abundantly on this day. Mothers are feasted, toasted, and showered with pre-sents. If a woman is also a mother, she is celebrated — even by people out-side her family. People send each other's mothers gifts and greetings. And, the family itself gathers for this day, the way families in the United States and Canada gather for Christmas.

Nuestra Señora de Aiquina

The peoples of the Andes who lived in the Empire of the **Inca** *(een-kah)* before the arrival of the Spaniards live according to many of their old beliefs to this day. Some of these beliefs, like the worship of Mother Earth, now take the forms familiar to Christianity and are just as deep-rooted and true as they ever were.

I have seen Andean Indians pour a bit of their drink to the ground, to offer it to **Pachamama** *(pah-cha-mah-mah)*, Mother Earth, before taking their own first sip.

The Indians who live in northern Chile celebrate the feast days of many dif-ferently named Virgins, all representing visual expressions of ancient devo-tions to the same Mother Earth. One of these Virgins is a figure of the Virgin of Guadaloupe, venerated in the tiny village of **Aiquina** *(ahee-kee-nah)*. She is not known by her real name, as the Virgin of Guadaloupe; everybody calls her **Nuestra Señora de Aiquina** *(nooehs-trah seh-nyoh-rah deh ahee-kee-nah)* (Our Lady of Aiquina.)

Aiquina, near the city **Calama** *(kah-lah-mah)*, is in a large highland area with a plateau at 9,000 feet. A very large area indeed, part of the driest desert on earth, called the *Atacama (ah-tah-kah-mah)* Desert which takes up large chunks of Peru, Bolivia, Chile, and Argentina. The **Cordillera de los Andes**, *(kohr-dee-yeh-rah deh lohs ahn-dehs)* (Andean Mountain Range) rises upward from this plateau. People up there live mostly in oases or close to very deep wells.

For centuries the devout to the **Virgen de Aiquina** *(bveer-Hehn deh ahee-kee-nah)* (the Virgin of Aiquina) have made the pilgrimage for the big holiday on September 7 and 8. Often walking for many days, these people chew coca leaves to silence their hunger and gain energy for the exhausting trek.

Of course, nowadays, many pilgrims can afford to travel to Aiquina via truck or bus.

Many pilgrims arrive a few days early to this small place and stay around a tiny church, outside of which they dance, sing, and drink for days on end. The Indians of this region of the world wear beautiful outfits, the women have many skirts, one on top of the other.

Nuestro Señor de los Milagros

During the whole month of October the people of Lima, Peru celebrate **Nuestro Señor de los Milagros** *(nooehs-troh seh-nyohr deh lohs mee-lah-grohs)* (Our Miracle Working Lord). This Lord is a figure of the suffering Jesus, called **Un Cristo Pobre** *(oon krees-toh poh-breh)* (A Poor Christ) in Spanish.

Many people are devoted to this figure of Jesus and pray to him for favors. When the devout believe that such favors are granted, they acknowledge this by wearing purple for the whole month of October. Men wear purple ties and women wear purple dresses.

Twice during October — the 18th and 28th — the figure of Jesus is taken to the streets in a procession. The procession starts and ends downtown, coming out of and returning to the church where people worship the image. The life size figure of Jesus is taken around on a slow moving **anda** *(ahn-dah)* (Literally: it goes), a platform weighed down by richly ornamented silver. Many men take turns carrying the **anda** during the long procession. These men belong to a religious association and take this difficult task as a sort of penance. The **anda** stops at any point where someone wants to add flowers to it. The flowers are made into four or five foot arrangements mounted on poles, which are added to the **anda**. As the day and the heat progress, the flowers multiply and the **anda** (ahn-dah) becomes heavier. An immense multitude surrounds the event.

Special bullfights — also throughout October — take place in Lima's bullring. The most important bullfight is held during the last day of the month. At this event, the best **torero** *(toh-reh-roh)* (bullfighter) wins the **escapulario de oro** *(ehs-kah-poo-lah-reeoh deh oh-roh)* (the gold scapular), a pair of medals that hang on the wearer's breast and back.

Día de los Muertos

On November 2, in the Andean countries and in Mexico, people celebrate the **El Día de los Muertos** *(ehl deeah deh lohs mooehr-tohs)* (the Day of the Dead), an event also celebrated in Spain. People in these countries believe that deceased family members come to visit on this day. They receive these relatives with offerings of all things the departed liked during their lifetimes.

Whole families, mostly among the Indian populations in Chile, Bolivia, Peru, Ecuador, Colombia, and Mexico spend the night in the cemeteries on November 1, eating and drinking with their beloved ones. Both children and adults participate, carrying flowers and food to the cemeteries.

In many communities, people set up altars and offerings of great beauty and abundance in their own homes. This remembrance of the dead is also a celebration of the harvests and of plenty. (Imagine inviting dead relatives to your Thanksgiving dinner and you have the right idea.)

Día de Santiago

The feast of the patron saint of Spain, St. James Day is celebrated throughout Spain on July 25 with fireworks and parades. In addition, throughout the year, pilgrims walk to **Santiago de Compostela** *(sahn-tee-ah-goh deh kohm-pohs-teh-lah)*, the Spanish city where the bones of Saint James are said to be buried, since the tenth century. **Santiago de Compostela** was declared a Holy Town by Pope Alexander II and pilgrims traveling there in a Holy Year are absolved of their sins. Pilgrims can be identified by a cockleshell, the symbol of Saint James, which many still pin to their clothing. The pilgrimage usually takes two months to complete, and the Cathedral of Saint James is the first stop they make at the end. A huge incense burner, requiring several men to pull it back and forth, can be seen in use during special masses at the Cathedral.

Your Own Holiday

Just you and a couple of Spanish-speaking Latin American friends are more than enough to drum up a wonderful holiday party. You can choose any day of the year and any locale for the party from your hometown or from a **Zapotec** *(sah-poh-tehk)* village in the south of Mexico, if you happen to be there. Get your friends to help you prepare delicious food, call in a group of **mariachis** *(mah-reeah-chees)* if you are in an area where you can find them (if not, use a recording of their music), and have a roaring good time.

Chapter 20

Ten Phrases That Make You Sound Fluent in Spanish

In This Chapter

▶ Phrases for the things that make you happy

▶ Phrases for the things that don't

Knowing just a few words — as long as they're the right words — can convince others that you speak Spanish fluently. Certain phrases can make a big difference, too. This chapter gives you not quite ten Spanish phrases to use at the right moments, in the right places. You'll impress your friends and have fun, too.

¡Esta es la mía!

The exclamation **¡Esta es la mía!** (*ehs-tah ehs lah meeah*) (This is my chance! [Literally: This one is mine!]) is a natural when you see an opportunity and go for it.

In this phrase, **la** (*lah*) (the) refers to **una oportunidad** (*oo-nah oh-pohr-too-nee-dahd*) (an opportunity), but you can use it in the sense of "I got it!" as well. For instance, you may be fishing, waiting for **el pez** (*ehl pehs*) (the fish). The instant the fish bites, yelling **¡Este es el mío!** is appropriate. You use the same phrase when you're waiting to catch **un vuelo** (*ehl bvooeh-loh*) (a flight) or **un bus** (*un bvoos*) (a bus). When you see your plane or bus arrive, you say, **¡Este es el mío!**

¿Y eso con qué se come?

¿Y eso con qué se come? (*ee eh-soh kohn keh seh koh-meh*) (What on earth is that? [Literally: And what do you eat that with?]) is a fun phrase that implies considerable knowledge of the language. The phrase is quite classical, and doesn't belong to one country or another. You say, "**¿Y eso con qué se come?**" when you run across something absurd or unknown.

Voy a ir de farra

When you're getting ready for a night on the town, you'll sound like a native if you say, "**¡Voy a ir de farra!**" (*bvohy ah eer deh fah-rrah!*) (I'm going to party!) You frequently hear the word **farra** (*fah-rrah*) (partying; good time) in South America. This word even has a verb form: **farrear** (*fah-rreh-ahr*) (to party; to have a good time).

If **farras** (*fah-rrahs*) (parties) are a jolly part of your life, you'll love this word. Alone, **ir de farra** means "going partying," "going to have a good time," and "going for it all the way."

An old, woeful tango goes, "**Se acabaron . . . todas las farras**" (*seh ah-kah-bvah-rohn toh-dahs lahs fah-rrahs*) (The party's over). No worse news could be had.

Caer fatal

You use the verb phrase **Caer fatal a uno** (*kah-ehr fah-tahl ah oo-noh*) (to strongly dislike something) to say that something unpleasant has befallen you. You can use **caer fatal** for almost anything that you don't like or that hurts you in some way. For example,

- You can say, "**Sus bromas me caen fatal**" (*soos bvroh-mahs meh kah-ehn fah-tahl*) (I can't stand her/his jokes) when someone's sense of humor really gets on your nerves.

- You can say, "**La comida me cayó fatal**" (*lah koh-mee-dah meh kah-yoh fah-tahl*) (The food made me sick) when suffering some painful consequence of eating food that didn't agree with you.

You can also use **fatal** (*fah-tahl*) (bad; rotten; unpleasant; fatal) alone to say that something wasn't good. For example, to tell someone that you saw a really rotten movie, you would say, "**La película estuvo fatal**" (*lah peh-lee-koo-lah ehs-too-bvoh fah-tahl*).

Nos divertimos en grande

The phrase **nos divertimos en grande** (*nohs dee-bvehr-tee-mohs ehn grahn-deh*) means "We had a great time." You can use **en grande** (*ehn grahn-deh*) (a lot; much; greatly; in a big way) for many things. For instance, you can say, "**Comimos en grande**" (*koh-mee-mohs ehn grahn-deh*) (We ate tremendously) after a feast, or "**Gozamos en grande**" (*goh-sah-mohs ehn gran-deh*) (We really, really enjoyed ourselves) after an extraordinarily pleasant event.

The verb **divertir** (*dee-bvehr-teer*) means to amuse or divert — just like this book amuses you and diverts your attention from other, less enjoyable things (or so we hope). **Divertirse,** (*dee-bvehr-teer-seh*) (to amuse [oneself]) is a reflexive form of the verb. (For more on reflexive verbs, see Chapters 3 and 16.) **Diversión** (*dee-bvehr-seeohn*) is the word for fun or entertainment.

Ver negro para

The idiom **ver negro para. . .** (*bvehr neh-groh pah-rah*) (to have a hard time of. . . [Literally: to see black to. . .]) followed by a verb beautifully conveys that a task is hugely difficult. Following are some examples of this phrase in action:

- ✔ **Las vimos negras para terminarlo.** (*lahs bvee-mohs neh-grahs pah-rah tehr-mee-nahr-loh*) (We had a hard time finishing it.)

- ✔ **Los refugiados se las vieron negras para salir del área.** (*lohs reh-foo-Heeah-dohs seh lahs bvee eh-rohn neh-grahs pah-rah sah-leer dehl ah-reh-ah*) (The refugees had a hard time leaving the area.)

- ✔ **Juana se las vio negras para aprender el inglés.** (*Hooah-nah seh lahs bveeoh neh-grahs pah-rah ah-prehn-dehr een-glehs*) (Juana had a hard time learning English.) That's because she had no *For Dummies* books to guide her.

Pasó sin pena ni gloria

You generally use the phrase **pasó sin pena ni gloria** (*pah-soh seen peh-nah nee gloh-reeah*) (it was neither here nor there) to talk about an event that had little echo with you or the public.

The verb **pasar** in this case signals the passing of time. **Pena** (*peh-nah*) is grief and **gloria** (*gloh-reeah*) is glory. Here you are saying that the event went by without pulling you down or lifting you up — it made no difference to you. Following are some examples of how you may use this phrase:

✔ **El concierto pasó sin pena ni gloria.** (*ehl kohn-see-ehr-toh pah-soh seen peh-nah nee gloh-reeah*) (The concert was neither here nor there.)

✔ **La reunión pasó sin pena ni gloria.** (*lah rehoo-neeohn pah-soh seen peh-nah nee gloh-reeah*) (The meeting was neither here nor there.)

✔ **La cena se acabó sin pena ni gloria.** (*lah seh-nah seh ah-kah-bvoh seen peh-nah nee gloh-reeah*) (The supper was eaten, but it was just so-so.)

¡Así a secas!

¡Así a secas! (*ah-see ah seh-kahs*) (Just like that!) is an idiom that conveys astonishment or disbelief. You can use this phrase in many ways — often with a snap of your fingers to help show just how quickly something happened. For instance, if you happen to know someone who always seems to be borrowing your money, you might say something like **"Me pidió mil dólares, ¡así a secas!"** (*meh pee-deeoh meel doh-lah-rehs ah-see ah seh-kahs*) (He asked me for a thousand dollars, just like that!)

¡La cosa va viento en popa!

The idiom **¡La cosa va viento en popa!** (*lah koh-sah bvah bveeehn-toh ehn poh-pah*) (It's going exceedingly well. [Literally: It's moving with the wind from the stern.]) comes from the language of sailing. The race is on and the wind is coming into the sail from the stern — nothing could go faster or better. You may also say the following:

✔ **¡El trabajo anduvo viento en popa!** (*ehl trah-bvah-Hoh anh-doo-bvoh bveeehn-toh ehn poh-pah*) (The job went exceedingly well!)

✔ **El partido salió viento en popa!** (*ehl pahr-tee-doh sah-leeoh bveeehn-toh ehn poh-pah*) (The game went exceedingly well!)

✔ **El aprendizaje del español va viento en popa!** (*ehl ah-prehn-dee-sah-Heh dehl ehs-pah-nyohl bvah bveeehn-toh ehn poh-pah*) (Learning Spanish is going exceedingly well!)

Part V
Appendixes

The 5th Wave   By Rich Tennant

"Do you mind NOT practicing your 'Olé's! while I'm vacuuming?"

In this part . . .

This part of the book includes important information that you can use for reference. We include verb tables, which show you how to conjugate a regular verb and then how to conjugate those verbs that stubbornly don't fit the pattern. We also provide a listing of the tracks that appear on the audio CD that comes with this book so that you can find out where in the book those dialogs are and follow along. We give you a mini-dictionary in both Spanish-to-English and English-to-Spanish formats. If you encounter a Spanish word that you don't understand, or you need to say something in Spanish that you can't find in the book, you can look it up here. And finally, we give you a brief overview of the 20 countries where Spanish is spoken.

Spanish-English Mini Dictionary

A

a pie/*ah peeeh*/walking (Literally: on foot)

abogado/m/*ah-bvoh-gah-doh*/lawyer

abril/m/*ah-bvreel*/April

abrir/*ah-bvreer*/to open

abuela/f/*ah-bvooeh-lah*/grandmother

abuelo/m/*ah-bvooeh-loh*/grandfather

actor/m/*ahk-tohr*/actor

adelante/*ah-deh-lahn-teh*/in front, ahead

adiós/*ah-deeohs*/good bye

aduana/f/*ah-dooah-nah*/customs

agencia/f/*ah-Hehn-seeah*/agency

agosto/m/*ah-gohs-toh*/August

agua/m/*ah-gooah*/water

aguacate/m/*ah-gooah-kah-teh*/avocado

ahora/*ah-oh-rah*/now

ají/m/*ah-Hee*/hot pepper (South America)

ajo/m/*ah-Hoh*/garlic

alfombra/f/*ahl-fohm-bvrah*/rug

algodón/*ahl-goh-dohn*/cotton

algún/*ahl-goon*/some

almuerzo/m/*ahl-mooehr-soh*/lunch

alto/*ahl-toh*/tall; high

amarillo/*ah-mah-ree-yoh*/yellow

apretado/*ah-preh-tah-doh*/tight

arroz/m/*ah-rros*/rice

ascensor/m/*ah-sehn-sohr*/elevator

asiento/m/*ah-seeehn-toh*/seat

atacar/*ah-tah-kahr*/attack

atún/m/*ah-toon*/tuna

auto/m/*ahoo-toh*/car (South America)

autopista/f/*ahoo-toh-pees-tah*/freeway

avenida/f/*ah-bveh-nee-dah*/avenue

ayer/*ah-yehr*/yesterday

ayudar/*ah-yoo-dahr*/to help

azul/*ah-sool*/blue

B

balcón/m/*bvahl-kohn*/balcony

baño/m/*bvah-nyoh*/bathroom

barrio/m/*bvah-rreeoh*/neighborhood

bastante/*bvahs-tahn-teh*/quite; enough

bello/*bveh-yoh*/beautiful

biblioteca/f/*bvee-bvlee-oh-teh-kah*/library

bicicleta/f/*bvee-see-kleh-tah*/bicycle

bife/m/*bvee-feh*/steak

bigote/m/*bvee-goh-teh*/moustache

billete/m/*bvee-yeh-teh*/bill

billetera/f/*bvee-yeh-teh-rah*/wallet

blanco/*bvlahn-koh*/white

boca/f/*bvoh-kah*/mouth

boleto/m/*bvoh-leh-toh*/ticket

bolsillo/m/*bvohl-see-yoh*/pocket

brazo/m/*bvrah-soh*/arm

brillo/*bvree-yoh*/shine

brócoli/m/*bvroh-koh-lee*/broccoli
bueno/*bvooeh-noh*/good
bulevar/m/*bvoo-leh-bvahr*/boulevard
buscar/*bvoos-kahr*/to search, to look for

C

caballo/m/*kah-bvah-yoh*/horse
cabeza/f/*kah-bveh-sah*/head
café/m/*kah-feh*/coffee
cajero/m/*kah-Heh-roh*/cashier [male]
caliente/*kah-leeehn-teh*/hot [temperature]
calle/f/*kah-yeh*/street
cama/f/*kah-mah*/bed
cámara de video/f/*kah-mah-rah deh bvee-deh-oh*/video camera
camarón/m/*kah-mah-rohn*/shrimp
camas/f/*kah-mahs*/beds
cambiar/*kahm-bveeahr*/change
camino/m/*kah-mee-noh*/road
camisa/f/*kah-mee-sah*/shirt
cancelar/*kah-seh-lahr*/to cancel
cantar/*kahn-tahr*/to sing
caries/f/*kah-reeehs*/cavity
caro/*kah-roh*/expensive
carrera/f/*kah-rreh-rah*/race; profession
carro/m/*kah-rroh*/car (Mexico)
carta/f/*kahr-tah*/letter
casa/f/*kah-sah*/house
cebollas/f/*seh-bvoh-yahs*/onions
cena/f/*seh-nah*/supper
cerámica/f/*seh-rah-mee-kah*/ceramic
cereales/m/*seh-reh-ah-lehs*/cereals
cereza/f/*seh-reh-sah*/cherry
cero/*seh-roh*/zero
chaqueta/f/*chah-keh-tah*/jacket
chico/*chee-koh*/little; small

chile/m/*chee-leh*/hot pepper (Mexico and Guatemala)
chofer/m/*choh-fehr*/driver
cine/m/*see-neh*/cinema
ciruela/f/*see-roo-eh-lah*/plum
cirugía/f/*see-roo-Heeah*/surgery
ciudad/f/*seeoo-dahd*/city
claro/*klah-roh*/light
cobre/m/*koh-bvreh*/copper
cocina/f/*lah koh-see-nah*/kitchen
cocinera/f/*koh-see-neh-rah*/cook [female]
coco/m/*koh-koh*/coconut
código postal/m/*koh-dee-goh pohs-tahl*/postal code [ZIP code]
colgar/*kohl-gahr*/to hang; to hang up
collar/m/*koh-yahr*/necklace
comida/f/*koh-mee-dah*/dinner
computadora/f/*kohm-poo-tah-doh-rah*/computer
computadora portátil/f/*lah kohm-poo-tah-doh-rah pohr-tah-teel*/laptop computer
congrio/m/*kohn-greeoh*/conger eel
contar/*kohn-tahr*/count
contento/*kohn-tehn-toh*/content; satisfied
corazón/m/*koh-rah-sohn*/heart
correo/m/*koh-rreh-oh*/mail; post
correo electrónico/m/*koh-rreh-oh eh-lehk-troh-nee-koh*/e-mail
cosa/f/*koh-sah*/thing
costar/*kohs-tahr*/to cost (as in price)
cuadra/f/*kooah-drah*/block
cuándo/*kooahn-doh*/when
cuánto/*kooahn-toh*/how much
cuarto/m/*kooahr-toh*/room
cuarto/*kooahr-toh*/fourth
cuarto/m/*kooahr-toh*/quarter
cuchara/f/*koo-chah-rah*/spoon

cuello/m/*koo<u>eh</u>-yoh*/neck
cuenta/f/*koo<u>ehn</u>-tah*/account
cuñada/f/*koo-<u>nyah</u>-dah*/sister-in-law
cuñado/m/*koo-<u>nyah</u>-doh*/brother-in-law

D

débito/<u>deh</u>-*bvee-toh*/debit
décimo/<u>deh</u>-*see-moh*/tenth
dedo/f/<u>deh</u>-*doh*/finger
dedo del pie/m/<u>deh</u>-*doh dehl pee<u>eh</u>*/toe
dentista/m/*dehn-<u>tees</u>-tah*/dentist
derecha/*deh-<u>reh</u>-chah*/right
derecho/*deh-<u>reh</u>-choh*/straight
desayuno/m/*deh-sah-<u>yoo</u>-noh*/breakfast
día/m/*dee<u>ah</u>*/day
diario/m/*dee<u>ah</u>-reeoh*/newspaper
dibujo/m/*dee-<u>bvoo</u>-Hoh*/drawing; the pattern
diciembre/m/*dee-see<u>ehm</u>-breh*/December
diente/m/*dee<u>ehn</u>-teh*/tooth
difícil/*dee-<u>fee</u>-seel*/difficult
dinero/m/*dee-<u>neh</u>-roh*/money
dirección/f/*dee-rehk-see-<u>ohn</u>*/address
disponible/*dees-poh-<u>nee</u>-bvleh*/available
divertido/*dee-bvehr-<u>tee</u>-doh*/amusing; funny
doblar/*doh-<u>bvlahr</u>*/turn
dolor/m/*doh-<u>lohr</u>*/pain
dolor de muelas/m/*doh-<u>lohr</u> deh moo<u>eh</u>-lahs*/toothache
domingo/m/*doh-<u>meen</u>-goh*/Sunday
dulce/<u>dool</u>-*seh*/sweet
durazno/m/*doo-<u>rahs</u>-noh*/peach

E

edificio/m/*eh-dee-<u>fee</u>-seeoh*/building
embotellada/*ehm-bvoh-teh-<u>yah</u>-dah*/bottled

empezar/*ehm-peh-<u>sahr</u>*/to begin; to start
empleo/m/*ehm-<u>pleh</u>-oh*/job
en taxi/*ehn <u>tahk</u>-see*/by taxi
encontrar/*ehn-kohn-<u>trahr</u>*/to find
enero/m/*eh-<u>neh</u>-roh*/January
enfemera/f/*ehn-fehr-<u>meh</u>-rah*/the nurse [female]
enfermo (a)/m,f/*ehn-<u>fehr</u>-moh (a)*/sick person
ensalada/f/*ehn-sah-<u>lah</u>-dah*/salad
entero/*ehn-<u>teh</u>-roh*/whole
entradas/f/*ehn-<u>trah</u>-dahs*/hors doeuvres
enviar/*ehn-bvee-<u>ahr</u>*/send
equipo/m/*eh-<u>kee</u>-poh*/team
escuchar/*ehs-koo-<u>chahr</u>*/to listen; to hear
escultura/f/*ehs-kool-<u>too</u>-rah*/sculpture
especial/*ehs-peh-see<u>ahl</u>*/special
esperar/*ehs-peh-<u>rahr</u>*/to wait
espinaca/f/*ehs-pee-<u>nah</u>-kah*/spinach
esquí/m/*ehs-<u>kee</u>*/ski
esquina/f/*ehs-<u>kee</u>-nah*/corner
estación/*ehs-tah-see<u>ohn</u>*/station
estacionamiento/m/*ehs-tah-seeoh-nah-mee-<u>ehn</u>-toh*/parking
estado/m/*ehs-<u>tah</u>-doh*/state
éste/<u>ehs</u>-*teh*/this one
estómago/m/*ehs-<u>toh</u>-mah-goh*/stomach
estreñimiento/m/*ehs-treh-nyee-mee<u>ehn</u>-toh*/constipation

F

fácil/<u>fah</u>-*seel*/easy
falda/f/<u>fahl</u>-*dah*/skirt
farmacia/f/*fahr-mah-<u>seeah</u>*/pharmacy
febrero/m/*feh-<u>bvreh</u>-roh*/February
fecha/f/<u>feh</u>-*chah*/date

feliz/*feh-lees*/happy

feo/*feh-oh*/ugly

fideo/m/*fee-de-oh*/pasta

fiebre/f/*feeeh-bvreh*/fever

fotógrafo/m/*foh-toh-grah-foh*/photographer

fresa/f/*freh-sah*/strawberry (Mexico, Central America, and Spain)

fruta/f/*froo-tah*/fruit

frutilla/f/*froo-tee-yah*/strawberry (from Colombia to the South Pole)

fuera/*fooeh-rah*/outside

G

galletas/f/*gah-yeh-tahs*/cookies; crackers

garantía/m/*gah-rahn-teeah*/warranty

garganta/f/*gahr-gahn-tah*/throat

gerente/m/*Heh-rehn-teh*/manager

gracias/*grah-seeahs*/thank you

grande/*grahn-deh*/big; large

gris/*grees*/grey

guayaba/f/*gooah-yah-bvah*/guava

guerra/f/*gheh-rrah*/war

guía/m,f/*gheeah*/guide

gustar/*goos-tahr*/to like

H

hablar/*ah-bvlahr*/to talk

hambre/*ahm-bvreh*/hungry

hecho a mano/*eh-choh ah mah-noh*/hand made

hermana/f/*ehr-mah-nah*/sister

hermano/m/*ehr-mah-noh*/brother

hígado/m/*ee-gah-doh*/liver

higo/m/*ee-goh*/fig

hija/f/*ee-Hah*/daughter

hijo/m/*ee-Hoh*/son

hombre/m/*ohm-bvreh*/man

hombro/m/*ohm-broh*/shoulder

hora/f/*oh-rah*/hour

hoy/*ohy*/today

huachinango/m/*ooah-chee-nahn-goh*/red snapper

hueso/m/*ooeh-soh*/bone

huevo/m/*ooeh-bvoh*/egg

I

identificación/f/*ee-dehn-tee-fee-kah-seeohn*/identification

idioma/m/*ee-dee-oh-mah*/language

imprimir/*eem-pree-meer*/print

incluido/*een-klooee-doh*/included

ingeniero/m/*een-Heh-neeeh-roh*/engineer

inmigración/*een-mee-grah-seeohn*/ immigration

intestino/m/*een-tehs-tee-noh*/bowel; intestine; gut

isla/f/*ees-lah*/island

izquierda/*ees-keeehr-dah*/left

J

jardín/m/*Hahr-deen*/garden

jueves/m/*Hooeh-bvehs*/Thursday

julio/m/*Hoo-leeoh*/July

junio/m/*Hoo-neeoh*/June

junto/*Hoon-toh*/together

L

lana/*lah-nah*/wool

langostino/m/*lahn-gohs-tee-noh*/prawn

lástima/f/*lahs-tee-mah*/pity; shame

leche/f/*leh-cheh*/milk

lechuga/f/*leh-choo-gah*/lettuce

lengua/f/*lehn-gooah*/language (Literally: the tongue)

libre/*lee-bvreh*/free

libro/m/*lee-bvroh*/book

limón/m/*lee-mohn*/lemon

limpiar/*leem-pee-ahr*/to clean

línea/f/*lee-neh-ah*/line

listada/*lees-tah-dah*/striped

llamar/*yah-mahr*/call

llave/f/*yah-bveh*/key

llegar/*yeh-gahr*/to arrive

lluvia/f/*yoo-bveeah*/rain

luna/f/*loo-nah*/moon

lunes/m/*loo-nehs*/Monday

M

madera/f/*mah-deh-rah*/wood

madre/f/*mah-dreh*/mother

madrina/f/*mah-dree-nah*/godmother

maleta/f/*mah-leh-tah*/luggage; suitcase

mañana/*mah-nyah-na*/tomorrow

mañana/f/*mah-nyah-nah*/morning

manejar/*mah-neh-Hahr*/to drive [a car]

manga/f/*mahn-gah*/sleeve

mango/m/*mahn-goh*/mango

manzana/f/*mahn-sah-nah*/apple

mapa/f/*mah-pah*/map

mar/m/*mahr*/sea

marcar/*mahr-kahr*/to mark; to dial; to punch in the number

marea/f/*mah-reh-ah*/tide

mareo/m/*mah-reh-oh*/dizziness

mariposas/f/*mah-ri-poh-sahs*/butterflies

marisco/m/*mah-rees-koh*/seafood

marrón/*mah-rrohn*/brown

martes/m/*mahr-tehs*/Tuesday

marzo/m/*mahr-soh*/March

más/*mahs*/more

mayo/m/*mah-yoh*/may

medicina/f/*meh-dee-see-nah*/medication; medicine

médico/m/*meh-dee-koh*/physician; doctor

medio/m/*meh-deeoh*/half

medio baño/m/*meh-deeoh bvah-nyoh*/ half-bathroom (a bathroom with no shower or tub)

mejor/*meh-Hohr*/best

melón/m/*meh-lohn*/melon

menos/*meh-nohs*/less

miércoles/m/*meeehr-koh-lehs*/Wednesday

minuto/m/*mee-noo-toh*/minute

moneda/f/*moh-neh-dah*/coin

montaña/f/*mohn-tah-nyah*/mountain

mora/f/*moh-rah*/blackberry

morado/*moh-rah-doh*/purple

mucho/*moo-choh*/a lot; much

mueble/m/*mooeh-bvleh*/furniture

mujer/f/*moo-Hehr*/woman

muñeca/f/*moo-nyeh-kah*/wrist

museo/m/*moo-seh-oh*/museum

muslo/m/*moos-loh*/thigh

N

naranja/*nah-rahn-Hah*/orange

nariz/f/*nah-rees*/nose

negro/*neh-groh*/black

nieta/f/*neeeh-tah*/granddaughter

nieto/m/*neeeh-toh*/grandson

niña/f/_nee_-nyah/girl

ningún/_neen_-_goon_/none

niño/m/_nee_-nyo/boy

noche/f/_noh_-cheh/night

novela/f/noh-_bveh_-lah/novel

noveno/noh-_bveh_-noh/ninth

noviembre/m/noh-bvee_ehm_-breh/
   November

nuera/f/noo_eh_-rah/daughter-in-law

número/m/_noo_-meh-roh/number

O

octavo/ohk-_tah_-bvoh/eighth

octubre/m/ohk-_too_-bvreh/October

ocupado/oh-koo-_pah_-doh/occupied; busy

ojo/m/_oh_-Hoh/eye

olla/f/_oh_-yah/pot

once/_ohn_-seh/eleven

oreja/f/oh-_reh_-Hah/ear

orina/f/oh-_ree_-nah/urine

oro/m/_oh_-roh/gold

oscuro/ohs-_koo_-roh/dark

otro/_oh_-troh/the other one

P

padre/m/_pah_-dreh/father

padrino/m/pah-_dree_-noh/godfather

pagado/pah-_gah_-doh/paid for

pagar/pah-_gahr_/pay

país/m/pah_ees_/country

pájaro/m/_pah_-Hah-roh/bird

pantalones/m/pahn-tah-_loh_-nehs/trousers

pantorrilla/f/pahn-toh-_rree_-yah/calf

papas/f/_pah_-pahs/potatoes

papas fritas/f/_pah_-pahs _free_-tahs/potato
   chips

papaya/f/pah-_pah_-yah/papaya

parque/m/_pahr_-keh/park

pasaporte/m/pah-sah-_pohr_-teh/document;
   paper; passport

paseo/m/pah-_seh_-oh/walk

pasillo/m/pah-_see_-yoh/aisle

patín/pah-_teen_/skate

pato/m/_pah_-toh/duck

peaje/m/peh-ah-_Heh_/toll

pecho/m/_peh_-choh/chest

pelea/f/peh-_leh_-ah/fight

pelo/m/_peh_-loh/hair

pensar/pehn-_sahr_/to think

pequeño/peh-_keh_-nyoh/small

pera/f/_peh_-rah/pear

perla/f/_pehr_-lah/pearl

pescado/m/pehs-_kah_-doh/fish

picante/pee-_kahn_-teh/hot [flavor]

pie/m/pee_eh_/foot

pierna/f/pee_ehr_-nah/leg

piloto/m/pee-_loh_-toh/pilot

piña/f/_pee_-nyah/pineapple

pintar/peen-_tahr_/to paint

pintura/f/peen-_too_-rah/painting

piscina/f/pees-_see_-nah/swimming pool

piso/m/_pee_-soh/floor

plátano/m/_plah_-tah-noh/banana

playa/f/_plah_-yah/beach

plaza/f/_plah_-sah/square

plomo/m/_ploh_-moh/lead

poco/m/_poh_-koh/a bit; a small amount

pollo/m/_poh_-yoh/chicken

por ciento/pohr see_ehn_-toh/percent;
   percentage

potable/poh-_tah_-bvleh/drinkable

precio/m/*preh-seeoh*/price

precioso/*preh-seeoh-soh*/gorgeous; beautiful; lovely

preguntar/*preh-goon-tahr*/to ask (a question)

presión sanguínea/f/*preh-seeohn sahn-ghee-neh-ah*/blood pressure

prima/f/*pree-mah*/cousin [female]

primero/*pree-meh-roh*/first

primo/m/*pree-moh*/cousin [male]

probador/m/*ehl proh-bvah-dohr*/fitting room

probar/*proh-bvahr*/to try

pronto/*prohn-toh*/right away, soon

propio/*proh-peeoh*/[ones] own

pulmón/m/*pool-mohn*/lung

pura/*poo-rah*/pure

Q

qué/*keh*/what

quedarse/*keh-dahr-seh*/to stay

queso/m/*keh-soh*/cheese

quién/*keeehn*/who

quinto/*keen-toh*/fifth

R

receta/f/*reh-seh-tah*/prescription

recibo/m/*reh-see-bvoh*/receipt

reembolsar/*reh-ehm-bvol-sahr*/to refund

reglamentos/m/*rehg-lah-mehn-tohs*/rules

repetir/*reh-peh-teer*/to repeat

reservación/f/*reh-sehr-bvah-see-ohn*/ reservation

responder/*rehs-pohn-dehr*/to answer

restaurante/m/*rehs-tahoo-rahn-teh*/ restaurant

retiro/*reh-tee-roh*/withdrawal

reunión/f/*rehoo-nee-ohn*/meeting

riñón/m/*ree-nyohn*/kidney

río/m/*ree-oh*/river

robar/*roh-bvahr*/to steal; to rob

rojo/*roh-Hoh*/red

rosado/*roh-sah-doh*/pink

ruinas/f/*rooee-nahs*/ruins

S

sábado/m/*sah-bvah-doh*/Saturday

sala/f/*sah-lah*/living room

salado/*sah-lah-doh*/salty

saldo/m/*sahl-doh*/balance

sandía/f/*sahn-deeah*/watermelon

sangre/f/*sahn-greh*/blood

seco/*seh-koh*/dry

sed/*sehd*/thirsty

seguir/*seh-gheer*/to keep going

segundo/m/*seh-goon-doh*/second

semana/f/*seh-mah-nah*/week

septiembre/m/*sehp-teeehm-breh*/ September

séptimo/*sehp-tee-moh*/seventh

sexto/*sehks-toh*/sixth

siguiente/*see-gheeehn-teh*/next

sol/m/*sohl*/sun

subterráneo/*soobv-teh-rrah-neh-oh*/ underground

suelto/*sooehl-toh*/loose

T

tabla/f/*tah-bvlah*/board [wood]

talla/f/*tah-yah*/size

tarde/f/*tahr-deh*/afternoon

tarjeta/f/*tahr-Heh-tah*/card
teclado/m/*tehk-lah-doh*/keyboard
tele/f/*teh-leh*/TV (colloquial)
tercero/*tehr-seh-roh*/third
tía/f/*teeah*/aunt
tierra/f/*teeeh-rrah*/land
tío/m/*teeoh*/uncle
típica/*tee-pee-kah*/typical
tobillo/m/*toh-bvee-yoh*/ankle
todavía/*toh-dah-bveeah*/yet; still
tomar el sol/*toh-mahr ehl sohl*/to sun bathe
toronja/f/*toh-rohn-Hah*/grapefruit
tos/f/*tohs*/cough
tráfico/m/*trah-fee-koh*/traffic
tranquilo/*trahn-kee-loh*/quiet
tren/m/*trehn*/train
trucha/f/*troo-chah*/trout

U

uva/f/*oo-bvah*/grape

V

vehículo/m/*bveh-ee-koo-loh*/vehicle
venta/f/*bvehn-tah*/sale
ver/*bvehr*/to see
verde/*bvehr-deh*/green
viaje/m/*bveeah-Heh*/trip
viajero/m/*bveeah-Heh-roh*/traveler
vida/f/*bvee-dah*/life
vidrio/m/*bvee-dreeoh*/glass
viernes/m/*bveeehr-nehs*/Friday
vino/m/*bvee-noh*/wine
violeta/*bveeoh-leh-tah*/violet; purple
violín/m/*bveeoh-leen*/violin

vivir/*bvee-bveer*/to live
vuelto/m/*bvooehl-toh*/change (as in money back)

Y

yerno/m/*yehr-noh*/son-in-law

Z

zanahoria/f/*sah-nah-oh-reeah*/carrot

English-Spanish Mini Dictionary

A

a bit; small amount/**poco**/m/*poh-koh*
a lot; much/**mucho**/*moo-choh*
account/**cuenta**/f/*kooehn-tah*
actor/**actor**/m/*ahk-tohr*
address/**dirección**/f/*dee-rehk-see-ohn*
afternoon/**tarde**/f/*tahr-deh*
agency/**agencia**/f/*ah-Hehn-seeah*
aisle/**pasillo**/m/*pah-see-yoh*
amusing; funny/**divertido**/*dee-bvehr-tee-doh*
ankle/**tobillo**/m/*toh-bvee-yoh*
answer/**responder**/*rehs-pohn-dehr*
apple/**manzana**/f/*mahn-sah-nah*
April/**abril**/m/*ah-bvreel*
arm/**brazo**/m/*bvrah-soh*
arrive/**llegar**/*yeh-gahr*
ask (a question)/**preguntar**/*preh-goon-tahr*
attack/**atacar**/*ah-tah-kahr*
August/**agosto**/m/*ah-gohs-toh*
aunt/**tía**/f/*teeah*
available/**disponible**/*dees-poh-nee-bvleh*
avenue/**avenida**/f/*ah-bveh-nee-dah*
avocado/**aguacate**/m/*ah-gooah-kah-teh*

B

balance/**saldo**/m/*sahl-doh*
balcony/**balcón**/m/*bahl-kohn*
banana/**plátano**/m/*plah-tah-noh*
bathroom/**baño**/m/*bvah-nyoh*
beach/**playa**/f/*plah-yah*
beautiful/**bello**/*bveh-yoh*
bed/**cama**/f/*kah-mah*
beds/**camas**/f/*kah-mahs*
begin; to start/**empezar**/*ehm-peh-sahr*
best/**mejor**/*meh-Hohr*
bicycle/**bicicleta**/f/*bvee-see-kleh-tah*
big; large/**grande**/*grahn-deh*
bill/**billete**/m/*bvee-yeh-teh*
bird/**pájaro**/m/*pah-Hah-roh*
black/**negro**/*neh-groh*
blackberry/**mora**/f/*moh-rah*
block/**cuadra**/f/*kooah-drah*
blood/**sangre**/f/*sahn-greh*
blood pressure/**presión sanguínea**/f/ *preh-seeohn sahn-ghee-neh-ah/*
blue/**azul**/*ah-sool*
board [wood]/**tabla**/f/*tah-bvlah*
bone/**hueso**/m/*ooeh-soh*
book/**libro**/m/*lee-bvroh*
bottled/**embotellada**/*ehm-bvoh-teh-yah-dah*
boulevard/**bulevar**/m/*bvoo-leh-bvahr*
bowel; intestine; gut/**intestino**/m/*een-tehs-tee-noh*
boy/**niño**/m/*nee-nyo*
breakfast/**desayuno**/m/*deh-sah-yoo-noh*
broccoli/**brócoli**/m/*bvroh-koh-lee*
brother/**hermano**/m/*ehr-mah-noh*

brother-in-law/**cuñado**/m/*koo-nyah-doh*
brown/**marrón**/*mah-rrohn*
building/**edificio**/m/*eh-dee-fee-seeoh*
butterflies/**mariposas**/f/*mah-ri-poh-sahs*
by taxi/**en taxi**/*ehn tahk-see*

C

calf/**pantorrilla**/f/*pahn-toh-rree-yah*
call/**llamar**/*yah-mahr*
cancel/**cancelar**/*kah-seh-lahr*
car (Mexico)/**carro**/m/*kah-rroh*
car (S. America)/**auto**/m/*ahoo-toh*
card/**tarjeta**/f/*tahr-Heh-tah*
carrot/**zanahoria**/f/*sah-nah-oh-reeah*
cashier [male]/**cajero**/m/*kah-Heh-roh*
cavity/**caries**/f/*kah-reeehs*
ceramic/**cerámica**/f/*seh-rah-mee-kah*
cereals/**cereales**/m/*seh-reh-ah-lehs*
change/**cambiar**/*kahm-bveeahr*
change (as in money back)/**vuelto**/m/
bvooehl-toh
cheese/**queso**/m/*keh-soh*
cherry/**cereza**/f/*seh-reh-sah*
chest/**pecho**/m/*peh-choh*
chicken/**pollo**/m/*poh-yoh*
cinema/**cine**/m/*see-neh*
city/**ciudad**/f/*seeoo-dahd*
clean/**limpiar**/*leem-peeahr*
coconut/**coco**/m/*koh-koh*
coffee/**café**/m/*kah-feh*
coin/**moneda**/f/*moh-neh-dah*
computer/**computadora**/f/*kohm-poo-tah-
doh-rah*
conger eel/**congrio**/m/*kohn-greeoh*
constipation/**estreñimiento**/m/*ehs-treh-
nyee-meeehn-toh*

content; satisfied/**contento**/*kohn-tehn-toh*
cook [female]/**cocinera**/f/*koh-see-neh-rah*
cookies; crackers/**galletas**/f/*gah-yeh-tahs*
copper/**cobre**/m/*koh-bvreh*
corner/**esquina**/f/*ehs-kee-nah*
cost (as in price)/**costar**/*kohs-tahr*
cotton/**algodón**/*ahl-goh-dohn*
cough/**tos**/f/*tohs*
count/**contar**/*kohn-tahr*
country/**país**/m/*pahees*
cousin [female]/**prima**/f/*pree-mah*
cousin [male]/**primo**/m/*pree-moh*
customs/**aduana**/f/*ah-dooah-nah*

D

dark/**oscuro**/*ohs-koo-roh*
date/**fecha**/f/*feh-chah*
daughter/**hija**/f/*ee-Hah*
daughter-in-law/**nuera**/f/*nooeh-rah*
day/**día**/m/*deeah*
debit/**débito**/*deh-bvee-toh*
December/**diciembre**/m/*dee-seeehm-breh*
dentist/**dentista**/m/*dehn-tees-tah*
difficult/**difícil**/*dee-fee-seel*
dinner/**comida**/f/*koh-mee-dah*
dizziness/**mareo**/m/*mah-reh-oh*
doctor/**médico**/m/*meh-dee-koh*
document, passport; paper/**pasaporte**/
m/*pah-sah-pohr-teh*
drawing; the pattern/**dibujo**/m/
dee-bvoo-Hoh
drinkable/**potable**/*poh-tah-bvleh*
drive [a car]/**manejar**/*mah-neh-Hahr*
driver/**chofer**/m/*choh-fehr*
dry/**seco**/*seh-koh*
duck/**pato**/m/*pah-toh*

E

ear/**oreja**/f/*oh-reh-Hah*

easy/**fácil**/*fah-seel*

egg/**huevo**/m/*ooeh-bvoh*

eighth/**octavo**/*ohk-tah-bvoh*

elevator/**ascensor**/m/*ah-sehn-sohr*

eleven/**once**/*ohn-seh*

e-mail/**correo electrónico**/*koh-rreh-oh eh-lehk-troh-nee-koh*

engineer/**ingeniero**/m/*een-Heh-neeeh-roh*

expensive/**caro**/*kah-roh*

eye/**ojo**/m/*oh-Hoh*

F

father/**padre**/m/*pah-dreh*

February/**febrero**/m/*feh-bvreh-roh*

fever/**fiebre**/f/*feeeh-bvreh*

fifth/**quinto**/*keen-toh*

fig/**higo**/m/*ee-goh*

fight/**pelea**/f/*peh-leh-ah*

find/**encontrar**/*ehn-kohn-trahr*

finger/**dedo**/f/*deh-doh*

first/**primero**/*pree-meh-roh*

fish/**pescado**/m/*pehs-kah-doh*

fitting room/**probador**/m/*ehl proh-bvah-dohr*

floor/**piso**/m/*pee-soh*

foot/**pie**/m/*peeeh*

fourth/**cuarto**/*kooahr-toh*

free/**libre**/*lee-bvreh*

freeway/**autopista**/f/*ahoo-toh-pees-tah*

Friday/**viernes**/m/*bveeehr-nehs*

fruit/**fruta**/f/*froo-tah*

furniture/**mueble**/m/*mooeh-bvleh*

G

garden/**jardín**/m/*Hahr-deen*

garlic/**ajo**/m/*ah-Hoh*

girl/**niña**/f/*nee-nyah*

glass/**vidrio**/m/*bvee-dreeoh*

godfather/**padrino**/m/*pah-dree-noh*

godmother/**madrina**/f/*mah-dree-nah*

gold/**oro**/m/*oh-roh*

good/**bueno**/*bvooeh-noh*

good bye/**adiós**/*ah-deeohs*

gorgeous; beautiful; lovely/**precioso**/*preh-seeoh-soh*

granddaughter/**nieta**/f/*neeeh-tah*

grandfather/**abuelo**/m/*ah-bvooeh-loh*

grandmother/**abuela**/f/*ah-bvooeh-lah*

grandson/**nieto**/m/*neeeh-toh*

grape/**uva**/f/*oo-bvah*

grapefruit/**toronja**/f/*toh-rohn-Hah*

green/**verde**/*bvehr-deh*

grey/**gris**/*grees*

guava/**guayaba**/f/*gooah-yah-bvah*

guide/**guía**/m,f/*gheeah*

H

hair/**pelo**/m/*peh-loh*

half/**medio**/m/*meh-deeoh*

half-bathroom (a bathroom with no shower or tub)/**medio baño**/m/*meh-deeoh bvah-nyoh*

hand made/**hecho a mano**/*eh-choh ah mah-noh*

hang; to hang up/**colgar**/*kohl-gahr*

happy/**feliz**/*feh-lees*

head/**cabeza**/f/*kah-bveh-sah*

heart/**corazón**/m/*koh-rah-sohn*

help/**ayudar**/*ah-yoo-dahr*

hors d'oevres/**entradas**/f/*ehn-trah-dahs*

horse/**caballo**/m/*kah-bvah-yoh*

hot [flavor]/**picante**/*pee-kahn-teh*

hot [temperature]/**caliente**/*kah-lee ehn-teh*

hot pepper (Mexico and Guatemala)/**chile**/m/*chee-leh*

hot pepper (South America)/**ají**/m/*ah-Hee*

hour/**hora**/f/*oh-rah*

house/**casa**/f/*kah-sah*

how much/**cuánto**/*koo ahn-toh*

hungry/**hambre**/*ahm-bvreh*

I

identification/**identificación**/f/*ee-dehn-tee-fee-kah-seeohn*

immigration/**inmigración**/*een-mee-grah-seeohn*

in front; ahead/**adelante**/*ah-deh-lahn-teh*

included/**incluido**/*een-kloo ee-doh*

island/**isla**/f/*ees-lah*

J

jacket/**chaqueta**/f/*chah-keh-tah*

January/**enero**/m/*eh-neh-roh*

job/**empleo**/m/*ehm-pleh-oh*

July/**julio**/m/*Hoo-leeoh*

June/**junio**/m/*Hoo-neeoh*

K

keep going/**seguir**/*seh-gheer*

key/**llave**/f/*yah-bveh*

keyboard/**teclado**/m/*tehk-lah-doh*

kidney/**riñón**/m/*ree-nyohn*

kitchen/**cocina**/f/*koh-see-nah*

L

land/**tierra**/f/*teeeh-rrah*

language/**idioma**/m/*ee-dee oh-mah*

language /**lengua**/f/*lah lehn-gooah* (Literally: tongue)

laptop computer/**computadora portátil**/f/*kohm-poo-tah-doh-rah pohr-tah-teel*

lawyer/**abogado**/m/*ah-bvoh-gah-doh*

lead/**plomo**/m/*ploh-moh*

left/**izquierda**/*ees-keeehr-dah*

leg/**pierna**/f/*peeehr-nah*

lemon/**limón**/m/*lee-mohn*

less/**menos**/*meh-nohs*

letter/**carta**/f/*kahr-tah*

lettuce/**lechuga**/f/*leh-choo-gah*

library/**biblioteca**/f/*bvee-bvlee oh-teh-kah*

life/**vida**/f/*bvee-dah*

light/**claro**/*klah-roh*

like/**gustar**/*goos-tahr*

line/**línea**/f/*lee-neh-ah*

listen; to hear/**escuchar**/*ehs-koo-chahr*

little, small/**chico**/*chee-koh*

live/**vivir**/*bvee-bveer*

liver/**hígado**/m/*ee-gah-doh*

living room/**sala**/f/*sah-lah*

loose/**suelto**/*sooehl-toh*

luggage; suitcase/**maleta**/f/*mah-leh-tah*

lunch/**almuerzo**/m/*ahl-mooehr-soh*

lung/**pulmón**/m/*pool-mohn*

M

mail; post/**correo**/m/*koh-rreh-oh*

man/**hombre**/m/*ohm-bvreh*

manager/**gerente**/m/*Heh-rehn-teh*

mango/**mango**/m/*mahn-goh*

map/**mapa**/f/*mah-pah*

March/**marzo**/m/*mahr-soh*

mark; to dial; to punch in the number/**marcar**/*mahr-kahr*

May/**mayo**/m/*mah-yoh*

medication; medicine/**medicina**/f/*meh-dee-see-nah*

meeting/**reunión**/f/*rehoo-neeohn*

melon/**melón**/m/*meh-lohn*

milk/**leche**/f/*leh-cheh*

minute/**minuto**/m/*mee-noo-toh*

Monday/**lunes**/m/*loo-nehs*

money/**dinero**/m/*dee-neh-roh*

moon/**luna**/f/*loo-nah*

more/**más**/*mahs*

morning/**mañana**/f/*mah-nyah-nah*

mother/**madre**/f/*mah-dreh*

mountain/**montaña**/f/*mohn-tah-nyah*

moustache/**bigote**/m/*bvee-goh-teh*

mouth/**boca**/f/*bvoh-kah*

much/**mucho**/*moo-choh*

museum/**museo**/m/*moo-seh-oh*

N

neck/**cuello**/m/*kooeh-yoh*

necklace/**collar**/m/*koh-yahr*

neighborhood/**barrio**/m/*bvah-rreeoh*

newspaper/**diario**/m/*deeah-reeoh*

next/**siguiente**/*see-gheeehn-teh*

night/**noche**/f/*noh-cheh*

ninth/**noveno**/*noh-bveh-noh*

none/**ningún**/*neen-goon*

nose/**nariz**/f/*nah-rees*

novel/**novela**/f/*noh-bveh-lah*

November/**noviembre**/m/*noh-bveeehm-breh*

now/**ahora**/*ah-oh-rah*

number/**número**/m/*noo-meh-roh*

O

occupied; busy/**ocupado**/*oh-koo-pah-doh*

October/**octubre**/m/*ohk-too-bvreh*

one's own/**propio**/*proh-peeoh*

onions/**cebollas**/f/*seh-bvoh-yahs*

open/**abrir**/*ah-bvreer*

orange/**naranja**/*nah-rahn-Hah*

outside/**fuera**/*fooeh-rah*

P

paid for/**pagado**/*pah-gah-doh*

pain/**dolor**/m/*doh-lohr*

paint/**pintar**/*peen-tahr*

painting/**pintura**/f/*peen-too-rah*

papaya/**papaya**/f/*pah-pah-yah*

park/**parque**/m/*pahr-keh*

parking/**estacionamiento**/m/*ehs-tah-seeoh-nah-meeehn-toh*

passport/**pasaporte**/m/*pah-sah-pohr-teh*

pasta/**fideo**/m/*fee-de-oh*

pay/**pagar**/*pah-gahr*

peach/**durazno**/m/*doo-rahs-noh*

pear/**pera**/f/*peh-rah*

pearl/**perla**/f/*pehr-lah*

percent; percentage/**por ciento**/*pohr seeehn-toh*

pharmacy/**farmacia**/f/*fahr-mah-seeah*

photographer/**fotógrafo**/m/*foh-toh-grah-foh*
physician/**médico**/m/*meh-dee-koh*
pilot/**piloto**/m/*pee-loh-toh*
pineapple/**piña**/f/*pee-nyah*
pink/**rosado**/*roh-sah-doh*
pity; shame/**lástima**/f/*lahs-tee-mah*
plum/**ciruela**/f/*see-rooeh-lah*
pocket/**bolsillo**/m/*bvohl-see-yoh*
postal code [ZIP code]/**código postal**/m/*koh-dee-goh pohs-tahl*
pot/**olla**/f/*oh-yah*
potato chips/**papas fritas**/f/*pah-pahs free-tahs*
potatoes/**papas**/f/*pah-pahs*
prawn/**langostino**/m/*lahn-gohs-tee-noh*
prescription/**receta**/f/*reh-seh-tah*
price/**precio**/m/*preh-seeoh*
print/**imprimir**/*eem-pree-meer*
pure/**pura**/*poo-rah*
purple/**morado**/*moh-rah-doh*

Q

quarter/**cuarto**/m/*kooahr-toh*
quiet/**tranquilo**/*trahn-kee-loh*
quite; enough/**bastante**/*bvahs-tahn-teh*

R

race; profession/**carrera**/f/*kah-rreh-rah*
rain/**lluvia**/f/*yoo-bveeah*
receipt/**recibo**/m/*reh-see-bvoh*
red/**rojo**/*roh-Hoh*
red snapper/**huachinango**/m/*ooah-chee-nahn-goh*
refund/**reembolsar**/*reh-ehm-bvol-sahr*
repeat/**repetir**/*reh-peh-teer*

reservation/**reservación**/f/*reh-sehr-bvah-see-ohn*
restaurant/**restaurante**/m/*rehs-tahoo-rahn-teh*
rice/**arroz**/m/*ah-rros*
right/**derecha**/*deh-reh-chah*
right away; soon/**pronto**/*prohn-toh*
river/**río**/m/*ree-oh*
road/**camino**/m/*kah-mee-noh*
room/**cuarto**/m/*kooahr-toh*
rug/**alfombra**/f/*ahl-fohm-bvrah*
ruins/**ruinas**/f/*rooee-nahs*
rules/**reglamentos**/m/*rehg-lah-mehn-tohs*

S

salad/**ensalada**/f/*ehn-sah-lah-dah*
sale/**venta**/f/*bvehn-tah*
salty/**salado**/*sah-lah-doh*
Saturday/**sábado**/m/*sah-bvah-doh*
sculpture/**escultura**/f/*ehs-kool-too-rah*
sea/**mar**/m/*mahr*
seafood/**marisco**/m/*mah-rees-koh*
search; to look for/**buscar**/*bvoos-kahr*
seat/**asiento**/m/*ah-seeehn-toh*
second/**segundo**/m/*seh-goon-doh*
see/**ver**/*bvehr*
send/**enviar**/*ehn-bveeahr*
September/**septiembre**/m/*sehp-teeehm-breh*
seventh/**séptimo**/*sehp-tee-moh*
shine/**brillo**/*bvree-yoh*
shirt/**camisa**/f/*kah-mee-sah*
shoulder/**hombro**/m/*ohm-broh*
shrimp/**camarón**/m/*kah-mah-rohn*
sick person/**enfermo (a)**/m,f/*ehn-fehr-moh (a)*

sing/**cantar**/*kahn-tahr*

sister/**hermana**/f/*ehr-mah-nah*

sister-in-law/**cuñada**/f/*koo-nyah-dah*

sixth/**sexto**/*sehks-toh*

size/**talla**/f/*tah-yah*

skate/**patín**/*pah-teen*

ski/**esquí**/m/*ehs-kee*

skirt/**falda**/f/*fahl-dah*

sleeve/**manga**/f/*mahn-gah*

small/**pequeño**/*peh-keh-nyoh*

small amount/**poco**/m/*poh-koh*

some/**algún**/*ahl-goon*

son/**hijo**/m/*ee-Hoh*

son-in-law/**yerno**/m/*yehr-noh*

special/**especial**/*ehs-peh-seeahl*

spinach/**espinaca**/f/*ehs-pee-nah-kah*

spoon/**cuchara**/f/*koo-chah-rah*

square/**plaza**/f/*plah-sah*

state/**estado**/m/*ehs-tah-doh*

station/**estación**/*ehs-tah-seeohn*

stay/**quedarse**/*keh-dahr-seh*

steak/**bife**/m/*bvee-feh*

to steal; to rob/**robar**/*roh-bvahr*

stomach/**estómago**/m/*ehs-toh-mah-goh*

straight/**derecho**/*deh-reh-choh*

strawberry (from Colombia to the South Pole)/**frutilla**/f/*froo-tee-yah*

strawberry (Mexico, Central America, and Spain)/**fresa**/f/*freh-sah*

street/**calle**/f/*kah-yeh*

striped/**listada**/*lees-tah-dah*

sun/**sol**/m/*sohl*

sun bathe/**tomar el sol**/*toh-mahr ehl sohl*

Sunday/**domingo**/m/*doh-meen-goh*

supper/**cena**/f/*seh-nah*

surgery/**cirugía**/f/*see-roo-Heeah*

sweet/**dulce**/*dool-seh*

swimming pool/**piscina**/f/*pees-see-nah*

T

talk/**hablar**/*ah-bvlahr*

tall; high/**alto**/*ahl-toh*

team/**equipo**/m/*eh-kee-poh*

tenth/**décimo**/*deh-see-moh*

thank you/**gracias**/*grah-seeahs*

the nurse [female]/**enfemera**/f/*ehn-fehr-meh-rah*

the other one/**otro**/*oh-troh*

thigh/**muslo**/m/*moos-loh*

thing/**cosa**/f/*koh-sah*

think/**pensar**/*pehn-sahr*

third/**tercero**/*tehr-seh-roh*

thirsty/**sed**/*sehd*

this one/**este**/*ehs-teh*

throat/**garganta**/f/*gahr-gahn-tah*

Thursday/**jueves**/m/*Hooeh-bvehs*

ticket/**boleto**/m/*bvoh-leh-toh*

tide/**marea**/f/*mah-reh-ah*

tight/**apretado**/*ah-preh-tah-doh*

today/**hoy**/*ohy*

toe/**dedo del pie**/m/*deh-doh dehl peeeh*

together/**junto**/*Hoon-toh*

toll/**peaje**/m/*peh-ah-Heh*

tomorrow/**mañana**/*mah-nyah-na*

tooth/**diente**/m/*deeehn-teh*

toothache/**dolor de muelas**/m/*doh-lohr deh mooeh-lahs*

traffic/**tráfico**/m/*trah-fee-koh*

train/**tren**/m/*trehn*

traveler/**viajero**/m/*bveeah-Heh-roh*

trip/**viaje**/m/*bveeah-Heh*

trousers/**pantalones**/m/*pahn-tah-loh-nehs*

trout/**trucha**/f/*troo-chah*

try/**probar**/*proh-bvahr*

Tuesday/**martes**/m/*mahr-tehs*

tuna/**atún**/m/*ah-toon*
turn/**doblar**/*doh-bvlahr*
TV/**tele**/f/*teh-leh*
typical/**típica**/*tee-pee-kah*

U

ugly/**feo**/*feh-oh*
uncle/**tío**/m/*teeoh*
underground/**subterráneo**/*soobv-teh-rrah-neh-oh*
urine/**orina**/f/*oh-ree-nah*

V

vehicle/**vehículo**/m/*bveh-ee-koo-loh*
video camera/**cámara de video**/f/*kah-mah-rah deh bvee-deh-oh*
violet; purple/**violeta**/*bveeoh-leh-tah*
violin/**violín**/m/*bveeoh-leen*

W

wait/**esperar**/*ehs-peh-rahr*
walk/**paseo**/m/*pah-seh-oh*
walking /**a pie**/*ah peeeh* (Literally: on foot)
wallet/**billetera**/f/*bvee-yeh-teh-rah*
war/**guerra**/f/*gheh-rrah*
warranty/**garantía**/m/*gah-rahn-teeah*
water/**agua**/m/*ah-gooah*
watermelon/**sandía**/f/*sahn-deeah*
Wednesday/**miércoles**/m/*meeehr-koh-lehs*
week/**semana**/f/*seh-mah-nah*
what/**qué**/*keh*
when/**cuándo**/*kooahn-doh*
white/**blanco**/*bvlahn-koh*
who/**quién**/*keeehn*

whole/**entero**/*ehn-teh-roh*
wine/**vino**/m/*bvee-noh*
withdrawal/**retiro**/*reh-tee-roh*
woman/**mujer**/f/*moo-Hehr*
wood/**madera**/f/*mah-deh-rah*
wool/**lana**/*lah-nah*
wrist/**muñeca**/f/*moo-nyeh-kah*

Y

yellow/**amarillo**/*ah-mah-ree-yoh*
yesterday/**ayer**/*ah-yehr*
yet; still/**todavía**/*toh-dah-bveeah*

Z

zero/**cero**/*seh-roh*

Appendix B

Spanish Verbs

Regular Verbs Ending in -ar: *hablar* (to speak)
Past Participle: *hablado* (spoken)

	Present	Simple Past	Future
yo (I)	hablo (speak)	hablé (spoke)	hablaré (will speak)
tú (you, informal)	hablas	hablaste	hablarás
Ud. (you, formal)	habla	habló	hablará
él/ella (he/she)	habla	habló	hablará
nosotros (we)	hablamos	hablamos	hablaremos
Uds. (you, formal)	hablan	hablaron	hablarán
ellos/ellas (they)	hablan	hablaron	hablarán

Regular Verbs Ending in -er: *comer* (to eat)
Past Participle: *comido* (eaten);

	Present	Simple Past	Future
yo (I)	como (eat)	comí (ate)	comeré (will eat)
tú (you, informal)	comes	comiste	comerás
Ud. (you, formal)	come	comió	comerá
él/ella (he/she)	come	comió	comerá
nosotros (we)	comemos	comimos	comeremos
Uds. (you, formal)	comen	comieron	comerán
ellos/ellas (they)	comen	comieron	comerán

Regular Verbs Ending in -ir: *vivir* (to live)
Past Participle: *vivido* (lived)

	Present	Simple Past	Future
yo (I)	vivo (live)	viví (lived)	viviré (will live)
tú (you, informal)	vives	viviste	vivirás
Ud. (you, formal)	vive	vivió	vivirá
él/ella (he/she)	vive	vivió	vivirá
nosotros (we)	vivimos	vivimos	viviremos
Uds. (you, formal)	viven	vivieron	vivirán
ellos/ellas (they)	viven	vivieron	vivirán

The Verb *estar* (to be: location, state of condition, w/compound tenses)
Past Participle: *estado* (been); Gerund: *estando* (being)

	Present	Simple Past	Future
yo (I)	estoy (am)	estuve (was)	estaré (will be)
tú (you, informal)	estás	estuviste	estarás
Ud. (you, formal)	está	estuvo	estará
él/ella (he/she)	está	estuvo	estará
nosotros (we)	estamos	estuvimos	estaremos
Uds. (you, formal)	están	estuvieron	estarán
ellos/ellas (they)	están	estuvieron	estarán

The Verb *ser* (to be: permanent state of condition)
Past Participle: *sido* (been);

	Present	Simple Past	Future
yo (I)	soy (am)	fui (was)	seré (will be)
tú (you, informal)	eres	fuiste	serás
Ud. (you, formal)	es	fue	será
él/ella (he/she)	es	fue	será
nosotros (we)	somos	fuimos	seremos
Uds. (you, formal)	son	fueron	serán
ellos/ellas (they)	son	fueron	serán

A Reflexive Verb *lavarse* (to wash oneself)
Past Participle: *lavado* (washed)

	Present	Simple Past	Future
yo (I)	me lavo	me lavé	me lavaré
tú (you, informal)	te lavas	te lavaste	te lavarás
Ud. (you, formal)	se lava	se lavó	se lavará
él/ella (he/she)	se lava	se lavó	se lavará
nosotros (we)	nos lavamos	nos lavamos	nos lavaremos
Uds. (you, formal)	se lavan	se lavaron	se lavarán
ellos/ellas (they)	se lavan	se lavaron	se lavarán

Irregular Spanish Verbs

		Present	Past	Future
almorzar	*yo*	almuerzo	almorcé	almorzaré
to eat breakfast	*tú*	almuerzas	almorzaste	almorzarás
	él/ella/Ud.	almuerza	almorzó	almorzará
Gerund:	*nosotros*	almorzamos	almorzamos	almorzaremos
almorzando	*ellos/ellas/Uds.*	almuerzan	almorzaron	almorzarán

		Present	Past	Future
cerrar	*yo*	cierro	cerré	cerraré
to close	*tú*	cierras	cerraste	cerrarás
	él/ella/Ud.	cierra	cerró	cerrará
Gerund:	*nosotros*	cerramos	cerramos	cerraremos
cerrando	*ellos/ellas/Uds.*	cierran	cerraron	cerrarán

		Present	Past	Future
comprar	*yo*	compro	compré	compraré
to buy	*tú*	compras	compraste	comprarás
	él/ella/Ud.	compra	compró	comprará
Gerund:	*nosotros*	compramos	compramos	compraremos
comprando	*ellos/ellas/Uds.*	compran	compraron	comprarán

		Present	Past	Future
conocer	*yo*	conozco	conocí	conoceré
to know	*tú*	conoces	conociste	conocerás
	él/ella/Ud.	conoce	conoció	conocerá
Gerund:	*nosotros*	conocemos	conocimos	conoceremos
conociendo	*ellos/ellas/Uds.*	conocen	conocieron	conocerán

		Present	Past	Future
conseguir	*yo*	consigo	conseguí	conseguiré
to get	*tú*	consigues	consiguiste	conseguirás
	él/ella/Ud.	consigue	consiguió	conseguirá
Gerund:	*nosotros*	conseguimos	conseguimos	conseguiremos
consiguiendo	*ellos/ellas/Uds.*	consiguen	consiguieron	conseguirán
dar	*yo*	doy	di	daré
to give	*tú*	das	diste	darás
	él/ella/Ud.	da	dio	dará
Gerund:	*nosotros*	damos	dimos	daremos
dando	*ellos/ellas/Uds.*	dan	dieron	darán
empezar	*yo*	empiezo	empecé	empezaré
to begin	*tú*	empiezas	empezaste	empezarás
	él/ella/Ud.	empieza	empezó	empezará
Gerund:	*nosotros*	empezamos	empezamos	empezaremos
empezando	*ellos/ellas/Uds.*	empiezan	empezaron	empezarán
encontrar	*yo*	encuentro	encontré	encontraré
to find	*tú*	encuentras	encontraste	encontrarás
	él/ella/Ud.	encuentra	encontró	encontrará
Gerund:	*nosotros*	encontramos	encontramos	encontraremos
encontrando	*ellos/ellas/Uds.*	encuentran	encontraron	encontrarán

		Present	Past	Future
entender	*yo*	entiendo	entendí	entenderé
to understand	*tú*	entiendes	entendiste	entenderás
	él/ella/Ud.	entiende	entendió	entenderá
Gerund:	*nosotros*	entendemos	entendimos	entenderemos
entendiendo	*ellos/ellas/Uds.*	entienden	entendieron	entenderán

hacer	*yo*	hago	hice	haré
to do; to make	*tú*	haces	hiciste	harás
	él/ella/Ud.	hace	hizo	hará
Gerund:	*nosotros*	hacemos	hicimos	haremos
haciendo	*ellos/ellas/Uds.*	hacen	hicieron	harán

ir	*yo*	voy	fui	iré
to go	*tú*	vas	fuiste	irás
	él/ella/Ud.	va	fue	irá
Gerund:	*nosotros*	vamos	fuimos	iremos
yendo	*ellos/ellas/Uds.*	van	fueron	irán

jugar	*yo*	juego	jugué	jugaré
to play	*tú*	juegas	jugaste	jugarás
	él/ella/Ud.	juega	jugó	jugará
Gerund:	*nosotros*	jugamos	jugamos	jugaremos
jugando	*ellos/ellas/Uds.*	jugan	jugaron	jugarán

		Present	Past	Future
leer	*yo*	leo	leí	leeré
to read	*tú*	lees	leiste	leerás
	él/ella/Ud.	lee	leyó	leerá
Gerund:	*nosotros*	leemos	leimos	leeremos
leyendo	*ellos/ellas/Uds.*	leen	leyeron	leerán

mostrar	*yo*	muestro	mostré	mostraré
to show	*tú*	muestras	mostraste	mostrarás
	él/ella/Ud.	muestra	mostró	mostrará
Gerund:	*nosotros*	mostramos	mostramos	mostraremos
mostrando	*ellos/ellas/Uds.*	muestran	mostraron	mostrarán

ofrecer	*yo*	ofrezco	ofrecí	ofreceré
to offer	*tú*	ofreces	ofreciste	ofrecerás
	él/ella/Ud.	ofrece	ofreció	ofrecerá
Gerund:	*nosotros*	ofrecemos	ofrecimos	ofreceremos
ofreciendo	*ellos/ellas/Uds.*	ofrecen	ofrecieron	ofrecerán

oír	*yo*	oigo	oí	oiré
to hear	*tú*	oyes	oíste	oirás
	él/ella/Ud.	oye	oyó	oirá
Gerund:	*nosotros*	oímos	oímos	oiremos
oyendo	*ellos/ellas/Uds.*	oyen	oyeron	oirán

		Present	Past	Future
pedir	yo	pido	pedí	pediré
to ask for	tú	pides	pediste	pedirás
	él/ella/Ud.	pide	pidió	pedirá
Gerund:	nosotros	pedimos	pedimos	pediremos
pidiendo	ellos/ellas/Uds.	piden	pidieron	pedirán
pensar	yo	pienso	pensé	pensaré
to think	tú	piensas	pensaste	pensarás
	él/ella/Ud.	piensa	pensó	pensará
Gerund:	nosotros	pensamos	pensamos	pensaremos
pensando	ellos/ellas/Uds.	piensan	pensaron	pensarán
perder	yo	pierdo	perdí	perderé
to lose	tú	pierdes	perdiste	perderás
	él/ella/Ud.	pierde	perdió	perderá
Gerund:	nosotros	perdemos	perdimos	perderemos
perdiendo	ellos/ellas/Uds.	pierden	perdieron	perderán
poder	yo	puedo	pude	podré
can	tú	puedes	pudiste	podrás
	él/ella/Ud.	puede	pudo	podrá
Gerund:	nosotros	podemos	pudimos	podremos
pudiendo	ellos/ellas/Uds.	pueden	pudieron	podrán

		Present	Past	Future
poner	*yo*	pongo	puse	pondré
to put	*tú*	pones	pusiste	pondrás
	él/ella/Ud.	pone	puso	pondrá
Gerund:	*nosotros*	ponemos	pusimos	pondremos
poniendo	*ellos/ellas/Uds.*	ponen	pusieron	pondrán

		Present	Past	Future
preferir	*yo*	prefiero	preferí	preferiré
to prefer	*tú*	prefieres	preferiste	preferirás
	él/ella/Ud.	prefiere	prefirió	preferirá
Gerund:	*nosotros*	preferimos	preferimos	preferiremos
prefiriendo	*ellos/ellas/Uds.*	prefieren	prefirieron	preferirán

		Present	Past	Future
querer	*yo*	quiero	quise	querré
to want	*tú*	quieres	quisiste	querrás
	él/ella/Ud.	quiere	quiso	querrá
Gerund:	*nosotros*	queremos	quisimos	querremos
queriendo	*ellos/ellas/Uds.*	quieren	quisieron	querrán

		Present	Past	Future
repetir	*yo*	repito	repetí	repetiré
to repeat	*tú*	repites	repetiste	repetirás
	él/ella/Ud.	repite	repitió	repetirá
Gerund:	*nosotros*	repetimos	repetimos	repetiremos
repitiendo	*ellos/ellas/Uds.*	repiten	repitieron	repetirán

		Present	Past	Future
saber	*yo*	sé	supe	sabré
to know	*tú*	sabes	supiste	sabrás
	él/ella/Ud.	sabe	supo	sabrá
Gerund:	*nosotros*	sabemos	supimos	sabremos
sabiendo	*ellos/ellas/Uds.*	saben	supieron	sabrán
salir	*yo*	salgo	salí	saldré
to leave	*tú*	sales	saliste	saldrás
	él/ella/Ud.	sale	salió	saldrá
Gerund:	*nosotros*	salimos	salimos	saldremos
saliendo	*ellos/ellas/Uds.*	salen	salieron	saldrán
servir	*yo*	sirvo	serví	serviré
to serve	*tú*	sirves	serviste	servirás
	él/ella/Ud.	sirve	sirvió	servirá
Gerund:	*nosotros*	servimos	servimos	serviremos
sirviendo	*ellos/ellas/Uds.*	sirven	sirvieron	servirán
tener	*yo*	tengo	tuve	tendré
to have	*tú*	tienes	tuviste	tendrás
	él/ella/Ud.	tiene	tuvo	tendrá
Gerund:	*nosotros*	tenemos	tuvimos	tendremos
teniendo	*ellos/ellas/Uds.*	tienen	tuvieron	tendrán

		Present	Past	Future
traer	*yo*	traigo	traje	traeré
to bring	*tú*	traes	trajiste	traerás
	él/ella/Ud.	trae	trajo	traerá
Gerund:	*nosotros*	traemos	trajimos	traeremos
trayendo	*ellos/ellas/Uds.*	traen	trajeron	traerán
venir	*yo*	vengo	vine	vendré
to come	*tú*	vienes	viniste	vendrás
	él/ella/Ud.	viene	vino	vendrá
Gerund:	*nosotros*	venimos	vinimos	vendremos
viniendo	*ellos/ellas/Uds.*	vienen	vinieron	vendrán
ver	*yo*	veo	vi	veré
to see	*tú*	ves	viste	verás
	él/ella/Ud.	ve	vio	verá
Gerund:	*nosotros*	vemos	vimos	veremos
viendo	*ellos/ellas/Uds.*	ven	vieron	verán
volver	*yo*	vuelvo	volví	volveré
to turn	*tú*	vuelves	volviste	volverás
	él/ella/Ud.	vuelve	volvió	volverá
Gerund:	*nosotros*	volvemos	volvimos	volveremos
volviendo	*ellos/ellas/Uds.*	vuelven	volvieron	volverán

Appendix C

About the CD

Following is a list of the tracks that appear on this book's audio CD, which you can find inside the back cover. Note that this is an audio-only CD — just pop it into your stereo (or whatever you use to listen to regular music CDs).

Track 1: Introduction and Pronunciation Guide

Track 2: Chapter 3: ¡Buenos días! Hello! Greetings and Introductions — greeting informally

Track 3: Chapter 3: ¡Buenos días! Hello! Greetings and Introductions — getting formal with strangers

Track 4: Chapter 3: ¡Buenos días! Hello! Greetings and Introductions — greeting colleagues

Track 5: Chapter 3: ¡Buenos días! Hello! Greetings and Introductions — greeting friends

Track 6: Chapter 4: Getting to Know You: Making Small Talk — asking about weather

Track 7: Chapter 4: Getting to Know You: Making Small Talk — talking shop

Track 8: Chapter 5: Dining Out and Shopping at the Market — making dinner reservations

Track 9: Chapter 5: Dining Out and Shopping at the Market — buying oranges

Track 10: Chapter 5: Shopping Made Easy — trying on a skirt

Track 11: Chapter 6: Shopping Made Easy — bargaining for a rug

Track 12: Chapter 7: Going Out on the Town — being invited to a party

Track 13: Chapter 7: Going Out on the Town — asking about the music

Appendix D

Spanish Facts

*H*ere are some facts about the Spanish language:

- ✔ Spanish originates in Spain.
- ✔ Spanish is the official language of 20 countries.
- ✔ Well over 325 million people speak Spanish.
- ✔ About one third of Spanish-speaking people are Mexicans.
- ✔ There are people talking remnants of Spanish in places like the Philippines (actually the Islands were named in honor of a king of Spain) and Morocco.
- ✔ Many people speak Spanish in the United States. Most of them have come to the States from Puerto Rico, Cuba, and Mexico. (The most numerous group is probably the latter.)

People Living in Spanish-Speaking Countries

The following list gives you some idea of the number of people who live in Spanish-speaking countries.

Country	Population
In Europe	
Spain	31.1 million
In the Americas; North, Central and South	
Argentina	34.5 million
Bolivia	4.0 million
Chile	14.2 million

(continued)

Colombia	37.7 million
Costa Rica	3.3 million
Cuba	11.0 million
Ecuador	11.4 million
El Salvador	5.8 million
Peru	3.9 million
Guatemala	10.6 million
Honduras	.4 million
Mexico	94 million
Nicaragua	4.4 million
Panama	2.6 million
Paraguay	4.9 million
Puerto Rico	3.7 million
Dominican Republic	7.8 million
Uruguay	3.1 million
Venezuela	21.8 million

Where in the World Is Spanish Spoken?

Word Search

R	Y	L	D	N	E	I	R	F	B	D
O	A	O	T	N	A	U	C	A	I	E
D	C	M	P	G	M	K	N	R	Q	R
I	V	A	A	C	Y	O	E	O	U	I
U	C	V	L	C	X	C	W	I	E	R
L	U	L	W	I	C	M	F	C	D	E
C	H	F	A	I	E	Z	O	E	A	F
N	E	I	O	M	M	N	H	R	R	E
I	R	N	Z	L	B	G	T	P	S	R
F	N	I	A	T	P	A	C	E	E	P
I	C	X	E	S	R	A	H	C	U	D

BANO	**DIRECCION**	**PRECIO**
CALIENTE	**DUCHARSE**	**PREFERIR**
CAMA	**FRIA**	**QUEDARSE**
CUANTO	**INCLUIDO**	

Answer key to word search in Chapter 13.

Index

• D •

• *G* •

Notes

Notes

Notes

Notes

Notes

Notes

Notes

Notes

Notes

Notes

Berlitz ® *The world's most trusted name in foreign language learning.*

Get one
Free
lesson

Redeemable at any
Berlitz Language Center in
The United States and Canada

Take a language lesson on us!

Millions of people have learned to speak a new language with Berlitz. Why not you?

No matter where you're going or where you're from, odds are Berlitz is already there. We are the global leader in language services with over 70 locations in the United States and Canada. And right now, you can get a free trial language lesson at any one of them and in any language! Experience the unique Berlitz Method® and start speaking a new language confidently from your very first class. Berlitz has over 120 years of proven success, so no matter what your language needs, you can be sure you're getting the best value for your money.

To schedule your free lesson, call Berlitz toll free at 1-800-457-7958 (outside the U.S. call 609-514-9650) for the Language Center nearest you. Or check your telephone book or visit our Web site at www.berlitz.com.

To confirm availability of a teacher for the language of your choice, you must call 24 hours in advance. No purchase is necessary.

Learn Spanish the Berlitz® Way!

There's no better way to understand more about other cultures and people than by trying to speak their language. Whether you want to speak a few essential phrases during your next business trip or vacation or you want to achieve real fluency, Berlitz can help you reach your goals. Here are some time-honored Berlitz tips to help get you on your way:

- Immerse yourself in the language. Read Spanish on the Internet, in newspapers, and in fashion magazines — you'll be surprised at how much you can understand already. Watch Spanish news programs on cable TV, rent Spanish language films, or consider hosting a Spanish-speaking exchange student for the summer. And check out your nearest Berlitz language center for information about special courses and cultural nights.
- Take home a self-study language course and set aside time to work with the material a couple of times a week. Berlitz courses are available in book, cassette, audio CD, and CD-ROM formats.
- Set your own pace, but try to put aside a regular block of time at least twice a week to work with your new language. It's more important to set a steady pace than an intensive one. Several 30-minute sessions during the week are better than one longer session a couple of times per month.
- Speak out loud. Don't just read to yourself or listen to a self-study program. Learning a language is as much a physical workout as it is an intellectual one. You have to train your vocal chords to do things they aren't used to doing. Remember: You only learn to speak by speaking!
- Talk to Spanish people! And don't be afraid to make mistakes. You'll notice that most people appreciate an attempt to speak their language.
- Try speaking English with a Spanish accent. Then, when you start speaking Spanish, your brain will already be in the mood.
- Keep an open mind. Don't expect your new language to work the same as your own, and don't look for a neat set of rules. Accept the differences.
- Enjoy yourself! Learning a foreign language can help you see the world and yourself from an entirely different perspective.

About Berlitz®

The name "Berlitz" has meant excellence in language services for over 120 years. Today, at over 400 locations and in 50 countries worldwide, Berlitz offers a full range of language and language-related services, including instruction, cross-cultural training, document translation, software localization, and interpretation services. Berlitz also offers a wide array of publishing products such as self-study language courses, phrase books, travel guides, and dictionaries.

Berlitz has programs to meet everyone's needs: The world-famous **Berlitz Method®** is the core of all Berlitz language instruction. From the time of its introduction in 1878, millions have used this method to learn a new language. Join any one of the classes available throughout the world, and immerse yourself in a new language and culture with the help of a Berlitz trained native instructor.

For those who may not have time for live instruction, **self-study language courses** may be the answer. In addition to several outstanding courses, Berlitz publishes **Bilingual Dictionaries**, **Workbooks**, and **Handbooks**.

Put the world in your pocket . . . with **Berlitz Pocket Guides** and **Phrase Books**, the renowned series that together are the ideal travel companions that will make the most of every trip. These portable full-color pocket guides are packed with information on history, language, must-see sights, shopping, and restaurant information; the Phrase Books help you communicate with ease and confidence.

Berlitz Kids™ has a complete range of fun products such as the **Kids Language Packs**, **1,000 Words**, and **Picture Dictionaries**. Parents and teachers will find **Help Your Child with a Foreign Language** especially informative and enlightening.

Berlitz Cross-Cultural™ **programs** are designed to bridge cultural gaps for international travelers and business transferees and their families. From vital information about daily life to social and business do's and don'ts, these programs can prepare you for life in any part of the world.

For more information, please consult your local telephone directory for the Language Center nearest you. Or visit the Berlitz Web site at www.berlitz.com, where you can enroll or shop directly online.